THE CONTEST FOR
SOCIAL SCIENCE

For Esther and the late Nat Janes

THE CONTEST FOR SOCIAL SCIENCE

Relations and Representations of Gender and Class

Eileen Janes Yeo

Rivers Oram Press
London

First published in 1996 by
Rivers Oram Press,
144 Hemingford Road,
London N1 1DE

Set in Baskerville by
N-J Design Associates, Romsey
and printed in Great Britain by
T.J. Press (Padstow) Ltd

British Library Cataloguing in Publication Data
A catalogue record for this book is available from the
British Library

ISBN 1 85489 068 9
ISBN 1 85489 069 7 (pbk)

CONTENTS

LIST OF ABBREVIATIONS

COS	Charity Organisation Society
DNB	*Dictionary of National Biography*
FWG	Fabian Women's Group
ILP	Independent Labour Party
JSSL	*Journal of the Statistical Society of London*
LSA	Ladies' Sanitary Association
LSE	London School of Economics and Political Science
MOH	Medical Officer of Health
NAPSS *Sess.*	*Sessional Proceedings* of the National Association for the Promotion of Social Science
NAPSS *Trans.*	*Transactions* of the National Association for the Promotion of Social Science
NCLC	National Council of Labour Colleges
NMW	*New Moral World*
NUWW	National Union of Women Workers
PMC	Professional Managerial Class
SBCP	Society for Bettering the Condition of the Poor
SDF	Social Democratic Federation
SDUK	Society for the Diffusion of Useful Knowledge
SSA	Social Science Association, the popular name of the NAPSS
WCG	Women's Co-operative Guild
WEA	Workers' Education Association
WIC	Women's Industrial Council
WLL	Women's Labour League
WUS	Women's University Settlement

PREFACE AND ACKNOWLEDGMENTS

This study has been in my life for a long time. It started first as an MA thesis exploring the changing ideas of the Owenite socialist movement and then continued as PhD research which placed the issues on a wider social canvas.[1] I put the finished thesis away for some years, both for negative and positive reasons. Negatively, I suffered from a kind of crisis of audience because at that time little work was being done on scientific knowledge in contests of social power. Positively, I changed intellectual direction and explored the creativity of working-class movements in the Chartist period, their contestation of key cultural areas like recreation, religion and education, and their insistence on participatory and democratic cultural forms despite the enormous constraints pressing in on their lives. Out of school, I also took an active part in community politics and publishing. Just as plebeian puritans of the seventeenth century preached 'the priesthood of all believers', so in community publishing we believe in the authorship of all readers and especially in facilitating access to print for working people.[2] This activity revealed the great enthusiasm which still exists for cultural production, once the space for self-expression opens. I was persuaded to reopen the social science project by colleagues who had found it useful and by the fact that the intellectual tide had turned in my direction. The original study had mapped the development of social science in relation to class but now my postgraduate students gently pressed me to explore the gender dimensions as well, which led to the excitement of having to redraw the picture anew.

I hope nobody will feel slighted if I single out for thanks the people who have helped me in this book production phase. I am most grateful to the following friends and colleagues who have read drafts of the manuscript in whole or part and who have given me the benefit of their expertise: Sally Alexander, Anna Davin, Ian Bullock, John Burrow, Philip Corrigan, Carol Dyhouse, John Harrison, Jane Lewis, Paddy Maguire, William Outhwaite, Hilary Rose, Gill Scott, Pat Thane and Robert Young. I rehearsed some of the book's arguments in 'Social Motherhood and the Sexual Communion of Labour in British Social Science, 1850-1950', *Women's History Review*, vol.I (1992) and wish to thank June Purvis for her help at that time. I would also like to thank the librarians and archivists for their welcome and permission to use material from the following collections: The British Library of Political and Economic Science Archives; The Goldsmiths' Library, Senate House; John Rylands University Library of Manchester; King's College London Archives; The Archives, The University of Liverpool; Manu-scripts and Rare Books, University College London; The Robinson Library, University of Newcastle. I am grateful to friends like Barbara Einhorn, Emily Furman, Vivien Hart and Françoise Hutton who gave me great support in the later stages of the work. I would also like to thank Linda Etchart for her skilful editorial interventions. Finally, my thanks goes to my sons, Jake and Ben, who valiantly helped compile the bibliography and print out the manuscript and who put up with my many moods while I finished this book.

INTRODUCTION

'Union is Strength and Knowledge is Power'
—Chartist banner, 1838

'Knowledge is, then, both power and safety'
—Lord Henry Brougham, National Association for the
Promotion of Social Science, 1857[1]

Despite their many differences, Chartist working men and a former Lord Chancellor could agree that 'knowledge is power'. Their perception, which figured strongly in pre-academic social science, has again come to the fore in cultural history and cultural politics. This book will chart the contested course of a powerful new knowledge in relation to class and gender in Britain. I take as a starting point the period of revolutions between 1789 and 1850 to indicate that the groups who created the 'new science of society' felt they were living through a time of profound social crisis which dictated urgent new priorities and discredited older modes of analysis and action. The book ends in the twentieth century with the movement of 'social science' into the university world, where other social sciences were also developing, and with the beginning of the transformation of students into trained professional social scientists and social workers. To clarify my approaches in this extended but selective historical journey, it will be useful first to map the keywords in the title: social science, contest, relations and representations of gender and class.

I treat social science as an historical category[2] which involves paying close attention to the practices which people in the past attached to what they defined as social science. This historicity becomes all the more important because I am partly in the business of recovering a lost tradition, which included what Jessie Bernard called 'a strongly reformist hodgepodge discipline of the nineteenth century' which still hung around until the 1950s, as A.H. Halsey observed, in 'oddly called departments of Social Science'.[3] The Department in Liverpool University did not change its 'odd' name from Social Science to Sociology until 1971, while the LSE department still carries its old name. This book provides neither a history of current-day academic disciplines, nor of the single disciplines, social policy or sociology, which are, perhaps, the closest surviving relatives of social science. Rather I am concerned to shed light on the process by which varieties of action-oriented social science, which made huge claims for being, variously, the science of happiness or of improvement or sometimes later of progress, came to occupy a place on the feminized margins of an academic map of learning. When tracking the history of 'social science', groups using the actual term from the 1820s onward make an obvious bid for attention; but it is also necessary to cast the net wider in order to consider practices which contributed to or conformed to the social science tradition but did not carry the name. Thus Chapter 1 explores the earlier emergence of 'the science of the poor' while Chapter 8 considers later strands of sociology which embraced ethics, analysis and action.

The social science tradition put great emphasis on the condition of the working class or the poor as an index to social happiness or improvement. Social science was evaluative and included a deep concern with moral and ethical issues, expressed both in terms of thinkers clarifying their own ideas of social purpose as well as highlighting the moral or ethical dimensions of the subjects they were studying. The new science of society developed dialectically, often as a critique (but not the only critique) of political economy, in a relationship that ranged from friendly supplementation to hostile repudiation. Most importantly, social action marked a necessary stage in the social science process; indeed pre-academic social science developed as an aid to action. The word 'practical' in this tradition carried very positive connotations. Expressions like 'practical fact' and 'remedial truth' indicated the concern to bring about social change on a lesser or greater scale, whether family reformation (a continuing concern of women) or total social transformation (the socialist ambition in Chapter 2). Such an omnibus science, which taught what human beings were and could become, which interpreted social actuality and potential and then proposed strategies to bridge the gap, became a glittering prize to try to capture and monopolize. For a long time, social science has remained deeply contested.

The idea of the essential contestability or undecidability of concepts has received attention from a number of directions recently. Some philosophers have argued that full agreement about the meaning of concepts is especially unlikely where judgements about value, for example about social values like happiness, utility, improvement, and progress, are involved.[4] Even more sensationally poststructuralists have asserted that essential meanings of texts (actions as well as words) simply do not exist and that the eye of the beholder or the mind of the reader supplies much of the interpretive gloss. Some feminist historians have insisted on the historical and therefore changing construction of key discursive categories like 'woman' or 'women', which masquerade as fixed and natural and have functioned, in their naturalized form, as huge constraints on the lives of real women.[5] I want to move the discussion of text into context in a different way.

While I explore some of the diverse practices of social science which indicate the unstable and contestable nature of the concept, I am also concerned to situate these practices as part of changing social contexts composed of equally unstable and dynamic power relations. As an increasingly influential legiti-mating discourse, social science helped to shape, as well as being shaped by, changing relations of power. I will particularly spotlight class and gender relations not only because these provided some of the central subject matter of pre-academic social science, but also because some working-class people and some women from the middle class or gentry became active producers of knowledge although they do not usually figure in histories of social science.[6] The dominant way of writing such histories has been to arrange a parade of great (male) thinkers whose discoveries anticipate the concepts and methods of present-day disciplines or schools within them. Intellectual historians have broken the mould by insisting on placing such theorists in context, but the idea of context remains somewhat circumscribed and confined to discussions and quarrels among formally educated men.[7] A closed circle can result. If scholars do not seek subaltern groups they do not find them. Without a more spacious idea of context which makes room for less privileged persons, scholars will go on constructing models of a scientific world and of the production of knowledge which allow no room for activity from below in the past or in the future. To enlarge the idea of context and to open up questions about science and power I have studied groups which drew adherents from a range of social backgrounds, which produced a variety of social science practices, and, where possible, which included women as well as men. I explore the lived experience which held groups together and shaped their constructions of science and probe how their analyses and representations functioned, often in unintended ways, within unstable contexts of social power.[8]

To explore the instability of contexts, I work with highly dynamic concepts of class and gender, in which every historical moment contains an untidy clutter of often contradictory practices, tendencies and possibilities. Within the Marxist tradition, which takes the most dialectical approach to class, E.P. Thompson provided a now classic formulation of class as a

> social and cultural formation (often finding institutional expression) which cannot be defined abstractly, or in isolation, but only in terms of relationship with other classes; and, ultimately, the definition can only be made in the medium of *time*—that is, action and reaction, change and conflict....class itself is not a thing, it is a happening.[9]

During the period covered by this study, when the key classes of industrial capitalist society were forming themselves, social science was not a product of any finished identity so much as an integral part of the continuing process of forming collective identities in relation to each other. Thus a range of middle-class venues of social science, not least the urban statistical societies (Chapter 3), provided a gathering point where religiously-divided groups could put forward a collective claim to knowledge and authority *vis à vis* the landed interest whom they charged with dereliction of social duty. Socialist science tried, by means of theory as well as action, to unify many disparate groups into a cohesive working class.

These attempted unities remained unstable. One important development, in a still-ongoing saga, has involved the growth of a professional and administrative sector within the middle class and its attempts to carve out a legitimate place in relation to the rest of its own class and to the classes seen as lying below. The story of this book partly concerns a huge take-over bid for social science. First developed largely by working people for their own emancipation, social science was later annexed by professional men and women to help establish their own indispensability on a foundation of science and service. Chapter 4 explores the mid-nineteenth century phase of this professionalization and the attempts of the 'older' professions to reposition themselves within an urban and industrial social order. Chapter 8 provides the next instalment of the story with the huge expansion of the professional managerial class: trained and often less powerful professionals some of whom ultimately came to take up places in university departments of sociology and social science as well as in active social work (Chapter 10).

Gender provided another dynamic element which interacted with class in complex ways in the social science story. Thanks to the pathbreaking work of Davidoff and Hall on the English middle class, which argues that 'the consciousness of class always takes a gendered form', it should no longer be possible to explore class relations without examining their gender dimension.[10] The British middle class, in particular, constructed the whole of reality around a deep gender divide. Social science became the discipline which could subject the supposedly feminine dimensions of existence to scientific scrutiny alongside the more masculine activities in pursuit of wealth and power.[11] Men as well as women inhabited this mental framework and even 'great' male thinkers now need to be studied with this in mind, not least men like John Stuart Mill (1806-73), who eloquently (and in ways that illuminate gender division in the culture) insisted upon his intellectual debt to Harriet Taylor (1808-58).[12] If gender division attended at the conceptual birth of social science from above, arguably it remained important for a very long time, even helping to structure a later rite of passage, the entry of social science and sociology into the university (Chapter 10). Because gender was so deeply implicated in the representation of reality, social science opened a field where actual women could respectably engage in public work. Social science became an important part of the negotiations between middle-class men and women about their gender roles and sometimes provided a trump card which women played in their dealings with men for access to public space (Chapter 5). At the same time, social science provided a public setting for relations between women of different classes where the very strategies which could appease men, could undercut the possibilities for sisterhood across a class divide (Chapters 1, 5 and 9).

The relations of race do not occupy a central place in the discussion here largely because anthropology, rather than social science, developed as the discipline structured around race. Early bodies, like the Ethnological and Anthropological Societies, explored whether all mankind had derived from a single or from multiple racial origins. Later anthropology studied the so-called 'primitive cultures' of non-European peoples often with immense sympathy but often, too, within a fundamentally unchallenged colonial paradigm.[13] The representations developed within social science could easily transfer into anthropology or shuttle between the two enquiries. Already full-blown in the period around the French Revolution, the science of the poor contained a language of domestic imperialism which represented Somerset peasants as 'savages' in parishes 'as dark as Africa' (Chapter 1) to be enlightened by 'domestic missionaries' just as 'foreign missionaries' would bring illumination to colonies abroad. Some people, like Hannah Kilham, literally moved between the two regions, starting as a visitor for the Society for Bettering the Condition of the Poor in Sheffield in the 1810s and ending as a missionary working in West Africa in the 1820s.[14] At the other end of the century, as empire became even more of a national obsession, Social Darwinists and eugenists positioned both British workers and colonial natives in the same way in their hierarchies although, according to Greta Jones, the readiness to devalue working people markedly declined once they won the vote and entered into the citizenry.[15]

The groups of people producing social science who feature in this book, besides living within class and gender relations, worked within definite institutional settings, from social movements to educational establishments, which both contained and formed part of relations of cultural power. Inspection of these sites of intellectual production, highlighting accessibility, control and place in a larger field of intellectual force, can give good indications of where power lay and to whom it was moving. How accessible was any form of cultural production to less powerful people is a key question and I ask it in many forms, on the level of epistemology, i.e. whose observations and experiments were regarded as scientific, as well as on the more mundane level of the organization, i.e. what type of people were recruited or allowed to join and, once there, how much control could they exert. Many cultural forms supplied from above, whether public libraries or mothers' meetings, urged participation but removed control.

Yet even the most enabling institutions, in terms of maximizing access and control, still operated in a larger ecology of knowledge production. What influence did a particular movement or institution have in the total equilibrium of intellectual power? In the 1820s, when some middle and working-class groups regarded universities with suspicion, all varieties of social science were being produced and comm-unicated in the same range of non-academic institutions: in learned societies, social movements, newspapers, journals, pamphlets and books. More of a relative parity of intellectual power existed, for example, between political economists, evidenced by the way in which economists in the 1830s turned to aggressive propaganda against socialist economics with the blessing of the government (Chapter 2). By the 1920s, the huge expansion of universities and polytechnics and the elaboration of state investigative machinery, together with the growing demand for training and qualifications for people involved in social research and social work, could make efforts carried on in the grand old style, in local statistical societies as well as in socialist Sunday schools, appear amateur and unimportant, even quaint (Chapter 10). The understandings and represent-ations produced in these different sites of intellectual production carried unequal weight in the culture as a whole.

As the title suggests, this book will be exploring representations as well as relations of power in social science. The social and intellectual dimensions cannot really be separated because knowledge and the language which articulates it play an integral role in creating, sustaining and challenging power relations. The interpenetration of knowledge and power has become a central concern of cultural analysts like Raymond Williams whose cultural materialism insisted that ideas and language were constitutive, not reflective, of social reality and production, and like Michel Foucault who put discursive practices and power-knowledge at the centre of his enquiry.[16] I will follow Foucault in my understanding of discourse as a system of knowledge (often claiming scientific authority from the Enlightenment onwards) which exercises power in specific historical situations and which is not only articulated in texts but operates in regulatory bodies (like professional associations), institutions (like hospitals) and in social relations (like those of doctor and patient).[17] As part of such discourses, I will be paying special attention to languages or representations by which I mean systems of resonant keywords or images which appear in repeating and patterned relationships, often of opposition, and which convey a pecking order of value which can justify a particular distribution of power. So, for example, in early socialist social science such giveaway oppositions of words included moral/immoral, productive/nonproductive, useful/useless, co-operation/ com-petition. In all these juxtapositions, working people placed themselves on the more valuable side of the line. In the language of the middle-class statisticians observing the same cities at the same time, very different resonant oppositions figured like immoral/moral, savage/civilized, animal/human, foreign (Irish)/ English, disorder/order, disease/health.

I am not playing lightly with empty words. These words shape ways of seeing and acting towards other people which affect, and sometimes shatter, their lives. As Helen Bosanquet of the Charity Organisation Society well knew:

> we have allowed to grow up amongst us the conception of another class, to which we apply a great variety of names, all tending to the degradation of those concerned.

> We call it the Residuum, the Poor, the Submerged, the Proletariat, the Abyss....This is one of the cases where a false idea of classification tends to mislead us in our action, and to create the very class which it has invented.[18]

This book will explore the large repertoire of imagery used in social science discourse which tended to dignify or disable, to liberate or subordinate groups of people. The repertoire included the more expected languages of class and gender but also a variety of borderlines to separate the human from the subhuman and a recurrent and mutating use of body metaphor to depict social hierarchy (Chapter 7). Of special interest are languages that women use and sometimes monopolize, like a prevalent and very contradictory language of motherhood, which could become, for women from the middle class and the gentry, an instrument of domination in their dealings with the poor (Chapters 1, 5 and 9). The question then follows about how the people being named reacted and whether they contested the social science languages which dignified or subordinated them.

The whole issue of contest in cultural production becomes exceedingly complex where the contestants have unequal power. When differences of experience, conflicts of interest, incompatibilities of perception, and divergences of analysis involve unequal parties, it would be unrealistic to expect open and sustained confrontation, particularly when more powerful groups can be prevailed upon to incorporate some of the agenda being urged from below. Especially where groups attempt to manufacture hegemony, that is, common sense about meanings and values, and try to operate through consent rather than coercion, movement often occurs towards more inclusive collectivities and away from overtly antagonistic relations. The historian needs to remain attuned to the many different forms through which contest modulates. Raymond Williams wrestled with this issue when he tried to respond to E.P. Thompson's critique that a way of life really amounted to a way of struggle. Williams made a useful distinction between class conflict (the basic fault line of conflicting interests which structure the capitalist social order) and class struggle, 'the moment at which structural conflict becomes a conscious and mutual contention, an overt engagement of forces'. He further suggested that 'almost by definition, some cultural institutions involve positive relations, whatever their strain, between classes. In these cases conflicts emerge as arguments over the extent of the institutions, the nature of their content or curricula, and so on'.[19] The art then becomes to detect conflict despite the absence of struggle.

This book tries to keep the activity of less powerful groups in focus whether they act as producers of knowledge, or as objects of scrutiny, or as clients of policy or as parties to negotiated outcomes which they affect but do not decisively influence. From this viewpoint, several different patterns of contest became apparent, for example, over language and discourse; these patterns were not mutually exclusive and could easily occur at the same time in the dense configurations of a cultural moment. One form, as Voloshinov suggested in 1929, involved a competition for the same legitimating language: 'different classes will use one and the same language. As a result, differently oriented accents intersect in every ideological sign. Sign becomes an arena of the class struggle'.[20] This kind of conflict could be deliberate or unintended. In the 1830s, many working-class movements showed real and conscious appetite for the discursive fray. Chartists, for example pitted radical versions of Christian and Constitutional rhetoric against ruling-class versions. Socialist proponents of social science openly disputed resonant concepts like happiness and utility in bourgeois science.

Another form of contest involved an objective incompatibility between alternative discourses available in the same cultural moment. Again discourses could either be developed in dispute with each other or without reference to each other but the point here is they provided alternative modes of understanding, expression and action in the same social context. In the late-nineteenth century, the middle-class progressives developing sociology used an organic analogy and a language of ethical citizenship which functioned as an alternative to the moral economy discourse still present in a revived socialist movement (Chapter 8).

A third pattern of contest involved subversion rather than confrontation. Trying to avoid being provocative, women became especially adept at investing resonant rhetoric with new meanings which opened up new possibilities for themselves. For example women from the middle-class and gentry reworked the idea of motherhood to suit the single woman and legitimate her work in the caring professions in the public sphere. Working-class housewives in the Women's Co-operative Guild stretched the rhetorics of production and of citizenship to allow space for themselves by arguing that homes were 'the workshops of many trades' and that 'citizenship is above sex, party, class and sect'.[21] Cultural critics need to remain on the alert for the different projects being operated within a shared language and, increasingly over the nineteenth and twentieth centuries, within the same institutions.

A provisional chronology of contest over social science can be suggested by this book. The period of revolutions between 1790 and 1850, which contained cultural offensives from above and below, probably witnessed the most explicit episodes of overt struggle over social science and, at the same time, revealed why such confrontation was so hard to sustain. Chapter 2 on socialist social science presents a key moment of encounter but also shows how the institutional settings for producing knowledge, like socialist Halls of Science, remained highly fragile given the relative poverty of working people and given the changing and more positive response of certain middle-class proponents of the social science, like the statisticians who lived in the same towns.

During the midcentury years, a pattern of co-option became widespread where inclusive institutions came into being, like the National Association for the Promotion of Social Science, which brought together previously antagonistic opponents (socialists and local capitalists for example) and also new and sometimes diffident challengers for social science space, like women. Such inclusive forums indicated the influence but relatively different degrees of power of the various parties. The dominant professional and business men in these associations certainly showed a new tolerance both for working-class combinations and women's public presence. At the same time they used a strategy of co-option, selecting the most acceptable or least threatening practices of these potentially intrusive groups: only certain forms of co-operatives and trade unions and only certain kinds of feminism received real support (Chapters 5 and 6).

The late nineteenth-century and early twentieth-century moment contained very complex and contradictory tendencies. The strategy of co-option reached its zenith with progressive social scientists making new constitutional blueprints which gave a central place to working-class combinations at the same time that a pattern of confrontation revived with the resurgence of the socialist movement although social science was not so much the disputed terrain as earlier in the century (Chapter 8). Again in the same moment a new tendency towards incorporation or monopoly emerged which moved in several directions at once. It involved the creation of a vastly expanded landscape of academic institutions and state agencies with new professionals policing the gateways, a process which tended to marginalize and discredit the older collective styles of producing knowledge in learned societies and social movements. Over time and particularly after the Second World War, these new institutions absorbed gifted scholarship boys and girls from all social groups and opened up opportunities for individuals while restricting the authority of the social groups from which they came.

As always, even this has remained an unstable process open to contestation, although increasingly the creation of diverse meanings and practices and even the mounting of fundamental challenges will probably occur within institutions not, as in the nineteenth century, by creating separate and rival initiatives. E.P. Thompson has eloquently characterized the massive bid for the entire social system that British working people mounted between 1944 and 1946 which then became

> assimilated and re-ordered within the system of economic activities, and also within the characteristic concepts, of the capitalist process. This entailed a translation of socialist meanings into capitalist ones. Socialized pits and railways became 'utilities' providing subsidized coal and transport to private industry. Private practice, private beds in hospitals, private nursing-homes and private insurance impoverished the public health service. Equality of opportunity in education was, in part, transformed into an adaptive mechanism through which skilled labour was trained for private industry: the opportunity was not for the working class but for the scholarship boy to escape from this class.[22]

Yet such apparent defeats also become partial victories in the sense that a system cannot incorporate such huge alternative potentials without being also changed.[23]

We live in apparently unpromising times. However, contests are now being mounted over the question of authority in the production of knowledge. The issue of objectivity has been brilliantly illuminated by a literature which explores the science question in feminism and which insists on shifting the discussion to take account of 'limited location and situated knowledge' in fields of social force. The new discussion is action-oriented and some participants highlight the need for co-operative 'politics and epistemologies of partial perspectives'.[24] As a code-name for legitimate scientific vision, 'objectivity' has been just as contested in the past as in the present. In the social science tradition 'experience, observation and experiment' have served as catchwords for authentic scientific practice and this book asks of diverse varieties of social science: whose experience most mattered, whose observation saw most clearly, whose experiments most counted. A clearer idea of the disputed history of such issues and of seemingly solid institutions and disciplines might produce some 'really useful knowledge', to borrow a phrase from our nineteenth-century predecessors, which could provide resources for present encounters and also empower new contests to begin.

Part I

SOCIAL SCIENCE IN AN AGE OF REVOLUTIONS 1789-1850

1

SOCIAL SCIENCE FROM ABOVE

Philanthropists and Utilitarians, 1789-1832

The contest for social science began in revolutionary times. Between 1789 and 1850, the people who rallied to the social science project felt they were living through a decisive age which they described as a 'great social revolution' or 'crisis'. Whether they spotlighted what we now call the French, the industrial or the urban revolutions, they saw unprecedented changes taking place in the relations of gender and class.[1] The first great upheaval of the period was the French Revolution which sent shock waves throughout Europe. It remained an enduring symbol, to different people, of a new awakening or a nightmare, of a regeneration or catastrophe, of a blissful dawn or the wrath of God.

Hannah More (1745-1833), the most influential Evangelical woman of her time, who earned the nickname of the 'Bishop in Skirts', chose the image of a disordered household to convey the horrors of French liberty. In 1790, she told an anecdote about a French lady who rang and rang to summon her maid. When finally the lady went to the kitchen to see why there was no response, she found the servant sitting idle, reading a pamphlet. The maid explained her impertinence, announcing with 'sang froid' that everyone was going to become equal and that she was preparing herself for equality ('nous allons tous devenir égaux, et je me prépare pour l'égalité').[2] As much as any lurid story of streets running with blood, this tale of an insubordinate woman, flirting with equality and straying into the masculine sphere of intellect and politics expressed the dangers of the French experience. Revolution could mean transgressions and even reversals of class and gender roles.

3

The early students of social science felt they were developing a new kind of knowledge as revolutionary as the situation they were trying to interpret and guide. This chapter focuses on the period beginning with the French Revolution and especially on the creation of two approaches which occupied an important place in the map of social science for at least the next 100 years. The first was the 'science of the poor' created in the 1790s which developed into scientific philanthropy, practical social science and then scientific social work. From a second direction the early writings and projects of Jeremy Bentham fed into a hard Utilitarian amalgam of the sciences of political economy and government, sciences of the public sphere which different versions of social science tried to soften and supplement or to destroy and replace. Both varieties of science also had gender implications which would ramify for years afterward. The social science tradition was contested but also had a coherence which can be illustrated in this chapter by the way in which early proponents, however much they disagreed with each other, ruthlessly brushed aside some pre-existing modes of social study and ways of treating the poor. Evangelical philanthropists, Benthamite materialists and incipient socialists also set a new agenda for dispute which included items like science, experience and social experiment.

THE FRENCH REVOLUTION AND THE SCIENCE OF THE POOR

The social turbulence of the 1790s traumatized the British ruling classes. As Lady Shelley observed, 'the awakening of the labouring classes after the first shocks of the French revolution made the upper classes tremble. Every man felt the necessity of putting his house in order.'[3] She could have added that the rich also wanted to order the houses of the poor. Scientific philanthropy, emergent in the 1780s, became part of this ordering project. The most important exponent of the science of the poor was the Society for Bettering the Condition of the Poor founded by Sir Thomas Bernard (1750-1818), a full-time philanthropist with Evangelical connections, who observed in 1797 that

The interests of the poor classes of society are so

interwoven with those of every part of the community, that there is no subject more deserving of general attention, nor any knowledge more entitled to the exalted name of science, than that in which their well-being is concerned....

Let us therefore make the inquiry into all that concerns the POOR and the promotion of their happiness, a SCIENCE—let us investigate *practically*, and upon system, the nature and consequences, and let us unite in the extension and improvement of those things which experience hath ascertained to be beneficial to the poor.[4]

The Bettering Society began its work in 1796 at the high tide of ruling-class panic. The previous year had been marked by a disastrous harvest, rocketing food prices, widespread food riots, soaring poor rates, intense radical activity and army disaffection. The following year threatened a French invasion and brought active Irish rebellion and mutiny in the fleet. This moment of crisis provoked an outpouring of literature in important new modes. Not only did Jeremy Bentham turn his attention in 1795 to the management of the poor but key Evangelical texts about social duty by William Wilberforce and the Reverend Thomas Gisborne appeared in 1797 along with Frederick Eden's monumental statistical survey of the *State of the Poor*. In 1798 the Reverend Malthus brought out his controversial first Essay which argued the natural tendency of population to grow faster than food supply and which disrupted ideas of divinely-composed harmony between man and nature and of Christian duty to the Poor.[5] The Bettering Society also took part in the cultural offensive which called for a new ordering of knowledge as part of a new ordering of social relations. The Society did not carry out its own investigations but served as a national clearing house, producing *Annual Reports* which contained hundreds of accounts of philanthropic experiments from all over the country, suitably annotated with deductions from the facts.

The Bettering Society used a rhetoric of science partly to devalue older modes of charity which they rudely called 'indiscriminate almsgiving', a name which stuck for the next hundred years. They used positive words to signify systematic and continuous effort leading to a clear end which they juxtaposed to intermittent, 'spontaneous', 'undirected' activity informed by equally disordered patterns of thought: 'speculation not fact', 'indefinite research', 'conjecture and hazard'. In fact the Society was attacking modes of charity which had definite but different logics where the justification lay as much in the process of giving as in the result. One such mode of charity valued alms as a personal act of Christian help and love and as a 'state of mind', a 'communion with the supreme spirit of love at work in the universe', to use Beatrice Webb's words in the late nineteenth-century phase of the battle with scientific charity. Another mode of giving was underpinned by Christian ideas of the divine right of the poor to subsistence particularly in times of dearth, with charity as a kind of compromise between the perfect state of community of property and the real estate of private property. In terms of *realpolitik*, charity featured in the dazzling theatricality of eighteenth-century rule which could step in occasionally and shower beneficence on the labouring poor to stifle smouldering discontent.[6]

The science of the poor functioned as a broad scientific church attracting many kinds of Christians but also other groups like the Benthamites to its project. Evangelical Anglicans took an especially active part in scientific philanthropy: indeed William Wilberforce, the scourge of slavery, and Shute Barrington, the Bishop of Durham, helped to start the Bettering Society. During the revolutionary crisis, the Evangelicals moved from being a marginal faction of zealots within the Church of England into the central role of the moral vanguard of the ruling classes. The inner circle of the 'Saints' were mercantile capitalists and politicians, who lived around Clapham Common, and had connections with landed interests and outposts in country places. In a Church notoriously relaxed about personal and social conduct, the Evangelicals believed deeply in human corruption and in the need for a vital religion to serve as a bulwark against the surging sea of sin. A key element in their personal faith was constant vigilance and painstaking self-inspection. Every minute of every hour of every day, Evangelicals surveyed and took account of their spiritual condition. William Wilberforce MP even kept statistical tables of the state of his soul (see p. 7.)[7]

Far from being in conflict with science, the Evangelical habit of mind was deeply rational in the Weberian sense that it methodically surveyed and interpreted experience in the light of

The State of William Wilberforce's Soul from R. & S. Wilberforce, *The Life of William Wilberforce*

	Major application. Study.	Minor application. Study.	Requisite company, &c. Visits, &c.	Unaccounted for, &c. Dressing.	Relaxation suâ causâ.	Squandered.	Serious reading, and meditation.	Bed.	Total.	House of Commons, business, &c. / Left out of plan.
Jan. 26th.		5¾	1¾	1¼	¼	½	1½	8½	24	4½
— 27th.			1	½	¼	2¼	1	8½	24½	11
— 28th.			8	¾			½	9¼	24	5½
— 29th.			5½	¼		1	¾	8¼	23½*	7½
— 30th.			8	1			¾	7¾	24	6½
— 31st.			7	½	¼	3¼	¾	9½	25	3¾
Sunday Feb. 1st.			4½	1	¼		8½	8¼	22½	
— 2nd.			~~4¼~~ 3¾	½	¼	2¼	¾	8¼	24¾	8½
— 3rd.			4½	¼			¾	9	23¾	9¼
— 4th.			8¾	1¼			¾	8	24	5¼

	Major application.	Minor application.	Meals, relaxation, &c.	Dressing, and undressing.	Squandered.	Serious reading, &c.	Necessary company.	Bed.	Total.
April. Thursday 9th.	7¾	1¼	4¾	¾		1		8¾	24¼
Good Friday, 10th.	5¾		4½	½		4½		8¾	24
— 11th.	9¼		5¾	¾		1		8	24¾
Easter Sunday, 12th.	3½		4¾	1	¼	5¾	¼	7	22½
— 13th.	9¾		6	¼		1¼		7¾	25
— 14th.	8¼		5½	¾		¾		7¾	23
— 15th.	10		6¼	½		½		9	26¼

chosen goals, and harnessed means to ends. Max Weber has suggested that only a motive as powerful as the desire for eternal salvation could have impelled people to re-form their customary mental patterns in this fundamental way.[8] Moreover, around the time of the French Revolution, when irreligion connoted Jacobinism, only a consonance between religion and science would have enabled science to gain purchase among groups with social power. Although other forces also moved in the same direction, Evangelical and Methodist religion in the period reinforced the scientific habit of mind. As a deeply-felt religious duty, at a time of social emergency, the Evangelicals then turned their practice of self-inspection outward towards the poor and became active practitioners of scientific philanthropy.

In the science of the poor, personal contact was still to be important. As Bernard insisted, using the word 'service' which later became conspicuous in social science, duty to the poor was 'A *personal* service, injoined by the highest authority, and cannot be commuted'. But the form of personal service was to change into more continuous modes of enquiry and intervention to transform character. The new science had breathtaking ambition. It aimed at nothing less than re-forming the mentality of the poor. New psychic habits were to be inculcated: obedience, 'industry, prudence, foresight, virtue, and cleanliness'.[9] 'To give without reforming, is but to pour water into a broken cistern' announced the Saints' own vicar, the Reverend John Venn, Treasurer of the Clapham Bettering Society, one of several local groups formed to put the new principles into practice.[10] Bernard, like Venn, stressed the need for the poor to help themselves but usually under supervision. He supported a vast array of parish agencies which would create more employment or enable the poor to make the best use of their meagre wages but which would also install the powerful in a continuous administrative role. He envisioned active patronage not self-government as the rule. Even more suspicious of working-class self-activity, Jeremy Bentham called for a national holding company for friendly societies to correct a situation where 'unlettered minds have been left to wander in the field of calculation without a guide'.[11]

The Clapham Bettering Society exemplified the 'new area in the science of managing the poor'. Before even starting their work of permanent improvement, they subdivided the parish into nine districts and took a census of poor families: they then assigned voluntary visitors to monitor eight to ten families on a weekly basis. Applicants for relief were even more carefully scrutinized by the visitors and by the 'Confidential Agent', one Mrs Clements of Bromells Road, who kept a stock of medical supplies and a register of nurses and charwomen to give practical help. 'By this plan', they felt, 'the benefits of information and inspection were attained in as perfect a degree as is usually the case in a very small country village.'[12] But, as Hannah More discovered, this vision of a small known rural community was a myth. In the Mendip villages of Somerset, she found such 'a great gulf' of ignorance and contempt dividing farmers and gentry from labourers, that they 'hardly thought they were children of a common father'.[13] Her work, like that of many Evangelicals in the countryside, aimed to turn myth into fact, not least by doing a survey of village families before starting up her usual cluster of new institutions, and then by making sure that the Sunday school teachers would also act as routine home visitors. In the country as well as the city, the thoroughness of the Evangelical attempt at 'surveillance' (one French word they continued to use) was impressive and seminal. It helped to set the pattern for surveys and social work over the next century, and eventually found its way into sociology in our time.

WOMEN AND THE SCIENCE OF THE POOR

Besides helping to pioneer a new approach to the treatment of the poor, the Evangelicals were important in shaping new models of the proper relations between the sexes. Social science became a setting where both projects intersected and thus a location for manifold tensions and conflicts. The Evangelicals believed in the essential difference between male and female nature and gave women a vital role to play in the fight against sin. Men were more robust, physically and intellectually. But women, although delicate, had a latent moral dynamism which could be released safely in the proper setting, usually seen as the family and the home. The public world of men was depicted as an arena for aggression and conflict: the domestic realm ruled by women as an abode of peace and love. No hypocrites, the Clapham Saints actually lived what they preached, much preferring an evening at home to an outing to a gentlemen's club.[14] By 1840, Evangelical ideas about gender had become dominant in the Church of England and were shared by most other Protestant denominations. These ideas ratified some earlier Enlightenment and medical thinking about gender division and more importantly prepared the way for the solid medical and scientific reinforcement which came in the mid-nineteenth century. As Davidoff and Hall have shown, these religious ideas converged with changes in forms of property and with shifts in work and leisure patterns to push the worlds of middle-class men and women ever-farther apart.[15] This interpenetration of religious teaching and capitalist institutions made evangelicalism supremely although not exclusively the religion of the middle class.

Despite the powerful pressures holding them in the home, women continually contested the boundary between public and private spheres. The idea of woman as a moral vanguard was dynamic and unstable, capable of breaking beyond any limits arbitrarily set down to confine it. Even in the earliest Evangelical days, and at the centre of the highest Evangelical circles, Hannah More, who never married, kept a public space open for women. 'Charity', she insisted in her novel *Coelebs in Search of a Wife*, 'is the calling of a lady; the care of the poor is her profession.'[16] Evangelical women reserved for themselves an important role to play in the 'science of the poor'. But they could move into public work only by transposing to it their role from the family and the home. Thus Evangelicals paradoxically allowed for a public role which both extended and confirmed a private identity. In addition to work in Sunday schools (where they could be 'nursing mothers to the poor'), and in public institutions like hospitals (where they could be what the 'judicious Mistress of a family is to her household'), Evangelical women took an active part in the district visiting societies which burgeoned before 1850 and aimed to keep routine contact with the poor in their own dwellings.[17] Thus rich women literally set out to put the houses of the poor in order, or rather order the poor and their dwellings into families and homes. However circumscribed their public space, rich women had continually to fight to keep it open. Even Hannah More had to defend herself against a malicious campaign by the local farmers who denounced her to the Bishop for preaching Methodist heresy and for practising and inciting insubordination.[18]

Hannah More's philanthropy in the Mendip villages of rural Somerset set a pioneering example. Having revolutionized her own life, Hannah did not hesitate to overhaul the lives of others. Once a best-selling author, an original blue stocking (part of the *bas bleu* circle), a pet of the aged Dr Johnson and an intimate of the theatrical Garricks, she converted to vital religion late in life.[19] She is best known as the author of lively religious tracts in the form of homely stories which circulated in their millions. She should be better known for opening a rare window onto the interactions of rich and poor women in the science of the poor. With her sister Patty, she set up Female Friendly Societies or Benefit Clubs which she used as key instruments for shaping a new practice of motherhood, a new pattern of sexual conduct and a new model of social relations.

Club members were asked to make a change in their customary behaviour in exchange for a material reward. In this rural area fertility was often tested first and women married, if they married at all, after they became pregnant. In order to reverse this order of events, the sisters offered to any member who could produce a certificate from her vicar attesting to her virginity, a marriage portion of one bible, five shillings and a pair of white stockings hand-knitted by Hannah or Patty. Similarly, a pregnant member, if she could produce proof of wedlock, would get the lying-in benefit.[20] The More sisters tried to load motherhood with a heavy responsibility for the surveillance of children and for securing their future prospects, temporal and eternal. The sisters used emotional blackmail freely: 'My dear women, which of you could bear to see your darling child condemned to everlasting destruction?' was a typical More reproach.[21] Shadowy indications suggest that a different pattern of child-rearing existed, with children left out of doors much of the time and subject to the 'great boys' of the village, seemingly adolescent youths whose authority the sisters were trying to break. Stand up to the boys' ridicule, the sisters urged the mothers, send your children to Sunday school, 'what do you think it most easy to endure—a little ridicule now, or everlasting condemnation hereafter'.

The sisters, like other Evangelicals, tried to transform class relations by speaking about spiritual equality. But undercutting this rhetoric, they also used three powerful representations, which endured in social science and which served to devalue and subordinate their poorer sisters and brothers. The first was a language of imperialism and colonialism. The More sisters saw their work in 'my little colony' as a civilizing mission and kept talking about 'savages' in Somerset parishes 'as dark as Africa' and about their astonishment at finding 'so much ignorant stupidity out of the interior of Africa'.[22] Naming people as dark, ignorant, savages who are less than human makes it easier to have few qualms about acting as cultural imperialists, riding roughshod over their customs and values, in order to colonize and civilize them. This representation of black savagery sometimes shaded into an image of demonic darkness marking out yet another borderline between human and nonhuman. The Nailsea glassmakers' workshop looked like hell:

> the great furnaces roaring—the swearing, eating and drinking of these half-dressed, black-looking beings, gave it a most infernal and horrible appearance.[23]

Evangelicals, secondly, saw the poor as diseased in a powerful representation of health and disease which linked the physical, moral, mental and political dimensions of life. All these levels could exist in an ordered or disordered state and social problems were seen as ailments for treatment. As all the levels interconnected, 'disorder' in one area could cause disease in another. The disease imagery was very powerful in the Evangelical mind and eventually in middle-class perception more generally. In the early Evangelical days, the disorders causing most concern were moral and political: religious infidelity and the French Revolution formed the most virulent poisons. If Tom Paine appeared as the arch-poisoner, even the historian Gibbon did not remain immune from Hannah More's jabs: 'how many souls have his writings polluted! Lord, preserve others from their contagion'. Conversely, vital Christianity was presented as health-restoring. The Reverend Venn preached that

> The Gospel is the great remedy supplied by God for the disorder introduced into the world by sin; and the dispensing of this remedy is entrusted to His Ministers.... He communicated spiritual health...in the same manner as He healed the sick by the hands of His Apostles and Prophets.[24]

The disease imagery also opened a space for women who had been the traditional family tenders of the sick. Thomas Bernard argued that women were needed as a kind of all-purpose *cordon sanitaire* to protect the nation from the French pestilence:

> A pestilential disease, of the most malignant nature, has corrupted the morals and mental sanity of a large portion of Europe. In order to exclude the infection, some line of demarcation is necessary to be drawn between Britain and the infected regions: and, if more cannot be done,—at least that sex to whose early care and instruction, we owe the religious and virtuous impression of the infantile and youthful age, should be preserved pure and immaculate; so as to be rendered the instruments of health and safety to others, whom curiosity or inattention may have exposed to the contagion.[25]

Physical contagion moved more centrally into the spotlight after the 1832 cholera epidemic (see Chapter 3) although the eighteenth-century science of hygienics had given it some attention.

Third, the Mores behaved as scolding mothers and antici-pated and prepared the way for a complex discourse of motherhood which was to become conspicuous in scientific social work. The Mores tended to treat their poorer sisters like naughty children. Even at the happiest time of the year, the Anniversary Day of the Women's Clubs, the More sisters man-aged to deliver an annual 'charge' which was more like an annual scolding. Although sometimes praised for being obedi-ent, the women were mostly reprimanded for Sunday shopping, dancing, gossiping, lax school attendance, sex before marriage.[26] To a modern ear, the tone of voice often sounds condescending and full of rebuke. Yet the Mores insisted that they were treating the poor with kindness and love. The discourse of motherhood and love was riddled with contradictions.

How did village women receive these messages? It is hard to hear their reactions because rural women are about the most silent of the silent majority in conventional historical sources. Nonetheless in addition to careful surmise about what the villagers could have found attractive or repellent, it is possible to find in the Mores' accounts of their work points of disagreement and even resistance which disclose the clash of different cultural values and the violation of precious taboos. There is evidence of complex interactions involving mutual give and take within a power relationship which was fundamentally skewed. Thus poor women got real material benefits from the clubs at a time of considerable hardship while their children received clothing, money and treats from the Sunday schools and even an avenue of social advance for those who became teachers. It would seem that the young women were not unprepared to re-form their sexual behaviour (perhaps to practise a bit of birth control). Hannah reported that she

> had the satisfaction of seeing the first dawn of hope on a subject of great difficulty and delicacy. My young women who were candidates for the bridal presents, which I bestow on the virtuous, gravely refused to associate with one who had been guilty of immoral conduct; whereas it formerly used to afford matter for horrid laughter and disgusting levity.[27]

Despite initial fears, it would seem that mothers did send their children to Sunday school and it may be that they were responding to a religion of spiritual equality which valued them for the first time.

But resistance erupted and women were prepared to vote with their feet over death and funeral practices. In this period, and in the following century, death provided a clear window through which to see fundamental clashes of cultural difference. Not only in the Mores' circuit but in other parts of the country the same situation developed. Rich patronesses wanted to give club benefits for marriage, childbirth and sickness. Poor women valued, above all of these, funeral payments. As a Rowberrow woman openly declared, 'What did a poor woman work hard for, but in hopes she should be put out of the world in a tidy way?' To the rich women, this notion of putting the dead before the living 'was a pitch of absurdity almost beyond bearing'.[28] Yet bear it they did because without the provision of funeral benefit, they found that poor women simply would not join or stay in the clubs. However unequal in power, poor women could influence the aims and conduct of the clubs and rich women could learn from the relationship.

Richer women made palpable gains. They could use the science of the poor to open public space for themselves. Largely under Evangelical influence, there was an explosion of philanthropic societies after 1790 in which women figured increasingly as subscribers (rising from 13 to 31 per cent of the Bettering Society list between 1798 and 1805). Even more strikingly, women began to run societies aimed at poor women. In 1804, the Bettering Society created a model Ladies' Committee for the Education and Employment of the Female Poor which started life by creating local groups and by making a survey to discover what work needed to be done. Yet a contradiction was also becoming apparent. Affluent women were trying to keep choices open for themselves about acceptable femininity, instead of allowing all possibility to shrink into the mould of married motherhood in the home. Yet it was precisely this narrower model of femininity that they began to try to impose through their philanthropy upon those poor women who were not domestic servants. The Ladies supported only home-based employment for the female poor, 'without withdrawing them from their habitations, or preventing a regular attention to their domestic concerns'.[29] Servants could be also be placed into the family discourse as the surrogate daughters of well-to-do mothers. An expanding social role for affluent women did not necessarily lead to the enlargement of sisterhood between women of different social classes. It could as easily drive a more 'scientific' wedge between rich and poor.

RADICAL UTILITARIANS VERSUS WHIG PHILOSOPHERS

The desire of early scientific philanthropy to secure a pre-industrial order provided just one impetus fuelling the complicated engine of social science. From other social locations and vantage points, the revolutionary crisis appeared to be less about social disintegration and more about the obstruction of positive new energies. During the French Wars, plebian radicals forged a new identity through struggle at the same time as an unprecedented growth of capitalist enterprise, in the face of government restraint, produced a surge of middle-class consciousness.[30] In this dynamic situation, radical thinkers became impatient to dismantle older or inhibiting intellectual

15

paradigms. For more than half a century after 1789, Utilitarian science stood in the vanguard of critical bourgeois intellect. Jeremy Bentham (1745-1832) was busily developing his theory of legislation and his Panopticon project around the years of the French Revolution but his intellectual approach became more influential in the 1820s in the proselytizing hands of his disciple James Mill (1773-1836) and in the 1830s, when his last secretary, Edwin Chadwick (1800-90), began to shape state projects for national improvement (see p. 76). Eager to sweep away the dead wood of the past, the Utilitarians, like radicals of other stripes, became impatient with intellectual approaches which prioritized historical methods and historical veneration.

This iconoclasm shaped the radical attitude to the Scottish Enlightenment and to the Philosophic Whiggism that developed out of it. At the Universities of Glasgow and Edinburgh in the last half of the eighteenth century, a group of thinkers including Adam Smith and Adam Ferguson created a discipline of moral philosophy which aimed to put the study of social life on an empirical basis. Not only did they work with an implicit idea of a social system but, being equally interested in social dynamics, they set out to periodize universal history and constructed a sequence of social stages from 'savagery' to 'civil society'. For the Scottish philosophers, significant change took place slowly and was the outcome of many small actions which often did not have their intended results: they left little room for purposive human agency in social change. In Ferguson's words, 'nations stumble upon establishments which are indeed the result of human action, but not the execution of any human design'.[31] Some Scottish thinkers were wary of tampering with any institutions which had served well enough. Ferguson even opposed extending the vote to the middle class.

The idea that the past and present formed a living, slow-growing organism which should be disturbed only with the greatest caution became ideological dynamite when thrown into the political arena in 1790 by Edmund Burke in his *Reflections on the Revolution in France*. To other intellectual and political contenders, this analysis was a reactionary smokescreen. Tom Paine jeered, 'the vanity and presumption of governing beyond the grave is the most ridiculous and insolent of tyrannies'. No democrat at this point, Bentham also insisted that 'of all tyranny the most relentless is that of the dead: for it cannot be mollified'.

An appeal to the wisdom of the ages, James Mill later dismissed it as 'an argument for everlasting postponement'.[32] Personal experience of the venerable constitution fed Bentham's intellectual exasperation. Samuel Bentham, Jeremy's younger brother, was appointed Inspector General of Naval Works in 1796 and found that his reforming broom, bristling with plans for rationalization and mechanization, ran straight into the stonewall of custom. Jeremy Bentham's pet scheme for the Panopticon prison was similarly frustrated by a government which withdrew support. Both brothers were then drafted into just that army of parasites on the public treasury they most despised. The government gave Jeremy Bentham a generous cash payment of £23,000 to compensate for his abortive efforts and forced Samuel out of his post with a hefty pension of £1,250 a year.[33] Perhaps the brothers had the last laugh after all. In 1824, Jeremy used his money to found the *Westminster Review*, the sworn enemy of aristocratic corruption and a powerful mouthpiece of Utilitarian science.

Radicals who wanted a science of society also wanted a perspective which would allow for more effective control of the social process and for immediate changes. Despite their fundamental difference in political views, it is significant how similar in logical structure were the analyses of the early Utilitarians and socialists. Both went outside history and put a model of essential human nature at the centre of their thinking. However incompatible their specific models, both groups thought in terms of human psychology with its drives, desires, capacities and potential. The socialists also endowed people with natural rights to realize this potential, which Bentham sniffed away as 'nonsense on stilts'. Whether from above or below, society was now seen as more of an artefact which could be designed and engineered to suit essential human nature, although the different groups proposed very different degrees of social intervention.

Utilitarian science rested on deceptively simple assumptions. 'Nature' announced Bentham 'has placed mankind under the governance of two sovereign masters, *pain* and *pleasure*.'[34] By nature, human beings sought after pleasure and tried to avoid pain. The job of the legislator was to engineer the greatest happiness for the greatest number and, in this way, effect the well-being of the community. In theory, no institutions, customs

17

or social classes could be justified on the grounds of historical survival, divine law or natural right. They had to pass the test of utility, that is, prove that they conduced to the greatest happiness of the greatest number. However, this simple formula concealed a Pandora's box of contestable concepts and ample room for internal inconsistency. Who was to define what happiness, pleasure and pain meant? Who would assess the greatest happiness and by what means? If the condition of the majority of the people, the labouring poor, was not given priority, did this not amount to a contradiction between premiss and practice?

Bentham's own thinking contained definite tensions between the democratic logic of his philosophy and the class-locked limits he laid down to contain it. Thus, although Bentham thought that the happiness of the labouring poor would be increased by more subsistence and greater equality, nonetheless he subordinated these to what he considered a greater good, security of private property:

> when security and equality are in conflict, it will not do to hesitate a moment. Equality must yield....if property should be overturned with the direct intention of establishing an equality of possessions, the evil would be irreparable. No more security, no more industry, no more abundance![35]

When it came to his remedy for indigence, the degrading surveillance in Panopticon was justified because the pain caused by deprivation of liberty or dignity amounted to less than the pain of starvation.

Overriding the happiness of the poor was one thing, but using the utility principle to challenge the legitimacy of historically established interest groups, indeed the doctrine of 'constitutional balance' itself, was quite another. James Mill's *An Essay on Government* of 1819 started from the premiss that men's 'desires are directed to pleasure and relief of pain as ends and to wealth and power as the principal means'. He argued that the monarchy and aristocracy would try to get as much power as possible and the only effective way to curb them was to make the interest of the community coterminous with that of the government by at least extending the franchise to the middle class: he was evasive about a more universal suffrage.[36] This essay provoked a furore, albeit a delayed explosion in the later

1820s when the issue of parliamentary reform became an active item on the political agenda.

The Utilitarians formed the abrasive cutting edge of middle-class intellect and repelled others who wanted to live more comfortably within older categories. The issue of scientific method and of respect for the past became bones of contention in an intellectual dogfight with the philosophic Whigs, grouped round the *Edinburgh Review*. The Whigs, through their spokesman, historian Charles Babington Macaulay, argued for a more inductive approach to the study of human motivation which took custom and culture into account. They stressed the Enlightenment view of the slowness of beneficial change, the Burkeian view of the proven serviceability of the Constitution and their own view that respect for constitutional tradition was what dignified the noble science of politics. From these vantage points, the Utilitarians looked suspiciously like some kind of Jacobin sect:

> as little inclined to respect antiquity, as enthusiastically attached to its ends, as unscrupulous in the choice of its means as the French Jacobins themselves—but far superior to the French Jacobins in acuteness and information, in caution, in patience, and in resolution.[37]

But the amount of dissension between the various factions of philosophers must not be exaggerated. They could find common ground and work together in organizations like the Society for the Diffusion of Useful Knowledge which tried to teach correct political economy to the working classes.

GENDER DIVISION AND THE SCIENCES OF THE PUBLIC SPHERE

By the 1820s, the Enlightenment synthesis had splintered. Taking its place beside the contested science of politics, a fragment of moral philosophy had developed into an equally riven science of political economy, the first discipline to specialize in the social sciences. The new pattern was durable and these enquiries became increasingly dominant while the Enlightenment's comparative historical approach, although it survived, slipped into a more recessive place. Both Parson Malthus (appointed the first professor of the subject in 1805) and banker David Ricardo were the brokers assisting at the new intellectual issue of political economy. The later arrival, Ricardo gained wider acceptance for his theorization of dynamic capitalism and managed to bridge the cracks which otherwise separated the Philosophic Radicals and Whigs. J.S. Mill recounted how his father and he welded this 'modern political economy' together with the Benthamite approach to government and other elements into a compound 'Philosophic Radicalism'.[38]

In the first instance, the new sciences developed largely outside academia within a cultural practice closely attuned to active politics and social issues of the day. Thus key texts in political economy often appeared in the periodical press, an important new feature of the cultural scene. By this means, the subject gained enough legitimacy by the late 1820s for new professorships to be established not least at University College which the Philosophic Whigs and Radicals had helped to found in 1828. Clubs and mutual improvement groups also proliferated. James Mill helped to form the Political Economy Club (1821) while J.S. Mill ran the Utilitarian Society (1822-6), which re-educated young Cambridge graduates and others in the principles of Philosophic Radicalism and held robust debates 'lutte corps à corps between Owenites and political economists'. The Philosophic Radicals tried to establish a parliamentary presence and only gave up the dream of leading the people when the growth of working-class movements revealed the fissure that existed between middle and working-class radicalism.[39] Women also featured in this cultural scene, as shown by the salon of Harriet Grote, the 'Queen of the radicals', but their role was becoming problematic.

The early Philosophic Radicals did not set out to create knowledge which mirrored emerging gender divisions; indeed some had a deep commitment to extending women's public role. Despite James Mill's own notorious views, both his son and Jeremy Bentham supported women's suffrage. More importantly, John Stuart Mill in partnership with Harriet Taylor later stretched the scope of political economy to relax some of the constraints I am about to explore. Nonetheless, in the early period, political economy and the science of politics were pre-eminently the sciences of the male elements of human nature and of male activity in the public sphere. The early Utilitarians worked with an abstract deductive method and erected at the centre of their science a male model of an egotistical individual whose happiness consisted in actively and rationally pursuing

> the leading objects of human desire; Wealth, Power,
> Dignity, Ease; including escape from the contrary;
> Poverty, Impotence, Degradation, Toil.[40]

It is interesting how limited was James Mill's rollcall of desire. The pleasures and pains itemized here were very much the glittering prizes and murky pitfalls of the public world of politics and commerce. Some leading objects of bourgeois desire were conspicuously missing from the list: salvation, morality, love, friendship, benevolence, family, to name but a few. These fell beyond the pale of the sciences of public life and were increasingly consigned to a separate science of morals and to the feminine part of human nature. It is also interesting how confined to the affluent were most of the Utilitarian juxtapositions. A working-class family would certainly have feared poverty but would have seen security, in the sense of absence of anxiety about subsistence, as its opposite.[41] A family of the working class would have hated impotence but aimed for mutuality and independence rather than individual power. Instead of ease, they would probably have juxtaposed useful work to toil.

From the 1820s onward, the socialists argued that the whole of human nature should be explored in a new field that they explicitly called 'social science'. These largely working-class Owenites, the subject of the next chapter, embraced the so-called feminine moral characteristics like love and compassion and built them into a sexless model of human nature (which sometimes sat uneasily with the actual practice in their local groups where men often governed while women made the tea!). Middle-class students tended to call for an expanded political economy or for an additional science to supplement political economy and focus the moral and intellectual dimensions of human nature and social life. Malthus was the first in a line of Christian thinkers, which included Archbishop Whately of Dublin and Rev. Thomas Chalmers of Glasgow in the 1820s, who wanted political economy to expand its conceptual framework beyond wealth to include national happiness and virtue or rather national happiness conceived as virtue.[42] The statisticians of the 1830s (Chapter 3 below) eagerly collected moral and intellectual statistics.

21

The gender dimensions took longer to confront. The subject matter of the public sciences made the entry of women either as thinkers or objects of scrutiny increasingly complicated. Aspiring women writers as well as the emergent intellectual community receiving them were often highly sensitive to the issue of gender division in intellectual work. The experience of Harriet Martineau (1802-76), one of the few 'lady Economists', makes this clear. In touch with the radical London circle of Unitarian Christians then revolving around the *Monthly Repository*, which had been Mary Wollstonecraft's set from the 1780s, and where Harriet Taylor moved in company with John Stuart Mill from 1830 onwards, Martineau might be expected to have been more daring than some other middle-class sisters. But she was also a Norwich Unitarian and very aware of the division between public and private spheres which she negotiated with care. Her *Autobiography* tells how her entry into public writing took place only with permission of male relatives. She invoked a secularized version of the calling to justify her ambitious project, first conceived around 1827, for monthly *Illustrations of Political Economy*. With 'the People' standing in for God, she argued that the wants of the People (in the double sense of needs and desires) made her work imperative. She told the story of her search for a publisher using the techniques of melodrama, including fainting fits and near collapse, to dramatize the difficulty involved.[43] Against all predictions, in 1832 the series became an immediate bestseller, established her as a professional author and made her financially independent for life.

Whether hostile or friendly, the periodical press, which played what Judith Newton has called a gatekeeping role for the still amorphous scientific community, tried to fix women's proper intellectual place when responding to Martineau's work. The conservative *Quarterly Review*, which published Malthus's economic writings while rejecting his population theories, attacked her as a gender transgressor, caricaturing her as a Utilitarian 'She Politician' and as a 'female Malthusian' who rejected all truly womanly views and roles:

> a *woman* who thinks child-bearing a *crime against society*! An unmarried woman who declaims against *marriage*!! A *young woman* who deprecates charity and a provision for the poor!!![44]

Despite its Whig views, the *Edinburgh Review* echoed some of the *Quarterly*'s opinions on women's intellectual place. William Empson, who later became the journal's editor, began his review by underlining women's long-standing reign over 'domestic economy' (as 'proper legislators for, as well as ministers of, the interior'). He also singled out one aspect of political economy 'in which women have an honourable and preeminent interest', namely 'its intimate connexion with the protection and comfort of the poor'.[45]

Empson welcomed the new 'priestesses' of political economy not as scientific authorities but as popularizers, particularly effective when they retailed the science in 'practical' tales, accessible not least to the poor. Martineau, however, kept eluding his categories. Empson admired her storytelling skill, which might appear faint praise, when novel-writing was increasingly seen as a female talent; indeed James Mill initially told her publisher that the project should be recast into didactic form. Empson felt differently and credited her with a real methodological breakthrough for using fiction (what she called her method of exemplification) to control, like a scientific experiment, the complex variables at play in 'the commingled mass of human affairs'. J.S. Mill thought the same method had reduced the '*laissez-faire*' system to absurdity...by merely carrying it out to all its consequences.[46] In the end, Empson wanted to suspend her somewhere between two gender poles and keep her from shrinking to 'mere circulating-library glory' while also warning her not to create 'a millennium of her own, in which our ladies will have taken out of our monopolising hands the cares of Parliament and public life'. He advised her, before publication, always to submit 'her writings to some dull friend' with a 'calm, sober eye' (a male censor?) for the 'detection of inadvertencies'.[47]

This consensus that women had a special affinity for the home, the family and the poor and a circumscribed relation to the sciences of public life supplied scientific reinforcement to teachings on gender division coming from the Evangelicals and elsewhere. These ideas fell on fertile social ground, which was not surprising. The doctrine of public and private spheres was exceedingly convenient to middle-class ambition. Karl Marx and others have noted how a rising social class always sees itself not as a sectional interest group, but as the carrier of the full potential of all humanity. The rising British middle class was no exception. In its political struggles, it presented itself as more intelligent and virtuous than either the barbaric aristocracy or the brutish populace. James Mill spoke of 'the class which is universally described as both the most wise and the most virtuous part of the community, the middle rank'.[48] By keeping much of the morality of the class at home in the custody of women, the middle class at once retained its virtue and also left its men free to pursue the amoral activities of politics and commerce on which real power rested. Women at home carried a heavy responsibility for the whole class. Not only did they have religious redemptive powers but they were put in charge of the very qualities which underlay the middle-class claim to embody human values. Gender division became part of the most positive middle-class sense of self and was difficult to dislodge.

Nonetheless, over time, women carved a pathway into public scientific work mobilizing, as resources, some of the very arguments used to distance them. Already both socialist scientists and Christian economists had made the moral and intellectual dimensions of life integral to the perspective with which they critiqued political economy. Both also privileged family in their enquiries although in diametrically different ways: the socialists attacked the nuclear family and tried to remake the public sphere on a more familial pattern while the Christian economists conceived the self-supporting reproductive family as the linchpin both of religious and economic well-being. The fact that family became such an integral part of the discourse about the 'social', a development observed by Denise Riley, created space for women's involvement.[49] But also the dialectical development of the idea of the 'social', in relation to the concept of the 'political' and 'economic', meant that the area of 'social' enquiry would tend to incorporate elements that had been marginalized by the public sciences.

The importance of the moral and intellectual aspects of life in the construction of a 'social' science immediately made room for the feminine dimension. While the radical Unitarians continued to safeguard women's rationality, other sections of the middle class began to regard morality as a feminine quality and intellect as primarily a masculine quality. In *Women's Mission* (1839), Evangelical Sarah Lewis advised that men be left 'the intellectual kingdom which is theirs', but added triumphantly, 'the moral world is ours'.[50] In one crucial area, however, the education of children, intellect entered even more abridged ideas of women's domain, and women could receive good educations to prepare them for this role. Scottish Enlightenment writers, like Adam Smith, had begun to stress the importance of the family in civil society as the place where morality and virtue would be learned particularly from the mother. When the Enlightenment synthesis fractured, education was hived off into what became the concerns of social science. By the mid-nineteenth century women were explicitly mobilizing their moral and intellectual capacity to stake their claim to a place in social science, whether, like Taylor and Martineau, they borrowed from Positivist sociology or found a comfortable niche in meliorist social science. The 'communion of labour' between the sexes was institutionally recognized in the National Association for the Promotion of Social Science where women and their male supporters argued the need to include the feminine as well as the masculine dimensions of life in order to make human nature, social analysis and social progress complete. They also accentuated the special role of women's experience in bringing about this synthesis.

SCIENCE, EXPERIENCE AND SYSTEM

'Experience' occupied an important place in the language of emerging social science. Since every human being has experience, a positive value on experience could logically open the way to a very accessible form of producing social knowledge or to a 'democratic epistemology', in Logie Barrow's striking phrase.[51] Hypothetically everybody could become the students as well as the studied in social science, the active researchers as well as the objects of scrutiny. But as Jeremy Bentham brutally declared when talking of working-class friendly societies, 'democracy is no more the essence of frugality, than it is of prudence, tranquillity, or science'.[52] To explore the boundaries being erected to mark out legitimate science, it is important to ask who was privileging whose experience and, conversely, whose experience was being devalued and by whom.

The whole range of people who rejected the Scottish Enlightenment approach also rejected one form of experience: experience as lessons from history to provide guidance in the

25

present. They felt that grand historical excursions were too circuitous, too leisurely and too irrelevant for understanding and managing a fast-changing, unprecedented reality. This kind of objection was already being articulated by the self-appointed custodian of the Enlightenment tradition, Dugald Stewart, but became more pressing from the 1820s onward when new social developments, in particular the industrial revolution and the accompanying growth of large towns, came to the forefront of concern. A clear illustration of the difficulty was provided by the developing work of William Cooke Taylor (1800-49) who was educated in Dublin not Scotland. But his book on *The Natural History of Society in the Barbarous and Civilized State: An Essay Towards Discovering the Origin and Course of Human Improvement*, which appeared in 1840 and occupied two volumes, betrayed its debt to the Enlightenment in more than title alone. In it he explored the major 'social relations' in 'concrete societies' from biblical times to the present. But this was his first and last effort at grandiose history and he said why. He noted the 'wondrous' development of steam power and machinery, and the massing of people in manufacturing districts. He was certain

> that they will modify if not direct the civilization of the coming age. But experience will give us little help in determining the nature of the influence they may exercise, for the steam-engine, the cotton-mill, and the rail-road, have no precedents; history furnishes no rule for their management.[53]

Like other students of social science, he felt the need was now for an intensive study of the present, perhaps in view of an immediate rural past, as the best way to clarify the direction of industrial development and its human consequences. Taylor's next writing in 1841 took the form of *Notes of a Tour in the Manufacturing Districts of Lancashire* and then a book on *Factories and the Factory System* (1844).

Originally, science had meant orderly knowledge. From the eighteenth century, a fissure developed between science and experience, which became a real juxtaposition between experiment and experience. The growth of social science enlarged the split in a complicated way. Since controlled experiments were not so possible in the social as in the physical world, students of social science devised what they felt to be equivalent scientific procedures. Closest to experiments, the attempt to organize human resources into social 'systems' burgeoned from the 1790s. But those championing a scientific approach also stressed rigorous modes of reasoning, systematic methods of empirical investigation and the wider application of discoveries from mechanical science to social life. Utilitarians, political economists and socialists all relied on an abstract deductive method which constructed essential models of human nature, distilled from experience ('the accumulated results of experience presented in an exceedingly condensed and concentrated state')[54] and then used them to clarify the complexity of the real world. Utilitarians tended to privilege the experience of powerful men in the public world when erecting their models while socialist science made more room for the experience of the oppressed and urged the testing of concepts from above with this experience.

A new rigour and scale was demanded of empirical investigation and inductive reasoning. Since at least the sixteenth century, according to the *Oxford English Dictionary*, the word 'survey' had mainly signified the state making inventories of property, provisions or people. Statistics had denoted facts useful to the state. In the Poor Law crisis of the 1790s, the pressure mounted to take a 'surview', a commanding view of the whole of the national poor in order to take command of them in reality. Sir John Sinclair, Frederick Eden, Arthur Young, Jeremy Bentham and John Rickman all championed a census project, and the first national census was taken in 1801 with Rickman in charge. Bentham felt certain that both diagnosis and cure would have to be worked out on a national scale and preferably through a national network of completely uniform Panopticons to be run by his National Charity Company.[55] In the same decade proponents of scientific philanthropy like the Bettering Societies devised more systematic ways to collect and present their local facts, which later reached a kind of apogee in the door-to-door statistical surveys of the 1830s. In few of these fact-collecting modes, however, did the experience of the people being studied figure as important.

But social science, whether practised by Evangelical Phil-anthropists or Utilitarians, made ample space for experiments in the form of social systems which would remake human nature. These contained built-in mechanisms for inspection from above and the observations of such monitors provided the experience from which science could be made. Jeremy Bentham's Pancopticon was a triumph of rationalized surveillance. First conceived as a supervisory device for labour in the Russian shipyards, then as a reformatory device for criminals, Bentham also saw its possibilities for dealing with the Poor Law crisis: it would provide relief to any child or adult willing to work and develop industrious habits. As Bahmueller argues, Bentham regarded the Panopticon principle as a paradigm for social survey and management in any area and used a string of revealing synonyms for it: 'central inspection principle', 'inspection-architecture', 'simultaneous-inspection principle', 'principle of omnipresence'.[56] In Panopticon, every worker, prisoner or pauper could be watched at all times by an inspector positioned at a central point. Even toilet needs did not defeat this compulsive surveillance: a screen could be carefully positioned 'which answers the purpose of decency' but prevents a person 'concealing from the eye of the inspector any forbidden enterprise'. Utilitarian systems tended to use policing and pain to bring about a change in character. The workhouse of the New Poor Law, later devised by Bentham's secretary Edwin Chadwick, bore the family resemblance: like the pauper Panopticon, it aimed to be so unpleasant that people would reform their character not only inside it but in order to stay out of it in the first place.

William Wilberforce was an enthusiastic proponent of the Panopticon. But Evangelical systems tended, more shrewdly, to extract a change of behaviour by offering some material advantage to the poor. Hannah More unashamedly used bribes and treats. To get the poor to come to church, the Reverend Glass of Greenford Middlesex set up a village shop offering good quality food at low prices which could only be used with a weekly entrance ticket issued by the parish clerk after worship each week. An even more impressive exercise in intrusion and inspection was the straw platting work in Avebury. The Bettering Society keenly supported this industry which required spotless cleanliness in the work of braiding long strands of straw for use in bonnet manufacture. In Avebury, the gentry and parish officers provided employment to poor children and seized the chance to instil new standards of hygiene at the same time. They visited the children's cottages and inspected the bedding. They boiled what they could salvage. They burned and replaced the rest. They whitewashed the walls. Finally they established an inner and outer workroom, the inner sanctum 'for those who are perfectly clean, and the outer room for those who wished to be neat and decent, and were gradually becoming so'. Promotion from outer to inner was 'eagerly sought', not surprisingly for it brought the prospect of secure employment.[57]

Evangelicals and Utilitarians again displayed their scientific cousinship in their concern with systems that could mass-produce improvement. This focus paralleled or even anticipated principles of factory organization but in the area of cultural production. Where the Utilitarians championed the work of Dr Joseph Lancaster who boasted that he could educate 1,000 boys with one master using the monitorial system, Thomas Bernard was committed to the principle of 'The Division of Labour' which he thought especially well developed in the educational work of the Reverend Dr Bell, who also subdivided pupils into smaller groups to be supervised by other boys. After quoting Adam Smith on the division of labour, Bernard went on to claim that its inventor

> did not more essential service to mechanical, than Dr Bell has done to intellectual operations. It is the division of labour in his schools, that leaves the master the easy task of directing the movements of the whole machine, instead of toiling ineffectually at a single part. The principle in manufactories, and in schools, is the same.[58]

Bernard saw wide social applicability for the division of labour which he considered not only a way to produce large-scale results but to achieve proper subordination: 'Divide and Govern is as correct a motto for a school, as for a cabinet'. (Significantly, Bell created this system to teach natives in Madras in India.) The district visiting system was another example of using subdivision to try to maintain contact with and supervision over the largest possible number of the urban poor. Panopticon was perhaps the most brutal form of subdividing to rule since it proposed putting those under surveillance, particularly in prison Panopticon, into virtually silent solitary confinement.

The practitioners of the science of the poor eagerly incorporated developments from the physical sciences into their social systems, perhaps partly to enhance their own claims to

29

scientificity but also out of real enthusiasm for the improving powers of science generally. The Bettering Society, in co-operation with Count Rumford (an American who had transformed poor relief in Munich), launched in 1799 an Institution for Applying Science to the Common Purposes of Life.[59] This body tried to develop better appliances for cooking, for heating and for ventilating houses. Bentham, who was in touch with Rumford, made mechanical as well as social engineering a part of his schemes. Thus the Panopticon was to have central heating as well as central inspection. As much as nature abhors a vacuum, the Utilitarian sensibility abhorred waste and devised endless systems for continuous recycling. In Panopticon a Ptenotrophium or chicken and egg factory was designed to make use of spoiled grain. Passing on to the next generation, the habit of mind continued in Edwin Chadwick who became obsessed with a total system to make towns clean and healthy (in all senses) by means of water closets whose waste could be piped as fertilizer direct to farms.

The emphasis on practical social experiments in early social science suggests the kind of experience that was valued. In the Bettering Society's science of the poor, the experience of running projects for improvement carried weight. Reports from affluent landed or middle-class patrons, or their administrative minions formed the facts, 'the useful and practical information derived from experience', and the opinions of the same kind of people made up the 'practical observations and deductions arising out of the facts'. The Benthamites developed a different view. For them too, the inspector occupied the best position to collect the facts and make unbiased judgements. But the inspector had to be under permanent scrutiny himself, his management 'transparent' (that is totally visible) and account-able to any number of observing eyes. His accounts

> will be scrutinized by many a benevolent, many a suspicious, many an envious eye; accounts under heads previously arranged with the declared purpose of giving the most perfect transparency to the whole management in every point of view imaginable.[60]

Bentham was partly trying to replace the slipshod and peculative styles of public management which characterized the Old Corruption of the eighteenth century with a new probity of behaviour which kept to a code of clearly-stated rules. Bentham dismissed the ruling elite and their professional henchmen, lawyers and judges, as sinister interests but he also held contradictory views on the role of the profit-making middle class in this critical area of inspection and management. Although he regarded them as the repository of many virtues when arguing for suffrage reform and saw them as good managers because their own money was at stake, he felt that they had a primary interest in their own profit and were not publicly accountable for their conduct. Unlike some political economists who assumed that an unseen hand would orchestrate a natural harmony of interests, Bentham had a clear idea of the clash between private and public interest and looked towards very visible legislation to accomplish an artificial harmonization of interests: 'law alone has accomplished what all the natural feelings were not able to do'.[61] Bentham helped lay the conceptual groundwork for an enduring later link between impartial scientific vision and the properly constituted state.

It would be oversimple to identify social experiments, the large-scale production of social results and technological romanticism only with social science from above. All these features can be found in socialist social science, which was first devised by a factory owner, Robert Owen, and then developed (not without contention), by a largely working-class movement. Indeed Owen first dreamt up his model community as a Poor Law reform, which accounted for its initially hostile reception from radicals, like William Cobbett, who detected an uncanny resemblance between 'Parallelogram' and Panopticon.[62] By the late 1820s, Owen's views had been incorporated into a social science which spoke to working-class experience and which transformed community from a device for managing the poor into a vision of democratic mutuality. The new moral world of socialism, which was often called 'the social system', was to be composed of communities of mutual co-operation, where the architectural layout aimed to engineer a change in human character which would extend a familial feeling beyond blood ties and where technology would ease household drudgery as well as man's toil. Community, however, formed only one dimension of a multilayered social science, which is the subject of the next chapter.

2

SOCIAL SCIENCE
FROM BELOW

Socialists and the New Moral World, 1824-1845

If cultural revolutionaries raised a banner of science from above, working-class radicals contested it with their own version of social science from below. Utilitarians and others may have founded a Society for the Diffusion of Useful Knowledge in 1827 but radicals retaliated with a Society for the Promotion of Co-operative Knowledge in 1829 and a concept of 'really useful knowledge' to enable them to liberate their full human potential. *The Poor Man's Guardian* even counselled 'the lass' (later the Queen) Victoria to 'learn *really* useful knowledge by being apprenticed to a milliner'.[1] We need a leap of imagination to appreciate the extent to which the production of knowledge became a battleground between 1830 and 1850. Today's common sense often narrows knowledge and education to what is transmitted in a classroom: like a dose of cod liver oil, it is good to have outgrown it. Although the link between education and formal schooling was first being forged in the early nineteenth century, radicals felt strongly that all of life was a learning activity, open to everyone. The possibility of creating relevant knowledge appeared very real. The need to break mind-forged manacles seemed urgent: the national socialist newspaper, the *New Moral World*, warned,

> The aggregate of knowledge, like the aggregate of wealth, is cut up into sections, to be subjected to individual appropriation and to stand forth in mutilated detachments, the excusers of social error and the postponements of remedial truth.[2]

Working-class radicals challenged all the forms of education being provided from above: from schools with a 'policing teacher' and monitorial system, to Mechanics' Institutions whose useful knowledge was 'profitable only to the unproductive'. They urged working people to 'think for themselves' and each person to 'become his own lecturer': they considered *mutual improvement*, not authority and deference, vital to the teaching and learning process. All the resonant languages of the time became contested territory. Radicals challenged them from within by producing their own democratic versions of legitimating discourse. The philosophic Whigs may have lived happily within a dignified constitutional rhetoric. But radicals from the period of the French Revolution onwards, from the members of the Corresponding Societies right through to the Chartists, appropriated that language, turned it upside down and moulded it into democratic shape. They dubbed the working class 'the People' (the legitimate source of power), renamed the ruling classes the rebel 'factions' and located the pure Constitution in democratic Saxon times before the imposition of the Norman Yoke. Chartists juxtaposed the 'false' Christianity of Anglican parsons to the 'true' Christianity being preached within their movement, which relied on biblical texts like Genesis, Exodus and the books of the Prophets.[3]

The co-operative and socialist movement used social science to challenge the vanguard of middle-class intellect and wage battle with political economy and Utilitarian science as well as with evangelical religions. To co-operators and socialists, the painful experience of a new capitalist industrial system made it imperative to move beyond narrow political contests and grapple with social and economic power. Manchester leader, E.T. Craig, whose fustian cutting trade was being replaced by machinery, reflected on the agitation for the 1832 Reform Bill which gave the middle classes the vote:

> political justice and equality before the law are highly desirable, but there are conditions essential to happiness and human progress which politics cannot reach. The claims of labor and the power of capital; the terribly harsh and enslaving influences of competition and the increasing power of machinery to create gluts and an evergrowing surplus population in relation to poverty;

the tendency of wealth to become concentrated in the hands of a few; make the study of Social Science a question of supreme importance to the industrial classes.[4]

The co-operative and socialist movement, which drew inspiration from Robert Owen, but which had an overwhelmingly working-class membership and a large national presence between 1824 and 1845,[5] called its analyses and strategies the new 'science of society' or 'social science'. For this alone it deserves mention in any history of social science, yet it is usually ignored. This chapter will restore the Owenite co-operators and socialists to the social science picture but will also indicate why their kind of independent scientific initiative and style of robust encounter proved difficult to sustain.

SOCIAL SCIENCE VERSUS POLITICAL ECONOMY AND UTILITARIANISM

As great inventors of social language, who introduced words like 'socialism', and 'capitalism' into the English vocabulary, the early socialists did not simply create words for the sake of it. They modified language when they felt that the existing connotations of terms could no longer convey the proper meanings. Whatever its positive attraction, the term 'social science' was created because political economy was no longer an adequate concept. By 1824, William Thompson, the maverick Irish landlord, former secretary to Jeremy Bentham and early challenger of the Ricardian economists, had to keep qualifying the term political economy. He argued that in order to make it useful to 'social science, the application of which becomes the art of social happiness, it is necessary always to keep in view the complicated nature of man, the instrument to operate with and the creature to be operated upon'.[6]

From the mid-1820s onward, a contest over political economy gathered momentum. In 1824 the Combination Acts were repealed, removing the onus of criminality from trade unions, wage bargaining and strikes. Trade unions multiplied vigorously, to the surprise of Utilitarian supporters of repeal who had thought that a more permissive climate would wither this unnatural growth. Utilitarians now considered it important to teach correct political economy to the labouring classes and to this end helped found the Mechanics' Institute movement and the Society for the Diffusion of Useful Knowledge. By the early 1830s, the continuing spread of 'subversive' ideas and the growing scale of working-class organization became even more intrusive. A co-operative movement which could mount three *national* delegate Congresses, and attempts at general union which culminated in the Grand *National* Consolidated Trade Union, so alarmed political economists that they diverted their energy from original speculation to zealous proselytizing. Using images of denigration which will be monitored more closely in the next chapter, James Mill warned that the spread of radical economic ideas 'would be the subversion of civilised society, worse than the overwhelming deluge of Huns and Tartars'. Charles Knight could conceive 'the triumphant song of "Labour Defended against the claims of Capital"' only 'amid the shriek of the jackal and the howl of the wolf'.[7]

The co-operators and socialists, who were developing the social science which included this defence, represented labour in a much more positive way. Far from being barbarian or animal, far from being an inert mass to be activated by capital, working people depicted themselves as 'the producing millions', the active producers of all the things people really needed to achieve happiness. All this went unrecognized by modern political economy which had dangerously narrowed its scope. It now focused only the production of a very limited kind of wealth measured in terms of *gross* national product and profit, capital accumulation and economic growth, a focus useful only to the rich. The issues most relevant to working-class well-being were excluded. To expose the fact that political economy was highly ideological despite claiming to be objective and value-free, co-operators and socialists used a string of other names, like 'moral' or 'social economy' to signify a more acceptable field of study, and contrasted 'co-operative' to 'competitive' economists.[8]

William Hawkes Smith (1786-1840), a key Birmingham activist, illustrated the linguistic dilemma about the term political economy and finally rejected it in favour of 'social science'. In 1834, he used the phrase 'enlightened political economy' and went on to pillory 'the Oxford professor' of the subject for being so unenlightened:

Mr Senior, the Oxford Professor, boldly declares, 'It is

35

not with *happiness*, but with *wealth*, that I am concerned as a political economist; and I am justified in omitting, but am perhaps bound to omit, all considerations which have no influence on wealth'. But surely political economy, to be valuable as a science should instruct in the rules which *ought* to govern the DISTRIBUTION as well as the *production* of wealth, or it may not be improperly defined—that science which determines the *best mode* of *production* and *distribution* of THAT SPECIES of wealth, which shall be most conducive to the physical, moral and intellectual improvement, and consequently, to the greatest happiness, of the WHOLE POPULATION.[9]

That a wine merchant and stationer should feel so free to attack 'the Oxford Professor' was indicative of the deep belief in universal intellectual capacity and the determination to break existing monopolies in the production of knowledge. Hawkes Smith gave much of his time to educational work in the Unitarian Sunday School and in the Birmingham Mechanics' Institution as well as writing prolifically for the socialist press.

Still wrestling with the term in 1838, Hawkes Smith spoke of 'aristocratic' and 'democratic' political economy. This time he characterized the aristocratic variety in a more subtle way, recognizing that it was also concerned with distribution but only

in the form of wages paid *to the many*, who are used as the implements of production, and petted as 'the useful class', so long as they are wanted by the few and frowned off as soon as their work can be performed by other agents.

By contrast, democratic political economy and the 'science of society' looked forward to a more equal distribution of means to bring about an equality of happiness. Finally, in 1839, in his *Letters on Social Science*, Hawkes Smith dropped the term 'political economy' and used instead 'social science' to describe the study concerned with the greatest happiness of the greatest number.[10]

As champions of happiness, the socialists also contested key concepts used by the Utilitarians. Their attack was aimed partly at the early Utilitarian model of human psychology which also stood at the centre of political economy, and partly at the scope and method of the sciences built around it. J.S. Mill argued in 1836 that political economy does not treat of the whole of man's nature as modified by the social state, nor the whole conduct of man in society. It is concerned with him solely as a being who desires to possess wealth and who is capable of judging of the comparative efficiency of means for ends.[11]

The socialists did not comment on the gendered nature of this construct but rather targeted its moral and methodological defects. They found it morally obnoxious because it privileged the least desirable components of human psychology and helped only the most privileged groups. In terms of a scientific division of labour, Mill proposed a blueprint for a specialized and co-ordinated model of social study in which a number of sciences, including political economy, would each take different aspects of human nature as its special concern and produce its own insights although all would have to be weighed together before any recommendations for action were made. The socialists belittled this circuitous exercise as 'palpably absurd'—why go such a long way around when one could as easily start with a holistic view of human nature and society? Moreover, however much Mill might protest that he was developing a value-free science and not an art, he himself admitted that it would be a 'useless' science if it did not lead to effective policy. These issues could not be left for leisurely intellectual consideration; nor was there time to comment on the way in which Mill's thinking was moving away from narrow Utilitarianism. The urgency lay in the fact that powerful interests ('capitalists and political governors') were using unmodified political economy to frame policy right now and producing results which contradicted the greatest happiness of the greatest number.

Even by its own criteria of wealth and power, the policies founded on economic and Utilitarian science had failed. Instead of bringing that kind of happiness to the greatest number, socialists painted a dark picture of the real effects upon working people: insecurity, redundancy and final incarceration in a Poor Law bastille, a segregated workhouse which separated wives from husbands, and children from parents. The key proponent of the new workhouse was Utilitarian Edwin Chadwick, standing foursquare in the Panopticon tradition. 'Take lesson from economical commissioners', the socialists warned, and learn that the true elements of bliss consist in brick floors, high windows, a spare dietary, and family separations. The very demand for pauper provision, is the most weighty proof that the commercial system, by which a superfluity of national wealth is so misappropriated as to give rise to this demand, is the most directly adverse to the happiness of the community.[12]

Returning to the theme in a later editorial, the *New Moral World* insisted that 'the point to which true Benthamism leads—the "Greatest happiness" demands not "Free Trade" in Commerce, but free Inquiry, freedom of action and total change of Social Systems'.

IDEAL SOCIAL SCIENCE

Social science would concern itself with the complexity of human nature, with all of social life and with the whole people. 'Social' was not a bland word but carried positive connotations of being inclusive, supportive, and concerned with the optimal way people could live together, as in 'the social system of society'.[13] Owenite social science was value-laden: it staked out and stood in an openly normative tradition which never came to dominate in the university. Whether early nineteenth-century socialists, or early twentieth-century sociologists, thinkers in this tradition worked with an explicit vision of social purpose which they used to evaluate actual social states. Of course there were significant differences in the methods they used to derive ethical imperatives. Early socialists, like other necessarians, believed that uniform laws of cause and effect governed the moral and social world and that inductive study could disclose optimal conditions and the processes which produced them. By contrast the later sociologists felt that ideas of social purpose could not be derived empirically but had to be supplied by philosophical speculation[14] just as their contemporary, R.H. Tawney, felt that only theology could clarify ultimate purpose.

Committed to holistic study, early socialist science did not have departments or branches, but three levels of concern can be distinguished: the ideal, the actual and the practical. The first level had at its heart a vision of optimal human nature and social arrangements. In 1831, 'Mr Owen's Institution for Teaching the New Science of Society' displayed two wall-charts. One contained

'The Five Fundamental Facts of Human Nature'. The other, in satisfying symmetry, listed five propositions about 'The Science of Society or the Social State of Man'.[15] Socialist psychology proposed a pliable model of human nature. Every individual, although born with a unique mixture of rudimentary physical, moral and intellectual capacities, would develop these in an interplay with 'external circumstances', a process of cultural conditioning in which the influence of the prevailing social ethos and institutions would be decisive. Happiness consisted of the fullest possible development of the physical, mental and moral faculties. Thus the Owenite view of happiness differed from the early Utilitarian, which selected from current 'objects of desire', and came closer to the concern of later Liberal sociologists with the development of the best possible self. Although physical well-being, in terms of health and material security, was the prerequisite for further growth, nonetheless in the fully developed human being, the moral and intellectual capacities would predominate. In the highest moral state, an individual would gain most pleasure from increasing the happiness of others; intellectual development involved free and fearless enquiry into the conditions of happiness. This optimal equilibrium meant not only that so-called 'masculine' and 'feminine' characteristics were reunited, but that the supposedly 'feminine' moral qualities like compassion, familial feeling, mutuality (not only the desire for public reputation) were regarded as the most human for both sexes.[16] All human beings, regardless of sex or class, had the same basic nature, which was capable both of infinite improvement and rapid change.

Individual potential could be released and developed only within supportive social relationships. Owen's wall-charts specified that the 'science of society' included 'a practical knowledge' of the best mode of producing and distributing 'the most beneficial necessities and comforts, for the support and enjoyment of human life', the optimal way of governing humanity as 'a great family of mankind' and of providing education in the broadest sense. In their fight with religious views on free will and individual responsibility, the Owenites brandished the slogan 'man's character is formed for him not by him' in order to underline the power of the environment rather than the individual in forming personality. But they saw this doctrine as enabling rather than disabling. In the usual

39

necessarian way, they believed that once people understood the process of character formation, they would seek to transform the environment and their effort could become a powerful link in the chain of cause and effect. The socialists were determined to 'surround each other with circumstances' and particularly with values and social relations which embodied the precept 'love thy neighbour as thyself' or the motto 'all for each, each for all'. The values of love and mutuality would saturate the public as well as the private sphere: any dividing line between the two would be erased not only by a movement of love beyond the home but an expansion of family beyond marital or blood ties. Socialists regarded 'communities of mutual interest', with around 2,000 residents, as the ideal social form which would facilitate this redefinition of the family: 'single families with separate interests' were to be eliminated so that 'communities...with one interest...arranged as one family' might flourish.[17] But even the more modest local and partial arrangements tried to embody the family principle in a public form.

To us the fixation with an abstract model of human nature might seem puzzling. But to working-class men and women of an earlier time the vision of infinite human potential developing in a supportive social setting appeared immensely enabling in a context where their adversaries were also giving primacy to models of human nature but of a more inhibiting kind. Socialists were engaged in battle with political economy, Utilitarian science and with evangelical religion which all put constructs of human nature at the centre of their systems. Indeed, it was the socialist vision of humanity which particularly attracted women and the small number of affluent activists to the movement. Many working men also gained a sense of value, confidence and hope from the socialist antidote to the evangelical propaganda, which most Anglican and Nonconformist groups were relentlessly directing at the poor, which preached human sin (and women's even more terrible sin) and which endorsed quietism in the face of suffering. The socialists saw evangelical Christianity as one of the most powerful custodians in the culture of disabling ideas of human nature for both the sexes. Each partly identified the other as the arch-enemy. 'To cure infidelity among the masses', an Evangelical missionary declared, 'we must cure Socialism.' During the late 1830s a Holy War broke out which reached a crescendo of hysteria after 1840 when the Bishop of Exeter used the House of Lords as his pulpit to denounce the socialists and demand they be outlawed as a blasphemous and seditious sect. At the centre of the religious campaign lay an assault on socialist teachings about women's nature, marriage and the family, all regarded as powerful representations of social order in general. The socialists counter-attacked in print and in the arena of public debate.[18] The weekly 'social martyrs' column of the *New Moral World* provided a casualty list of those victimized in the struggle.

The Reverend Francis Close, nicknamed 'the Pope of Cheltenham', epitomized the kind of ideas that Evangelicals were preaching about woman's nature. Shortly before he began to hound socialist George Jacob Holyoake with a blasphemy prosecution, he read the theological riot act to Chartist women demonstrating in his church in 1839. He told them God had punished Eve for tempting Adam by giving to women a nature that was thrice-cursed. First, women were to experience pain more sharply than men because of 'the delicacy of their nerves and the excitability of their feelings'. Second, they were to suffer pain in childbirth and third, they were to suffer subjection to their husbands. When God chose Mary as the vessel of salvation, woman was partly restored 'to her paradisiacal level'. Now instead of being forced into submission, in her proper domestic sphere, she could voluntarily and cheerfully submit to it:

> the centre of all your virtues, and the fountain of all your influence in society, is your home—your own fire-side— and it is amongst your children, it is in the bosom of your family...where your legitimate influence must be exercised; there you are born to shine....Be the pious mother; be the obedient wife; yield that voluntary and cheerful submission to the wishes of your husband, which was extorted from you, till Christ removed the curse.[19]

The Reverend Close mustered an arsenal of damning images to attack women who strayed from home into the public sphere of politics. Like Eve, they were satanic temptresses, 'inciting rather than allaying bad passions'. They were unfeminine and destitute 'of female decorum, of female modesty and diffidence'. They were unEnglish and more akin to their French sisters, who 'glutted themselves with blood; and danced like maniacs amidst the most fearful scenes of the Reign of Terror'![20]

By contrast with this kind of preaching, women of different

41

social classes, as Barbara Taylor has shown, found socialist ideas liberating although problematic. Emma Martin of Bristol (1812-51) first converted to the stern Calvinism of the Particular Baptists when she married Isaac Luther, 'whose company it was a humiliation to endure' and had three children by him. As for some other middle-class feminists, her smattering of education, frustrated career efforts, and deeply unhappy marriage made her receptive to the teaching of socialist missionary Alexander Campbell—except that he rejected the divine origin of the Bible. She challenged the socialists to debate, but found that during the public encounters she herself became converted. Finally she gathered up her daughters, ran away from her husband, and moved out of bourgeois respectability into the socialist movement where she tried to make her livelihood as a lecturer. At the height of her powers, at the 1841 socialist Congress, she testified that

> three years ago a new sun broke upon her, and that was Robert Owen. (Cheers) On looking at the position of woman, she had seen that all remunerating employment was taken from her,—that all institutions for mental improvement were confined to males, and that even the morals of the female sex were of a different stamp to those of the male. She saw no remedy for this till she saw the remedy of Socialism.[21]

And yet as Emma's story also shows, socialist women lived out exhausting contradictions. Emma's uncompromising advocacy of women's rights, her unrelenting attack on Christianity and her provocative public style (she especially liked preaching rival sermons in Anglican churches) led to her being regarded as an extremist even within the movement. Despite the theoretical teaching about the equality of women's nature, the posture for women which was most permissible in the movement was that of the militant married mother. Public space was treacherous terrain for the working class of both sexes. Working men were trying to establish their right to public speech in this period against firm resistance which sometimes erupted into violence as at Peterloo (1819) or during the Chartist Sacred Days (1839). What Chartists called a 'public meeting', magistrates saw as an 'illegal meeting'. Chartist 'public speech' (like socialist teaching) was seen by the ruling class as 'sedition': the Chartist 'people' were the 'mob'. Working men were understandably concerned about their own credibility and tried to occupy the high moral ground. But one way they tended to assure their own respectability was by ensuring that women, to the extent that they did speak in public, did so in an impeccable family pose.

Many socialist women co-operated in this presentation of themselves. A 'public woman' at this time meant a prostitute. Antagonists continually branded female socialists as whores and community as 'one vast brothel'. Unlike Emma, many socialist women made their public utterance apologetically as though they were being watched. Even 'the bondswoman', Frances Morrison, who helped her painter-decorator husband edit the *Pioneer* and then made a living as a socialist lecturer after his death, at first felt reluctant to go into print. In the *Pioneer* she spoke to women as wives and mothers, urging them to unshackle their minds 'and get knowledge'. Although she knew that 'men in general, tremble at the idea of a reading wife' nonetheless 'the mother is the first to sow the seed of instruction in the youthful mind'. To seek liberating knowledge was not a selfish pursuit, but the duty of patriotic motherhood: 'your children's, your own, your country's interest demand it'.[22] Like women from oppressed groups today, many socialist women were unwilling to take stands which would produce dissension in their own families in a situation where they and their menfolk were being oppressed by outsiders. This created a contradictory situation. On the one hand, the posture of militant motherhood genuinely enabled women to move into public space and take new kinds of action. On the other, it contradicted the socialist theory of equal nature and equal activity and put limits around what women could do in the public sphere. Their sphere of action was at once extended but circumscribed. Their basic identity was not only as equals but as wives and mothers, and this identity obviously posed problems for single women.

Another and perhaps more surprising group attracted by the socialist vision of human nature was a small contingent from the middle class. Thin on the ground, they usually numbered no more than one in each town. The exception was the cluster of adherents in Birmingham, a city of workshops where masters and men co-operated, albeit with increasing difficulty, in political campaigns. The moving force in Birmingham Owenism, William Pare, who owned a coffee house and tobacconist's, also played a key buffer role between working- and middle-class groups in the Political Union and became the town's first registrar of births and deaths. The middle-class socialists were prosperous, well-integrated local figures. A well-to-do Coventry ribbon manufacturer, Charles Bray (1811-84), was a lapsed Evangelical who had become a necessarian and who stood at the centre of an advanced intellectual coterie including the young George Eliot. They explored new theories of human nature, such as phrenology (see p.45), and applied the historical method to the study of Christianity.[23] Several of the more affluent socialists moved in Unitarian circles where the improvability of humanity through education was an accepted tenet. But these socialist recruits tended to have far greater expectations of human capacities than their fellow-chapelgoers some of whom will be introduced in the next chapter. Hawkes Smith for example, began his political life as a constitutional radical after the French wars. By 1831 he had converted to social science, believing that 'the BOUNDLESS powers of machinery' within capitalist social relations had created 'an alarming crisis' for the working classes who now needed to emancipate themselves from the shackling categories and realities of class. He urged the people to think of themselves

> not as a class or caste of WORKERS, but as human beings, capable of infinite improvement; and to whom, under wise arrangements, work—labour—sufficient for the production of every reasonable enjoyment, physical or intellectual, may be so reduced, as to form only a pleasant and healthful recreation.[24]

Socialist social science spoke even more directly to the experience of working *men*. No matter from what part of the country or from what occupation they came, workers attracted to socialism had a sense of vast human capacity being stifled (and humiliated) by oppressive social relations. Thus George Jacob Holyoake (1817-1906), also from Birmingham, entered the Eagle Foundry where he worked alongside his father as a skilled smith in white iron and burnished steel for 13 years. Here one of the owners, who saw himself as a caring Christian, was perceived by the men as totally blind to the dignity of labour. Holyoake described his own fascination with machinery and love of craftsmanship, and insisted that there is more independence in pursuits of handicraft, and more time for original thought, than in clerkship or business. That which made me desirous of escaping from the workshop was the hopelessness of sufficient and certain wages, and the idea of personal subjection associated with it.[25]

To the oppressive relations of the workshop was added the weight of oppressive religious teaching. Raised as a Methodist, Holyoake despaired of doctrines which crippled the artisan who, as he later put it, was involved in an 'imminent struggle against wrong and injustice':

> what has he, the struggler to do with Christianity, which tells him *not* to resist evil—which forbids him self-trust—which brands him with inherited guilt—which fetters him by an arbitrary faith, which denies saving power to good works—which menaces him with eternal damnation.[26]

For Holyoake any form of knowledge which posited a lawful universe and rejected special interventions by an angry God provided an energizing tonic. Enrolling in the Mechanics' Institution, Holyoake came into contact not only with socialist teachers like Pare and Hawkes Smith, but encountered phrenology, a science of human nature popular with reformers. Phrenology taught that the mind was situated in the brain and that the various animal, moral and intellectual faculties appeared as bumps on the outer contour of the head; it offered a 'cranioscopic' method to diagnose deficiencies and prescribed largely educational remedies.[27] Whereas phrenology assigned heredity a large role in the permanent improvement of the human race which would take place over generations, socialism provided a more plastic model of human nature and a more optimistic timescale for social transformation. In 1838, Holyoake formally joined the socialists and in 1840 was appointed as a paid social missionary to Worcester and then to Sheffield. During this period he became a socialist martyr. Arrested for remarks in Cheltenham, after conducting his own defence for more than nine hours, he was imprisoned for blasphemy. Undeterred, he went on to champion freethought and to become the leading propagandist and later the historian for working-class co-operation after 1850. His dedicated activity sprang from a conviction that the unique accomplishment of Mr Owen and his movement was 'the development of Social Science', which enabled 'workmen to reason upon their condition' for the first time.[28]

CRITICAL ANALYSIS OF THE ACTUAL STATE OF SOCIETY

The second level of socialist science provided a pioneering analysis of the capitalist system as a whole. Since the whole of social relations needed restructuring, what was to be remade had to be understood as a whole. William Pare insisted that the 'evils...are inherent in the very frame-work of society itself, and consequently admit of no permanent and effective remedy until this be changed'. Owen spoke of the need for 'a radical change in the general structure of society'. John Watts of Manchester argued that 'if we are to have a *system* of society, knowledge of all kinds must be given forth, upon system'.[29]

The spotlight fell on different areas of the system at different times, depending upon the focus of the agitational struggle. But socialists had a consistent concern with the interplay between social ethos and social arrangements, between social values and social relations of power. They saw consciousness as a key part of a system: institutions both embodied values and meanings and helped to create them. Thus the socialists spoke more often of the competitive system than of the capitalist system to signify that competition was becoming the dominant value and practice in every area of social life, diametrically opposed to the co-operation and mutual support the socialists wanted to prevail. Between 1829 and 1834, co-operators and socialists placed great emphasis on the economic sphere, on the value of working people there, on the ethos and practice of competition, on the unequal power relations between capitalists, middlemen and workers, and on the role of machinery in this setting. However, a concern with religion, education and the family, as key sites for the production of social meanings, existed from the beginning. It became the central preoccupation after the defeat of the Grand National Consolidated Trade Union in 1834 and was fixed in the spotlight by the Holy War.

The earlier analysis of the economic dimensions of the

system revolved around three paradoxes. Paradox was a good way of showing the moral and material bankruptcy of the system by keeping linguistically visible at the same time the discrepancy between what actually existed and what could or should exist. The first paradox formed a key part of the working-class self-image: the working classes who made the most valuable contribution to society were the least valued. Or in the words of the Ripponden Co-operative Society, 'the working class although the producers of wealth, instead of being the richest, are the poorest in the community'.[30] William Thompson and John Gray, both members of the London Co-operative Society, provided explanations of this paradox and representations of labour's value which resonated in labour movements long after the end of the Owenite period. They argued that manual labour was the truly productive force which was systematically defrauded of the value it had created by capitalists who paid wages synchronized only to subsistence and creamed off the surplus as profits. In this way the co-operators inverted the arguments of a line of political economists from William Petty to Ricardo. They also considered labour to be the source of value but deemed capital the indispensable catalyst to set inert labour into productive motion and was thus entitled to the surplus.[31]

Gray also made a robust re-evaluation of the social utility of all the existing groups in the population, which asserted the true utility of the working classes, turned the status pyramid of landed society upside down and also challenged the rival middle-class vision of social value. In *A Lecture on Human Happiness*, 1825, Gray insisted that only manual labour could be called productive:

> they only are productive members of society who apply their own hands either to the cultivation of the earth itself, or to the preparing or appropriating the produce of the earth to the uses of life.[32]

Everyone else was not only an 'UNPRODUCTIVE' member of society and a 'DIRECT TAX upon the productive classes' but also 'USELESS unless he gives an equivalent for that which he consumes'. Although utility could have become a very elastic category, Gray offered a limited inventory of useful persons which included those distributing goods, governing, protecting, amusing and instructing mankind and, for good measure, 'the medical profession'. Not surprisingly, he found the 'working classes' to be overwhelmingly both productive and useful (although they could be useless when producing luxuries for the rich). By contrast, he judged all the middle classes nonproductive and the majority of them useless too. Using Patrick Colquhoun's statistical breakdown of groups in the English population, Gray insisted that manufacturers employing capital played a useful role only when directly engaged in management while three-quarters of eminent merchants and bankers were unnecessary. The landed classes, 12,900 temporal peers and 402,915 gentry, together with the 720 bishops were damned as both nonproductive and useless.

In the counterpoint between productive and nonproductive, useful and useless, industrious and idle, value-creating and parasites, labour and capital, the co-operators gave the working classes the moral resonance. They were the active producers not only of the surplus value of the market system but of all that was useful for genuine social happiness. Like socialist psychology which granted full humanity to every person regardless of social class, this discussion of value enhanced the self-esteem of working people. However, the co-operative economists' discussion of value was largely about the realm of public production, exchange and distribution, which made it more relevant to men although women figured in their capacity as waged workers. Gray judged 'umbrella and parasol makers, silk lace workers, embroiderers, domestic spinsters, clearstarchers etc.', as both productive and useful, while he designated prostitutes as both nonproductive and useless. Despite the central concern of socialist science with happiness and not simply with the market, theorists did not explicitly develop the resonant categories 'productive' and 'useful' to cover all activities and persons expending energy which contributed to social happiness, including women doing unpaid work. Although socialists had a clear analysis of women's devaluation in the family and drudgery in the home, this language of women's oppression never quite meshed with the discourse of labour exploitation which dignified the real producer. The working-class language of the producer remained problematic for women, especially from the midcentury onward when the labour movement tended to screen women's oppression either in public or private out of the analytic focus. In the early period, however, the Bondswoman noted, 'the contemptible expression is, it is made by woman, and therefore cheap. Why, we ask, should woman's labour be thus undervalued?'.[33]

Socialists and co-operators usually answered the question in terms of men and pointed to competition and unequal relations of power which resulted in the two remaining paradoxes of critical social science: 'machinery which is naturally a blessing to the human race is converted into an absolute curse' and 'distress in the midst of abundance'.[34] Among the first to appreciate the promise of new technology, the socialists argued that machinery was being misused within the present system by competing employers to replace labour wherever possible in a bid to lower production costs. Redundancy and lowered wages meant shrinking national purchasing power just at the very time when productive capacity was increasing by leaps and bounds. This routine convergence of overproduction with underconsumption would lead to endemic crises: 'we must necessarily', at certain intervals, argued William Pare, 'be subject to such sudden and dreadful revulsions as were experienced in 1810, 1817, 1819, 1825 and are again being suffered but with increased calamitous effects and with a greater fear of their continuance'.[35]

Socialist science made it conceptually possible to unify the different sections of the working class in a situation of very uneven capitalist development. All workers became to some degree the devalued victims of competition and unequal power and all were potential if not actual victims of machinery.[36] Artisans who owned their tools found themselves exploited by competitive middlemen; factory operatives were exploited by competing mill owners; skilled and unskilled workers in competition with each other were both being robbed by capitalist or middleman of the value they were creating. Although this theory of exploitation gave good weapons with which to wage class war, most co-operators and socialists were concerned to free themselves from the power of others by collectively becoming their own capitalists. This would happen by introducing the family principle into public working-class action: 'by the increase of capital', the Ripponden Co-operative Society insisted,

> the working classes may better their condition, if they only
> *unite* and set their shoulder to the work; by uniting we do
> not mean strikes and turning out for wages, but like men

of one family, strive to begin to work for ourselves...[37]

Social science, then, subverted middle-class values by debunking the competitive system as a lurching and inefficient mechanism. Instead, it proposed a range of possible forms for a more familial organization of public economics.

In a similarly iconoclastic way, socialist feminists used the social science from the 1820s onward to take a microscope to the bourgeois sanctum of the nuclear family. What they saw did not resemble the abode of peace and love separated from the conflict of the outside world. Instead they represented the marital family as a key site for the manufacture of competitive values and as deformed by unequal power as any part of the public sphere. For William Thompson and his partner Anna Wheeler, the position of a wife was that of a slave: 'a domestic, a civil, a political slave, in the plain unsophisticated sense of the word— in no metaphorical sense—is every married woman'.[38] A *femme couverte* devoid of political rights, with no identity in the civil courts, with no exit from loveless or violent unions, without rights to the custody of children, an unpaid and often unappreciated domestic worker, whose drudgery was equivalent to the toil of a public wage slave (and sometimes that as well), the married woman could hardly be represented as the valued redeeming angel. No harmonious nest, the marital family provided a psychic nursery where habits of domination and subordination were early engrained:

> Every family is a centre of absolute despotism, where of course intelligence and persuasion are quite superfluous to him who has only to command to be obeyed: from these centres, in the midst of which all mankind are now trained, spreads the contagion of selfishness and the love of domination through all human transactions.[39]

Not so attuned to the dissonance of patriarchy, Owen was more concerned with the nuclear family as a keystone of the competitive structure which ensured the transmission of private property and which inculcated a deformed family mutuality that fed public competitiveness. In his Lectures on the *Marriages of the Priesthood in the Old Immoral World* (1835), which brought him as much opprobrium as his denunciation of all religion in 1817, Owen spoke of nuclear families as 'dens of selfishness and hypocrisy' where children are taught to consider their own individual family their own world, and that it is the duty and interest of all within this little orb to do whatever they can to promote the advantages of all the legitimate members of it.[40]

The socialist discourse about the family proved both attractive and threatening to women. On the one hand, it created the linguistic space to voice frustration and anger about the experience of marriage, a space unavailable in the middle-class romance of the family. But however alluring the promise of lighter housework in community (and much socialist ingenuity was spent on working out ways to reorganize or to mechanize it) and however attractive Owen's proposals for easier divorce and more harmonious relationships in community, the issue of marriage and divorce proved the area where women felt most susceptible to religious pressure, fearing a concealed Casanova's charter. All the women socialist lecturers moved carefully, urging strict enforcement of the marriage laws while the old immoral world continued, and then held out the promise not of free love in community but of a secure family life.[41]

PRACTICAL SOCIAL SCIENCE

The distance between the first two levels of socialist science, between the ideal and the actual, set up a dynamic tension. 'The student of practical *Social Science*', could not 'stand in dreamy wonder, moodily gazing at defects in what we call "the progress of society"' insisted Hawkes Smith.[42] The pressure built up on the third level of social science to find practical strategies to bridge the gap. Class conflicts existed within the movement about different possible routes. Owen and other reformers from above advocated immediate community on the land funded by government or philanthropy. Working-class socialists tended to try to do it for themselves more slowly in stages and did not always see rural communities as the ultimate way to embody the values and practices of mutuality. As part of the constructive strategy, socialists were keen to contest powerful ideologies, to create relevant knowledge, to raise consciousness as widely as possible and to experience supportive social relations. They produced a vigorous and various cultural practice which tried to be relevant to the material situation of working people, who

51

were largely poor and who had little spare time when employed and no spare money when out of work. At one extreme, small mutual improvement classes met in members' houses.[43] At the other extreme stood large multipurpose institutions increasingly called Halls of Science. Given the material constraints in the lives of working people, the pressures against postponed gratification were enormous. Socialists tended to put their pennies into local facilities rather than into the Community Fund.[44] These Halls of Science became for most socialists their experience of the New Moral World and even these proved too expensive to sustain.

Manchester and Salford exemplified the possibilities and problems for practical social science in a context of local class relations. This conurbation had the largest, most working-class and most enduring socialist movement outside London. Here cultural concerns cut across occupational lines and provided the cement that held the socialist core group together. Many of the leading activists, including E.T. Craig, had met as students in the Manchester Mechanics' Institution which was founded in 1824 by Nonconformist bankers and millowners (who will feature again in the next chapter as activists in the Manchester Statistical Society). The Mechanics' Institute movement, under the national patronage of Lord Henry Brougham, aimed to teach correct political economy and more especially to provide a scientific curriculum for working men to enable them to become more inventive and upwardly mobile in their trades.

From the early case of the London Mechanics' Institution onward, working men often used and contested these facilities at the same time.[45] The Manchester students launched additional ventures to make a relevant education more available to working families, like a Scientific Society which met at night, and a Utility Society Sunday School which taught grammar and reading from co-operative texts. Finally, in 1829, they seceded from the Mechanics' Institution in protest at its undemocratic mode of government and narrow curriculum and founded a rival New Mechanics' Institution where working men were both governors and teachers and where really useful knowledge and pleasurable recreation could be found.[46] An evening school for forty women was running by 1834. The parent Institution, under the presidency of Unitarian banker and statistician Benjamin Heywood, was not unresponsive to this challenge: they changed the composition of their committee to allow for student representation and put some lighter items into the intellectual menu.

Socialist educational work became even more ambitious and more costly after 1831.[47] To a Manchester and Salford Association for the Dissemination of Co-operative Knowledge, they added the production of a weekly newspaper. By 1836 the First Salford Co-operative Society had moved its cultural activities into a purpose-built Social Institution. These projects proved expensive to run. Salford benefited from inventive modes of federating pennies (groups from all over the country were urged to buy the *Lancashire and Yorkshire Co-operator*). Salford also received donations of handicraft (Sheffield gave penknives with buckhorn handles), services (teachers received no pay) and money (a sum of £850 from local socialist Joseph Smith to pay for the Hall). Once again the cultural initiatives did not go unnoticed. By 1838 three Lyceums had opened in the area bearing an uncanny resemblance to the socialist Institution except for the controlling presence of bourgeois patrons like Benjamin Heywood. A pattern of middle-class response to working-class initiative was taking shape which eventually ended in a stifling incorporative embrace.

From 1839, socialists faced a crisis about physical and cultural space. The prohibition of meeting places to radicals of any stripe during the Chartist climax of 1839, and the increasing persecution of socialists by Christians made the creation of independent self-controlled territory urgent. By 1841, the socialists had actually built Halls of Science in Huddersfield, Ratcliffe Bridge, Sheffield, Worcester, Yarmouth, Macclesfield, Manchester, London, Bradford, Liverpool, Bristol, Halifax and Stockport, while Birmingham and Glasgow bought and converted chapels. By 1842, twenty-nine branches had social institutions of some size. The halls were usually financed from one-pound shares which could be paid in weekly instalments of as little as 3d. The most elaborate halls were built on two storeys and included two large rooms, each capable of holding more than 2,000 people, kitchen and cloakrooms (sometimes with baths) and smaller rooms housing libraries and classes. These were multipurpose cultural centres.[48]

Such imposing and intrusive assertions of working-class science could not be ignored. In Manchester, the world headquarters of industrial capitalism, it was the socialist Hall of Science in Camp Fields which could boast the largest meeting room in the town. Initial reactions were hostile and even violent: an arson attempt on the unfinished Manchester building was followed by a court case brought by the local vicar, charging illegal Sunday meetings, in an early bid to get the hall closed down. But by the mid-1840s, the strategy of counter-attraction had shifted into a new and powerful gear.[49] After the Chartist climax of 1842, Benjamin Heywood threw his considerable energy and wealth completely behind the Lyceum movement as the most promising agency of social improvement and reconciliation. From then on his money figured conspicuously in attempts to provide new 'public' spaces for working-class life after work: £1,000 towards Peel public park, a large donation to the public library movement. Always hard for working people to finance, the Hall of Science was bought (cheaply) and presented to the Corporation in 1851 as the first free public library in Britain. In 1877, it was torn down and its memory erased.

From the late 1840s onward, in Manchester as elsewhere, local Liberal and Tory governors made space for the active working class in a new concept of a civic community and in a new public landscape, where participation was welcomed but control was denied. Given their own experience of the difficulty of running independent ventures, working people began to think in terms of acceptable forms of 'public' provision and even of state schooling in the gentler climate of middle-class embrace. Socialist pupils in Salford in 1833 had persuaded their teachers not to apply for a government grant 'as it might subject the school to some tyrannical restraint'.[50] By the 1860s a national system of state education was becoming a plank in labour movement platforms.

Nonetheless, tensions continued. As Peter Gurney shows, the co-operative movement, which grew rapidly again during the midcentury years, remained uneasy about the kind of education being provided under the Elementary Education Act of 1870: Holyoake insisted that the 'National Instruction' had little to do with real education which taught how to reason independently. Local societies were also worried about the censorship both of school curricula and public library holdings in response to pressure from local traders to screen out co-operative materials. The societies operated a twofold strategy, trying both to keep their own libraries and newspapers going, which was easier than in the Owenite period because funding was available from store profits, as well as trying to get some purchase on state education by seeking election to local School Boards. When the 1902 Education Act abolished the Boards, at a time when the tabloid press was growing fast and relying on advertising revenue from private traders, the co-operators recognized that they had a full-scale cultural crisis on their hands.[51]

SOCIALIST OBJECTIVITY

The early socialist thinkers saw themselves as empiricists, working from 'the Facts of Science, which they have ascertained by observation and experience, and the legitimate deductions from those Facts'. Yet their effort was directed more towards developing a general interpretive framework than towards the systematic collection and presentation of facts. As a result their analyses seem abstract, although enlivened by a tone of indignation, and remarkably similar, no matter from what part of the country they came. Although they constructed general theory, they used the word 'theorist' as a term of abuse. Before the next chapter considers middle-class investigators, it will be useful to establish what socialists considered to be valid empiricism. Fundamentally the question of reliable fact, observation and experience involved issues of class and commitment. The early Benthamites and Evangelicals were convinced that the authoritative gaze was that of the inspector observing a system in which he had power, in other words, a system as seen by the controller from above. The socialists rejected social distance as an ingredient in true perception. Those who were socially distant did not see more clearly but were in danger of not seeing at all and becoming 'mere theorists': nothing about the competitive economists was surprising

> when we reflect upon whom they are and how they are situated. Though talented and deeply read, yet...are persons removed by their conditions from that intercourse with their poorer brethren which can really make them acquainted with the condition of society, and all their writings prove them, to be not practical men but mere theorists.[52]

Science did not start from outside but from within. 'Practical fact' and valid experience were, importantly, what working people experienced. Taking the phrase 'greatest happiness of the greatest number' quite literally, socialists gave the experience of the greatest number of the working classes a valued role as the litmus test of the real tendency of a social system. What was felt and thought by people from other class backgrounds could also be 'good useful knowledge', but only if they repudiated the spread of science on an 'exclusive system', and were committed to the 'general acquisition of Science' and 'the universal upraising of Human Nature'[53] which would make them genuinely interested in working-class experience.

But experience needed further patterning because the facts were often known by working people in a partial, local and confused way. These rough and ready empiricists argued from their limited experience and created divergent and conflicting interpretations. What was needed were clear general theories of the purpose of social life which provided standard criteria for evaluation, general theories of capitalist development which gave partial and local experience general significance, and uniform programmes for total social change. Dr McCormac of Belfast worried about 'biassed...professional or local views' and urged a person to 'gather a few certain demonstrable truths...taking nothing on trust that the narrow sphere of his own observation does not render necessary'. 'A rigid comparison of theory with fact', counselled Leeds Chartist and socialist J.F. Bray, 'should be the first great object of the productive classes and the prelude to all demands for change'.[54]

Before total social reconstruction became possible, competitive society had to be seen as a whole, a socialist alternative had to grasped as a whole and social action had to be undertaken by the working class as a whole. To help make this cohesion, the socialists took a different approach from other working-class movements at the time. Rather than suppressing ideology to conceal differences, they provided a social science on a high enough level of abstraction to have relevance and appeal to all occupational groups and their specific problems. Moreover, the picture of the equality of all working people as possessors of vast human potential who were victims of an anti-social system could soften customary gender and status differences and jealousies and lay the groundwork for a unified movement.

Even though socialists tended to stress general theory for sound agitational reasons, they were well acquainted with their localities and, like members of other labour movements, kept internal statistics important for their work.[55] Socialists were also involved in some of the few radical attempts to make systematic surveys. Two years before the first statistical society came into being, the Birmingham Political Union sponsored a survey in which Pare and Hawkes Smith took an active part. Yet the Birmingham survey illustrated the point that different types of empiricism were considered necessary for different audiences. The Council of the Union did not think they were starting an activity vital to keep abreast of local developments. They felt they already knew and had interpreted the local situation well enough but now needed a more systematic gathering and presentation of facts, which resembled a Royal Commission, to convince an outside body, the government, that the Birmingham currency theories were the remedy for economic depression. Every Monday, Thursday and Saturday evening over several months Pare chaired a committee which heard evidence about wages and regularity of employment from workmen in various trades.

Hawkes Smith, who helped to write the final report, was part of a committee that went from house to house in selected working-class areas to assess the impact of employment conditions on the standard of living. This survey was one of the few in which socialists took part.[56] Hawkes Smith probably expressed the representative attitude of the socialists towards statistical investigations, once the social survey became identified with local middle-class statistical societies. Having congratulated the Reverend John Johns, the Unitarian missionary stationed in the Liverpool slums, for producing a report which was 'highly valuable as statistical data, though collected without expensive and especial organization', Smith went on to observe:

> In truth, statistical researches are principally called for by the contented scepticism and satisfied errors of the uninquiring prosperous and influential. They are laborious exhibitions of truths, tabulated and figured, which in the gross, are generally known and felt.[57]

For Smith, collecting statistics was a timewasting exercise which delayed action and sometimes served as a shabby substitute for action. Manchester, the home of the most active statistical society, 'the city most studied by statists', still remained the 'most victimized by the so-called prosperity'. Middle-class investigators deeply disagreed.

3

MIDDLE-CLASS SOCIAL SURVEY AND URBAN SOCIAL DISORDER, 1832-1850

While the socialists created general theory, middle-class investigators set out to find the facts. The years between 1832 and 1850 became an age of enthusiasm for the statistical idea and for investigations into the condition of the working class. The London Statistical Society exulted in 1838 that

> The spirit of the present age has an evident tendency to confront the figures of speech with the figures of arithmetic; it being impossible not to observe a growing distrust of mere hypothetical theory and *a priori* assumption, and the appearance of a general conviction that, in the business of social science, principles are valid for application only inasmuch as they are legitimate inductions from facts, accurately observed and methodically classified.[1]

'Statistics' grew rapidly, not so much as a discipline developing theory, but as an aid to reform, in the influential words of Sir John Sinclair, as 'the knowledge of the present state of the country, with a view to its future improvement'. One of the intriguing features of the period was the rise and demise of the voluntary statistical societies and their creation, the town-wide, door-to-door survey into the condition of the working class. This chapter will begin by exploring the context and work of the statistical societies and go on to signpost the increasing presence of the central state in the investigatory project. Finally it will examine the survey work of the maverick Henry Mayhew and show how his innovative directions came to be submerged by powerful new intellectual currents.

A NEW PATTERN OF CRISIS

The investigative engine started in earnest in 1832, a key year that marked the first in a series of moments when political crisis and epidemic cholera converged, producing an explosive mix which recurrently sparked the social scientific imagination. Events of that year also forged a closer link between social investigation and the rising urban middle class. The political triumph of the 1832 Reform Act gave the middle class a parliamentary vote and a place in the Constitution alongside the landed interest. But the campaign for reform had exposed dangerous potentials. The working class had erupted not only in the Swing riots in the countryside, but in the urban Reform riots, particularly in Bristol in 1831, which remained deeply etched in many middle-class minds and seemed to preview the nearly continuous state of working-class disorder over the next twenty years. (To other eyes, the disorder could look impressively orderly with socialist, trade union and political movements achieving a nationally organized presence.)

The Reform agitation cleared one item from the social agenda but added another. The middle class was always forging its identity in relation to the classes both above and below. Having won the battle with the landed interest for parliamentary representation, the middle class could use its new powers to continue its thrust towards political ascendancy nationally and locally, and it could now turn its attention more systematically to the working class. Back from a short stint in the Commons, where he supported the Reform Bill in 'one of the most memorable struggles in the history of our country', Benjamin Heywood, soon to become the president of the Manchester Statistical Society, announced his new priorities:

> I return with one deep conviction upon my mind, that the improvement of the condition of the working classes is an object of paramount and urgent importance; and as it is the duty of every man to mark out for himself some sphere of active usefulness to his fellow-men, I would select the furtherance of this object as mine.[2]

Service to the local working class now became an important part of the bourgeois claim to moral and political authority in contrast to the classes above and in relation to those below.

Already the middle class had pressed its moral weight in terms of its gender ideals, comparing its responsible Christian masculinity in the family enterprise to the aristocratic irresponsibility of debting, gambling, duelling, drinking and wenching.[3] The middle class had already insisted on its political and commercial probity compared with the jobbery of the landed interest. From now on, Christian service to the working class also became a key component of middle-class virtue. Making the class comparison, Dr James Kay-Shuttleworth of Manchester (see p.62) argued that the indifference of the aristocracy, cocooned in their large country parks, 'cannot invite surprise' and made a sharp contrast to 'the enlightened manufacturers of the country acutely sensible of the miseries of large masses of the operative body...and the most active promoters of every plan which can conduce to their physical improvement or their moral elevation'.[4]

Before the Reform crisis had been resolved, the 1832 cholera epidemic struck and helped to set an urban agenda for middle-class science and service. A very divisive episode, the poor experienced the epidemic as yet another encounter in an ongoing contest over their bodies and death. At first radicals dismissed the cholera as a ploy to divert attention from Reform. Later they accused doctors of using the epidemic as an excuse to build fever hospitals, lure the poor into them, kill them there and use their bodies for dissection. As Ruth Richardson has shown, a head-on collision took place between the attitudes of a medical profession trying to put itself on a scientific footing and make anatomy a part of the training of surgeons and the beliefs of poor people who felt that the corpses of their loved ones could not find permanent peace unless buried intact.[5] Fever hospitals were regarded with great suspicion and provoked riots in many places. In Glasgow, for instance, Reverend Chalmers had to plead in his sermons against violence towards doctors. In Manchester, a crowd that forced a coffin open and found a decapitated boy corpse with a stone substituting for his head, burned the hospital down.[6] Local doctors received powers to form Boards of Health which not only built these fever hospitals but carried out systematic surveys of poor people's dwellings, burned contaminated bedding and whitewashed walls at will. Dr Kay-Shuttleworth wanted such Boards turned into 'permanent organized centres of medical police, where municipal powers will be directed by scientific men, to the removal of those agencies which most powerfully depress the physical condition of the inhabitants'.[7]

DOCTORS AND SOCIAL INVESTIGATION IN THE 1830s

The cholera investigations or intrusions, depending upon your position in the affair, formed an important prelude to the outburst of survey work after 1832. Local cholera doctors who had carried out door-to-door investigation on an unprecedented scale became active in the statistical societies and contributed to several Royal Commissions. But it would be a mistake to see social investigation as a medical monopoly in this period or to speak of new attitudes to social study 'derived from medicine rather than religion'.[8] Doctors were products of their decades, as well as innovators, and their analyses expanded and contracted accordingly. Some early studies of the working class by medical men were strikingly comprehensive when contrasted with the studies made by doctors little more than a decade later, once public health had crystallized as a new field for exploration.

The raging debates about the factory system and the Poor Law in the early 1830s occasioned two revealing studies: Manchester surgeon Peter Gaskell's work on *Artisans and Machinery* (1836), which impressed both co-operative socialists and Friedrich Engels and Dr Henry McCormac of Belfast's *Appeal on Behalf of the Poor* (1830).[9] Despite differing political views, both men considered economic and social change over the preceding fifty years as decisive in shaping the life chances of working people. Moral indiscipline was secondary and derivative. Gaskell showed how large-scale capitalist landlords had squeezed out small farmers and then how factory production had destroyed the domestic system of cotton manufacture. Not only did redundancy result for the handworkers but the factory population, with a place in the sun for the moment, would eventually be overshadowed by the threat of increasing automation. McCormac's work, too, began by showing how the introduction of machinery had created widespread redundancy in certain trades in Ireland at the same time that the system of absentee landlordism kept the peasants from being fully employed. Gaskell worried less about the unfolding panorama of physical destitution than he did about the disappearance of two key agencies for social discipline: the supervising family and the hierarchical rural community. McCormac was more troubled by the consequences of low wages: bad food, crowded dwellings in filthy neighbourhoods, strained human relations, all leading to a craving for the 'rudest and most transient gratifications'.[10]

By contrast, Dr James Kay-Shuttleworth felt basically satisfied with the new industrial system. His investigation of *The Moral and Physical Condition of the Working Classes Employed in the Cotton Manufacture in Manchester*, arising out his work during the cholera epidemic, went through two editions in 1832 and was probably the most influential survey by a medical man in the decade. His diagnosis of social problems and his remedies, indeed his whole sensibility both expressed and helped to shape the scientific outlook of the urban middle class. An evangelical Congregationalist from a pious mill-owning family, he can be interpreted not simply as a doctor but as a spokesman of the religiously committed urban bourgeoisie, intent on increasing its local power and deeply concerned with the working class.[11] Kay-Shuttleworth's influence also extended into the central state when he became an Assistant Poor Law Commissioner in 1835 and then, in 1839, Secretary to the new Privy Council Committee on Education.

Like his fellow Manchester statisticians and like the Utilitarians and the Ricardian economists, Kay-Shuttleworth thought that the 'natural tendency' of capitalism was sound and healthy but that 'foreign and accidental causes' at present restricted the system. Although desirable, shorter working hours and higher wages could only come as a result of action to abolish the Corn Laws, establish totally free trade and ensure the constant expansion of foreign markets which would create a larger wage fund.[12] This issue would dominate the contest between the industrial and the landed interest in the 1840s. In 1832, an individual could do little to make improvements on the industrial front. One of the consequences of a diagnosis like Kay-Shuttleworth's was to move the industrial system out of the centre of the investigative gaze.

Instead he and the statisticians moved the residential condition of the poor in cities to focal point. His book considered the deleterious effects of factory work, prolonging an earlier debate to which he had already contributed in the *North of England Medical Journal*. But his more novel contribution was to present the residential situation of the poor as an independent and potent influence. In a preface addressed to Reverend Chalmers, Kay-Shuttleworth quickly identified himself as a cholera doctor working with the local Board of Health. He went on to enlarge a syndrome of disorder which had existed since the time of the Napoleonic Wars, when moral and political disease had been regarded as the urgent problems (see p.12). Visualizing the city as a social body, he diagnosed two further symptoms of social malfunction: organic disease, especially of epidemic proportions, and derangement of urban space:

> He whose duty it is to follow the steps of this messenger of death (cholera), must descend to the abodes of poverty, must frequent the close alleys, the crowded courts, the overpeopled habitations of wretchedness, where pauperism and disease congregate round the source of social discontent and political disorder in the centre of our large towns, and behold with alarm, in the hot-bed of pestilence, ills that fester in secret, at the very heart of society.[13]

Disordered urban space consisted of closed communities: impenetrable thickets of houses, teeming with working-class people, secret because closed to the upper-class gaze. The pauperism mentioned in the passage above was a moral condition caused by 'sufficient' wages being 'too often consumed by vice and improvidence'.[14] The links between spatial, physical, moral and political disorder were not only metaphorical, they also expressed a view of causation. Disturbance on one level could cause disorder on another; disturbance on two or more at once, as in the case of political crisis and cholera coming together, created an explosive mix.

The statisticians, including Kay-Shuttleworth, began to use a rhetoric about their work being objective and accurate science. But it is important to monitor contradictory undercurrents like the strong languages of denigration and even of loathing which surfaced in their texts. Kay-Shuttleworth produced tabulated statistics collected by the District Boards of Health. But to depict moral disorder he also used resonant opposing images which conveyed a contrast between human and subhuman. Like the

63

early proponents of the science of the poor, he set up a savage/civilized polarity and then added an animal/human juxtaposition. Obsessed with the Irish as lurking on every borderline between human and nonhuman, Kay-Shuttleworth added a contrast between wholesome English labour and the 'debased' foreign Irish. The most potent representation of moral disorder was sexual confusion, usually imaged as indiscriminate herding in bed which carried overtones of incest:

> a whole (Irish) family is often accommodated on a single bed, and sometimes a heap of filthy straw and a covering of old sacking hide them in one undistinguished heap, debased alike by penury, want of economy, and dissolute habits. Frequently, the inspectors found two or more families crowded into one small house, containing only one room, in whose pestilential atmosphere from twelve to sixteen persons were crowded. To these fertile sources of disease were sometimes added the keeping of pigs and other animals in the house, with other nuisances of the most revolting character.[15]

Raising the linguistic temperature, Kay-Shuttleworth depicted political disorder in more explosive terms. Again a case of provocation by outsiders, peaceful English workers were being 'excited by the inflammatory harangues of demagogues'. The labouring population, 'a slumbering giant' has already been woken into 'turbulent riots', 'machine breaking' and

> secret and sullen organization which has suddenly lit the torch of incendiarism, or well nigh uplifted the arm of rebellion in the land....political desperadoes have ever loved to tempt this population to the hazards of the swindling game of revolution, and have scarcely failed.

If more appropriate outsiders like the more powerful classes did not begin to do their duty 'to promote domestic comfort, virtue and knowledge among them' then working people would 'prove volcanic elements, by whose explosive violence the structure of society may be destroyed'.[16]

THE LOCAL STATISTICAL SOCIETIES

In this heated atmosphere of disorder, the local statistical societies set out to do their duty. Manchester founded the first Statistical Society and the British Association for the Advancement of Science added a statistical section in 1833. Thereafter local societies appeared in London, Birmingham, Bristol, Glasgow, Belfast, Liverpool, Leeds, Aberdeen, Dublin and as far afield as New York and Boston. Distinctly middle-class, the provincial societies were dominated by local businessmen but also included a contingent of doctors, often with cholera experience, and religious ministers who were mainly Unitarian and Anglican, and often in routine contact with the poor.[17] The London Society was exceptional in boasting a majority of professional men, including civil servants and academics. The provincial statisticians were the newly enfranchised men who now sought political dominance in their localities. They based their claim to public authority on their probity, their industry, the comprehensiveness of their knowledge and on their religious service towards the local working class.

The service ideal clearly figured in Manchester which had the closest-knit membership. Mainly Unitarians and largely from the cotton industry and banking, the members belonged to the same chapel, family and friendship networks. These adherents of wage-fund economics could be easily dismissed as insensitive to working-class misery; early on they arranged to deliver Lord Brougham's lectures on political economy at the Mechanics' Institution. Quite accurately, however, they considered themselves to be deeply religious and active philanthropists. Many were the largest employers of labour in their neighbourhoods like Thomas Ashton of Hyde, Henry Ashworth of Bolton and Samuel Robinson of Dukenfield who built model villages around their factories and reigned supreme in their domains until the Factory Acts, which they at first resisted, challenged some of their authority. They regarded their villages as experiments both in social welfare and social discipline. Samuel Greg supplied workers at his Bollington mills with

> fair wages, comfortable houses, gardens for their vege-
> tables and flowers, schools and other means of
> improvement for their children, sundry little accommo-
> dations and conveniences in the mill, attention to them
> when sick and in distress, and interest taken in their

general comfort and welfare;—everything, in short, which can make the place a home to them, and attach them to it and to their employer.[18]

It is interesting that he saw the paternalist village as 'home' compared with the 'restless and migratory' habits of the unregulated workers, a representation with both savage and animal overtones. In statistical circles these factory villages were regarded as the ideal form for industrialism: a resident employer meant routine and cordial social contact which served as a discipline against pauperism infinitely preferable to the New Poor Law. One middle-class vision of the good society was a small community but one organized along fundamentally different lines from the proposed settlements in the socialist new moral world.

For the resident rich, the focus of service was clear. Benjamin Heywood, president of the family bank and trustee of the Cross Street Unitarian Chapel, supported many projects in Miles Platting, a village of handloom weavers, where he lived, and insisted that his son do the same: 'I am anxious now that you should give both money and time to the improvement of the people in your neighbourhood'.[19] However, serving the poor in the large cities like the Manchester-Salford conurbation, which was losing its upper class to the suburbs, was more problematic. Besides his educational projects for working men (reviewed in Chapter 2) Heywood, with Kay-Shuttleworth, helped to found the Manchester and Salford District Provident Society in 1833. This divided the city into 1,042 sections for district visiting in order to give working people advice and to recruit them into a savings scheme.

The wives of the statisticians were also active in urban philanthropy but took no part in the statistical investigations or the penumbra of local learned societies. They were thus embedded in hardening gender divisions in social science and intellectual work more generally. Reverend William Gaskell, minister to many of the statisticians, and his novelist wife Elizabeth illustrated the outer limits for married couples in this circle. Besides his duties in the Cross Street Chapel, he serviced the educational and scientific side of Manchester life. A model wife, she managed the household, looked after family and friendship networks, taught Sunday school and other classes for boys and girls and visited for the District Provident Society. She moved into public writing via fiction, an approved route for women, although her first novel, *Mary Barton*, drew criticism from some statisticians and from her friend Lady Kay-Shuttleworth for being too sympathetic to working-class radicals. Paradoxically, her writing for publication became her really private space, 'the refuge of the hidden world of Art' from the 'daily small Lilliputian arrows of peddling cares'.[20]

Religious developments helped to shift the attention of the statisticians to the urban scene. From different denominational directions, Christian thinking had been converging to highlight the poor in cities as the most urgently in need of service. The Evangelical effort which had been prominent at the time of the French Wars received powerful reinforcement from the work and writing of the Reverend Thomas Chalmers (1750-1847) who remained a demigod of scientific philanthropy right into the twentieth century. In 1820, Chalmers began a famous experiment in his Glasgow parish of St John's which eliminated the Poor Rate and slashed the cost of poor relief. His system relied on the dedicated work of voluntary upper-class deacons who had responsibility for a district of the parish and who combined 'firmness with kindness' while exercising 'the privilege of a strict search and entry upon the question of every man's state, who should claim relief'.[21] As his book title attested, Chalmers deeply believed in *The Supreme Importance of a Right Moral to a Right Economical State of the Community* (1832) and felt the service of the rich in the moral education of the poor offered the best way to 'obey' the laws of political economy and to create the proper *Christian and Civic Economy of Large Towns* (the title of his most famous book).

Nonconformists now joined Anglicans in bodies like the local statistical societies where Unitarians often predominated. The Unitarian theology preached in Manchester, Bristol and Liverpool came across the Atlantic from the Reverend W.E. Channing and the Reverend Joseph Tuckerman of Boston. Enhancing Priestley's merely human Christ with a moral divinity, they taught that each person had the seeds of a god-like moral perfection within them which must be nurtured. It was the duty of each Unitarian to follow Christ's example and serve the poor whose capacities for improvement were the most neglected and attend particularly to the urban poor who were cut off from contact with their richer brethren. Tuckerman, the first slum missionary, toured Britain in 1833 and, 'like the angel descending to stir the sleeping waters', gave added force to already-influential ideas.[22] Christians who could not meet elsewhere, like Evangelical Anglicans and Unitarians, who denied the Trinity and even doubted the full divinity of Christ, discovered common ground in their concern with the urban poor. They co-operated in statistical societies, which helped to bridge deep differences and create a more unified local middle class.

Statistical surveys strongly buttressed the middle-class claim to comprehensive knowledge. As we have already seen, the word survey had been associated from the sixteenth century onward with state inventories of people, property or provisions for purposes of governance. Now the local middle class were going to gain commanding knowledge of their town to strengthen their claim to local command. While the resident country gentry had found it easy to know the state of their poor (if they wished to enquire), in the new urban conditions, where rich and poor did not live in proximity, Christian service required new modes of enquiry and action. As Unitarian minister and vice-president of the Bristol Society, the Reverend Lant Carpenter insisted,

> in the present very complicated relations of society they could only look to the operations of such institutions as theirs for a secure means of improving the social condition. In country places he was aware that it was not so difficult for benevolent individuals to discriminate and to bestow their claims so as to benefit society; but in large cities and towns statistical enquiries were of the greatest moment.[23]

With part of their time, the local societies acted as embryonic town councils collecting civic statistics. Bristol, for example, annually tabulated local vital statistics, trade figures and returns from prisons and police. Once their boroughs were incorporated under the Municipal Corporations Act of 1835 (another middle-class victory over the old style of Tory-gentry rule), the new town council often took over these statistical tasks. The new Leeds Town Council continued the survey begun on a voluntary basis.[24] The Liverpool Society had such identical personnel to the newly incorporated Borough, that it disbanded after two years, probably because it played a duplicating role.

But the most important area of town life which preoccupied the statistical societies was the condition of the local working class.

Door-to-door surveys of the working class took up most of the investigatory timetable. Even the London Society fit the pattern. They started by glancing back to the Scottish Enlightenment and across the Channel to the more theoretical concerns of Adolphe Quételet and devised a classification to make it possible to compare statistical profiles of societies in the past and present. But they ended up making surveys of the London poor.[25] Carried out by paid agents, the statistical society investigations were large-scale undertakings. The Manchester Society offered apologies for not contacting all working-class families in Manchester and Salford although the 4,102 families visited did include every household 'below the rank of shopkeepers' in Dukinfield, Staleybridge and Ashton-under-Lyne. The Bristol Society interviewed 6,000 families; in the London parish of St George's in the East, the number of families totalled 1,954.[26] There was no question of sampling. Although cripplingly expensive, completeness seemed to be mandatory as a measure of religious service and evidence that an overview necessary for governance had been achieved.

The investigations were social discipline surveys not poverty surveys. The Manchester Society set the pattern for the questionnaire and made a significant negative contribution. It shifted the focus away from the employment situation and cut out any discussion about wages or working conditions, about unemployment or regularity of employment. This was partly a conscious decision. Initially, one faction had wanted to organize the study around the trades of the city and even go into workshops and factories to question people, an apparent way to prolong the debate about the effects of the manufacturing system. After some argument, Dr Kay-Shuttleworth won out with his idea of a residential survey, which facilitated the investigation of what were generally called moral and intellectual statistics. Although Kay-Shuttleworth still included questions about wages, when the actual survey was published, it gave no information at all, explaining in a defensive way that

> the only subjects on which any disposition to mislead, or to resent inquiry was manifested, were those connected with the question of wages and hours of labour; but it

will be seen that no direct inquiries on these points were attempted, not because their importance was under-valued, but because it was feared that they could lead to no correct results, and might endanger the success of matters of greater moment.[27]

This was not a very convincing excuse when the Society had such easy access to the company books of millowners in the cotton industry at least. They certainly could have obtained information and even presented it, if need be, in the form of conflicting tables which summarized what the company accounts read and what working people said. Later the Society kept pursuing a line of questioning about numbers of people to numbers of beds although informants appeared just as reluctant to give information. The Society was coy in 1836 mainly because they assumed, unlike Drs Gaskell and McCormac and later Henry Mayhew, that wages and unemployment were not fundamentally connected with 'matters of greater moment' which their action could immediately affect. This was also a point of fundamental difference with socialist analysis and with working-class surveys like the Chartist census of the regions in 1839. The Chartists asked comprehensive questions about the wages of men, women and children by trade as well as about the cost of living.[28]

The Statistical Society questionnaire quickly became stand-ardized and revolved around domestic habits and about membership in organizations which were at once seen as indices and agencies of moral improvement. The key institutions which would perform the function of the once-resident rich were the church and the school. Statisticians considered participation in one or both as the necessary credentials for moral respectability. All of the surveys asked about religious affiliation and whether the family attended worship. Beyond this, Manchester, Bristol, London and even the Leeds Town Council made censuses of the church accommodation actually available to the poor. In all cases, they found it lamentably wanting.[29] The door-to-door surveys always asked about educational attainment—whether children were at school, whether parents were literate, what books were in the house. Analogous to the church censuses but much more elaborate, the societies conducted investigations into the state of local education for the poor. They found the results staggering. The educational surveys chronicled such failure that some of the statistical societies, like Manchester, became convinced that voluntary effort could not cope and wrote into their reports spirited demands for a state system of education and teacher training.[30]

Intent on providing institutions for the working class, the attitude of Society members towards collective working-class self-help was ambivalent and in marked contrast to their later midcentury tolerance. Friendly societies were acceptable (although informants were loath to give information about membership) because they revealed a capacity for planning and a desire to provide for sickness and old age. Socialist educational ventures were mentioned in only two Manchester surveys but with a benignity which probably denoted ignorance of their full aims.[31] Trade unions, however, were anathema. John Cleland's tirade against the useless and pernicious nature of trade unions in the face of the wage fund would doubtless have been echoed by the president of the second Glasgow Statistical Society, Archibald Alison, the Sheriff of Lanarkshire. Better known among working people for his strong-armed way of breaking the 1837 strike of the Glasgow cotton spinners and for his merciless conduct of the subsequent trials, his hostile feelings towards unionists were heartily reciprocated. As Alison put it, 'in one day I was denounced by name as a public enemy by placards posted simultaneously during the night in every city of Great Britain and Ireland'.[32] Even cooler assessments betrayed an underlying suspicion of unions. In 1835 the London Statistical Society set up a Committee on Strikes and Combinations which designed a searching questionnaire about the causes, course and effects of strikes but did not send it to even a single trade union.[33] Studies of strikes in this period laid the blame on trade unions whose supposed 'ignorance' of political economy was alleged to have caused misery for all.

Returning to the standard questionnaire, only the Bristol and London Societies explored the sanitary state of the streets, but all the societies asked about housing conditions: the number of rooms, the number of people in them, the amount of rent, the condition of the furnishing. Manchester regretted that it did not try to learn the number of beds possessed by families (which would allow for the calculation of a people to bed ratio) until it had extended the survey to Bury, a deficiency which Bristol tried

71

to put right. Both societies 'encountered considerable reluctance to give the requested information' but nonetheless published such facts as they could glean. The domestic economy of the poor intensely interested the statisticians who remarked on the findings in this area with a vehemence and emotion which undercut their claims to a dispassionate and objective scrutiny. The two groups, investigators and investigated, stood in a revealing reverse relationship. The middle-class statisticians were just the type of men who staked their class and masculine virtue on a version of proper family life which was connected with the dividing and ordering of domestic and public space. Public space was mainly allotted to men and private space largely reserved for women and the family. The safe home was juxtaposed to the dangerous streets, the family with a home to the migratory and restless poor who inhabited lodging houses or the streets. Within domestic space, further class and gender division took place. The family were separated from the servants who were confined to the back parts or the lower parts of the house (a spatial analogy to the parts of the body less consciously valued by the bourgeoisie). Children were divided from adults and segregated by sex for sleeping.[34]

A bourgeoisie so concerned with the ordering of its own family lives would naturally be sensitive to the absence of such organization in the lives of others. To the investigators, the sleeping arrangements of the working class epitomized confusion. The theme of mixing up age and sex, which horrified Kay-Shuttleworth, was again spotlighted by the Bristol Society, in the cumulative statistics:

> out of 6,028 children who are above seven years of age, 4,752 sleep in the same room with their parents, or with both sexes in the same room; and at least 1,247 of them must be above the age of 14.

They also highlighted the same point in individual vignettes: not only the 'one instance where there was only one bed for the parents and six children, and the mother...shortly expecting her confinement' but in the 'singular case' where 'a man, aged 40, to save fuel apparently, slept in the same bed with his mother', and in the case of the 'drunken father reviling his daughter...in the most indecent terms'.[35] Incest became the ultimate embodiment of disorder because it invaded the most intimate social cell of all, the family, and, when joined with syphilis, it ensured the deterioration of the race for generations yet to come.

The devaluing way in which middle-class social investigators often constructed the poor did not come from or lead to mutual respect. Kay-Shuttleworth's adjectives of 'loathsome', 'noisome', 'squalid', 'disgusting', and 'revolting' to signify some of the customs of poor people, blocked the recognition of separate and valid cultures among the working classes. People 'rubbished' in this way were not likely to be regarded as having legitimate access to the arena of public speech, and their representation of their own experience was likely to be excluded from scientific space. There was one exception in J.R. Wood, the Manchester agent for the education surveys, who was interested in the views of his informants and squeezed these into footnotes which make some of the most lively as well as informative reading.[36] On the whole, the middle-class investigators had an affinity for statistics partly because they did not need to develop methods of inquiry and presentation which would allow cultural facts about meanings and values, habits and customs, to be expressed. The presence or absence of an activity or of membership in a school or church was a sufficient register of intellectual and moral condition. This kind of information could be expressed statistically.

In 1839, Thomas Carlyle savagely attacked the statisticians on many grounds including their neglect of how the poor perceived 'well being'.[37] But the early statisticians never questioned their own assumptions about social order, and remained convinced that departure from their rules denoted dehumanization not cultural difference. Thus the Bristol Society could only point to 'a strange degree of misery and degradation' to explain the working-class reluctance to spend a little more money on an extra sleeping room which would ensure the separation of parents and children and allow for one sex in one bed.[38] The virtue of the middle class was now firmly tied to its practice of proper gender and family relations and also to its service to the working class. Service meant redeeming the working class from disorder seen as deviation from middle-class patterns. The construction of the poor became so integrally linked to the construction of middle-class identity that the structures were hard to dismantle.

Nonetheless the surveys did change over time. From the onset of a severe economic depression in 1837, there was a growing awareness that environmental forces beyond the control of the poor could block or even prevent moral development. The preoccupation with moral order remained but there was a growing recognition that its improvement required new analyses and even new strategies. A crop of surveys of Glasgow, Nottingham and Manchester highlighted the desperate situation of domestic outworkers like the Paisley weavers whose 'religious, moral and intellectual condition...was long of a very high grade' but whose 'character is fast deteriorating' because poverty prevented their attendance at worship or school.[39] A house-to-house survey completed by the Leeds Town Council in 1839, with active Chartist participation, stressed the importance of public health, in the Council's power to regulate, and also of wages and regularity of employment in the improvement of moral and social condition.[40] This survey greatly impressed Edwin Chadwick who was just starting his consideration of the social role of public health.

In the northern cities, it was the depression of the early 1840s and the Anti-Corn Law League agitation that put questions of wages and expenditure into the centre of middle-class enquiry for the first time. Statistical Society members, particularly from Manchester, felt that the time was finally ripe to press for their way, through abolition of the Corn Laws, to engineer a situation where ever-expanding foreign markets could ensure an ever-increasing wage fund. A number of surveys now appeared which explored the social and moral effect of economic depression. Henry Ashworth, millowner and leading figure on the statistical committee of the Anti-Corn Law League, for the first time produced wages and budgets from Bolton showing that the lower the income, the larger proportion of it was spent on subsistence. Only when the wages of a family of six topped a pound a week would expenditure on moral and intellectual improvement be possible:

> with this enlargement of income we observe the prudential habits, money savings, benefit societies, a dread of pauperism, and an inclination to educate and take every care to provide for their offspring.[41]

Nor were the difficulties confined to one class: they rippled outward to the shopkeepers who lost their working-class customers.

74

London statistical surveys took a slightly different course, which was also marked by a growing interest in environmental forces affecting the morality of the poor. While asking the usual questions in 1839, the agents received constant complaints about high rents and found that Londoners were actually paying more for one room than Manchester families were paying for entire cottages. Rather than talk about bad housing as the result of bad habits, the London Society argued that bad housing created bad habits, and they singled out the problem of rents as the key to getting respectable accommodation for the working class.[42] Very nervous about interfering with the sacred law of supply and demand, they called for voluntary efforts to provide an alternative supply of housing; London members became leading figures in the model dwellings movement which took shape in the mid-1840s. Yet in its last survey, the London Society showed that it had learned from the new focus on wages and expenditure in the northern towns. Begun in 1844 and completed in 1848, the survey of 1,954 families in a Stepney parish tried explicitly to correlate employment and wages with the kinds of questions which had been asked in earlier surveys about housing, furnishings and education. To test Malthusian views about the dangers of early marriage, it also included vital statistics about the ages of mothers, numbers of births and child mortality which again could be correlated with conditions in the trades.

The most comprehensive of all the door-to-door surveys and the most attentive to the environmental pressures working on the poor, this investigation marked the last survey to be done by a voluntary body for the next twenty years. It provides a natural and intriguing chronological breaking-point. It is interesting that London saw itself preserving an older tradition of enquiry in the face of a new surge of interest in those 'lowest sinks of barbarism and vice, which sanitary and other reports have recently placed with such painful truth before the public'. They offered the survey as a study of the true working classes and as an 'example of the average condition of the poorer classes of the metropolis'.[43] London detected a shift in the focus of investigation, which will be the concern of the next chapter, and pointed to the fact that new social groups and new agencies were taking over the work of social survey, not least the municipal and central state. The transfer of survey work from the voluntary societies to the new Town Councils in Leeds, Liverpool and

Sheffield has already been noted.[44] Central state activity requires more detailed examination.

STATE INVESTIGATIONS INTO THE WORKING CLASS

The increasing role of the central state in investigatory work had profound implications both for the development of social science and for the civil service. Although relations between the voluntary societies and the state commissions usually stayed cordial and personnel moved easily between the two,[45] state effort nonetheless tended in a different direction, and ultimately marginalized the kinds of local businessmen and citizens who had pioneered the survey work (Chapter 8). The period between 1832 and 1846 witnessed a huge acceleration in state activity. Over 100 Royal Commissions set to work in those years alone and new agencies came into being, such as the Board of Trade's Statistical Section and the Statistical Branch of the Registrar General's Office, in which Utilitarians held key posts.[46] Like the proverbial jack-in-the-box, wherever state investigations between 1830 and 1850 focused upon working-class life, Edwin Chadwick popped up in an influential role. Disciple of Jeremy Bentham, Chadwick perhaps more than anyone else inherited the master's mantle (an appropriate transfer since he laboured, according to his biographer, under the strong impression that 'the best things in Scripture had been said by Jeremy Bentham').[47] During his long life, he arguably became the most influential of the Benthamites, turning a new concept of the state into a reality. He had clear ideas about 'statesmanship as a science' and about the intimate relations between true science and the state which he acted upon and later theorized.

Chadwick tried to use science to give civil servants credibility and in turn proposed certain kinds of civil servants as the only truly scientific observers. This appeared a preposterous claim when Chadwick started his work with the Poor Law Commission but he made it seem more like common sense in the end. The civil service in the 1830s formed a notorious part of the 'Old Corruption', where aristocratic patronage showered jobs on friends and allies and on kith and kin. Indeed the Assistant Commissioners on the Factories Inquiry emerged from 'a riot of jobbery'. Lord Althorp supposedly recruited the medical member, who had attended his family, by hailing him in the street with the words, 'Hallo, Loudon would you like to be on a Commission'. Althorp also replaced Chadwick on the Poor Law Commission with his own land steward who Chadwick described as, 'a very worthy accomplished and excellent man, but about as fit to act for the Poor Law Amendment Act as a delicate girl would be to assist in performing an amputation'.[48] To rescue the civil service from aristocratic corruption, and to reposition it as a strategic and positive element in emerging urban industrial society, Chadwick tried to give it the task of bringing into harmony conflicting public and private interests. Chadwick extended over a far broader social canvas Bentham's idea of using legislation to force a harmonization of interests.[49] To the civil service employing scientific procedures he gave the task of preparing the way for suitable legislation and then, via the new inspectorates, the job of enforcing the law.

Both tasks contained a built-in element of investigation. To prepare the way for legislation Chadwick proposed an 'Open Method' of investigation by Commission which would establish national reality by taking evidence from all interested parties in breadth and depth: 'complete investigation as to the state of information and opinion in the most obscure nook and corner of society'[50]. The idea was that the members of the Commission and their employees would be 'men of distinction outside the political arena', 'neutral to all but evidence' and thus be able to adjudicate among interested parties. As the list of investigations lengthened so too did the rogue's gallery of 'interested' parties. To party politicians were added local vestry officials pressured by greed or fear, and then even capitalists as well as labourers. In the Factories Inquiry *First Report*, the Benthamite co-signers, Chadwick, Tooke and Southwood Smith, insisted on the need for an impartial inspectorate since the recommended measures for limiting the hours of child labour,

> are not directly conducive to the immediate interest
> either of the master manufacturers, or of the operatives,
> or of any powerful class and are not therefore likely to
> receive continuous voluntary support.[51]

The only untainted groups began to be seen as educated men, often professional men like Chadwick (who had trained as a criminal lawyer), recruited into government service as paid officials. Chadwick helped to dignify a connection between the state and professional men by identifying these with impartiality and science.[52] In the light of the new call for nationwide investigations and for 'disinterested' state employees to do them, both the local scope and commercial affiliation of many of the statisticians could begin to look dubious—although in fact relations between the public and private enterprises remained friendly while the latter still persisted. Indeed Chadwick had entered the Manchester cottonopoly by marrying one daughter of John Kennedy, Vice President of the Statistical Society whose other daughter married Samuel Robinson, brother-in-law of Benjamin Heywood.

Measured by his practice, Chadwick's manifesto for scientific investigation sometimes amounted to little more than hypocritical cant. He shamelessly gerrymandered investigations to produce the findings he wanted: not only did he engineer the packing of the Commissions, he ignored unwelcome facts at the Report stage and sometimes falsified the meaning of inconvenient evidence, even managing, for example, to list petitions against the New Poor Law as though they were in favour.[53] Moreover, no matter how much he won the confidence of middle-class citizens eager to dissociate themselves from aristocratic corruption, his efforts still looked suspicious to many working-class subjects. The 1833 Factory Commission in particular was widely regarded as the outcome of 'the unjust and mercenary influence of the mill-owners in Parliament', and as a tactic to overturn the findings of a previous Select Committee investigation, which had strong working-class support, and sabotage a Ten Hours Bill which had already received its second reading. A Delegate Conference of Short Time Committees instructed every locality in England and Scotland to appoint a 'Select Committee' of two workers to tail every sub-Commissioner and report on all his activities as well as to stage large protest demonstrations. Activists often regarded the new inspectorates as yet more honeypots of patronage, and for the rest of the century had trouble seeing them as neutral and unbiased, while they remained the hirelings of an unrepresentative state.[54]

The major Royal Commissions which looked into aspects of working-class life between 1830 and 1850 examined the administration of the Poor Laws, the condition of women and children in various industries, and the state of health in towns. The investigators produced massive volumes of text. Here I will discuss only a few reports which can illustrate how the state inquiries both reinforced and extended the statistician's concern with urban disorder. Chadwick's *Report...on...the Sanitary Condition of the Labouring Population of Great Britain*[55] both followed up the pilot survey carried out by Dr Kay-Shuttleworth and other doctors as well as previewing some of the concerns which would dominate first the Health of Towns agitation and the Royal Commission in the 1840s and then the field of public health or sanitary science during the midcentury years. Together with this pivotal inquiry, I will consider the investigations into Factories and Mines and the way in which they constructed women as a powerful contradictory symbol both of order and disorder.

The timing of the Sanitary *Report* was as significant as its content. Chadwick began work during the first Chartist climax of 1839, and presented his findings to the House of Lords in July 1842, barely a month after parliament's rejection of the second mammoth Chartist petition and at the lowest point of the worst economic depression of the century. A month later, a general strike would spread over fifteen counties and be met with a severity of repression and sentencing unrivalled since the Swing riots of 1832. Disorder spread. Yet despite the facts of trade depression and widespread unemployment, Chadwick still put the spotlight onto the residential rather than the industrial life of the poor and saw the social problem as one of interlocking physical, moral, spatial and political disturbance. Using the national network of Poor Law Medical Officers as informants together with local statisticians, Chadwick cobbled the *Report* out of large slabs of quotation, giving the appearance of overwhelming unanimity from disparate places and thus of unassailable national truth.

Compared with the statistician's surveys, there was a new emphasis on 'atmospheric impurity' and a sharper focus on the state of the streets where piles of animal and vegetable refuse putrefied and produced the miasma held responsible for physical disease and moral debility. Moving indoors, the investigators highlighted the bad ventilation and damp caused by poor construction and compounded by the overcrowding and 'moral depravity' of the poor. Repeatedly featuring in investigatory texts as the epitome of disorder, low lodging houses for the homeless poor brought promiscuous sleeping and miasmatic stench to their most 'abominable' extremes:

> the crowded state of the beds, filled promiscuously with men, women, and children; the floor covered over with the filthy and ragged clothes they have just put off, and with their various bundles and packages, containing all the property they possess, mark the depraved and blunted state of their feelings, and the moral and social disorder which exists. The suffocating stench and heat of the atmosphere are almost intolerable to a person coming from the open air.[56]

Chadwick's suggested remedies for multilayered disorder included a new central authority appointed by the crown with powers over sewerage, street cleansing, water supply etc., together with a large dose of regulation from above. In a watered down and permissive form some of these proposals became part of the 1848 Public Health Act which left considerable initiative to local councils.

It is worth noting the lack of enthusiasm that working-class activists showed for Chadwick's public health reforms. This is not to suggest thatthe poor preferred to remain poorly housed, dirty and sick. But issues about social analysis and power were at stake. The socialists saw disease as the result of the inequality of life chances within capitalism, to be remedied, in the words of Elijah Dixon, a Manchester Owenite, by

> wholesome food, comfortable clothing and dwellings, cleanliness and temperance, and above all a knowledge of pharmacy; advantages which would be secured to each member of a co-operative community.[57]

The public health reforms became entangled with the heated issue of controlling unaccountable authority in a situation where most working men had neither a parliamentary nor, after the Municipal Corporations Act of 1835, a local vote. Chadwick became the chief centralizing bogeyman to those involved in the battle of 'Local Self-Government versus Centralization', the title of the book by the leading theorist on the self-government side, Joshua Toulmin Smith, son of socialist Hawkes Smith. Working-class activists even tried to devise alternative democratic routes to public health reform. In the extraordinary case of Sheffield, socialist and Chartist Isaac Ironside, powerfully influenced by Smith's ideas, managed to introduce an element of direct Saxon democracy into the new system of town councils. He then started a People's Gas Company to break private monopolies over local services and helped press for the construction of one of the first modern sewer systems independently of the 1848 Public Health Act.[58] In this atmosphere of contest, it is not surprising that working people did not welcome the kind of surveillance that Chadwick and his colleagues, already tainted by their association with the hated New Poor Law and the county police, so lavishly proposed.

Chadwick would root out all secret sources of miasma: a middle-class gaze and regulation would cure the disease of disorder. Medical Officers of Health and their team of Sanitary Inspectors would eliminate nuisances inside and outside, inanimate and human. Police would patrol low lodging houses. The chief advantage of factories was 'constant general supervision' and factory villages could be kept 'under observation' by employers in order to improve the standard of domestic economy. In the city, working-class dwellings were best separated to check the 'frequent instances of ... social disorder arising from the too close contiguity of residences'. Apartment blocks were such seething cauldrons of chaos that 'a power and discipline almost as strong as that of a man-of-war, is requisite to preserve order in such communities'. Common bakehouses, communal wash-houses, and common water pumps provided stagesets for disorder: 'for perpetual quarrels and frequent assaults among females'.[59]

It is interesting how often the situation of women became emblematic of the condition of the whole group, whether family or class. Women at the water pumps transgressed the ideal of bourgeois femininity: the loudmouthed fighting fiend was the opposite of the modest, soft-spoken, gentle wife whose efforts were devoted to keeping her family physically as well as morally clean. In a Glasgow tenement with three interconnecting courtyards full of dung, the inside horror story was expressed in terms of pathetic women imprisoned all day in bed while their clothes were being worn by female friends out of doors.[60] Again and again, working-class women were portrayed in a contradictory way. They were both actively out of control and yet at the same time pathetic victims of the incapacity of their unruly menfolk to protect them. Disciplinarians from outside the class were needed to contain the rampant gender chaos.

The same tendency to depict disorder in the image of woman was to be found in the *Report* of the Royal Commission on the Employment of Children (Mines) also published in 1842. The state studies of the working class in industry in this period focused upon women and children rather than men whose situation could not be adjusted without 'violating' the laws of political economy. Just as essential bourgeois masculinity protected vulnerable women and children in the family, so middle-class investigators believed that working-class women and children in the public sphere were obvious candidates for public protection by means of legislation. Indeed women and children were conceptually conflated to the point where the Factory Commissioners actually used the same questionnaire for both which included queries like: 'do you go to any school now whilst you are at the factory?', 'have you any play-ground?' and 'are you, or other children in your works, in the habit of frequenting public-houses?'. Understandably grown women had trouble relating to these questions: Margaret Jackson, aged 18, and Ann Cook, aged 23, both answered the question about schooling, 'I go to a Sunday-school, and I am a teacher'.[61]

The Mines inquiry was particularly interesting because the Sub-Commissioners had no brief to investigate women, but widened the terms of reference on their own initiative because they were so shocked by what they found once down in the pits. This was also the only Royal Commission Report in the period to contain illustrations, many of which represented women transgressing boundaries in predictable directions. For example, women were depicted in animal poses (drawing carts of coal on all fours), in masculine poses with erotic overtones (with hands in trouser pockets yet also wearing unbuttoned blouse, necklace and earrings), and as savages with the blackness of the skin accentuated. Sophie Hamilton has shown how the Sub-Commissioners and the Commissioners excluded from their analysis evidence they collected which went counter to their case that women working in the black of the pit displayed a sexuality so rampant that, in the memorable words of J.C. Symons, 'no brothel can beat it'.[62] To give just one of Hamilton's examples,

Mary Barrett's testimony appeared in the final *Report* but without its final phrase which changed its whole meaning:

> I wear nothing but my chemise; I have to go up to the headings with the men; they are all naked there; I am got well used to it; I was afraid at first, and did not like it; *they never behave rudely to me* (italics added to indicate the deleted part).[63]

The Commissioners could not conceive that morality could coexist with nudity. Equally the Commissioners suppressed evidence that women in public work could nonetheless shoulder a double burden, and manage their domestic economy in a satisfactory way. Depositions like that of Dr Barham about pit women being 'tender mothers and industrious wives' never reached the First Report stage.[64] Instead, the Commissioners at all levels bemoaned the fact that such unbridled women, who worked not merely in the public sphere but in its dark underground places, had spoiled (soiled) themselves for marriage and motherhood, their true vocation. By overstepping the limits of femininity, they had put their families and the whole class in jeopardy: the man would leave his house for the pub (already a charged symbol of hidden disorder) and the 'cheerfulness and physical comfort which his fireside did not afford'.[65] Once again state investigators revealed their contradictory view of women, assigning women the power to ruin the family and class or to redeem them, to rip up the social fabric or knit it together. Not surprisingly the first clause in the Mines Regulation Act of 1842 prohibited the employment of females underground.

HENRY MAYHEW, *LONDON LABOUR AND THE LONDON POOR*

In the long run, state investigators established more of a monopoly over social survey work than any other social group, with the possible exception of academic researchers. But in the short run, investigatory work was also passing from the local statistical societies into the hands of other groups like journalists. In October 1849, the *Morning Chronicle* newspaper launched its massive enquiry into Labour and the Poor in the agricultural, manufacturing, mining and metropolitan districts of Great

Britain. This example spurred several provincial journals, like the *Newcastle Chronicle* and the *Edinburgh News*, to undertake similar investigations often out of a grandiose sense of professional mission. The *Morning Chronicle* sponsored its unprecedented enquiry at another moment of convergence between political crisis and pestilence. Hard on the heels of the Chartist climax of 1848, enacted against the backdrop of European revolutions, came a cholera outbreak which peaked in September 1849. What made the *Chronicle* survey remarkable was the work of Henry Mayhew (1812-87) the correspondent who had written vividly about the cholera districts of Bermondsey and was now hired as the metropolitan 'commissioner' to investigate the whole of London.[66]

The son of a staid solicitor, Mayhew had strayed off the parental path to make a precarious living by constantly concocting new publishing and theatrical ventures in a literary bohemia which was irreverent if not radical. *Punch* came from this circle, as did the satirical cartoons of George Cruikshank. Obviously, Mayhew was not the same kind of ultra-respectable bourgeois man who had shaped the developing genre of social surveys. This is precisely what makes the tensions in his work so illuminating. He made radical departures from the usual middle-class agenda, and yet was still constrained by the symbolic repertoire of the bourgeois imagination. He was able to hear, understand and incorporate the analyses of working people and to move much further down paths that middle-class investigators had only tentatively begun to explore. Yet he was also magnetically attached to certain constructions of the poor which were to dominate mid-century social science from above. He was the bourgeois renegade who still revealed the power of middle-class meanings.

For the first year of the survey until he engaged (and enraged) nearly every vested interest in the metropolis and broke with the *Chronicle*, Mayhew had the most secure job of his life and did his best work. After that he continued the survey on his own but in a situation where he had to write what would sell or go under: this financial constraint must be kept in mind when evaluating the directions of his work. I would still argue, as I did in the *Unknown Mayhew*, that he set out to conduct the first empirical survey into poverty as such. He started with the first-ever attempt to define a poverty line:

Under the term 'poor' I shall include all those persons whose incomings are insufficient for the satisfaction of their wants—a want being, according to my idea, contra-distinguished from a mere desire by a positive physical pain, instead of mental uneasiness accompanying it....I shall consider the whole of the metropolitan poor under three separate phases, according as they will work, they can't work, and they won't work.[67]

Turning first to 'those who will work', whose poverty he attributed to low wages, high prices or improvident habits, he decided to begin by focusing on occupations which were notorious for their low wages: Spitalfields silk weaving, dock labouring and needlework. But he quickly felt that he could not understand a low-paid branch of a trade without considering the trade as a whole. He developed a method of interviewing a representative cross-section of workers (and employers when they would co-operate) which enabled him to explore the power relations, the organization and dynamics, the conditions and wage levels in a trade. Thus he created a mode of industrial survey which at once established the levels of wages and the causes for them. This approach was very different from the retreat of the statisticians who, even when they found that low wages were an impediment to high morals, did no empirical study of the industrial causes of low wages but simply prescribed their nostrum of free trade as the remedy for all industrial problems. Indeed it was Mayhew's growing conviction that workmen were right to urge protective tariffs that led to the break with the *Chronicle* which militantly championed free trade.

What made Mayhew so different from other investigators was his willingness to make room for the voices of working people in his investigative practice. He gave the poor space to speak their experience in their own words (although in answer to his questions). Those words were written into his articles (a source of great pleasure to the informants, including residents of a common lodging house who were 'much delighted at finding themselves in print').[68] He did not automatically assume that the qualities of the poor were the opposite of middle-class order and virtue. Possibly it was because he didn't suffer from the usual middle-class 'moral halitosis', that he inspired confidence: probably he communicated his real interest in others and respect for them and this made people more responsive. Even in a cheap lodging house, for other investigators the modern equivalent, in microcosm, of Babel, Sodom and Gomorrah all rolled into one, Mayhew laid on a dinner for thirty informants. When fifty showed up to eat, Mayhew left it to those residents entitled to the meal to decide about the others, a gesture of respect towards the competence of the guests that no other investigator would have made in this period. Not surprisingly, 'the answer from one and all was that the newcomers were to share the feast'.[69] People talked to Mayhew at length and however much they tailored their speech to their perceived audience, he was receptive and willing to absorb many of their analyses into his own. He became increasingly aware of conflicting vantage points, the facts from the employers' point of view and from the workers' and usually ended up attributing greater accuracy to the perceptions of the workers.[70]

His painstaking studies of the tailoring, shoemaking and woodworking trades revealed the recent development of a slop or cheap section, or in the workers' moral economy parlance, a 'dishonourable branch'. This was a jungle of rampant competition inhabited by a new competitive type of employer and untamed by trade union organization or legislative regulation. As unionized artisans and honourable masters testified, competition from the cheap branch tended to depress conditions in the honourable section. Wages descended rapidly once the border between honourable and dishonourable labour had been crossed.[71] However provident a workman might try to be, poverty stubbornly accompanied the low wages and irregularity of work in the slop part of a trade. Indeed from his very early work on the docks, Mayhew began to feel that a more subtle process was at work where, to turn the usual argument on its head, poverty was creating improvident habits. Noting that a docker's wages plunged from fifteen shillings one week to nought the next, he argued that it was psychologically improbable that such a workman could develop a routinized and respectable way of life:

> Regularity of habits are incompatible with irregularity of income; indeed the very conditions necessary for the formation of any habit whatsoever are, that the act or thing to which we are to become habituated should be

repeated at frequent and regular intervals. It is a moral impossibility that the class of labourers who are only occasionally employed should be either generally industrious or temperate—both industry and temperance being habits produced by constancy of employment and uniformity of income. [72]

Yet if Mayhew came increasingly to value 'those who will work' and even, in a neat inversion of the usual middle-class use of the imagery of savagery, to see them as the decent prey of capitalistic 'cannibals', he took a very different view of 'those who will not work'. As the survey proceeded, he came to divide them off and linguistically to devalue them. Increasingly when analysing them, stereotypes and symbols began to take the place of people, even though (and this was Mayhew's greatness) real people could still break in through the medium of their own words. Early in the survey, in order to interview dockers, he visited the lodging houses where they lived, which middle-class social analysis represented as such demonic places. His attitudes were revealingly contradictory. Starting from a position of ignorance his views hardened and his imagery became more denigrating during his seven letters on vagrancy and shelters for the homeless (lodging houses, casual wards of workhouses and refuges for the destitute). In his usual way, he tried to interview inmates as well as conductors of these places and managed to make some less usual discriminations as well as give space for people's experience. He noted the sections of the vagrant population who wanted to find work and also refused to demonize the Irish, saying that they had been 'starved out of their own country'.[73] In a sense he performed a conceptual and linguistic rescue by removing these groups from the subhuman.

However, he also became increasingly fixated upon young criminals among the migratory population and came to see the various hostels as schools for crime and vice. Later he attacked ragged schools for the same reasons and infuriated pillars of the Evangelical philanthropic establishment like Lord Shaftesbury who replied with letters in the *Chronicle* which were roundly supported by the proprietors of the paper.[74] As usual, females, this time girls and young women, were made to carry the clearest messages about disorder. Thus in his last letter, devoted entirely to the role of lodging houses as schools for scandal, a 'good-looking girl of sixteen' disclosed 'a system of depravity, atrocity, and enormity, which certainly cannot be paralleled in any nation, however barbarous, nor in any age, however "dark"'.[75] Mayhew rarely indulged in this kind of hyperbolic condemnation. Like that of many of the young people, her story was one of being mistreated by an employer and then of being orphaned, and in this defenceless and friendless state taking up with groups of youths at a lodging house to survive by beggary, petty theft and prostitution. For Mayhew it was the young away from adult supervision, whether from their own families or from different classes, who posed the greatest social problem. Their disorder, as usual, was 'horrifically' depicted in terms of promiscuous sleeping arrangements in a lodging house with an added scene of satanic rituals of dancing half-naked at midnight:

> We lay packed on a full night, a dozen boys and girls squeedged into one bed. That was very often the case— some at the foot and some at the top—boys and girls all mixed. I can't go into all the particulars, but whatever could take place in words or acts between boys and girls did take place, and in the midst of the others. I am sorry to say I took part in these bad ways myself, but I wasn't so bad as some of the others. There was only a candle burning all night, but in summer it was light great part of the night. Some boys and girls slept without any clothes, and would dance about the room that way. I have seen them, and, wicked as I was, felt ashamed.[76]

Mayhew restored a large number of working people to the category of dignified human beings, where many previous social investigators, like the statisticians and Chadwick, had seen the working classes as a whole but portrayed them with devaluing imagery as disordered. At the same time Mayhew helped to reinforce what became a dominant midcentury conceptual divide, however it was named, between the true working class and the 'perishing and dangerous classes'. Drawing upon the ethnology of the day, Mayhew tried to develop his own category of wandering tribes in civilized society. He endowed the members of migratory tribes with features which had pejorative animal and savage associations:

[they] are all more or less distinguished for their high cheekbones and protruding jaws—for their use of a slang language—for their lax ideas of property—for their general improvidence—their repugnance to continuous labour—their disregard of female honour—their love of cruelty—thcir pugnacity—and their utter want of religion.[77]

He first put this concept to work when he left the *Chronicle* and continued part-publication on his own with a return to the subject of the costermongers. When Mayhew first studied the costers, he saw their role in a setting of political economy: as that 'large portion of the poor' 'through whom the working people obtain considerable part of their provisions and raiment'.[78] Now he placed them in a more charged landscape of disorder and desire.

Nonetheless his actual account of the costers showed that their life was in fact organized, although around different values. Even in the symbolic heartland of social stability, he showed that differences in sexual and marital behaviour, which he did not condone, did not inevitably lead to social chaos. The costers cohabited and seldom married, yet family and community continued. 'The married women', Mayhew observed,

associate with the unmarried mothers of families without the slightest scruple. There is no honour attached to the marriage state and no shame to concubinage. Neither are the unmarried women less faithful to their 'partners' than the married: but I understand that, of the two classes, the unmarried betray the most jealousy.[79]

As for the children, Mayhew insisted that '"chance children", as they are called, or children unrecognized by any father are rare among the young women of the costermongers'.

The more Mayhew had to sell his publications quickly to survive, the more his focus turned to the magnetic underside of Victorian respectability: costers, street cleaners, prostitutes and, finally, exterminators of rodents and vermin. In the three volume version of *London Labour and the London Poor*, the industrial survey was virtually concealed under the weight of the repellent and therefore fascinating opposites of urban order: the people of the street or of the sewer.[80] Over time, Mayhew's work was merging into a powerful midcentury mainstream. During the 'hungry forties', new and narrower fields of social study had emerged for dealing with the condition of the working class. These were dominated by new professionals and specialists who fragmented the study of the poor just as they dismembered Mayhew's survey when they took any notice of it.[81] Many of the new experts concentrated on just those 'lowest sinks of barbarism' which the London Statistical Society had tried so carefully to sidestep in its last survey and which Mayhew found himself exploring increasingly in the last phases of his investigations. Where the statistical societies survived, an influx of professional men reshaped their way of studying the working class.[82] These experts largely defined the issues of pressing social concern during the midcentury, shaped social research inside and outside the state and coloured the approach of bodies like the National Association for the Promotion of Social Science.

Part II

SOCIAL SCIENCE
AND THE
COMMUNION
OF LABOUR
1850-1890

4

PROFESSIONAL MEN, SCIENCE AND SERVICE 1840-1880

In this period, an intimate relationship began between social science and middle-class professionalization. The older professions, law, medicine and the clergy, together with the often overlapping civil service, grew between 1851 and 1881.[1] But increasing numbers do not automatically mean an affinity for social science. This chapter will explore how professionalising men began to use a formula of science and service to close a huge credibility gap and establish themselves as indispensable to modern social life. In recent controversial literature about the nature of salaried brainworkers, some writers have depicted professionals as the possessors of cultural or intellectual capital, a kind of income-yielding property that takes the form of valuable expertise.[2] This chapter will emphasize how hard professional men worked to accumulate their intellectual capital and make plausible their claims to indispensability and how they utilized social science in the process.

All the older professions were deeply implicated in the 'Old Corruption' of the eighteenth century. Broadly speaking, during the nineteenth century, the professions tried to break the remaining links with the landed interest or aristocratic order and reposition themselves firmly in the middle class, indeed to mark out a place as its intellectual and moral vanguard. Each of the older professions had deeply tarnished images to refurbish. If the memory of the fox-hunting, hard-drinking, absentee cleric was becoming dimmer as a result of Evangelical effort, many middle-class Nonconformists would still have agreed with the Chartist banners calling for 'More Pigs Less Parsons'. In the

1820s even the middle class sneered at doctors who gained professional distinction simply through their connection with the landed interest, while the poor regarded some medical men, especially after the passing of the Anatomy Act in 1832, largely as legally-sanctioned grave-robbers. The middle class and the poor also shared a view of lawyers as hearse-chasers, incorrigible litigators (for their own profit of course) and toadies to the aristocracy. Although Chadwick was trying to shift this view, civil servants were often reviled as jumped-up placemen created by aristocratic patronage. The case of Dr Loudon, mentioned in the last chapter, amounted to double jeopardy. Not only did Lord Althorp recruit him to the Factories Inquiry in the most casual fashion, but Loudon responded in the most self-interested manner, thinking 'it might lead to something good, I said "Yes" and his Lordship put me on'. Critics saw Oxford and Cambridge universities as training establishments for the parasitic clergy and landed polloi (the rich poll men who scraped by with pass degrees).[3]

In an effort to transform this situation and create a more responsible and credible role, some professional men modified a formula of service and science already familiar in scientific philanthropy and urban statistical work. This chapter will explore a range of attempts, by individual professionals whose careers had a paradigmatic quality, and by collective bodies, to give the ideal of service new meaning. Whether in terms of service to clients, or, more often in social science, to a section of the working class or, later, to the nation as a whole, professional men were altering the mantle of service in ways which fitted them particularly well.

But it would be crude in the extreme to suggest that professional men intended to use a language of service only for opportunistic advantage, even if redefining service did function to legitimize the professions: intention and function did not neatly coincide. The commitment to service was already deeply engrained in the consciousness of many members of the middle class, either because enjoined by God, or, as became more common among the educated middle class from the midcentury onward if they had lost their Christian faith, because, in the spiritual wreckage, the ethical impulse to duty remained. George Eliot encapsulated the usual way of navigating religious crisis when she spoke of God, Immortality and Duty, explaining 'how inconceivable was the *first*, how unbelievable the *second*, and yet how peremptory and absolute the *third*'.[4]

Social science became a strategic part of professional service. The last chapter showed how Chadwick used science to rehabilitate civil servants. This chapter will explore how other groups of professional men used their expertise to develop sciences in response to social crisis. The sequence of revolution in 1848 followed by cholera in 1849 provided a splendid chance for professionals to establish their legitimacy and value. In language reminiscent of Lady Shelley during the first French Revolution, G.S. Trevelyan, one of the architects of civil service reform, spoke of how 'the revolutionary period of 1848 gave us a shake, and created a disposition to put our house in order'.[5] To put the social house in order, professional men took over emerging social science fields and established themselves as the indispensable experts who could remedy the very social problems they had helped to define. They set in motion a decisive shift and began to take over the social science project from the working people who had pioneered it from below and the local citizens who had developed it from above.

DOCTORS AND SANITARY SCIENCE

The new field of 'sanitary science', or public health, opened up a community role which could dignify medical skill—if only doctors could find a way to dominate it. For some time, images of health and disease had been key ways of representing social problems and it would be a great prize if medical men could establish a monopoly over that language. But at first, laymen like Chadwick wielded considerable power in the field of public health. Although he placed doctors like Kay-Shuttleworth, Southwood Smith and William Farr in strategic state jobs, and largely created the posts of Poor Law Medical Officer and Medical Officer of Health, nonetheless he remained basically suspicious of doctors. He dismissed medical skill as 'nothing but *consolatio animi*...pretending to alleviate disease which if they had the will they had not the skill to *prevent*'.[6] He stubbornly opposed the appointment of a medical commissioner to the Poor Law Board and would not tolerate a permanent medical officer on the General Board of Health. As he became convinced that prevention would be achieved through a system of 'arterial drainage', his definition of the science of public health became synonymous with sanitary engineering. His ideal Medical Officer of Health was an engineer.

Doctors, like John Simon (1816-1904), challenged this definition and tried to establish the idea that medical men, by virtue of their professional expertise, could make the most important contributions to sanitary science. His model career as Medical Officer of Health in the City of London dating from 1848 (the second such post in Britain) and then his powerful role as Medical Officer first at the General Board of Health (1855-8) and later to the Privy Council (1858-71), gave his ideas force. Despite owing his appointment in the City as much to the string-pulling of his father, a wealthy insurance broker, as to his own competence as a surgeon and scientist, Simon worked assiduously to give medical skill more influence. In 1854, the General Board pensioned Chadwick off, and, partly as a result of Simon's pressure, appointed twelve doctors as cholera inspectors and set up a medical 'Committee for Scientific Inquiry'. These events symbolized the advent of a new union between medicine and public health. Electing him the first president of the Metropolitan Association of Medical Officers of Health in 1856, his professional colleagues 'agreed on all sides that it is Mr. Simon who has given sanitary science its present status and popularity'.[7] But the conflict must not be exaggerated. Both Chadwick and the doctors saw the state as integral to public health and concurred in the way they depicted and treated social problem groups. Simon, however, wanted to establish doctors as the legitimate experts to speak these shared truths.

Like Chadwick, Simon saw routine inspection as central to the project of 'improving the social conditions of the poor'.[8] His ideal, only realized at the height of the 1849 cholera epidemic, was to receive weekly reports about the 'personal habits' of the sick, including 'temperance, nourishment, kind of occupation and exposure', together with facts about 'domestic conditions—overcrowding, ventilation, light, warmth and water supply' and about 'local circumstances as to ventilation and drainage, nuisances and other causes of unhealthiness'.[9] Simon added to the public health agenda a concern with the employment situation but only as far as workshop conditions directly affected physical health. Firmly convinced that the real causes of disease were not sufficiently understood, he also encouraged doctors to undertake scientific experiments.

Doctors of the Simon stamp became the most active figures in the Public Health Department of the Social Science Association of which Simon was a founder-member. A typical figure, Edwin Lankester (1814-74), became editor of the Association's *Journal of Social Science*. The son of a Suffolk builder of modest means, Lankester was rebuffed by the still-exclusive Royal College of Physicians in 1847 and abandoned private practice for public service, becoming best known from 1862 for his work as Coroner for the Central District of Middlesex.[10] Here he became an active patron of the Ladies' Sanitary Association, delivering lectures and writing pamphlets particularly on physiology, and encouraging the women to undertake household visiting and keep a careful eye on infant mortality.[11] He had an abiding interest in microscopy, nutrition and physiology and, with Dr Snow, did a microscopic examination of drinking water which demonstrated the waterborne nature of cholera. This investigation marked the beginning of the end of the miasmatic theory of disease.

Many high ideals and hopes attached to the 'sanitary idea'. In his more expansive moods, Simon even felt that medical skill channelled through public health had the most important contribution to make to community welfare. He told the penny-pinching City burghers:

> In the great objects which sanitary science proposes to itself, in the immense amelioration which it proffers to the physical, to the social and indirectly to the moral condition of an immense majority of our fellow-creatures, it transcends the importance of all other sciences, and its beneficent operation seems most nearly to embody the spirit and to fulfil the intentions of practical Christianity.[12]

Nonetheless the function of thought and action in this field was to give further authority to the representation of the poor as already diseased or at risk of becoming so. Medical attention was confined to a more narrow notion of the environmental factors shaping the lives of the poor than had been the case twenty years before. Even Dr McCormac of Belfast could not resist the attraction of sanitary science offering its special role for medical competence in community service. He was like a new man writing *Moral-Sanatory Economy* in 1853. Gone was any analysis of structural economic change or of the economic determinants of social conditions. Now he focused on city nuisances, not on capitalism, as the problem and devoted the greater part of the book to standard public health concerns, among them

> The pallor and defective stamina of town-bred populations, decimated and devastated by foul drinking waters, imperfect sewage, miserable cleansing, defective ventilation, intramural interests, the local slaughter of animals for food, in short every imaginable impurity.[13]

From this time onward, he became obsessed with demonstrating the connection between foul air and all kinds of diseases from malaria to tuberculosis. How completely he had succumbed to prevailing midcentury perspectives can be seen from the rest of the book. A chapter on employment was simply a discussion of pauper relief. Such attention as he gave to preventative action was taken up with the rescue of prostitutes and with the education of that other favourite midcentury problem group, the children of the 'perishing and dangerous classes'.

LAWYERS AND REFORMATORY SCIENCE

During the 1840s, often growing out of their professional work, some lawyers shifted their interest to selected groups of the urban poor. Lawyers figured as the most numerous occupational group in the Social Science Association and featured prominently in other varieties of midcentury social science. Some lawyers, it is true, came to the SSA to discuss jurisprudence and technical legal matters. But others came to talk about the working class. The Hill brothers, especially Matthew Davenport Hill and Frederic Hill, prove especially interesting examples because, like Dr McCormac, they had been concerned with the condition of the working classes earlier, in the 1830s. Through their professional experience, they came to isolate a segment of the working class, the criminal element, most frequently to be found in 'the rookeries' of large cities. The Hills were instrumental in marking out as a new special field, 'reformatory science', the study and treatment of the criminal classes.

The Hill brothers were born into a first-generation middle-class Unitarian family who ran an 'experimental' Boys' School in Birmingham. All the five sons taught in the school, and formed a mutual improvement society among themselves to further their own educations.[14] Not unlike artisans themselves, their early thinking about the working classes was shaped by the Birmingham scene. Frederic Hill, who was deputed by the family to serve on the Council of the Political Union, shared the currency views of townsman Thomas Attwood and thought of poverty in terms of the plight of artisans and mechanics degraded 'into the rank of paupers' by an economic system inhibited by dear money and high taxation. The family was also 'on terms of friendly intimacy' with Robert Owen and brother Rowland, later famous as the inventor of the penny post, even flirted with a scheme to make the family the centre of a communitarian experiment.[15]

In 1822, the family found a patron in Jeremy Bentham, who had been impressed by their educational ideas. He introduced all the Hill brothers to his own networks and opened a way to public success based on professional expertise, state service and reform.[16] At first the Hills remained inveterate Birmingham men. They were all active in the Society for the Diffusion of Useful Knowledge from its inception, but saw it not as a political economy propaganda machine but very much as a way to extend the self-education of artisans. Without success, they tried to get the Society to publish Dr William King's *Co-operator*, one of the foundation texts of the early co-operative movement. The Hill brothers thought of the working class as the artisans and mechanics of Birmingham who had co-operated with them in the Political Union. Working-class distress had nothing to do with the peculiar features of urban living. If anything, there were conspicuous 'advantages which a dense population can command', ranging from greater sociability to more help in times of need.[17]

Their preoccupation with a more limited section of the poor and with forms of urban destitution grew out of their professional experience. Both M.D. and Frederic Hill read for the Bar, a novel undertaking for Birmingham men, and then Frederic realised a childhood dream by entering the civil service.[18] The passing of the Great Reform Bill furthered the family fortunes of the Hills. Matthew sat as Reform MP for Hull until 1834, long enough to put his legal practice on a firm financial footing, and to build a network of government contacts which his brothers could use. Through his influence, Frederic was appointed the first Inspector of Prisons for Scotland, Northumberland and Durham in 1835. During his first year of office, Frederic toured the Scottish prisons and became friendly with lights of Edinburgh society like Sir John Murray and James Simpson, barristers who were interested in criminal jurisprudence and prison discipline. His interest shifted to the study of the 'criminal classes' and the possibility for their social rehabilitation. His occupation and his *Annual Reports* qualified him to speak as an expert in debates on criminality. In 1853 he published his observations in more systematic form as *Crime, its Amount, Causes and Remedies*. His interest in crime spread to his brothers. Edwin brought out a book in 1870 on *Criminal Capitalists* which was not an indictment of the capitalist system but a study of the city areas where criminals lodged and of urban patterns for disposing of stolen goods.

M.D. Hill practised as a barrister until he was appointed Recorder of Birmingham in 1839. If he had little mercy for the Chartists, his compassion did go out to juvenile offenders. His daughters, who later took up this work, stressed his reluctance to send young children to prison. 'It was perhaps not unnatural', they explained,

> that the public whose only knowledge of the young criminal was derived from the newspaper reports of his trial, should remain indifferent to his downward course; but among his judges were those who meeting him face to face were moved to compassion by his inevitable fate. They recognized the futility of expecting any benefit to the child, or to society from immuring him, often so small that his little head was hardly visible above the top of the dock, within the gloomy walls of a gaol. They were thus led to seek wiser and more humane means of dealing with him.[19]

Hill put children in the care of their employers and was so pleased with the system that he tried to get it adopted in the metropolis. But the magistrates of the Middlesex Sessions informed him that scarcely any of their juvenile delinquents had either employers, parents or friends. The idea that there existed a class of city children, abandoned and friendless, bereft of all the family ties which had given his own life form and purpose, clearly struck him with great force. From 1848, Hill became active in the reformatory movement, learning from people like Mary Carpenter who had had more direct contact with the urban poor. In his testimony before the Select Committee on Destitute and Criminal Juveniles in 1852, Hill connected the emergence of a dangerous class with the growth of large cities. He spoke of the movement of the higher classes from the centre of towns to the suburbs, and insisted that this trend led to a breakdown of regulating forces and to the appearance of a criminal class.[20]

Within the new field of 'reformatory science', which had an adult and juvenile branch, issues about the criminal poor and about the causes and cure of crime were thrashed out. As in the case of sanitary science, the general condition of the working class was subordinated to the study of special groups among the poor and special features of the social environment, like dysfunctional families (see p.123) or urban pathology. Yet the lawyers in the reformatory movement, like the doctors in public health, argued that their reduced and specialized perspective was the key factor in the move down the road from revolution to reconciliation. J.C. Symons, now a barrister and an Inspector of schools, wrote *Tactics for the Times as Regards the Treatment of the Dangerous Classes* (1849) which, despite the climactic title, was only about the education of criminal children. Alexander Thomson's book, *Social Evils: Their Causes and Cure* (1852) was similarly about juvenile delinquency and the need for industrial schools: Alfred Hill, another barrister from Birmingham, insisted in 1856, that 'the management and diminution of the criminal and vagrant population of this country is one of the most pressing problems of the age'.[21] The reformatory field offered few state posts for lawyers comparable to those available to doctors in public health. Even if their interest had been awakened through their work, lawyers tended to become active in philanthropic ventures or outside pressure groups or else they entered the civil service and took up posts which led to a different expertise. Voluntary work in the juvenile rescue field was popular, especially with ragged schools or groups employing pupils like the Ragged School Shoe Black Society, where young lawyer-helpers were as conspicuous as the lads who wore striking red uniforms.[22]

THE PROFESSIONAL IDEAL AND COMMUNITY SERVICE

Service formed an integral part of middle-class identity and middle-class groups on the move upward regularly found service a useful validating ticket. From the 1840s, a number of separate but reinforcing developments suggest that professional men began to claim the mantle of service as particularly their own, even compared with other sections of their class. In a generalized way, observers began to theorize the professional class in relation to other sections of the middle class accenting both its morality and command of knowledge. Appropriating the language that had been used in the 1820s to dignify the middle classes in contrast to the landed interest, H. Byerley Thomson effusively insisted in 1857 that

> the importance of the professions and the professional classes can hardly be overrated, they form the head of the great English middle class, maintain its tone and independence, keep up to the mark its standard of morality and direct its intelligence.[23]

In contrast to the businessman whose conduct was regulated at best only by 'general rules of honesty and regard to his own interest', A.V. Dicey insisted, in 1867, that members of a profession submitted themselves to regulation by their peers in the interest of a service ethic which meant that they had to 'sacrifice a certain amount of individual liberty in order to ensure professional objects'. Even if created mainly by insecure, status-seeking men, the professional ideal was just the kind of conception which could grow far beyond the conditions of its originating moment: it seemed capable of infinite expansion and extensive application.[24] Later socialists, like Tawney and the Webbs, felt that professional self-regulation and high standards of service prefigured the attitude they wished to inculcate into all citizens of the modern socialist industrial state.

The early attempts to characterize a professional class were partly occasioned by important institutional developments in the professions and in higher education. From the 1820s, the medical hierarchy was restructured on the basis of competence rather than social standing. Professional associations, like the Provincial Medical and Surgical Association (1832) and professional journals like the *Lancet* (1823) and the *British Medical Journal* (1840) came into being largely to fight the heated battle over qualification. This contest involved approving some knowledge as legitimate, outlawing other practices, establishing courses of training and, finally, policing the boundaries between the qualified and the excluded practitioners. This phase reached a climax with the Medical Act of 1858 which gave the state power to approve courses of training and examinations and also to license qualified practitioners.[25] In the legal profession, solicitors also made educational standards a main topic of debate during the same years and barristers even toyed with the idea of a course of training a bit more rigorous than statutory dinners. The Law Society, founded in 1825, managed to get the government to agree to substitute for a merely formal interview, written examinations for solicitors in 1836 and for attorneys in 1837.

By the mid-1840s, a new phase was gathering momentum with corporate attempts to moralize the professions and accent their service role to clients and to the community. The Manchester Medico-Ethical Association, founded in 1847, wrote the first code of etiquette in the belief that 'a high sense of honour and gentlemanly conduct are inseparable from the right discharge of professional duties'.[26] These high-sounding words should not obscure a vital concern with respectability to be secured by exclusion and policing. Practitioners of homeopathy, hydropathy or mesmerism were denied membership; the Society even expelled its own vice-president for unwittingly consulting a homeopathist. The code also established an ethos of service as the unique component of medical respectability, when it recommended scaling fees to the patient's ability to pay: 'the profession, unlike all other trades and professions, continues to claim its remuneration, not according the abstract worth of its service, but according to the ability of its clients'. Adopting the Manchester model, ethical societies formed all over the country, eventually merging into the body which became the British Medical Association in 1856. Similarly, many local law societies which aimed to 'promote fair and liberal practice', federated in 1847 to become the Metropolitan and Provincial Law Association.

Sanitary science and reformatory science extended professional service beyond the individual client to the community. The appearance of professional organisations to deal with community problems, like the Association of Poor Law Medical Officers (1846), the Epidemiological Society (1850), the Society of Metropolitan Officers of Health (1856), and the Sanitary Institution (1867), helped to solidify the impression that doctors were particularly qualified to speak as experts in sanitary science. By the time the National Association for the Promotion of Social Science came into existence in 1857, the rhetoric about medical men as social benefactors through public health was fully developed. The *British Medical Journal* boasted before the first Congress:

> We rejoice that an occasion is about to arise in which medicine will be enabled to assert its position in the face of the world as one of the most philanthropic professions. The science of Public Health has been built up and maintained by the leading men of our own body, and it behooves us to keep the lead we have so worthily obtained.[27]

The Social Science Association, which had a Department of Public Health as well as Departments of Punishment and Reformation and of Jurisprudence and the Amendment of the Law, forming supposedly permanent branches of social science, further buttressed the professional claim to unique community relevance. The SSA grew partly out of the Society for Promoting the Amendment of the Law, a Benthamite grouping which had a small but highpowered and expert membership. The majority had taken a legal training and were practising lawyers or judges, or had entered parliament or the civil service. They had come together to press for law reform in a wide range of legal and social areas. Frederic Hill's son remembered well how his father 'used to talk to us children, even when very young about his work there, and explain to us the reforms that he was assisting to promote. We always felt that we were giving up the pleasure of his company for a good cause'.[28]

Midcentury university developments not only cemented a connection between professional men and higher education but also reinforced the growing association with some vision of community service. The trend to more effective professional training helped to catalyse the foundation of civic universities in a number of ways. London came first into the field with the secular University College which boasted a Medical Department from its opening in 1828, as did its religious rival King's College in 1829. When the two combined into London University in 1836, one of their most successful ventures was to function as a 'vast examining machine' to which nearly all the medical schools in the country affiliated. In the localities the medical schools often made the first move to launch a campaign for a civic university. When these eventually came into being over the second half of the nineteenth century, they were conceived within a ethos of service to the municipal community. Thus a resolution submitted to a Liverpool Town Meeting urged the establishment of a college for town residents providing all the branches of a liberal education together with such training 'as would be of immediate service in professional and commercial life'.[29]

Oxford and Cambridge had to scramble quickly to make themselves relevant in the midcentury period. Royal Commissions from 1850 and legislation from 1854 onward signalled the enormous pressure for university reform coming from Utilitarians, from Whig-Liberals and from the urban, Nonconformist middle class. The ancient universities responded by reforming themselves, making more improvements in twenty years, according to one Oxford don, than in the 'three centuries since the Reformation'. Some of the informing ideas and institutional changes had material relevance to professional practices of science and service. To detach themselves from too narrow an association with the aristocratic interest, dons began to present their universities as the true custodians of the culture of the nation. In 1868, Mark Pattison, the Rector of Lincoln College and an active presence in the Education Department of the Social Science Association, described a properly-reformed Oxford as

> no longer a class-school, nor mainly a school for youth at all. It is a national institute for the preservation and tradition of useful knowledge. It is the common interest of the whole community that such knowledge should exist, should be guarded, treasured, cultivated, disseminated, expounded.[30]

James Bryce, the Cambridge student of democratic institutions, saw the key question as: 'how to make the universities serviceable to the whole nation, instead of only to the upper classes'. To do this job, Pattison favoured the creation of an 'organised profession' of academics, headed by professors who received proper funding (from endowments) and whose primary function would be research in their chosen disciplines: or, in Pattison's words again, 'a body of learned men, devoting their lives to the cultivation of science and to the direction of academical education'. Interestingly the emphasis on academics as researchers seemed to go along with a view of research as disinterested and neutral, making the academic profession, at least in its research aspect, virtually the only nascent profession to underplay its capacity for social service or even social reform. This attitude of detachment would play an important role later at the point where it became separated from a larger cluster of responsibilities.

For the moment, in their teaching capacity, the same academics could perform an important service as tutors in public duty to the future leaders of the nation. They would further extend the Coleridgean and Arnoldian ideas of a clerisy, already gaining ground in the universities and in reformed public schools like Rugby.[31] Just as the universities would transcend narrow class interest by enlarging their focus to the nation, so a service ethic would transfigure the outdated aristocratic ideal into a useful model of the professional gentleman. The dispute between two parties of dons, one wishing the colleges to remain preeminent as teaching institutions and the other wanting the university to become predominantly a research institution, reached a negotiated truce where both objectives were pursued at the same time. On the college side, both in Oxford and Cambridge, there emerged during the midcentury period a cluster of truly charismatic teachers whose invocations to service inspired many prominent men. At Cambridge, from 1866 the Reverend F.D. Maurice (who will be discussed later in this chapter) and J.R. Seeley, who was elected Regius Professor of History in 1869, played this role.[32] At Oxford, Benjamin Jowett's influence was eclipsed from the late 1860s by his student, philosopher T.H. Green, who had earlier been a pupil at Rugby.

Green fired undergraduates with his insistence on the duty of closing the gap in society between the inadequate present self and 'the best possible self', which made morality 'an effort, not an attainment, a progressive construction of what should be, not an enjoyment of what is'.[33] A little extravagantly perhaps, both

Asquith and Bryce credited Green's version of Idealism with unseating Utilitarianism as the dominant philosophical school in the universities. For Green, a life of praxis became a necessity: 'the reformer cannot bear to think of himself except as giving effect...to his project of reform; and thus, instead of merely contemplating a possible work, he does it'. Green became the model scholar-citizen, who served for many years after 1875 on the Oxford Town Council, and sent out into the world 'a stream of serious young men dedicated to reform in politics, social work and the civil service'. Many of Green's protegés passed through social settlements like Toynbee Hall or became key figures in voluntary work like the Charity Organisation Society, all dedicated to service on a neighbourhood level. But starting in Green's time and coming to a climax in the crisis situation of the 1890s, influential university figures groomed the elite of young graduates to see the nation as the proper focus of service.

The consciousness of 'the nation' sharpened in the wake of the 1867 Reform Act, which allowed the vote to only a minority of working men but had a symbolic impact out of all proportion to the real changes it brought about.[34] With the working class and nation coinciding to a greater extent, professional service to sections of the working class could be developed and articulated as service to the new citizenry or in the less felicitous phrase 'our new masters'. Depicting themselves as fountainheads of national culture, the reformed universities created Extension lectures, classes and examinations to carry the 'stream that runs from the mountain tops of the university...over the whole land'.[35] But the University Extension service, begun by Cambridge in 1875 and by Oxford in 1878, did not amount to a simple top-down operation. In a situation of threatened reform, Oxbridge used Extension work to demonstrate its capacity to serve the national interest, and it tried to respond to real demand from women of the provincial middle class and from working-class co-operative societies for access to university resources.

These demands from outsiders helped to transform Oxford and Cambridge into what they wanted to become: widely accepted national centres of knowledge and learning. Oxford and Cambridge took their place among a range of institutions, including the public schools, the professional associations, and social science groupings, all of which helped to homogenize the culture of a powerful *couche* of mid-Victorian politicians, professionals and administrators. Indeed Oxbridge gained a new kind of special relationship with that *couche* when in 1870, the Northcote-Trevelyan reforms of the civil service introduced the first competitive examinations in 'the subjects which then constituted the education of a gentleman' which meant, to Chadwick's dismay, testing the Oxbridge curriculum.[36] A university education began to become a necessary preamble to a powerful career in the public service, although in the midcentury period, some key men like Simon, Lankester and the Hill brothers had arrived by another route.

METROPOLITAN PROFESSIONALS, THE POOR AND THE *POUVOIR SPIRITUEL*

The midcentury commitment to scientific altruism can further be illuminated by bringing into focus some groupings of university graduates who aligned with different social science traditions and created influential styles of professional service. These men differed from the doctors and lawyers developing sanitary and reformatory science because they did not find their community vocation primarily through their occupational work. Rather they came to social service through their commitment to different varieties of social science which they then stamped with their professional imprint. Two of the most interesting groups came from different scientific directions: one, a group of London lawyers, adapted older practices of scientific philanthropy to new professional personnel while the other, the English Positivists, tried to integrate imported sociology with that peculiar feature of the English landscape, the growing professional class. Both groups illustrate the extent to which professional ideas of social service in the midcentury period involved a relationship with a scientifically selected section of the working class—albeit diametrically opposite strata in these two cases. Both also indicated how the revaluation of the organized working class could open new possibilities for midcentury class co-operation.

The group of lawyers, which included C.B.P. Bosanquet, Edward Denison (1840-70) and A.H. Hill (1839-1906), made its first contact with the urban poor through the established mode of district visiting within scientific philanthropy. Literally the urban gentry, since all came from powerful landed county

108

families and then settled in London, they were devout Anglicans, who had attended Oxford or Cambridge and wished to transpose country patterns to the metropolis. 'I well remember my own first plunge', Bosanquet testified. 'I had for some time felt that I ought to have acquaintances amongst my poor neighbours in London as I always had in the country.' Voicing the usual worry of scientific philanthropists, he stressed that 'the want of neighbourly feeling is one of the great evils of large towns'.[37] In his book on *London* (1868), he tried to recruit 'young professional men' into neighbourhood service. While serving as almoners in the Society for the Relief of Distress, Denison, Bosanquet and Hill became disillusioned. They sounded the familiar cry for an end to doles of food (however discriminate) and a concentration on 'more solid and permanent schemes of assistance'. District visiting provided contact with the poor but revealed enormities of destitution which it could not radically change.

By 1868, these lawyers shared a widespread feeling that philanthropy and the Poor Law were in crisis. Like most experts in the Social Science Association, the gentry lawyers had considerable respect for the members of working-class organisations and linguistically promoted these newly-enfranchised working men into the more dignified ranks of the citizenry. So completely did Denison identify trade unions with respectability, that he tried to guide workers towards religion by drawing 'parallels with trade unions and benefit clubs'.[38] The gentry lawyers now concentrated on the remaining poor, finding ways to categorize them which might also allow for some linguistic and material rescue. All played a strategic part in the development of the Charity Organisation Society (COS) which began in 1869 and became the main embodiment of scientific philanthropy until the First World War. Each of the lawyers by the late 1860s had also carved out his special area of expertise and his special segment of the poor. Bosanquet, the first paid secretary of the COS, became recognised as an expert on questions to do with the integration of statutory and philanthropic relief and a master at arranging the poor into categories according to whether they would benefit from Poor Law or voluntary provision. Denison, in his few remaining years, became a pioneer 'settler' and moved to Philpott Street in the East End of London. He made trips to France and Edinburgh to study alternative systems of legal relief and became recognised as an expert on the Poor Law. Becoming more interested in the problem of underemployment and casual labour, Hill (another early secretary of the COS), developed typologies of the 'unemployed', set up the Central Labour Agency, an early employment exchange, and edited the *Labour News*, a directory to available jobs in the metropolis. All then isolated the very poorest segment of the working class, or those teetering on the brink of pauperism, as their focus for study and service.

By contrast, the English Positivists were largely concerned with the skilled and organised working class. The way in which foreign ideas are assimilated or selectively adapted into a new home can reveal much about the hosts. For mid-Victorian men and women who were suffering doubts about their religious faith, positivism had much to offer. Auguste Comte's system provided a substitute secular Religion of Humanity which claimed to be scientifically validated by the laws of history. His protean demonstration of the lawfulness of the natural and social universe attracted Harriet Martineau, who translated and condensed Comte's *Positive Philosophy* (1853), as much as it did Frederic Harrison and his cohort at Oxford in the early 1850s. However, Martineau, like many other Protestants and Liberals, including J.S. Mill, could not abide what they saw as Comte's reinvention of a Catholic-type priesthood; T.H. Huxley pilloried positivism as 'Catholicism minus Christianity'.[39] But a group of Oxford undergraduates, who had come under the influence of Positivist tutor Richard Congreve, had a different way of interpreting the *pouvoir spirituel* to which Comte gave an exalted role as a vanguard of social change and as an estate in the Positive polity.

Comte had hoped to fill the ranks of the intelligentsia or *pouvoir spirituel* with scientifically trained recruits from the École Polytechnique. But his English followers, who donned the mantle of Positive philosophers, largely entered the growing professional sector of middle class. Frederic Harrison, the Lushington twins, Henry Crompton and E.S. Beesly became barristers and later some became civil servants; Richard Congreve, having resigned holy orders and his Wadham fellowship, and J.H. Bridges studied medicine and then Bridges became a Factory and later a Medical Inspector. Ironically, Comte regarded lawyers as a 'secondary', 'transitional' and generally disreputable group, while 'men of letters', another category which almost fit many English Postivists, were dismissed as unscrupulous hacks. Undeterred by the verdict of the master, Harrison urged Beesly to 'come at once to the Law and to the Bar'; it was an occupation allowing for leisure and for access to government levers of power. Even if they did not try to rewrite the Comtist bible, to make the intelligentsia identical with the professional classes, the British Comtists were, in fact, working professional men.[40] As such, they added an important item to the repertoire of social roles available to professional gentlemen. The Comtist conception of the *pouvoir spirituel* did have affinities with already-existing notions, stemming from Coleridge's idea of a Clerisy and permeating the Oxford atmosphere of the 1850s, of a gentlemanly elite of talent whose mission was to raise the standard of national civilization. But Comtism added two vital new ingredients: science and the definition of service in terms of a relationship with a definite social group, the working class.

From the Comtist perspective, history was nearing a final climax. The last critical period, characterized by conflict between capital and organised labour and by the dominance of intellectual views stressing individualism and competition, was poised to give way to the final organic period of positivism—a stage of highly regulated corporate capitalism. Only the two social classes with an enlarged and disinterested sensibility, the unionized working classes and the *pouvoir spirituel*, were competent to spearhead the transition. Seen as natural allies, the intelligentsia and the workers, marching arm in arm, would usher in the Positive Polity:

it is only through their combined action that social regeneration can become a practical possibility. Notwithstanding their differences of position, a difference which indeed is more apparent than real, there are strong affinities between them, both morally and intellectually. Both have the same sense of the real, the same preference for the useful and the same tendency to subordinate special points to general principles. Morally they resemble each other in generosity of feeling, in wise unconcern for material prospects, and in indifference to worldly grandeur. This

111

at least will be the case as soon as philosophers in the true sense of that word have mixed sufficiently with the nobler members of the working classes to raise their own character to its proper level. When these sympathies which unite them upon these points have had time to show themselves, it will be felt that the philosopher is, under certain aspects, a member of the working class fully trained; while the working man is in many respects the philosopher without the training.[41]

Frederic Harrison took Comte's advice about mixing seriously. His life 'Agenda', drawn up in 1861, determined, first, to clarify his views on religion and then to acquire 'Knowledge of the working classes', preferably by getting 'to know the best of them personally as friends'.[42] The working class, through Comtist eyes, was the section of the working class which belonged to trade unions. This perspective was criticized for its 'unconsciousness...of the existence of a class beneath the artisan'.[43]

For two decades, the English Postivists who were active in politics used their positions and expertise to win important gains for the unionized working class. In Royden Harrison's words, they 'played a decisive role in securing a satisfactory legal basis for Trade Unionism'.[44] From 1867 to 1869, Frederic Harrison served on the Royal Commission on Trade Unionism and was responsible for the crucially important Minority Report. Beesly, Harrison (now Secretary to the Law Digest Commission), Crompton (Clerk of Assize) and Lushington (Home Office Counsel to advise on the drafting of all Bills) helped to frame legislation at every stage and advised the Trade Union Congress on strategy throughout the struggle. After 1875, and victory, Positivist influence in the labour movement declined. Welcomed as practical allies, they had failed to convert their trade-union protégés to their religion of science. When they turned inward to building up the institutional side of their sect, few labour movement figures followed them. But the Positivists also lost their direction as anxiety about the economy began to replace midcentury confidence and as they became uncomfortably aware of the poverty of the unskilled and ununionized with whom their perspective was unequipped to deal.

CHRISTIAN SOCIALISTS AND SLUM PRIESTS

For many professional men, Christian duty rather than Christian doubt formed part of the call to service. The Reverend F.D. Maurice, first in post at King's College and as chaplain to Lincoln's Inn and then Grote's successor at Cambridge, gave the most charismatic utterance to this call. He exerted an extraordinary influence on many earnest law students and made an impact far beyond the confines of the actual Christian Socialist group. Positivist Frederic Harrison, for example, came into his orbit and taught at the Working Men's College before moving his history lectures into a Secular Hall; Unitarian women like Mrs Gaskell gave his projects support.[45] The clergy conferred a special dignity onto professional service to the poor by identifying it as religious work. Even if not the conscious aim, the clergy also secured their own professional status by establishing their position as tutors in social duty to other rising professionals; Maurice depicted the clergy as veritable professors of sacrifice 'who could set forth the whole mystery of sacrifice as involved in the least acts'.[46] When Maurice was hounded out of his King's College professorship in 1853, persecution and martyrdom only strengthened his influence.

In 1849 he had been stung into an awareness of Lincoln's Inn as an island of privilege floating in a sea of poverty by J.M. Ludlow's relentless requests for guidance about doing service to the local poor and by Mayhew's cumulative, darkening picture of exploitation in London's industrial world. Increasingly, he came to feel that the Church, the body of Christ in the world, could be healthy only when active attempts were made to transform neighbourhoods into loving Christian families. Professional men had a key part to play in this social alchemy, as he pointed out to Ludlow:

> Lincoln's Inn is a very powerful body of cultivated men in the midst of as bad a neighbourhood for health and probably education as most in London. If a small body of us could unite to do something for that place our bond would be surely a quasi-sacramental one—a much better one than that of any club or league....I speak as a clergy-man to you as a lawyer. May we not by God's blessing help to secure both our professions from perishing?[47]

This thinking became flesh in 1849 in the form of a Band of Brothers, a mixed group of professional men including barristers like Thomas Hughes, doctors like Charles Mansfield and, of course, the Reverend Charles Kingsley. For a short moment, they managed to occupy a place close to the centre of the co-operative movement, with their workshops in the London tailoring and building trades. Maurice's powerful repudiation of competitive capitalism as the incarnation of 'a hateful devilish theory'[48] enabled his disciples, briefly, to straddle the whole of the working class with their work of reconciliation.

Before taking on the midcentury role of tutoring other professionals in social service, ministers had usually pioneered less subversive modes of relating to the poor as part of their own idea of clerical duty. If Glasgow had had its Evangelical Dr Chalmers for a short period of time, London had its much more durable Bishop Blomfield (caustically nicknamed 'Rt Reverend Utilitarian') who set out from the mid-1830s to create effective religious parish machines throughout the metropolis. This involved constructing new 'iron churches' as well as schools in slum districts and providing each new parish with a resident vicar and auxiliary help in the form of curates and deacons who would establish a routine superintendence over the poor.[49] By the 1850s, according to one historian of the Church, the vocation of the slum priest was being taken seriously, not least after Maurice's teaching had glossed the parish machinery with a spiritual aura.[50] One of the pioneer slum clergymen, the Reverend Brooke Lambert (1834-1901), vicar of St Mark's Whitechapel, was also an activist in the Social Science Association where he served as Secretary to the Education Department for some fourteen years.[51]

Lambert's special interest in education related to the fraction of the poor carved out by the clergy as their particular concern. Just as midcentury doctors became experts in diagnosing the diseased poor in the field of sanitary science, and members of the legal profession in treating the criminal poor in the area of reformatory science, so the clergy were the main analysts of the immoral or vicious poor in the field they dominated: moral science. These segments of the poor and the sciences which constructed them all overlapped. But, as Chapter 6 will argue, the various experts would achieve a comprehensive view of these lowest of the poor by co-ordinating their work rather than by any one specialist having the exclusive overview. The Reverend Sidney Godolphin Osborne, brother-in-law of the Reverend Charles Kingsley, borrowed language from public health to characterize the immoral fraction of the poor in his famous 1853 essay on 'Immortal Sewerage' (see p.185). Although a constant offence, these poor usually stayed stagnant or apathetic. But they could be stirred into turbulence in revolutionary moments like the one just gone by. In language reminiscent of the Reverend Close in 1839 evoking the horrors of the French Revolution, Reverend Osborne warned of

> streets crowded with women almost unsexed, men almost unhumanized; children, such in form, but with the worst vices of the adult stamped upon them. These are the creatures that in the days of revolution work out barbarisms and cruelties, with the language and demeanour of fiends. The horrors they commit become the marvels of history.[52]

As well as being the chief diagnosticians of moral disease, the clergy also became the main spokesmen for the therapy which would not so much expel the vicious poor or 'immortal refuse' from the body social as recycle them, namely a truly religious education. Osborne's essay ended with a plea for a national effort to create National Samaritan Schools and Preaching Stations in every large town, to serve as 'schools for humanizing'...'seeking to get the lowest of our kind, step by step, out of the depths of mere animal ignorance'.[53]

Clergymen active in social science also paved the way for a relationship with women in the work of service. The language of the clergy from the late 1860s onward resonated with images of neighbourhood and of family. Like the earlier statisticians, the clergy depicted healthy social relations in terms of patriarchal social families: country gentlemen 'like fathers of the old school' who looked after their tenants, merchants and tradesmen who lived with their employees, even first-generation factory owners who personally knew their workers.[54] But matriarchal relations now also became important in science and service. For Kingsley 'the power of the mothers and wives of the higher class' seemed the only force strong enough to end the massacre of the innocents, the dramatic phrase he used for infant mortality which he blamed on mothers among the poor who ignored the laws of health.[55] The language of family provided a meeting ground for professional men and women who wanted a respectable role in the public sphere. Several of the professional men already mentioned, Lankester the doctor, M.D. Hill the lawyer, and Canon Augustus Barnett, just starting his work in the East End in 1867, were integrally connected with, not to say deeply dependent upon, the kind of women who will be the focus of the next chapter.

JOHN STUART MILL AND
HARRIET TAYLOR

So far this chapter has explored how professional men, through their occupational work, through their professional associations and through their informal groupings committed to social science, were creating new practices of service often in relation to sections of the working class. The Christian socialists and the Positivists, whatever their religious disagreements, managed, through their praxis, both to disrupt political economy and secure new alliances with working men. The Christian socialists also actively supported women's entry into social service work while the Positivists were asserting the role of women as vital tutors in social altruism although confining them to the home or the sect.[56] The most symbolic curtain-raiser on the new possibilities for class and gender relations in social science at the midcentury has not yet been mentioned.

In 1848 John Stuart Mill published the *Principles of Political Economy*, which he insisted owed a great debt to Harriet Taylor. This and his other book entitled *A System of Logic*, were identified by the Social Science Association as 'the chief text-books throughout Europe and America'.[57] *The Principles of Political Economy* went through three editions in four years. Here the thoroughbred with an impeccable Utilitarian pedigree marked out new space for social and intellectual rapprochement in a number of different directions. Even if Mill and Taylor were more daring, both in intellectual and gender terms, than some other professional men and feminist women of their time, they nonetheless helped to mark out new paths down which others moved with more circumspection.[58]

When they met in 1830, Mill was already moving away from 'sectarian Benthamism', a distancing he only felt able to articulate after his father's death in 1836. In the *Logic*, which he began in 1837, and more particularly in the *Principles*, he mobilized a view of history gleaned from Saint Simonian writings and from Auguste Comte which enabled him to destabilize key elements in the structure of Utilitarianism and political economy. The idea that the progress of the human mind and of society took place over critical and organic stages of history enabled Mill to identify the scope of political economy, its 'laws' of distribution and its central character, the enlightened egotist, not as natural but as historical constructs, which belonged to what would hopefully be the final critical period before a stage of social altruism came into existence. By a nice turnabout, where the early Utilitarians had used the propositions about essential nature to upset Enlightenment historical methods, now John Stuart Mill used a version of history to disturb Utilitarian constructs of laws of nature. *The Principles*, Mill insisted,

> set the example of not treating those conditions as final. The economic generalisations which depend, not on necessities of nature but on those combined with the existing arrangements of society, it deals with only as provisional, and as liable to be much altered by the progress of social improvement.[59]

Mill also credited his growing dissatisfaction with political economy to Harriet Taylor. This is not the place to enter the debate about how much Taylor really influenced Mill. Instead I want to argue that the way he described her influence was consonant with some feminist constructions of gender at the time, and also moved his thinking closer, in some respects, to the social science developed by the Owenite socialists. He insisted that the book's chapter on 'the Probable Futurity of the Labouring Classes', which had 'a greater influence on opinion than all the rest', was 'entirely due to her'. As well as attributing to her whole dimensions of intense moral feeling that he lacked, especially a (com)passion for both justice and benevolence, he continually credited her with the ability to make ideas practical both in terms of being more able than he to envision a different social future and also to embody ideas in 'concrete shape' and identify workable strategies of advance:

What was abstract and purely scientific was generally

117

mine; the properly human element came from her: in all that concerned the application of philosophy to the exigencies of human society and progress, I was her pupil, alike in boldness of speculation and cautiousness of practical judgement.[60]

She excelled on what in socialist science could be called the ideal and practical levels of enquiry; he was master of abstract analysis. While he also invested her with the best analytical intellect as well, and indeed constructed her as the complete human being who embraced the full communion of masculine and feminine qualities, other feminists at the time more modestly stressed the contribution to social science to be gained from women's moral sensitivity, intuitive intellect and active practicality (Chapter 5).

Mill insisted that it was largely due to Taylor that the *Principles* 'treated Political Economy not as a thing by itself but as a fragment of a greater whole: a branch of Social Philosophy'. The nature of this enlargement built new bridges to women and to working-class movements. Taylor chivvied Mill to take a broader view of human motivation, persuading him to delete a long passage where he worried, in the old Malthusian way, that 'freedom from anxiety as to the means of subsistence' would enervate people into torpor. She tried to make him more optimistic about the pace at which human nature could change. He attributed to her the two 'conflicting theories, respecting the social position desirable for manual labourers', which allowed moral considerations about the quality of social relationship to enter the discussions and opened new space for inter-class accommodation. Again mobilizing history, Mill devalued the first type of social relationship based on paternalism or a coupling of dependence and protection as appropriate to an earlier historical stage. The theory of self-dependence which assumed that others should treat working people as equals and not as children was identified as the characteristic of an advanced civilization.[61]

Mill and Taylor also coupled the oppression of workers with the oppression of women making the project of advancing progress one which took both class and gender issues on board at the same time. When surveying the evidence of independence, they identified working-class movements as the providers of a 'spontaneous education' and singled out co-operative enterprise as a middle way between unbridled capitalism and regimented communism. That a prodigal son had seen the light, that the scion of the house of political economy now put a seal of approval on working-class movements and co-operation was welcomed by radicals who were reworking some of their earlier analyses. Holyoake felt grateful that Mill 'as an authority in political economy, extended co-operation scientific recognition, and subsequently promoted, befriended, and advised all who worked for it'.[62] Feminists like Bessie Rayner Parkes welcomed the Mills' widening of economic analysis. The stage was now set for greater degree of class and gender co-operation in social science than ever before.

5

SOCIAL MOTHERS AND SOCIAL SCIENCE 1850-1886

The influx of women into social science was connected with a midcentury crisis in femininity. After the revolutions of 1848 and after the censuses of 1851 and 1861, women seeking a public role found themselves working in a fraught atmosphere. Once again, ruling-class nerves were very exposed. Revolution had dramatized the dangerous potential of the working class, but now a great cloud of anxiety also settled on women—or rather the section of women insultingly called 'surplus', 'redundant' or 'superfluous', namely women above the age of thirty who had not married. Mayhew's sensational revelations about the 'surplus' needlewomen who had turned to prostitution to augment their paltry pay had probably started the public discussion. Then the censuses revealed a larger number of women in the population than men, and alarmists accused middle-class women in particular of shirking their duty to wed. Insult became the name of the game: the *Saturday Review* categorically announced that 'married life is a woman's profession', and delivered the verdict that women who stayed single had 'failed in business'.[1]

The nastiness in the tone could perhaps be attributed to the way in which these unnatural shirkers appeared to be a danger not only to sexual hierarchy but to class. The most positive bourgeois self-image placed much of the virtue of the middle class in the keeping of married mothers in the home. So single women who evaded domestic, marital and maternal duty posed a threat to the dignity of the class. Yet, paradoxically, the very spinsters who lived outside the approved bounds of femininity actually enjoyed more legal rights. Unlike married mothers, but just like men, they were persons in the eyes of the Common Law and had rights over their own property. By contrast a married woman was a *femme couverte*: in Blackstone's famous words, 'husband and wife are one person and the husband is that person'. The paradox that the most unsexed had the most legal rights added fuel to the fire of conservative rage. Some of the solutions proposed to the 'surplus woman problem' were as insulting as the way of defining the problem. Rewriting the prescription previously supplied to the needlewomen, W.R. Greg from the Manchester mill-owning family who had been stalwarts of the Statistical Society, urged that single women become marital exports to the colonies where they would find an ample supply of willing mates. As an alternative, he also proposed that spinsters could partly imitate successful courtesans at home to make themselves more womanly and attractive to men![2]

The women who figure in this chapter contested this negative view and tried to find ways to dignify the single woman and validate her work. From different class and religious backgrounds and from different generations, they moved into the orbit of the Langham Place circle either by taking part in campaigning committees, by writing for the *English Woman's Journal* (the first feminist periodical) or by becoming active in the cultural centre at Langham Place which, from 1859, ran classes, clubs, a library and reading room for women.[3] They also participated in the National Association for the Promotion of Social Science in relation to which their practice of social science clarified and developed. These women never totally abandoned key features of bourgeois femininity and masculinity but rather remodelled to enable women to move respectably into the public sphere. The .Social Science Association became a key public arena where this remodelling and repositioning process took place. Other contemporary strands of sociology did not allow women such a smooth passage. Theorists like Herbert Spencer and August Comte not only ratified sexual division in their evolutionary schema but kept women fairly firmly fixed in the private sphere.[4] This chapter will explore two key strategies that women devised, the conception of *social* motherhood and the sexual *communion* of labour, which structured their social science and subverted conventional ideas of gender division. It will also examine how these strategies received support from many professional men in social science, but at a price which involved the co-option of safer varieties of feminism and contradictory relations with women among the poor.

SOCIAL MOTHERHOOD IN SOCIAL SCIENCE

Rather than abandon the resonant language of motherhood and home, many women active in social science enlarged and altered it to fit the single woman. Alongside the image of the married mother, they set up another icon of the virgin mother doing self-sacrificing work in the public world with the poor and needy, and extending a home influence into it. When constructing the new ideal of social motherhood as legitimate femininity, women emphasized sacrifice to counter the charge that spinsters were selfish shirkers. 'Not selfishness', Frances Power Cobbe (1822-1904) insisted, 'but self-sacrifice even more entire than belongs to the double life of marriage is the true law of celibacy'.[5] The daughter of an Evangelical Irish landowner, she never married in the heterosexual sense but lived in a partnership with another woman, and supported herself with a small inheritance, her pen and the Anglo-American lecture circuit, while also doing regular voluntary work first with juvenile delinquents, then with workhouse girls, and finally, and passionately, against vivisection.

Her early mentor, Mary Carpenter (1807-77), was trained to teach by her father, the Bristol Unitarian minister, the Reverend Lant Carpenter, whose Lewins Mead School educated and helped to homogenize the whole generation of prosperous, powerful, provincial Unitarians who figured so prominently in the statistical societies. To establish the sacrificial capacity of single women, Mary turned to the Gospels which showed that the women among the disciples of Jesus stood more steadfast and endured more suffering than the men:

they followed him from Galilee, and ministered to him of their substance, and did not desert him in his last trial when his chosen Apostles forsook him and fled; they could not be driven back by angry Pharisees, nor by cruel soldiers from the foot of the cross; they did not sink under the weight of their own harrowed feelings while aught remained to be done, nor were they deterred by 'the watch, the stone, the seal', from seeking to bestow their last offices of love and reverence on the sacred remains.[6]

A vision of the Madonna or the virgin mother appeared frequently even in evangelical Protestant writing. Carpenter, who pioneered work with juvenile delinquents, began an article on 'Women's Work in the Reformatory Movement' (1858) with a glowing reference to a sermon on 'The Glory of the Virgin Mother'. She appealed to single women 'who are mothers in heart, though not by God's gift on earth'. They 'will be able to bestow their maternal love...on those most wretched moral orphans whose natural sweetness of filial love has been mingled with deadly poison'.[7] Just as the Madonna offered a powerful example of spiritual motherhood without full biological maternity, so the moral motherhood of single women could override the claims of bad biological parenting which created moral orphans. Basically an inter-class relationship, social motherhood could violate the usual age differences between parent and child. The adult poor could be considered as children, while middle-class adolescents like Octavia Hill (1838-1912), aged fourteen when she ran a toy-making workshop, could even talk of her often-older charges as her 'dear, dear children'.[8] Her later work, carving out a new career for single women like herself in housing management, gave scope, according to one biographer 'for her maternal instinct and pastoral gifts in the care of the tenants'.

The new social mothers regarded a large number of social groups as needing adequate parenting, or put in another way, as needing their intervention. The focus of the social mothers helped to shape the analytical framework of some fields of midcentury social science as well as to set their agendas for practical action. Reformatory science provided a good example with its adult and juvenile branch. Carpenter developed the latter, which dealt with juvenile delinquents, in ways which allowed for the influx of women workers in their capacity as social mothers. She identified dysfunctional or nonexistent families as the primary cause of juvenile crime. She created a typology of family circumstances which could be useful in matching children to the appropriate remedial institutions, all of which served as surrogate families often presided over by a 'matron' or social mother. Thus children of poor but honest parents could be left in their existing families but would attend a ragged day school and be taught by a good maternal model. Children of negligent parents or vagrant orphans would be removed to boarding industrial schools if they had not yet committed a crime or, if they were already offenders, to reformatory schools run more on a family system instead of prison.[9]

Many of the varieties of social science represented in the Social Science Association also held bad parenting responsible for creating social problem groups, thereby opening up an area of public work which women could legitimately enter. Since then, the problem family syndrome has endured in the analytical apparatus of social work right into our time. The domestic branch of sanitary science, developed largely through the efforts of the Ladies' Sanitary Association and the Social Science Association, put great emphasis on the need for mothers among the poor to apply the laws of health in their childraising practice. In the scientific philanthropy of the midcentury period, where the relations between voluntary work and state provision occupied the spotlight, women especially focused on 'the children of the State', namely workhouse children whether orphaned or not, and tried to provide effective family settings for them. Substitute families took the form of separate residential workhouse schools, or approved foster families, or a job placement for the child which carried with it an adequate home dimension.[10]

'Home' was another part of the paraphernalia of femininity that had to be refurbished to accommodate the virgin or social mother. In the midcentury period, discussion about enlarging home and transposing a home influence into the public sphere went along with devising a range of experiments to accomplish this. Josephine Butler, just before entering the lists of the crusade against the Contagious Diseases Acts, responded to that majority of Englishmen who dreaded that women would 'revolutionize society' or, more particularly, 'revolutionize our Homes'. Agreeing that home was the source of all virtues, she argued

that a great enlargement of hearts and a free opening

out and giving forth of the influences of homes, as reservoirs of blessing for the common good, would ultimately result in the restored security of all the best elements in our present ideal of Home.[11]

Butler was perhaps unusual in being a publicly active married mother. Her husband, the Reverend George Butler, clearly thought her a prophet or saint and gave her latitude unusual for a middle-class wife. He supported her public campaigning and would sit patiently in railway stations into the small hours of the morning awaiting her return from speaking engagements. Beautiful, flamboyant, charismatic, she had an extraordinary effect on other people. A member of a Royal Commission which took testimony from her in 1871 commented, 'I am not accustomed to religious phraseology but I cannot give you any idea of the effect produced except by saying that the spirit of God was there.'[12]

Few of her socially-equal sisters would have agreed with her verdict that the comfortable bourgeois home came 'near to selfishness'. Few would have agreed that families should open their doors to lunatics and strangers, or, as she did, to dying prostitutes. But they would have joined her in a plea, dating at least from the early Evangelical days, that philanthropic mothering and the home influence be introduced into public institutions like hospitals and workhouses. They would also have ratified the established practice of extending home influence by visiting the poor in their dwellings and helping to transform the people and the abodes into families and homes.

A characteristic midcentury way of extending the idea of home, women philanthropists created a new type of residential institution often called a Home, where social mothers could care especially for children and young women in sexual danger. Mary Carpenter's own experience traced the shifting directions of philanthropic effort. Having been dissuaded from marriage by a composite vision of Christ, her father and Dr Tuckerman, Carpenter turned to serving the poor through the conventional practice of district visiting. But she decided that children at risk could not be rescued for God until they had been removed from their biological families: indeed rescue came to mean transplantation to a substitute home and family in the midcentury period.[13] She spent her life devising just such institutions. Hers became only one of many initiatives. Emily Shirreff ran a Home for factory girls in Birmingham, Jessie Boucherett a Home for trainee clerical workers in London.[14] Cobbe became involved in providing Homes for workhouse girls training to be servants or factory workers,[15] for workhouse epileptics and for discharged female prisoners. The fascinating experience of providing Homes for prostitutes, which proliferated during the midcentury, will be examined later in this chapter. But the women social workers (as they began to call themselves in the period), cut off from the paternal or marital family, also needed a variety of family and home for themselves. This period witnessed the vigorous growth of Protestant sisterhoods of various kinds ranging from the controversial monastic orders which stirred up lurid fantasies about religious harems at the disposal of lusty priests, to the more acceptable Deaconess Houses under the supervision of parish vicars.[16] Secular homes also appeared for women active in some branch of social work, like homes for nurses in the midcentury period and later Settlement Houses.

In the same moment that the concept of motherhood was being destabilized by allowing it to spill beyond biological maternity and the marital family, so too, ever so carefully, some of the more radical women in the same circle were trying to stretch the conception of what married mothers could be permitted to do. Emily Davies (1830-1921), campaigning for women's university education, insisted that while she would never disrupt women's familial duties, nonetheless since only one hour a day was really necessary for supervising a well-organized household, a married woman could legitimately spend the rest 'in definitely professional work...or in unpaid public services, which, when seriously undertaken, constitute something of a profession'. Radical Unitarian Barbara Bodichon (see p.139) felt certain that biological mothers could be trusted to strike a sensible balance: 'maternal love is too strong ever to be weakened by any love of a science, art or profession.' Moreover social mothering was also mothering; the services of women in the medical profession were especially needed to treat 'delicate young womanhood'. The new spacious concept of social motherhood enabled both single and married women to expand their social roles.[17]

COMMUNION OF LABOUR IN
SOCIAL SCIENCE

A second key conception that women developed to assure their place in social science was the sexual communion of labour which both endorsed and undermined the pervasive idea of the sexual division of labour. In an article in *Macmillan's Magazine* (1861) on 'Social Science Congresses and Women's Part in Them', Frances Power Cobbe most clearly proposed how sexual division could both be accepted and subverted in social science. She followed in the more meandering footsteps of art critic Anna Jameson whose two drawing room lectures on 'Sisters of Charity' and 'Communion of Labour' enjoyed such popularity that they were brought out in a second edition in 1859 under the auspices of the Social Science Association.[18] Cobbe argued that God was androgynous, but human men and women, she insisted, could not be androgynous since they had different, equivalent and complementary natures. Both natures were needed to make a full humanity and produce what she called 'a stereoscopic view'. This unity could only come about through the 'communion of labour', that is, men and women working together on divided tasks in every area of public and private life. The kind of complementarity that she had in mind was conveyed by her coupling of opposites:

> Surely, surely, it is time we gain something from woman of her religious nature! And we want her moral intuition also. We want her sense of the law of love to complete man's sense of the law of justice. We want her influence inspiring virtue by gentle prompting from within to complete man's external legislation of morality. And, then, we want woman's practical service. We want her genius for detail, her tenderness for age and suffering, her comprehension of the wants of childhood to complete man's gigantic charities and nobly planned hospitals and orphanages.[19]

Love was to complete justice; inner spirit to complement external law. Intuition was to supplement abstract intelligence; attention to the individual and the particular to enhance the capacity to plan large-scale institutions and systems. Since the communion of labour was to extend into every area of life and science, this kind of thinking did open the way to an enlarged public role for women but one still circumscribed by the idea of gender division. Even women, like Barbara Bodichon and Emily Davies, who started from a premise of theological equality tended to end up in the same place by proposing gendered contributions to shared public work.

When Cobbe referred to Social Science Congresses she meant the annual five-day long meetings of the National Association for the Promotion of Social Science, which took place in a different city each year between 1857 and 1886. The Social Science Association, as it was popularly called, will be discussed more fully as an institution and in relation to class in the next chapter. Since women's ideas on the communion of labour developed so intimately in relation to this body, their most empowering mixed-sex setting, the relevant gender dimensions of the Association's work will be examined now. Throughout its life, the SSA embraced the sexual communion of labour. In 1859, veteran reformer Lord Shaftesbury applauded having 'added to our forces one half of creation' and went on to

> insist on the value and peculiar nature of the assistance; men may discover principles, write big treatises, and indicate, and do what must be done on a large scale—but the instant the work becomes minute, individual, and personal, the instant that it leaves the open field and touches the home; the instant it requires tact, sentiment, and delicacy; from that instant it passes into the hands of woman. It is essentially their province, in which may be exercised all their moral powers, and all their intellectual faculties. It will give them their full share in the vast operations that the world is yet to see.[20]

Ten years later, the man whose name became attached to civil service reform, Sir Stafford Northcote, insisted that 'to examine social questions aright, we must approach them from a feminine as well as from a masculine point of view'. The Association embodied the communion of labour principle in its choice of paid staff. The General Secretary typified the new professional man: barrister G.W. Hastings, the son of Dr Sir Charles Hastings, founder of what later became the British Medical Association. His Assistant Secretary, Miss Isa Craig (1831-1903), represented the independent single woman: a journalist and prize-winning poetess from Scotland, she held the post only until she married, when she immediately retired from paid work.

Feminists considered the Social Science Association to be vitally important and praised it enthusiastically: 'its beneficial effects on women generally cannot be over-estimated.' They found its facilities 'incalculably useful to women, and Social Science has thus acquired a title to the grateful consideration and remembrance of all those who are working for their elevation'.[21] Women could become members in their own right and family groups with a plethora of wives and daughters figured conspicuously among the Congress attenders. The Association was the first middle-class forum in Britain to welcome the public voice of women. Early in the Association's life women began to speak in public, presenting their papers *viva voce*. The Association was predictably barracked by conservative voices like the *Saturday Review*, for an ingenious solution to

> the problem of female loquacity....It is a great idea to tire out the hitherto unflagging vigour of their tongues by encouraging a taste for stump-oratory among them....We heartily wish the strong-minded ladies happiness and success in their new alliance; and do not doubt that they will remember to practise the precept of one of their debaters, 'not to mind being thought unladylike'. It is always better not to mind that which is inevitable.[22]

Women used the Association's protective umbrella to launch or to shield initiatives which now grew rapidly along communion of labour lines: the Ladies' National Association for the Diffusion of Sanitary Knowledge (Ladies' Sanitary Association, founded 1858), the Workhouse Visiting Society and the Society for Promoting the Industrial Employment of Women (1859). In 1869 the SSA spawned the Charity Organisation Society which would become such an important force in the development of professionalized social work for women. The Association acted as an important ally in the middle-class feminist struggle to legitimize a place for single women in the public sphere and to achieve equal civil rights for wives. Nearly all of the major initiatives concerning secondary education for girls or university education for women came before the Association and received sympathetic consideration. The whole issue of employment opportunities for women of different classes also received a sympathetic hearing. The Jurisprudence Department continually lent its expertise to the campaign for a Married Women's Property Act. Yet the line was drawn at women's suffrage which was hardly ever discussed.[23] Despite the palpable elation and sense of release experienced by women, the Association helped restrict as well as liberate them. The new public space became available but women tended to remain assistants and auxiliaries rather than become equal associates.

Having briefly explored what the SSA offered to women, it is necessary to turn the issue round and ask what women and the communion of labour idea offered to the kind of social science embodied in the Association. Even if subordinate, women were essential. Just how essential now needs to be spelled out. The feminine element would help to resolve four contradictions and help to avoid four pitfalls in the path of middle-class social science. First, women, together with the clergy, would harmonize any conflict between science and religion. Already considered as a moral vanguard and as spiritually superior, the presence of respectable women could give any organization or gathering a brighter moral aura. In the anti-slavery movement and the Anti-Corn Law campaign, British women had been allowed onto public platforms as visible symbols—to be seen but not heard— to underline the moral legitimacy of these causes. Now women's very perceptual peculiarities were going to help redeem science. If John Stuart Mill argued for an inverse-deductive method in social science, Frances Power Cobbe pointed to women's capacity to practise what could be called an intuitive-inductive method.[24] According to Cobbe, God had inscribed the simple laws of the moral universe on the heart and these could only be known through intuition. Women's superior intuitive powers equipped them to know these laws which also revealed the ultimate ends towards which all scientific activity had to be directed.

Social Science Association spokesmen and clergymen reinforced this idea of lawfulness which in turn ratified the claims of women. Hastings informed the first Congress 'that Newton foreshadowed in his *Principia*, a unity throughout creation, a vast expansion of purpose based on a few simple laws' and Hastings went on to ask: 'are the moral laws of the universe, promulgated by the same Divine Legislator, less uniform, less simple and less sure?' Whatever quarrels raged elsewhere between biologists and bishops, the clergy and women in the

Social Science Association accented the harmony of science and religion. Canon Richson of Manchester insisted that 'such a harmony existed between the aims of sociology and the moral and practical life upon which Christianity insisted, that the purposes of the one received their most powerful sanction from the intention of the other.'[25] In addition to their sensitivity to moral law, women would also be valuable practitioners of induction, operating social schemes, observing and comparing results, supplying 'the experimental basis of facts on which the moral law is to take effect'. By championing an intuitive-inductive method, Cobbe was not attacking evolutionary theory as developed by Darwin or Spencer. Rather she targeted the early Utilitarians whom she placed in the inductive camp and attacked for trying to induce ultimate principles from empirical facts. Fortunately women would be able to stem the slide from morality to egoism and expediency.

Second, women would humanize political economy and the state. Women added their power to the moral critique of political economy. Bessie Rayner Parkes (see p.139), editor of the *English Woman's Journal*, paid homage to political economy's laws which 'stand up like rocks amidst the wild waves of theory' but observed that 'natures in whom love and reverence predominate insist on supplementing their shortcomings by a higher principle'. Aligning herself with J.S. Mill and the Christian socialists, she called for 'anxious care to build up the new theory; in connection with the old reverence for all that makes a woman estimable',[26] not least to secure a kind of moral safety zone for women in their public work. The workhouse was another suitable case for feminine treatment. Castigated as 'abodes of political economical discomfort', Anna Jameson, the coiner of the phrase 'community of labour', regarded the workhouse as the exemplary case of how 'the element of power disunited from the element of Christian love, must in the long run become a hard, cold, cruel machine'. Workhouses could be transformed simply by ladies visiting the inmates: 'it is not an alteration of the system...that is demanded', argued Louisa Twining (1820-1912), Secretary of the Ladies' Workhouse Visiting Society, 'rather the introduction of the law of love into it'.[27] However, the course of the law of love did not always run smooth. Women sometimes met with strong resistance from the Guardians of the Poor who were often men of their own or a lower class.[28] This treatment

131

and their outrage at what they found in the workhouse impelled some women, including Miss Twining, to move beyond their categories and take action which began to look suspiciously like a bid to take over the system. Twining stood for election as a Guardian and helped found the Society for Promoting the Return of Women as Poor Law Guardians.

Third, women's initiatives would help to moralize the professions. Professional men found the communion of labour idea particularly attractive. They were creating an identity in which science and service formed key elements. Their service credentials could be ratified by a relationship with the most undisputed serving group within the middle class, namely women. The Reverend F.D. Maurice, in his 'Plan of a Female College' (1855-7) on the communion of labour principle where women could train to work alongside professional men, clearly argued that sacrifice was a key feminine contribution whether in the public or private sphere:

> it is no novelty for women to make sacrifices; that is their ordinary business and vocation; that every home duty demands the same spirit of sacrifice as the hospital work at Scutari.[29]

Women trying to establish the legitimacy of their public work not only stressed their capacity for service but for self-sacrifice to rebut charges of selfishness. They welcomed any male support to buttress their project. The communion of social working women and professional men might also be interpreted as collusion of labour with each group reinforcing the service or the science claims of the other. Already during the 1840s, a pattern of professionals allying with feminist philanthropy had become visible. The creation of reformatory science with its juvenile rescue branch, its women ideologues and its new emphasis on quasi-professional training for women was the first area. With women thus associated, the new science could be presented not simply as punitive but as caring and as an authentic form of social service. When in danger of stepping on masculine toes, feminists went out of their way to stress their special moral contribution to professional work. While Emily Davies called attention to 'the profession of modern growth which has been called "management"', she did not want to clone the male manager but rather urged that 'women of the employing class' act as social mothers and bring women workers under 'womanly influence'. Bodichon put an embargo on professions based on conflict and thought it 'unlikely' that women would consider 'being in the army, mixing in political life, going to sea, or being barristers'. She felt certain they would prefer professions 'congenial to their moral natures', and 'destined to be perpetual, being consistent with the highest moral development of humanity, which war is not'.[30]

The Social Science Association co-opted two sets of women's initiatives in the medical field. The whole area of women and medicine was a minefield of contradictions. Doctors were consolidating their professional position in this period not least by discovering a staggering number of specifically female illnesses which not only reinforced theories of sexual difference but supported the idea of a woman primarily as a mother and disease as a departure from her biological destiny (e.g., hysteria meant a disorder of the womb). Some feminists, like Frances Power Cobbe, who had been misdiagnosed after a fall from a railway train and then left to 'rest' until she had grown to gargantuan size, felt that doctors were more the cause than the cure of female illness.[31] Although some medical knowledge and practitioners were restricting women's development within narrow confines, nonetheless other doctors in the SSA moved in a contradictory direction to help widen women's sphere.

Elizabeth Garrett Anderson received a hearing when she urged that women become doctors to treat women and children, although from her sick bed Florence Nightingale fired off a salvo of letters attacking any suggestion that nurses be demoted in the process.[32] SSA doctors more enthusiastically welcomed hospital nursing on the communion of labour pattern. A star celebrity, Nightingale sent papers to the Congresses and became a symbol, to Dr Sieveking, of how even that most masculine Department of State, the War Office, could benefit 'from the co-operation of the female sex' and demonstrate 'as one of the essential constituents of modern progress and Christian civilisation, The Communion of Labour between Man and Woman'.[33] Nursing would create a surrogate family on the ward where the nurse-mother would do sanitary and moral healing while the doctor-father did physical curing. The presence of redemptive mothers would protect doctors from the more brutal charge of being experimental anatomical butchers.

Doctors also supported the Ladies' Sanitary Association, which served the interests both of medics and of women social workers. Sanitary visiting, which involved distributing tracts about the laws of health, upgraded traditional philanthropic visiting or its supervision into scientific activity. Indeed voluntary visiting, eventually, in the first decade of the twentieth century, developed into paid careers for women as health visitors and sanitary inspectors.[34] The presence of women was helpful to public health doctors who could now give to inspection a more human and loving face. The medical journal, the *Lancet*, praised the LSA attempt to

> proselytize in quarters where masculine and rougher apostles could scarcely gain a hearing. Health Committees, and Sanitary Boards, Officers of Health and Inspectors of Nuisances performed fundamental and extensive parts, but rather of a public than a fireside nature. The Ladies' Sanitary Association, on the other hand, entered the mechanics' room and the poor man's cottage, and talked, in a woman's voice, to mechanics' and poor men's wives.[35]

The *Lancet* added significantly that 'hygienically regenerated wives and daughters, would do more to wean our working-men from skittle grounds and gin-shops than a millennium of Exeter Hall demonstrations'.

The fourth key transformation that women social workers would accomplish would be to change class separation and antagonism, so disturbing in Hyde Park demonstrations, into the loving relations of family. Public mothering provided a key ingredient in this social alchemy. Women working as matrons or teachers acted as social mothers and instilled a proper model of family life into their charges. Women visiting the poor whether from the Ladies' Sanitary Association, the Charity Organisation Society or the local parish used the authority of mothers to help poor women to become proper mothers. Octavia Hill, pioneer of housing management, urged her lady rent collectors to think of the poor 'primarily as husbands, wives, sons and daughters, members of households as we are ourselves, instead of contemplating them as a different class'.[36] Soaring to rhetorical heights, the Reverend Brewer urged women visitors to spread the gospel of the bourgeois family and especially provide an image of the professional family to the poor in order to ensure the perpetuation of national greatness:

> for an English household of the educated classes is not the growth of a year, or a life, or a century; it is the very marrow of our national life—the essence of our national experience.[37]

Perhaps the biggest prize that the women in social science offered to the men was the promise that the language of family rather than the language of class would quiet social struggle, civilize working people and create social harmony. Class conflict and rhetoric could be replaced by a common national vision of proper family life.

CO-OPTION OF FEMINISM IN SOCIAL SCIENCE

The communion of labour in social science, which sometimes looked suspiciously like a collusion of labour between feminist women and professional men, also involved a co-option of some strands of feminism and rejection of others. Not only men who kept a more distant watching brief, but many of the professional men who wanted to create a public working relationship with women found maternal feminism more tolerable than two other strains active on the midcentury scene: equal rights feminism or sexual feminism. They could more easily accept maternal feminism which upheld sexual difference and argued for an extension of women's social role in terms of the need for her feminine and especially her maternal qualities in every area of social life. They could less easily come to grips with Langham Place demands for equality of access to political rights as well as to educational and employment opportunities. There is evidence that some professional men welcomed and fostered maternal feminism, not least to discredit or even to tame other strains of the feminist beast. They made an artificial selection among species of feminism and helped those they preferred to survive. Thus the Reverend F.D. Maurice reassured professional men who felt threatened by female competition and by women's demands for 'free entrance into the College of Physicians and the Inns of Court' or into the ministry via that most preposterous of routes, 'Romish sisterhoods', that a Ladies'

135

College which supplied training for work among the poor on communion of labour lines would

> remove the slightest craving for such a state of things, by giving....a more healthful direction to the minds which entertain it. The more pains we take to call forth and employ the faculties which belong characteristically to each sex, the less it will be intruding upon the province which, not the conventions of the world, but the will of God, has assigned to the other.[38]

Such a College would both skill women and teach them their proper limits: 'they need education not only to show them what they can do, but what they cannot do and should not attempt'.

In the Social Science Association women overstepped their limits from time to time and reminders of safer directions had to be signposted. The Newcastle Congress in 1870 seemed to crackle with feminist energy of all kinds. For the second year running, a Ladies' Conference met for several days forming a kind of Congress within a Congress, with Lady Bowring in the chair. A crowded session endorsed an effective Married Women's Property Bill drafted by the Jurisprudence Department. On the next day another gathering, 'composed of ladies exclusively' but not formally connected to the Congress, met to inaugurate the Ladies' National Association for the Repeal of the Contagious Diseases Acts.[39] At the Social Science Congress the year before, doctors had tried to launch a campaign to extend these Acts to the whole civilian population and had been immediately obstructed by a voluble opposition meeting. The women now determined to use the SSA theatre once again for a dramatic initiative. Theirs became the most controversial of the midcentury feminist campaigns: not only did it move into the public sphere and work as a pressure group to change the law but it turned the searchlight on to the most shrouded topic of all, sex. The CD Acts empowered police in designated military towns to stop women suspected of being prostitutes and order them to submit to medical examination for venereal disease, while in no way troubling their male clients. The Ladies' National Association mercilessly exposed the double standard operating in every social area from sex to constitutional rights and spotlighted the behaviour of affluent men whether customers, politicians, doctors or police. The repealers also often argued that male lust had created the moral sewer of prostitution and that the only way to achieve moral hygiene was for men to become equal in conduct to women and to abstain from sex outside the marital bed. Significantly, the repealers pointed the finger of blame not at defective working-class families, but at respectable upper-class men. Ladies' Conferences ceased suddenly after 1870 ostensibly to enable women to take more part in mixed meetings but probably also to put a stop to awkward fringe meetings of women at Congress time. The Contagious Diseases issue proved very divisive even among the men in the SSA: doctors in the Public Health Department tended to support the Acts, while the Jurisprudence Department opposed them. After 1871, the issue disappeared from the repertoire of debate: scientific harmony had been achieved by means of evasion.

For a wide spectrum of male opinion, the Ladies' Sanitary Association epitomized the acceptable face of feminism, compared with equal rights or sexual campaigns. In 1870, the *Leeds Mercury* underlined the unquestionable 'propriety' of the work of the LSA:

> Such work cannot justly expose them to sarcasm or ridicule, as has been the case with reference to the Contagious Diseases Act....surely instruction in such matters is woman's legitimate work and there is nothing repulsive in it and no man of right feeling or intellect can object to see such work undertaken by them.[40]

Even the *Saturday Review* could find a place in its misogynist heart for the LSA in comparison to unsexed equal rights feminism: if

> ladies would read, mark, learn and inwardly digest the tracts of the Ladies' Sanitary Association, preach on them, practise them, they would be much better sociologists than by discussing the question of woman's franchise, or by aping the institutions which encourage female lawyers, clerks, doctoresses in medicine, and petticoated preachers.[41]

Kingsley too could champion the LSA at the same time that he branded political feminists as failures in femininity and even attacked single women playing at being maternal feminists. Mixing together all the vitriol he could muster, in images of hyperactive, overbearing, loudmouthed, querulous women, he poured contempt on

> strong-minded and emancipated women, who prided themselves on having cast off conventionalities, and on being rude and awkward and dogmatic and irreverent, and sometimes slightly improper; women who have missions to mend everything in heaven and earth, except themselves; who had quarrelled with their husbands, and had therefore felt a mission to assert women's rights and reform marriages in general; or who had never been able to get married at all, and therefore were especially competent to promulgate a model method of educating the children whom they had never met.[42]

Women active in social science welcomed male support but did not regard their maternal feminism as an absolute alternative to other feminist strategies. Their positions were often ambiguous, containing strands which both asserted women's equality and women's difference. Depending upon the actual situation, they could pull harder at the strand which seemed most likely to widen women's opportunities at the time. Emily Davies, seen by historians as one of the most egalitarian of the midcentury feminists, was predictably complex. An Evangelical who then embraced Christian socialism, she asserted a theological equality between the sexes ('God had created man and woman in his own image'), and a common call to duty ('love the Lord thy God with all thy heart and thy neighbour as thyself'), precisely to discredit a bogus 'dual theory'. Determined to achieve a common university curriculum for both sexes, she cited as a powerful precedent that 'the theory of education of our English Church recognizes no distinction of sex'. She eventually succeeded in founding Girton College Cambridge on the basis of curricular equality. On the other hand, she accepted the existence of gender difference although, like most other women in social science, she argued that women's real nature and true femininity could not yet be known because for centuries these had been socially constructed or, more accurately socially constricted in virtually every sphere. Nonetheless when she came to discuss the actual professions which would be relevant for women with well-trained intelligence, she mobilized conventional ideas of women's special moral and nurturing qualities. Even her most adventurous suggestion that women could minister in the workhouse and replace the chaplain there, would not involve their taking an authority role either in the learning or organization of the church. Rather they would read prayers to the poor, visit the sick and supervise the children.[43] Other feminists, like Josephine Butler, considered Davies 'too masculine aiming' and supported an alternative strategy for establishing women's place in universities by proposing a separate and flexible curriculum, the course followed at Newnham College Cambridge.

Tensions between equality and difference should come as no surprise. Many of the midcentury women labelled as equal rights feminists[44] tended to come from radical Unitarian circles which could trace their feminist pedigree back at least to Mary Wollstonecraft's time. Yet from the Enlightenment onward, the 'equal rights' tradition of feminism had contained ambiguities not to say unresolved contradictions. Wollstonecraft herself held that women and men shared an equal capacity for reason and morality: their only difference resided in relatively unimportant physical strength. Yet even in her vision sexual difference and ideas of femininity as maternity crept back. She saw the social roles of male and female citizens as gender divided: public duty for the men—maternal citizenship for the women whose primary job would be raising and educating the future citizenry. Women's 'first duty', she asserted, 'is to themselves as rational creatures, and the next,...as citizens, is that which includes so many, of a mother'.[45] In the early socialist movement, national figures as well as local women celebrated the special role of socialist mothers in shaping the future of the human race while at the same time speaking about the equal faculties of men and women.[46] If the most daring of feminists were in fact so ambiguous it is not surprising that mid-Victorian, upper-class women seeking an expanded social role should often move into the maternal mode. And, of course, the fact that men also beckoned them into that space made it appear a hopeful way forward.

Even among the more unorthodox of midcentury women, maternal feminism figured in personal life as well as politics. Barbara Bodichon (1827-91) and Bessie Rayner Parkes (1829-1925) came from unconventional Unitarian families. Barbara was the eldest of the five illegitimate children of Anne Longden, a milliner's apprentice, and Benjamin Leigh Smith, a wealthy brewer and radical Norwich MP who took an unusually active role in raising the children when their mother died.[47] The parents of Bessie Rayner Parkes did not get on and kept separate households; her father, another rich MP and an associate of the Philosophic Radicals, had a house in London, while her mother's Birmingham home deeply disappointed her because she found it so lacking 'in real happiness'.[48]

Bodichon and Parkes became leading figures in the Langham Place Group which illustrated the complex interplay between feminist activity premissed on sexual equality or difference. Their first foray into active campaigning concerned equal property rights and ended with the defeat of the Married Women's Property Act in 1857.[49] They then turned their effort towards founding the *English Woman's Journal* and securing the Langham Place premises. Within this framework, other issues which had also preoccupied them moved more energetically ahead. Several of these, like the concern with employment and social work opportunities, brought into play the theme of maternal feminism. Parkes, for example, took a keen interest in the Ladies' Sanitary Association.[50] When a political path reopened, they followed it, first to support J.S. Mill's parliamentary candidacy, and then to back his amendment for an ungendered franchise in the 1867 Reform Bill. After the defeat of this campaign, they could revitalize work in other ongoing directions.

Both Bodichon and Parkes show how deeply motherhood was etched in the psyche of feminists and how various were the ways of handling this area of desire. A singular marriage to French doctor and Positivist Eugene Bodichon enabled Barbara sometimes to live as a married and a single woman at different seasons of the year, depending upon whether she was in Algiers where he was based, or in England on her own.[51] She tried desperately to become pregnant, but remained childless. In the end, she did what Anna Jameson had done for her and acted as informal mother to many young women striving to make an independent life.[52] Parkes took a more conventional path. At the age of thirty-eight, she 'fell in love' with an invalid Frenchman. Many strands of motherhood were tangled here: in his mother she found the mother she had always craved, whose house was 'a paradise of joyous lightness and buoyancy'. Told by doctors she could not have children, she might have wanted to offer him 'the affection of a mother, as well as that of a wife', a 'sacrifice' his mother thought 'too much to ask'.[53] Against all predictions, she conceived almost immediately and, in quick succession, gave birth to two children. She virtually retired from British public life to attend to her demanding family situation.

FACES OF MOTHERHOOD IN SOCIAL SCIENCE

The discourse of social motherhood which dominated women's social science resonated with words about family and love. This language endured for a very long time, long after philanthropy began to turn into professionalized social work. Thus, some fifty years on, in 1909, the object of district nursing was, according to Queen's Nurse M.E. Loane, 'the completion of family and neighbourhood'.[54] Seventy years on, in 1929, Ellen Chase promised that a successful lady rent collector, working in new-model dwellings for the poor, would find that 'in time, the property with which one is connected comes to hold almost the place of an enlarged family, tied together by mutual affection and service'.[55] This language of family and love can be seductive. But it is important to take account of the less gentle words and actions of the same women which make their motherhood and love seem highly disciplinarian and even punitive. Motherhood was not a unitary experience or idea. Depending on your position in the relationship and your point of view, it could be a many-headed monster or a many-splendoured thing!

Midcentury women active in social science seemed to split motherhood into at least three different faces. There has been very good historical writing on the tendency of Victorian middle-class men to split key parts of themselves and their reality. In one of the most striking examples, men detached maternity from sexuality, divided women into mothers and whores and pointed the fragmented pieces in different class directions: maternity towards bourgeois women, sexuality towards working-class women and whores. Thus Dr William Acton, in his 1858 work on *Prostitution*, could speak of the prostitute as 'a woman with half the woman gone, and that half containing all that elevates her nature, leaving her a mere instrument of impurity'.[56] However, historians have not yet explored the possibility that middle-class women also tended to split themselves. Their splitting, I would argue, was more complex than any simple collusion with middle-class men would suggest. Many middle-class women certainly shared the tendency to sever the maternal from the sexual. The burgeoning area of midcentury work with prostitutes opened up a space where the split segments of womanhood could encounter each other. But the negotiation between them seemed to be mediated by a more underlying perceptual grid which contained three facets of motherhood.

The rest of this chapter will explore three key archetypes in women's social science: the empowering, the protecting and finally the disciplining or punishing mother. The disciplining mother presents a very unattractive figure to modern eyes. By using this concept, I do not want to detract from the enormous commitment and courage of the women, especially the single women, who devoted their lives to social mothering. To stretch their role beyond the conventional script of godly wives, dutiful daughters or supportive sisters required immense bravery and sometimes exacted a devastating psychic toll. Florence Nightingale never nursed again after the Crimea but virtually spent the rest of her life in a sick bed in an attempt to manage powerfully ambivalent feelings about her mother and sister while at the same time running ambitious projects by proxy.[57]

Nonetheless the practices of social motherhood which women like Nightingale helped to create contained tensions and produced unintended consequences especially when it came to relations with poor women. These complexities need to be understood just as much as the courage of the social workers deserves to be appreciated. By proposing a typology of three faces of motherhood, I am not suggesting that real women expressed only one of the tendencies: real women are always more complex and contradictory than that. Mary Carpenter, whom I use to illustrate a disciplining face of motherhood, depended on the love of her institutional children for her fragile sense of self-esteem; Josephine Butler, whom I cite to illustrate protective motherhood, also lived within a deep commitment to the essential equality of all human beings.[58] Nonetheless, the typology can serve as an analytical tool that can make it easier to identify patterns in the confusion of real life and especially make it more possible to monitor dissonances and contradictions in women's social science.

Women in social science circles often acted out, both in fantasy and in reality, the nurturing and empowering side of mother love in relation to women of their own class. Thus many women waxed lyrical about the tenderness and support they found with women they mothered (in feeling not biological fact) or by whom they were mothered. Frances Power Cobbe spoke of her mother as 'the one being in the world whom I truly loved...the only one who really loved me'. The other most important relationship of her life, with the sculptress Mary Lloyd, enabled her both to work productively and to re-experience her mother's love, in 'a friendship which has been to my later life what my mother's affection was to my youth'.[59] Social workers continued to articulate their yearning for a nurturing relationship with another woman. At the turn of the twentieth century, nurse Loane shared her fantasy about how every district nurse really needed a 'Dark Star', a kind of mother-wife from the same social background, who would give personal and professional nurture:

> by making the nurse's domestic life thoroughly comfort-
> able, by providing her with cheerful companionship,
> by saving her about two hours work daily, and by
> enabling her to undertake duties which she must other-
> wise distress herself by refusing, the Dark Star could
> make even the most difficult district manageable.[60]

However, when turned to the poor, two other faces of mother love appeared. The first was a protective face, the second a disciplining face. What linked them both and informed them both was a tendency to infantilize the adult poor. The protective attitude made continual use of the biblical language of oppression, bondage and slavery. Young single women, prostitutes and, increasingly from the 1860s onwards, working-class wives were seen as powerless victims, as defenceless children in need of protection and advocacy. In the campaign against the Contagious Diseases Acts, the language of victimization was very salient. Butler in *The Duty of Women in Relation to our Great Social Evil* (1870) spoke of the campaign's mission

> to release the enslaved, loaded with chains of sin; women
> crushed by want and woe, and now pressed down

beneath the heel of a powerful tyranny, and of a
grievous, cruel oppressive law, by which they are made
legal slaves, the official slaves of a great, regulated, and
sanctioned iniquity.[61]

Butler made an extensive inventory of oppressors. She pointed
to an employment system which offered women only starvation
wages, a state, a police and a medical profession which violated
the constitution (in the double sense of women's bodies and the
body politic) in addition to focusing the villain more usually
identified by female repealers and later by social purity
feminists: predatory lusting males. The language of victims was
often tied, in Butler's rhetoric, to a plea for maternal advocacy:
'I address these words to you, as a mother to mothers. Listen to
me while I plead for the children.'[62]

Being the extraordinary person she was, Butler's flow of
rhetoric also contained contradictory currents which did not
surface in the speech of other middle-class women repealers.
Thus womanhood was a key category in her thinking and
included women of all classes and all moral shades. Not only
were the prostitute victims extending a hand and asking for help
(like the Levite's concubine, pushed from the house and raped
all night, stretching out her hand on the doorstep). But also the
'respectable' wives, 'the Sarahs are beginning to repent and
stretch forth their hands to the Hagars and to bridge over the
gulf which has so long separated them'.[63] This united
womanhood Butler saw as much more than a tribe of dominant
mothers and dependent daughters. They were all citizens with
constitutional rights ('it was as a citizen of a free country first and
as a woman secondly, that I felt impelled to come forward in
defense of right').[64] Together with allies like working-class men,
women united would work out their own liberation.[65] But it is
important not to try too hard to tidy up the contradictions.
While a radical thrust in Butler's thought moved towards self-
enacted liberation, she also told a contradictory story about
protective mothers helping to rescue prostitutes and propelling
them into a new life as servants—not only of God but of middle-
class households.

Another face of motherhood turned towards the poor
appeared more disciplining and harsh. Mary Carpenter may
have spoken of children brought to the virgin mother 'by the

hand of the law and she receives each one as led to her by the Saviour, makes it her own, gives it a mother's love and devotes herself to save it'. 'Yet', she continued, 'in the wild and undisciplined condition of many of the children there must be an admixture of the prison element of compulsory power'.[66] Reformatories became 'moral hospitals' for youngsters who had tangled with the law: hospitals acted as 'moral reformatories' for the sick poor. Penitentiaries were the name often given to reformatories where prostitutes would penitently re-form their characters under religious surveillance. We are again moving into the harsh country of cultural imperialism where people with power try to force human nature into their preferred moulds.

We have already noticed how prominent features in this landscape are languages of subordination which distance and devalue other human beings and which open the way for their wholesale re-formation. We have already explored discourses likening people to savages, to animals and to disease. The language of motherhood is perhaps the most interesting of all the discourses of denigration. It was a gendered language of subordination, a woman's language of authority from the mid-Victorian period onward. There have been historical times when men have appropriated even this discourse, as in the twelfth century when Cistercian abbots tried to adopt people into a new monastic life by likening themselves and Christ to nursing mothers.[67] But in nineteenth-century Britain, motherhood was a woman's discourse and the most paradoxical of the languages of devaluation because it tried to force renovation while talking of love. Middle-class feminists often spoke to the poor of any age as though they were naughty children. The posture of the scolding mother was an exceedingly useful stance, and deeply rooted both in psyche and class. It kept femininity intact, by preserving motherhood, and it kept hierarchy intact, by creating the need for dominant maternal authority figures to look after the infantilized poor.

Disciplining or punitive mothering was conspicuous in the penitentiary movement which provided Homes for the rehabilitation of prostitutes. Frances Finnegan tells a story about the York Female Penitentiary Society which the juvenile rescue movement had already rehearsed and which, in many essentials, could be repeated about other institutions created by midcentury feminist philanthropy. The middle-class Committee of the York Society did not connect the causes of prostitution with male sexuality as did the women active in the campaign against the Contagious Diseases Acts. Instead, they sometimes pointed to foolish female friends who 'seduced' girls from home, but mainly laid the blame on inadequate parenting:

> the majority have known little, if anything, of the pure and hallowing influences which we attach to Home; while many have been left by the indifference of their parents to become the prey of temptations incident to their time of life. Many have had in their parents bad examples which they only too naturally followed; and some had been actually initiated in sin by those who should have been their protectors from evil influences.[68]

The York Refuge was to be an adequate Home presided over by a social mother, for more than thirty years the Matron Miss Briddon, who offered a strictly disciplined version of loving care. York people in the 1970s, old enough to remember the Home, remained 'adamant that it was—a female prison'.[69] Strict rules governed every hour of the day, and most of 'the monotony of the life' was spent working in the laundry (as symbolic a choice of occupation as earlier straw platting) with religious rebuke as a constant refrain. Finnegan suggests that this harsh regime reduced some girls to demoralised dependents with an obsessive need to get approval from the matron who had become 'a rather authoritarian mother figure'.[70]

Like many total institutions which aim at transforming character, the Home tried to devalue and break down the old sense of identity (one London penitentiary even gave all the inmates new names) in order to create fallow ground in which to seed the new.[71] However, the dependence suggested above was not the majority experience which seems rather to have been an ongoing saga of tension and resistance. Of 412 who had dealings with the York Home between 1837 and 1887, only 142 were placed in service. The remainder left the Home, usually by running away or being thrown out. Beyond discipline problems, usually involving misdemeanours of the voice like shouting, swearing, insubordination, sometimes a veritable epidemic of disorder broke out, as in 1858 when all except two girls left.[72] In terms of its formal objective, of re-forming the girls through a kind of loving, this case of disciplinary mothering cannot be adjudged a great success. The contours of failure will be further explored in a later chapter on social science and social work.

But in another way the strategy of maternal intervention produced real gains for the social workers themselves. The new view of public femininity combining maternal service and science was part of the incipient professionalization of social work which took place in the midcentury period. Loosely analogous to what was happening in the male professions, charity workers began to exchange expertise and even to establish training of sorts. In the reformatory field proto-professional developments took place earliest and fastest. For example, in 1851, Mary Carpenter and M.D. Hill organized a conference of specialists and repeated the 'sacred day' in 1853. The state, as would become the pattern in many areas of social science, supplied a further impetus. The passing of the Juvenile Offenders Act of 1854 which provided state funds to voluntary groups to run institutions set the stage for a vast expansion of work. In response, Hill and Carpenter and the Law Amendment Society's paid secretary, G.W. Hastings, launched the National Reformatory Union with a conference in Bristol in August 1856, while in the same year the Reformatory and Refuge Union was also established—for Anglicans only.[73] The Reformatory and Refuge Union continued as a professional-type group for some years, holding conferences and even bringing out a journal which legitimized certain theory and practice, shared approved experience and advertised job opportunities. The National Reformatory Union ran a different course. Within a year it had been absorbed into the National Association for the Promotion of Social Science.

6

THE SOCIAL SCIENCE ASSOCIATION

Division and Communion of Labour, 1857-1886

The Social Science Association was a peripatetic extravaganza and a forceful pressure group.[1] Modelled on the British Association for the Advancement of Science, it moved to a different city each year to hold its five-day Congress, and then in the mid-1860s added regular London meetings to its itinerary. The Association operated on a huge scale attracting thousands of participants and hundreds of papers which found their way into large volumes of *Transactions* and *Sessional Proceedings* over a period of nearly thirty years. Besides helping to generate a popular culture of social science all around the country, the SSA also organized powerful national specialist groups which made an influential mark on state and voluntary action. The Association won admirers abroad who practised the sincerest form of flattery by imitating it: a Brussels-based Association Internationale pour le Progrès des Sciences Sociales formed in 1862 and an American Association for the Promotion of Social Science started in 1865.[2]

Such a large-scale presence requires attention but will probably always elude any one interpretative frame imposed upon it. Early interpretations assessed the Social Science Association as a gigantic non-event on the grounds that it contributed little to the development of social theory. Most recently, Goldman has turned this view on its head arguing that the Social Science Association embodied just the kind of science a powerful Liberalism would create, whereas frustrated and failed bourgeois effort in other countries, like America and Germany, led precisely to a more exclusive concentration on theory and to faster academic professionalization.[3]

My focus is on the Association in relation to class and gender issues. Having considered the situation of women in the last chapter, I will now turn the spotlight more fully onto men and their relations and representations of class in the Social Science Association. The Association produced a version of social science which embraced the communion of labour between men and women and then extended the principle to include co-operation between specialists and communication with the labour movement. Within this formula of division but communion of labour, the Association furnished a scientific house with spacious accommodation for a range of social residents. Professional men and philanthropic women moved in quickly. Bessie Rayner Parkes noted that 'the amelioration of humanity under its varied phases of misfortune has now become a science' and identified the recipe for success as 'the spirit of association involving unity of purpose and division of labour'.[4] Edward Denison approved 'the resurrection of the old instinct of union in the form of active associations for carrying out a practical purpose'.[5] They were joined by more surprising newcomers: figures from the midcentury labour movement and practitioners of socialist social science trying to navigate the wreckage of some of their earlier projects.

MOVEMENTS TOWARDS CO-ORDINATION FROM BELOW

The collapse of the Queenwood Community, which had been a main focus of socialist activity and generosity between 1837 and 1845, dealt a severe blow to radical hope. The rejection of the third Chartist Petition just three years later delivered another body blow. But all was not despair. New avenues of advance seemed to be opening at the same time that old strategies were turning out to be dead ends. For example, local socialists and Chartists had sustained smaller-scale co-operative and cultural ventures during the 'hungry forties', even while the national campaigns were floundering. The socialists conducted postmortems on Queenwood with the analytic tools of their social science: thus the discussion topic on 7 June 1846 for the London A.1. branch was 'why have the attempts to reduce co-operative principles to practice hitherto failed? Is the failure attributable to the ignorance of professed Co-operators, or the incompatibility of the principles with human nature?'[6] They used the

Queenwood experience to interrogate their models of essential human nature and the ultimate social stage, to test their analysis of the competitive system and, on the practical level, to review their transitional strategies.

Most socialists began to feel that human nature changed more slowly than they had previously assumed and that people remained too selfish at the moment to sustain full community life. Many socialists retained community as the ultimate goal although some, like Holyoake, later insisted that competitive energies had been undervalued and that community would never be the appropriate setting for the realization of human potential.[7] A perhaps surprising number of socialists retained their analysis of capitalist society even during the years of so-called midcentury prosperity. After all, a glaring gap still remained between the actual situation and the ideal: a chasm marked out by continuing unemployment, a rash of industrial disputes, competitive social relationships and an absence of educational opportunity. William Pare, now the prosperous manager of iron works in Clontarf, Liverpool and Chepstow, published a second edition of William Thompson's *Inquiry into the Distribution of Wealth* in 1850, and brought out yet another in 1869. Responding to the Preston strike and lockout of 1854, he stressed the inherent opposition of interests between capital and labour as the permanent source of industrial conflict ('the labourers have not received...more than a small share of the fruits of their industry') and underlined the tendency of capitalists to replace people with machines, creating a pool of 'cast off' labour.[8]

On the practical level of social science, all agreed that the slower rate of change invalidated a dramatic single remedy solution, like the Charter or community on the land. What were needed were more limited and slower-acting strategies, which might still have eventual transformative effects, and a co-ordination of partial reforms. Ex-Chartist Thomas Cooper called for a 'General Progress Union' while William Lovett urged a General Association of Progress to effect communication and co-ordination between 'various classes of Reformers'.[9] In 1852, the Co-operative League brought together a range of groups committed to conflicting versions of co-operation, including orthodox old socialists, like Owen himself and his inflexible acolyte Henry Travis, and Christian Socialists, like E. Vansittart

Neale. Once fiercely ideological, socialists now became fastidious about avoiding sectarian offence. The Co-operative League gave the assurance that no member

> is called upon in any way to conceal his individual convictions, or pledge himself to the opinions which other members of the League may entertain:...the kind of union asked for is a union as permits each of the various schools included under the name of co-operative to retain its distinctive peculiarities, and calls upon them only to recognize in each other a community of objects and ideas, as shall make them mutually disposed to impart the one, and ascertain how far they can unite in effecting the other.[10]

In his 1851 *Lectures on Social Science and Organization of Labour*, James Hole, the Leeds socialist, also mooted a 'National Union of Association which collected and diffused the actual experience of associations in Great Britain and elsewhere'.[11] The desire for co-ordination created a ground for a degree of consensus or at least a space for discussion with the middle-class professionals keen on some form of service to the working classes.

This chapter will explore the main social science arena for inter-class dialogue, but it is important to note that midcentury working-class movements, and the co-operative movement in particular, continued to carry on a vigorous and assertively working-class cultural practice. Local societies, which ran their co-operative stores, also produced newspapers, provided libraries and classes and supplied a rich menu of convivial activities.[12] Such activities enjoyed a greater measure of support from above than ever before. National newspapers like the *Co-operator* and the *Social Economist* welcomed contributions from now friendly thinkers like John Stuart Mill. However much of a bourgeois rag Marx and Engels thought the *Bee-Hive* while edited by the Reverend Henry Solly, the ex-Chartist, the newspaper had been started by trade unionists, provided good coverage of the labour movement and carried working-class contributions like William Lovett's 'ABC of Social Science'.[13] Despite new collaboration, tensions remained, which occasionally surfaced even in the generally sympathetic SSA literature. Thus William Mattieu Williams from the Edinburgh Secular School, which tried to teach the social science curriculum developed by William Ellis, told of his experience with socialist parents, who opposed 'the social economy nonsense' and remained convinced that Williams was 'a special pleader for the capitalists'. Although they kept the children at school, the parents made sure to counteract the political economy lessons with their own teaching at home.[14]

These Edinburgh parents acted like a miniature epitome of labour figures within the Social Science Association who utilized its facility, without illusions, and sometimes carried on quite dissident activity outside its perimeter. The new inclusiveness of the Social Science Association also involved selectivity. The dominant groups within the Association practised the same kind of co-option towards labour movements as towards varieties of feminism, and gave an enthusiastic audience to acceptable perspectives and activities while curtailing discussion and even censoring publication of less favoured items. The exclusion from the annual *Transactions* of a paper read by William Dronfield, Secretary of the United Kingdom Alliance of Organized Trades, at Sheffield in 1865 caused a furore in the labour world.[15] Moreover, even when people talked to each other in the same institution, their common agenda could come from very different vantage points and their tacit co-operation could still quietly vibrate with tension. Whatever the complications once such inclusive bodies came into existence, working-class activists feeling their way in a new situation called for associations of reformers.

THE NATIONAL ASSOCIATION FOR THE PROMOTION OF SOCIAL SCIENCE: MEETINGS AND MEMBERS

The Social Science Association was the most spectacular response to the call for inclusive associations coming from above and from below.[16] However hard it may be to imagine social science as a highlight of the social season, the annual Congresses became splendid local events, often involving thousands of people and organized by committees of prominent citizens months in advance. The Congress proceedings followed a ritual formula. The first day featured a sermon in the parish church, often preached by a bishop, and opening addresses from the Departmental Presidents, well-known national figures who were often peers. The following four days were devoted to reading and discussing papers at meetings which took place in the most important local public buildings. In London, the judges even adjourned the sittings at *Nisis* to make the Law Courts available.[17] But work took up only part of the time. Lavish soirées hosted by the Mayor and *conversazioni* given by local learned societies occupied the evenings. In London, even the staid Royal College of Physicians, to the amazement as well as the amusement of the medical press, laid on a soirée.[18] Daytime activity included social scientific sight-seeing. In Manchester, the itinerary for inspection included local factories, the new workhouse, the Athenaeum, the Moral and Industrial Training Schools, the Free Library, the Asylum for Female Penitents and the grand opening of the showpiece of the working-class co-operative movement, the Cobden Memorial Mills at Sabden Bridge.[19]

In 1864, the Association merged with the Law Amendment Society and took over its London office and library. Now the buoyant provincial Congresses were supplemented by a more stable London membership, which provided an income of some £900 annually until June 1878. Activities expanded to include fortnightly sessional meetings in London and the SSA became even better placed to act as a pressure group on government. But during the 1870s, Congress attendances and remittances began to drop and then took an accelerated nosedive in 1879; visits to cities a second time round excited far less interest. From 1880 even the subscriptions received at the London office began to fall steadily.[20]

From the beginning to the end, the social profile of the membership remained fairly constant. After the London Congress of 1862, London members formed the majority and came mainly from the midcentury professions: in 1866, 1869, 1872 and 1880 members of the legal profession comprised around 30 per cent, Members of Parliament 10 per cent, City businessmen 10 per cent falling to 6.6 per cent, doctors and civil servants 12 per cent taken together, women and aristocrats made up a rising 7 per cent, and architects, clergy, engineers and military men figured in smaller percentages as later did teachers and accountants. The provincial membership cut a different pattern. Here businessmen who financed local philanthropic projects or whose firms were regarded as key social experiments formed the single largest group, although each city showed its own variation. Bristol had 51 members when the Association met there in 1869, of whom ten were businessmen, eight barristers and solicitors, five clergymen, four doctors, three teachers and one a woman, Mary Carpenter, but during non-Congress years the membership fell to a core of between seven and twelve, of whom three to four were businessmen. By contrast, in the Leeds area, large model manufacturers formed more than half the local membership and, with the exception of the occasional clergyman, no professional people joined at all.

Nearly everybody who was anybody in the field of social improvement attended. The key civil servants of the central state, men like Chadwick, Simon, Kay-Shuttleworth and the Hill brothers featured as did the leaders of voluntary action of the day, like Mary Carpenter, Octavia Hill and the Charity Organisation brigade. Old socialists, midcentury co-operators and new model unionists participated alongside new model employers. Intellectuals active in social reform, like the Christian Socialists and the Positivists made their mark in the social econ-omy discussions; J.S. Mill served faithfully as a longtime Council member. Professional men like doctors, lawyers and clergymen gravitated to the Public Health, Jurisprudence and Education Departments while women seeking a public role made their presence felt across the Departmental board. Parliamentary members and Cabinet Ministers of both parties appeared on the governing Council and as Departmental Presidents. Right across the political spectrum, the old generation as well as the new made their appearance, including the venerable Whig Lord Brougham, veteran Tory Lord Shaftesbury and even the Rational Socialist Father himself, Robert Owen, before he died. Without illusions, G.J. Holyoake congratulated

> Mr Owen on having lived to witness the triumph of his views. We are quite aware that very few of the eminent men present at this conference would accept Mr. Owen's plan for remedying social evils; but the existence of social evils is recognized in the most conspicuous manner— they have become subject of public study, and every member of the conference has agreed that they must be remedied somehow.[21]

This incredibly broad scientific church has been conceptualized, by Philip Abrams, as a surrogate political party which acted as an 'institutional filter for social concern' between the middle class and the legislature before the modern party system solidified, and by Goldman as 'a type of research institute attached to the emergent Liberal Party under Gladstone, which it supplied with blueprints for social legislation'.[22] These useful frameworks do not cover, however, the range of people who affiliated and did not define themselves, in this forum, primarily in political terms: indeed political ideology or social theory was deliberately underplayed in order to facilitate practical co-operation. This attempt at total inclusion brought in voluntarists as well as advocates of legislation and the 'unenfranchised' who proved to be fickle supporters of the Liberal Party when they felt their interests were not being properly served. In the scientific world, the SSA created a surrogate nation which the political system did not yet fully recognize, as the *Daily News* sarcastically noted in 1870, when it drew upon Chartist language and called the Association a 'peripatetic Parliament',

> in which every man is his own representative, in which women are already enfranchised, in which small minorities may find a voice for their crotchets, and in which unappreciated philosophers of both sexes may meet together to talk over the welfare of the world.[23]

Nonetheless widespread inclusion did not mean that all parties had equal weight in setting the scientific agenda or laying out the grounds for consensus.

THE ASSOCIATION'S IDEA OF SOCIAL SCIENCE

The Association was closely tied to professional men who often had a connection with the central state and to newly specialized social workers, many of whom were women. Indeed the Association's idea of social science should be extracted from its origins and practice as much as from its quasi-theoretical statements. The midwives attending at its birth were the two representative organizations for 'socializing' professional work and for 'professionalizing' social work: the Law Amendment Society and the National Reformatory Union. Anna Jameson also attended the initial meeting. After ten months of national tours, soundings, discussions, and cajolings, a decisive moment was reached at a meeting at the home of Lord Brougham. The high-powered gathering created Five Departments which corresponded to their special preserves.[24] 'Jurisprudence and the Amendment of the Law' covered the special territory of the Law Amendment Society to which both Brougham and Hastings belonged. Mary Carpenter, M.D. Hill and Reverend Sydney Turner, head of the Red Hill Reformatory School and newly appointed Government Inspector of Reformatories, represented the juvenile branch of Reformatory Science in the Punishment and Reformation of Crime Department. William Newmarch of the London Statistical Society and Dr Farr, the Assistant Registrar General, represented statistics, which, significantly, did not get a department to itself, possibly a reflection of the fact that the statistical societies were increasingly being dominated by the professionals. John Simon, now Medical Officer to the General Board of Health, and the veteran public health campaigners, Viscount Ebrington and Charles Adderley, would have spoken up for Sanitary Science. Once launched, the Public Health Department was piloted by a Committee with a majority of people professionally active in the work, especially doctors and civil servants.[25] Mrs Baines represented the Ladies' Sanitary Association.

The fourth Department covered Education, already such a key concern of Evangelical as well as Nonconformist reformers. Ministers of religion, many of whom ran schools, comprised one third of its long-serving Committee members; 15 per cent were civil servants (including now-retired Kay-Shuttleworth) or Inspectors of Schools and Factories (like Cooke Taylor), and 15 per cent were women active in educational work like Mary Carpenter, Jessie Boucherett of the Society for Promoting the Employment of Women and Emily Davies. A Department of Social Economy completed the original rollcall and concerned itself especially with 'questions relating to Capital, Labour and Production'. Significantly even here professional men dominated the Department Committee which had nine civil servants (from the Poor Law Board, the Board of Trade, the Committee on Education and the inevitable Hill brothers from the Post Office), five barristers and three political economists, W. S. Jevons, R. Torrens and W. N. Hancock, as against five identifiable businessmen.

Even if it started as a marriage of convenience, the departmental structure worked well and, with one change, was elevated in 1863 to the status of being 'scientific and therefore exhaustive and final'. At this point the Punishment and Reformation Department was amalgamated with Jurisprudence (the 'prominent questions relating to the treatment of prisoners, whether adult or juvenile, are either solved or in process of solution'). Instead an Art Department was proposed and finally added in 1876. The final departmental inventory, Jurisprudence, Education, Health, Economy, Art, seemed 'to exhaust the entire conditions of society'.[26] This structure dignified midcentury fields of social reform by giving them scientific credentials and also allowed for a co-ordination of effort. If Karl Marx was unifying social science by forging the analytic tools of historical and dialectical materialism, and if J. S. Mill was talking of integrating the work of specialized sciences which dealt with analytically separable aspects of human nature, the Social Science Association largely wanted activists to talk to one another. As Hastings put it from the first: 'the plan advocated for a union of social reformers is not to compel every one to master the occupations of his colleagues, but to establish a mutual interchange of opinion, experience, and information.'[27]

Association spokesmen paid serious lip service to the lawfulness of the social and moral universe but the Association did not concern itself with the 'more abstract labours' of elucidating the simple laws. This moratorium on theory accounted for some of the missing presences, like that of Herbert Spencer. Even if he had not suffered from an acute allergy to its 'over-legislation', the discouragement of theory would probably have kept him away. His evolutionary sociology did not feature. The Positivists and J. S. Mill did not consider the SSA an appropriate arena for rehearsing theoretical issues although they valued its importance in its chosen province. The Association concerned itself with the 'practical field of social science...which is nonetheless scientific in its real character'. 'It is not within the power of this or any similar body', Hastings observed,

> to investigate abstract truth at a popular meeting. The good effected by such gatherings is to encourage discussion, to stimulate inquiry, to collect the materials on which scientific induction can afterwards be founded. But the Association can and ought to deal with practical details in a scientific spirit, and under the guidance of a

scientific method; for it should never be supposed that science can be lost sight of, even in the most practical details, without the danger of error and illusion. No amendment of the law is likely to be sound or permanent which is carried out without reference to the philosophy of jurisprudence; no social legislation can afford to defy the principles of economic science; no attempt at national or local organisation is free from danger if it ignores sanitary truths.[28]

This emphasis on a practical science directly linked to policy-making and social reform put the Association into the middle of the mainstream tradition of British social science dating back to the French Revolution. Indeed at that earlier point in time, radical thinkers from all social classes had rejected the comparative historical method and long-scale historical periodization largely because these perspectives seemed to inhibit urgently-needed social action and align with do-nothing or reactionary political positions. Neither Utilitarianism, political economy nor socialist social science could be called untheoretical, but all led quickly to praxis. The re-engagement with developmental schema at the midcentury either in the form of Positivism, which functioned as a reformist science before it retreated largely into being a secularist church, or in the form of evolutionary thought (Chapter 7) changed the intellectual ecology. Nonetheless, action-oriented varieties of social science still dominated and continued growing vigorously into the twentieth century. SSA activists were often well read in the new evolutionary theory but still, as Goldman reminds us about Lord Stanley, located their scientific praxis in the SSA.[29]

In the discourse of practical science, from the 1790s onward, 'facts' and 'experiments' had occupied a central place. Whose facts and experiments counted at the midcentury? The SSA endorsed, as scientific fact and valid experiment, the experience and judgement of people in state agencies and in positions of command within voluntary institutions, including labour movements. Expertise safeguarded the reliability of results. But in this period, expertise did not so much attach to training as to having direct experience of exercising power over a period of time. R. E. Warwick intended to treat the issue of the Poor Law 'as one of pure social science and to lay before you the knowledge I have obtained and the opinions I have framed having for the last twenty-five years been practically engaged in the administration of the Poor-Laws'.[30] Experiments now meant the results of legislation or the effects of institutions as reported and interpreted by people who administered them. M. D. Hill spoke of the reformatory movement being in the 'tentative or experimental stage' and of 'diversity of action in different Reformatories' as essential 'to the advancement of our science'; Lord Brougham cited the Maine Liquor Law as a successful 'experiment in the history of social science'.[31]

The statistical Eden of objectivity of the 1830s, where the numerical representation of facts assured truth, seemed to dissolve from view. While the encounter between interviewer and informant did not become problematized until later in nineteenth-century social work, nonetheless Mary Carpenter indicated that some statistics carried more weight than others. Accuracy seemed to be guaranteed by a vantage point from above and by length of service in that position:

> Though it may be impossible from mere statistical tables to form a true estimate of the real relation between ignorance and crime in this country, so variable are the criterions on which such tables are founded, so easily may the most accurate be led into error by the misstatement, intentional or otherwise, of the prisoners—yet the testimony of such a man as Mr. Clay, who for more than a quarter of a century has been anxiously and watchfully fulfilling the painful yet most important duties of Chaplain at the Preston House of Correction, must be entitled to great weight.[32]

Doubly ratified, Reverend Clay was a clergyman of the state church who worked in a state institution.

The Association made a few attempts to carry out its own investigations, most notably its enquiry into Trade Societies and Strikes which received full union co-operation after overcoming suspicions about its being an 'employers' movement in disguise'. On the whole, however, the Association left it to the state to collect the facts and made powerful representation that the Censuses of 1861 and 1871 should include a compulsory industrial survey which would show the distribution of manufacturing industry, the 'extent and description' of the labour employed, the average wages in different trades and which would provide 'the necessary and only reliable basis for investigating many of the social problems for the elucidation of which this Association was called into existence'.[33] The Association marked a further stage in the process begun in the 1830s in which investigatory commissions, new inspectorates and state departments served authorize certain kinds of knowledge as scientific and beyond dispute. Now the Association gave its name, Social Science, to ratify state apparatuses of fact collection.

This recipe for science would seem to have offered paltry fare to those with less power. Yet the SSA provided contradictory space for the working class. On the one hand, a large measure of condescension figured in the Working Man's Meeting which became a staple part of the Congress menu. Even the *Law Magazine and Law Review* found this item indigestible:

> Certain of the speakers seemed to think they could not talk down sufficiently low to the 'working classes', and there was an Exeter Hall-ishness, a platformitude and sabbath school teacherism, about one at least of the speeches, which, we dare to say, are now-a-days utterly unacceptable and nauseous to the British working-man.[34]

Yet, as the last sentence suggests, the recognition was growing that British working men had 'come of age', most importantly in their ability to run their own large organizations. Some of the most important social facts and most hopeful social experiments were being created by working people. Working-class associations and activists played a central role in the Departments rather than only being hived off and put in their (lower) place at separate lecture-meetings.

In yet another way, the Association's practice of social science moved closer to the ideas of some working people and women, in the space opened up by J. S. Mill and Harriet Taylor. Like the earlier Owenite socialists, Association spokesmen argued the need for a science which would encompass the moral and intellectual dimensions of human life and become 'the science of promoting the prosperity, happiness and welfare of the human race'.[35] The new enlargement of focus went together with an attack on the scope of political economy. In the 1820s when the sciences of political economy and of government had first crystallized out of a broader matrix of moral philosophy, they formed themselves preeminently as sciences of the public sphere, working with an egotistical male model of human nature which equated happiness with wealth and power. Now feminist women, together with professional men and working-class proponents of moral economy, could ally in the SSA to question this reductive idea of the science. Hastings felt it

> enough to say that the Association sprang out of the belief that many of our political economists have illogically narrowed their investigations by ignoring all view of moral duty, and that a union was needed between the moral and economical sciences, in order to constitute a philosophy which would embrace in its inquiries alike the conditions of social prosperity and the rights and obligations of citizenship.[36]

The Association provided an important middle-class arena for a concerted critique of political economy which did not always take the form of a friendly call for a (comm)union of moral and economical concerns. Sometimes the encounter became more robust when cocky individuals threw down the gauntlet to dignified professors of political economy and made them squirm onto the defensive. At a Sessional Meeting on Wages and Capital, John Ruskin ceremoniously read out ten embarrassing questions. Dr W. B. Hodgson (1815-80), soon to be appointed Professor of Commercial and Political Economy at the University of Edinburgh, nervously rejoined:

> it was commonly assumed that political economy was a selfish science, that it advocated selfishness and taught every man to look to his interests as opposed to those of his fellow-men. He altogether denied that man was a predatory animal, following predatory instincts. The object of political economy was to ascertain the interests of the community, and the interests of individuals as members of the community. Every man who promoted his own interests to the injury of the community, or even without benefit to the community, was so far from being a sound political economist that he was a traitor to political economy.[37]

In his 'Address' as President of the Economy and Trade Department in 1868, Henry Fawcett MP (1833-84), holder of the new chair of Political Economy at Cambridge, also felt obliged to redeem the political economist from his popular image as 'a selfish hardhearted being'. Fawcett laid stress, like the old socialists and like his friend J. S. Mill, on distribution and on happiness:

> the practical end which the political economist has to attain, is to show how the labour and capital required for the production of wealth may be economised; and how wealth may be distributed and exchanged so as to confer the greatest amount of happiness on mankind.[38]

In good communion of labour fashion, Millicent Fawcett read out this speech 'with singular clearness and enunciation'. She was not only the perfect helpmeet to her blind husband but also taught political economy in the Ladies' Department of King's College and wrote on the subject, in the approved womanly style, producing a textbook for school children in 1870 and *Tales in Political Economy* in 1874.[39]

The moral critique of political economy dominated in the SSA. Other intellectual rumblings against the subject remained muffled. The stormy debate launched by Professor Ingram in the British Association in 1878, which centred around the comparative scientific merits of positivist sociology compared with political economy, entered SSA debate only twice when Professor Bonamy Price and William Westgarth picked up Ingram's gauntlet to oppose him. Only one contribution to 'the historical method of political economy' appeared when J. E. Thorold Rogers spoke on ideas of *laissez-faire* and collective regulation in his presidential address to the Economy and Trade Department in 1883.[40]

REPRESENTATIONS OF THE WORKING CLASS IN THE SSA

To many members, men and women alike, the condition of the working classes still presented the single most important issue facing social science. Given the departmental structure, however, the treatment of this all-important subject tended to be fragmented as each year each Department dealt with only some aspects of working-class life. Nonetheless it is possible to focus on dominant representations of the working classes which were shared across Departments and gave a coherence of approach and a real basis for communion of labour despite specialization. Throughout the long career of the Association, members did not think in terms of a unified working class. Underlying many specialist analyses, and many different typologies of the poor, was a fundamental division of the working class into at least two groups, whether the division was based on individual psychology, social capacity, occupational position or resonant metaphor. On the one hand, there were the 'perishing and dangerous classes'; on the other 'the true working classes'. The representation of the two major sections of the working class did not remain static between 1857 and 1880. The huge corpus of SSA papers, along with other writings where members developed their ideas more fully, offer a rich and complex source for a chronology of representations. Here a powerful consortium of the industrial, professional and administrative middle class can be seen constructing themselves in relation to their most significant 'Other'—the working class.

Just how far the problem pendulum had swung from the 1830s could be measured by the fact that the factory population no longer ranked high on the agenda for concern. During the 1830s, social observers had spent a good deal of their energy trying to analyse the tendencies of the new mechanical leviathan. They used lurid language about its evils, apocalyptic language about its promise, and images of energy or indeed explosiveness to depict the people working within it. The SSA indicated how defused the issue had become. The Social Economy and the Public Health Departments spent a comparatively small amount of time on the factory system, placed factory workers in the true working classes and discussed them in a sober and uncontentious way.[41] Association members ascribed the tranquillity of the factory scene to a new partnership between capital and the state, brought about by the more enlightened attitude of employers going hand in hand with the Factory Acts, which limited working hours for women and children mainly in textiles, regulated the sanitary conditions of work, and instituted a compulsory schooling principle. Indeed the discussion often displayed the new moral economy of the capitalists. The Association served as the pulpit where capitalists came to recant their earlier hostility and publicly to affirm their conversion to limited protective legislation.

Edward Ackroyd, a devoted SSA member and self-styled political economist, owned a large worsted firm in Copley and Halifax, employing nearly 5,000 workers. He interpreted recent history as a kind of morality tale of how cash-nexus attitudes had led to terrible conflict, how sobered employers had reviewed their stewardship and how the Factory Acts had helped them to take a new approach which had created more harmonious class relations:

> For years the relative positions of employers and employed had been one of growing antagonism, the workmen looking upon the master as a groping and selfish tyrant, when the ill feeling found vent in the popular and violent agitation for the restriction of a Ten Hours Bill which eventually passed into an Act of Parliament....The fierce animosity displayed against mill-owners during this agitation and the unmeasured abuse heaped upon masters by their own workpeople, led me and doubtless other employers, seriously to review our position and to ask ourselves if we had done our duty to those over whom Providence had placed us?[42]

At first, Ackroyd and his father had opposed the Bill. But when it became law 'they had striven to give it their most earnest and practical support'. After searching his conscience, Ackroyd had also provided model villages for his workpeople which included well-built houses, allotments, recreation grounds, sick and funeral clubs, penny savings banks, canteens managed by working men, and, like Owen's New Lanark, a community store which undercut standard retail prices. By his own reckoning, thanks to 'an intelligence that was the offspring of the Factory Act, a much better feeling had prevailed between employers and employed in their works'.

Ackroyd epitomized the model employer of the Social Science Association and moral economy or morally-adjusted economics as seen by the capitalist. Just as the Association provided ratification for the social commitment of professional men, so too it validated the moral credentials of certain kinds of capitalists. The new model employer bore a family resemblance to the ideal of the earlier mill-owning statisticians who had provided a model village which aimed to make a factory family out of themselves and their employees. The attempt to extend family into class relations (also the project of the women social workers) characterized the social morality of the employer and provided the moral corrective to the deficiencies of political economy. Compared with the old statisticians, the new model employer now supported regulatory legislation for women and children and accepted working men as adult members of the social family. The latter recognition involved support for collective working-class self-help, not only the easy kind which admitted patronage (like the Ackroyds' benefit clubs and canteen) but sometimes even trade unions.[43]

This capacity to combine and organize into groups to achieve an objective identified the true working class in the discussions of the Social Economy Department. Before 1868, discussion in other Departments assumed that the 'respectable' working class and the 'residuum' had altogether different individual psychologies and moral natures. Specialists in reformatory work tended to argue that the respectable working man had self-discipline which enabled him to carry on regular work, postpone immediate gratification and plan for the future. A member of the perishing and dangerous class, by contrast, lived only for the moment. But the Social Economy Department emphasized the social capacity of the respectable working class rather than individual psychology. The increasing tendency towards combination marked a healthy sign of maturity and progress. Mobilizing the language of development from child to adulthood and allowing the working classes to grow up, the Reverend Blaikie observed how

classes of society, like individuals have their periods of infancy and childhood, when they are so far dependent on others; but if the spirit of dependence survive the natural period of feebleness, nothing but evil can ensue. The working classes of this country have recently been discovering that they can do far more for themselves especially by the union of their energies and resources, than they used to think possible. It is no longer an idle dream to think of building their own houses, relieving their own sick, providing for their own old age, and even, as the co-operative experiment has shown, carrying on for their own benefit large and remunerative

165

undertakings. The discovery of what self-reliance can do, under wise regulation, and above all under God's blessing, seems likely to bring in a new era for the working masses of our country.[44]

Collective self-help supplied at once an index and an agency of improvement. In the words of political economist W. Stanley Jevons, 'association...is alike the sign and means of civilisation'.[45] Even the most ambivalent form, trade unions, provided an important 'education in the art of self-government'.[46]

This new-found middle-class tolerance towards working-class combinations provided a ground for discussion and even some space for consensus which had not existed before. Working-class activists read papers, took part in discussion and received an attentive hearing as experts in the Social Economy Department. When the question of industrial partnership as a form of co-operation first came up in 1865, socialist and co-operator G. J. Holyoake, not a factory owner, gave the keynote paper. The area of shared assumption was broad, even if some large fences of partition remained. Many unionists and co-operators also saw a crucial division in the working class between self-maintaining labour and the poor. Although this distinction did not often occur in their SSA papers, other works contained the dual model. Christian Socialist J. M. Ludlow, and active co-operator Lloyd Jones began their account of the *Progress of the Working Class* (1867) with an emphatic definition

> The terms 'working class', 'working men', will...be taken in their every-day acceptation, as meaning those who work, chiefly with their muscles for wages, and maintain themselves thereby....It is not indeed intended to deal with 'the Poor',—i.e., those who may work but cannot habitually maintain themselves otherwise than by an occasional glimpse at some of their efforts to raise themselves into the true working class.[47]

There was further agreement that the true working class could be identified by membership in a combination: 'if there is one thing more axiomatically certain than another', Ludlow and Jones insisted, it is that the worst work is and must always be done by others than the members of such societies....the East End workers being either entirely without organization, or their attempts at organization proving repeatedly abortive through the lowness of their wages and the demoralization thereby produced among them.

A fundamental difference remained. The writers from the working-class movement recognized that the respectable workers and the poor did not belong to separate species of human being. The capacity to organize was constrained by environmental factors beyond the control of individual acts of will and no constraint operated more powerfully than low wages. The SSA provides a window for observing how some sections of the middle class, from 1868 onward, moved to the same point of view.

How far they had moved before 1868 also needs underlining. Between 1830 and 1850, the middle class had regarded labour combinations and especially trade unions, as anathema. The statisticians, for example, had represented them as social dynamite ignited by that most dangerous of social types, the outside agitator, who fired up honest but gullible working men. Now SSA members dismantled this construction and moved the organized working class to more dignified linguistic ground. Interestingly the language now being used to analyse the relation between capital and labour became the metaphor of the market, with the working man depicted as a 'seller' or 'commodity' in the market place or, at best, a labouring capitalist who could sidestep the worst pitfalls in the market square. Even the Christian Socialists and co-operators who took exception to employers putting 'the lives of their men on the same principles as those on which they treated a dead commodity', still used the market model. Instead of being a detraction from humanity, some like Reverend Blaikie felt that the use of political economy categories to depict a group signified a tribute to its development. Only as a group progressed did it become able to conform to the 'laws of political economy'.[48]

In a complete turnabout from the position twenty years before, the majority of SSA spokesmen now joined working-class figures in defending trade unions as necessary to equalize the power of capital and labour in the bargaining process. Only trade unions could give single working men the power to produce a genuine trial of strength. Even Sir Archibald Alison, once the sworn enemy of trade unions in deed as well as word, arrived at this position. In 1860, Alison accepted that

> trades unions are indispensable to compensate for the weight of capital in an advanced community; that such is the concentrated power of capital...that, unless men combine together and meet the power by the organisation of numbers...there must inevitably ensue from the principle of competition, the prostration of industry manacled in the fetters of capital....trades unions in themselves are not only proper, but a necessary balance in the fabric of society. I think without them capital would become far too powerful, and workmen would be beaten down.[49]

New model manufacturers like Samuel Pope, and trade unionists like J. Dunning of the Consolidated Society of Bookbinders used the same arguments to put their case. Even former socialist missionaries, Lloyd Jones and Alexander Campbell, once the prophets of the New Moral World which would transcend the pathetic rivalries of the market place, now preached the vital defensive role of trade unions.[50]

But strikes remained the stumbling block. Of all the avenues of working-class advance, the SSA gave trade unions the rockiest passage. Just as they had dealt with varieties of feminism, SSA members now selected from the working-class movement those forms of organization which looked most attractive or least threatening, and helped these to survive and grow. The Committee on Trades Societies and Strikes suggested two alternatives. A majority proposed that unions keep their present form but that independent arbitration machinery be created, possibly by the government. A minority suggested that unions be turned into friendly societies and their bargaining powers be turned over to 'united associations' of capitalists and workmen.[51] From the mid-1860s the printed papers tended to deal with arbitration rather than the legitimacy of trades unions. Practising what it preached, in 1870, the Association's Labour and Capital Committee, with Liberal MP and Nottingham hosiery manufacturer A. J. Mundella as a leading member, began to offer its services as an independent mediator in a series of labour disputes across the country.[52]

From the first Congress, SSA members preferred some form of co-operative enterprise as the way forward. Many contributors to the debate on combinations not only worried about strikes but more profoundly about the model of the market place which perpetuated competition between classes and made strikes an intrinsic tendency of economic life.[53] At an important Sessional Meeting in 1868, co-operators, Christian Socialists and even trade unionists urged the need for a new vision of the relations between capital and labour. Chaired by Gladstone, the meeting attracted a wide cross-section of influential people to consider a set of resolutions incorporating SSA 'party lines'. But any resolution which suggested, even inadvertently, that the present interests of capital and labour were identical sparked such heated opposition that several had to be amended or withdrawn, while the contentious meeting went on for so long that it had to be adjourned.

Old conventional wisdom visibly toppled. Dr Kay-Shuttleworth moved the first resolution which deplored strikes and claimed that they showed 'lamentable ignorance of the natural laws which regulate wages'. J. M. Ludlow briskly rejoined that strikes, on the contrary, proceeded naturally from

> a scientific education in political economy...erected into a rule of society and of mutual relations between man and man. Upon that footing, which started from the self interest of each class, there was no reconcilement possible.

Seconding Ludlow's amendment to cut out the offensive passages, Robert Applegarth, general secretary of the Amalgamated Society of Carpenters and Joiners, said that he disliked strikes but 'believed that as long as the present competitive system lasted they could not be put an end to, and they would cease only when there was an identity of interest between workmen and masters'. Ludlow's amendment carried.[54]

Co-operative theory and institutions would accomplish the social alchemy of welding together the interests of capital and labour. As Professor Fawcett argued,

> a completely effectual remedy would be provided if the capital which is needed to support and assist labour were owned by the labourers themselves....The interests of

capital and labour would be merged and would therefore cease to be antagonistic. Such an association as that just described would represent a very high form of social and economic development.[55]

While consumer co-operation got the SSA seal of approval, it was co-operative production and industrial co-partnership which really caught the imagination of members. These forms of industrial organization enabled the workman, although often in the most limited way, to share in the profits and thus to become a capitalist of sorts, instead of a mere vendor of labour. Some members, like John Holmes, felt that co-operative factories, financed and run by working men, like the Rochdale or Leeds flour mills, represented the ultimate development of the principle. Other members, like H. C. Briggs, owner of the Whitwood Collieries, advocated partnerships in which workers could buy shares or where, as in his own firm, a fixed proportion of the annual profits was added to wages.[56] Industrial partnership had the attraction for employers that it motivated workers but did not expropriate the capitalist or indeed abrogate his power. Most members in the Social Economy Department thought all forms of co-operation good and were still discussing the subject long after trade unions had disappeared from the agenda. Co-operation promised a veritable philosopher's stone, bringing harmony where there had been hostility, transforming conflict into ethically defensible mutual aid.

FROM THE DANGEROUS CLASSES
TO THE UNEMPLOYED

An organized working class, capable of militant class consciousness and concerted class action, might be expected to cause the most anxiety in the SSA. Instead, the urban destitute who did not have the capacity for collective self-help provoked the maximum concern and possibly fear. Anthropologists have noticed that the forces which are socially central in any culture may not be symbolically central so that the real dynamic of power may not occupy the centre of social attention or become the focus of desire.[57] The next chapter will explore some of these (subterranean) directions. Here the context of class relations in

Britain in the mid-1860s will be further probed. The year 1868 keeps recurring as an important moment in SSA discussion. Besides the turbulent Sessional Meeting on Wages and Capital, another took place, chaired by the Bishop of London, on 'How to Deal with the Unemployed Poor of London and with its "Roughs" and Criminal Classes'.[58] In the end this meeting led to the formation of the Charity Organisation Society, the dominating feature in the landscape of scientific philanthropy until the First World War. The year 1868 marked a shift of focus onto the adult male poor and the beginnings of new ways to classify 'the dangerous class' which removed some sections from this linguistic refuse bin.

Until 1868, the perspective of women social workers dominated in the Social Science Association and the spotlight often fell on the children of the dangerous class. The concept of the dangerous class had been building cumulatively since 1848 and had become an accretion of criminal, pauper, ignorant, immoral and organically diseased elements, a comprehensive syndrome of disorder which, as the 1850s drew on, began to shed its political layer. A large number at risk also stood on the periphery, in danger of contamination, invoking the disease metaphor, or sliding fast into the mire, if the imagery of falling and rescue or raising prevailed. In 1849, in his book on educating children, J.C. Symons argued that 'every country has its dangerous class. It consists not only of criminals, paupers and persons whose conduct is obnoxious to the interests of society, but of the proximate body of people who are within reach of its contagion and continually swell its number'.[59] Central for the SSA, Mary Carpenter formulated a definition of the children of the 'perishing and dangerous classes' as

> those who have not yet fallen into actual crime, but who are almost certain from their ignorance, destitution, and the circumstances in which they are growing up, to do so, if a helping hand be not extended to raise them:— these form the *perishing classes*—those who have already received the prison brand, or, if the mark has not yet visibly set upon them, are notoriously living by plunder—who unblushingly acknowledge that they can gain more for the support of themselves and their parents by stealing than working—whose hand is against

every man for they know not that any man is their brother:—these form the *dangerous classes*.[60]

Despite the damning names 'perishing and dangerous', the children raised in these classes were not held responsible for their condition. *Sans discernement*, in Carpenter's words, their character had been shaped by a family environment that lay beyond their control. Early discussion in the SSA revolved around supporting the existing family or supplying a more effective replacement family usually in the form of a institutional Home. In the Punishment and Reformation Department, the range of institutions proposed by Carpenter and being established 'experimentally' in many places received attention. The causal analysis did not extend far beyond problem families, although, following the lead of the Public Health Department, the urban environment of overcrowded, dilapidated housing and public filth was seen as a cause of family disintegration.[61] In the Social Economy Department, the discussion about pauperism or the Poor Law borrowed liberally from the reformatory movement. Before 1868 the discussion centred very much on 'children of the state' and the institutions which could remove them from the contaminating atmosphere of an 'indiscriminately' mixed workhouse.

In 1868, the spotlight shifted dramatically from children to able-bodied adults. Yet again this refocusing took place in the aftermath of a multiple crisis. That powerful mixture of plague and riot, which automatically raised the level of ruling class alarm, occurred again. In 1866, during a trade recession, the last cholera epidemic of the nineteenth century hit London. In the same year, as part of the campaign to give working men the vote, a demonstration in Hyde Park escalated into riots lasting for several days. The prospect of allowing working men into the citizenry provoked an outpouring of hyperbolic literature, pulsating with millenarian hope or fear.[62] For some, like Carlyle, this 'leap in the Dark', to use the Earl of Derby's phrase, amounted to a headlong plunge into catastrophe. For the progressive Liberals and the Tory philanthropists of the Social Science Association, the prospect did not appear so terrible because the line had been so carefully drawn to bring only the organized working class into the pale of the Constitution, and keep out those who could accurately now be called 'the residuum', the people excluded from the body politic. To a hostile observer like Matthew Arnold whose polemic *Culture and Anarchy* (1869) was written in response to the 1866 riots and the 1867 reform, a deadening alliance had been formed between the industrial middle class and the organized working class: both were philistines. Arnold saw the residuum as a different animal, and actually described it as an awakened beast, getting wildly intoxicated on the heady brew of Englishmen's freedoms.[63]

The 1867 Reform Act marked the culmination of a process of class accommodation which had probably begun in the 1840s. Between the French Revolution and the repeal of the Corn Laws in 1846, the attitude of the groups with social power, including Evangelicals, capitalists, local authorities and successive governments, had been consistently hostile to the organized working class. Even the repeal of the Combination Acts in 1825, which made trade unions legal, was expected to result in unions just withering away. Whether using a velvet glove of criminal law and due process (e.g. transporting the Tolpuddle martyrs or the Glasgow Cotton Spinners) or the iron fist of physical force (Peterloo right through to the Plug Plot suppression), the basic aim was to defeat and destroy working-class combination. But the seemingly endless resurgence of working-class effort, the unstoppable tides of trade unions, socialism, Chartism, coming in continual waves, finally helped to channel effort from above into new directions. The working-class movement could not be wished or bludgeoned away: increasingly perceived as a permanent feature on the landscape, it began to win the respect due to a formidable foe.

From the mid-1840s, as Chapter 3 indicated, the urban Liberal plutocracy who were priming themselves to take political power in their localities and who were beginning to savour the sweet smell of midcentury business success began to operate a new strategy. Instead of confrontation, they provided counter-attraction and offered selective solidarity. Their local Tory counterparts often began to follow suit. They all created a rival notion of citizenship which did not yet include the franchise but which stressed participation in civic life and cultural institutions, providing a safer alternative to the cultural forms that working people, with great financial difficulty, had provided for themselves. Hence the outcropping of 'public' facilities like libraries, parks and Town Halls which absorbed or dwarfed working-class efforts like the Halls of Science. The working-class movement through its resistance had forced concessions. The concessions produced a compromise solution which did not give any of the contenders exactly what they wanted but offered enough that could be accepted by all.

The 1867 reform can be seen as one further move in the same game. To a bourgeoisie already skilled in counter-attraction or in finding tolerable versions of problematic social forms, the franchise could be hedged around to allow entry only to the most skilled working men who belonged to labour movements which might be guided to become even more acceptable. M.D. Hill admitted, however grudgingly, that trade unions no longer demanded 'the equal division of unequal earnings'; Lord Brougham, President of the SSA until his death, contrasted Owen's old-style 'communistic principles' with the mature co-operation of the present which 'gives all the rights and independence of individuals with all the benefits of joint labours'.[64] Many SSA members supported the extension of the vote to self-governing working men and then helped in the succeeding decade to construct a legal framework which enabled some forms of labour combinations to exist rather than others. Co-opting a part of the working class into the citizenry still left out the lowest of the poor who still preoccupied so much midcentury social science and professional service. The franchise crisis also led to their being considered in a new way.

With the 1867 searchlight so glaringly directed onto adult males of the population, the adult males in the perishing classes were also thrown into bold relief. In the SSA, the return of 'good times' occasioned what became the continuous obsession with relief for the able-bodied adult male pauper. Most puzzling was the revelation that London pauperism was actually increasing at a time of 'extraordinary prosperity'. The workhouse as a satisfactory means for coping with this emergency came into question. As Dr Stallard argued, 'one insuperable objection to indoor relief for the able-bodied....was that it practically prevented their seeking work'.[65] In 1868 the Social Economy Department set the special question 'to what Classes and on what Conditions should Outdoor Relief be Administered', while in the same year, W.R. Lloyd offered a prize for the best essay 'on the Employment of Workmen in Casual Distress'. The discussion, which had been conducted before in terms of the 'dangerous classes', now began to revolve around the 'unemployed' as well.

The smoke had not yet cleared from the 1867 eruptions and the scent of political danger still lingered in the air. But rather than use the Arnoldian image of the beast awakening and rampaging, Social Science Association members talked of industrious men falling downward into the perishing 'roughs'. If allowed to become frustrated and desperate, they would become brutalized and ripe for manipulation by the real dangerous classes, either hardened criminals or revolutionary agitators. Thomas Webster, QC, and his colleague in land reclamation schemes, C.P. Measor, made these arguments, as did the Reverend Henry Solly, a dedicated patron of the Working-Man's Club and Institute Union and soon to become editor of the *Bee-Hive*. Solly spoke of the wholesome extension of the vote to a respectable portion of the working class but pointed out that a huge residue remained:

> the great mass of rough, unmoral and uneducated physical force which we have been contemplating, some portion only half employed and half fed, another portion already tainted with dispositions to crime, is always in danger, under provocation, of combining with the actually criminal and violent cases for the illegal assertion of its power, or for purposes of plunder.[66]

Solly proposed a package of measures including a radical version of supervision and organization, the first involving the revival of the Saxon system of 'frank pledge' and the second involving the extension of friendly societies to the roughs. But the most important lifeline of rescue was to be employment.

In its most baffling form, the problem of unemployment was seen as an urban problem rather than as a problem of the factory system or of capitalism in general. The issue of factory unemployment had arisen only once in SSA discussions, during the unique emergency of the Lancashire 'cotton famine' caused by the American civil war. It is true that R. Arthur Arnold, an Inspector of Public Works, carried off first prize in the Association's essay competition by drawing upon his Lancashire experience and urging that public works be provided on a temporary basis. But his solutions attracted social science colleagues only to the extent that they could be applied to an altogether different group, now beginning to be noticed again for the first time since Mayhew's survey—the chronically unemployed or underemployed in the great cities. London became the paradigm city, East London the critical laboratory. Not least, discussions became London-centred because a familiar group of London-based professional men made the study of the labour market and unemployment their speciality.

Barrister A. H. Hill won the second prize for his essay. He began by distinguishing between the temporary unemployed of Lancashire and the urban unemployed 'in a chronic state of difficulty—though not in chronic destitution'. Hill then isolated two groups of underemployed workmen who previously would have been lumped, more or less indiscriminately, into the perishing and dangerous classes. The first contained labourers trapped in the annual cycle of seasonal employment like dockworkers and building labourers 'whose employment at the best of times is but casual and uncertain, and dependent as they literally are on wind and weather for their bread, their incomes must always be of a slender and fluctuating nature'. The second category contained redundant labour displaced by technological innovation, 'the class...which draws its scanty wages from the rapidly dying trades which still survive in East London and elsewhere—especially hand-loom weaving'. The residue again were depicted as a 'semi-criminal', perishing and dangerous class:

> this Class which is a very large one, I can only designate by the name of 'the incompetent class', and consists of the great mass of the weakly poor, as well as the rough, idle and unemployed fellows whom the accretion of great cities, the inefficiency of our Poor Laws, and the want of a thorough system of industrial training have bred up in our midst.[67]

Colleagues of Hill's, like Denison and C. P. B. Bosanquet, supplied variations on this theme of classifying the poor submerged beneath artisan level. Their categories did not prove to be watertight compartments but phases on an urban employment continuum which moved from an artisan ceiling down to quasi-criminal depths. Significantly, as Mayhew had earlier recognized, many of the phases were distinguished by factors beyond individual control like the level of wages and the regularity of work. The poor in these phases began to be represented as victims rather than villains, as social casualties rather than vicious dropouts, although middle-class analysts found it impossible to rid themselves of their moral disgust.[68] However much Hill, Denison and Bosanquet wanted to cling to the midcentury truism that thrift offered the remedy for destitution, the idea came under severe strain in their minds.[69]

Unlike Mayhew, however, these professional men were not prepared to press beyond the limits of capitalist political economy to discover some dynamic responsible for creating all forms of unemployment. Their solutions were more evasive than subversive. To the question of why some urban jobs provided only low wages and intermittent work, they had the hackneyed old answer—over-supply of labour. Within this framework they practised what could almost be called the SSA golden rule: divide and remedy. Hill's nostrum, supported by all the others, did not involve remodelling the structure of industry, but rescuing surplus men from it by increasing their mobility. By means of a national system of Labour Exchanges, linked to the Post Office, men in redundant or seasonal trades could be matched with available jobs all over the country. For the 'incompetents', Hill suggested evening industrial training centres which could be attached to the Labour Exchanges as well as public works programmes sponsored by philanthropic backers with the help of low-interest government loans.[70] The irredeemables would be consigned to the slender mercies of the Poor Law.

As a new twist in the analysis, Hill discovered the source of surplus labour in the accelerating migration of people from the countryside. He observed that the new arrivals to the city made up a large part of the vagrant population who then tended to drift into the range of unskilled jobs which inevitably led to urban pauperism. The focus on migration produced a noteworthy change in attitude to yet another section of the poor: some vagrants won a reprieve from the charge of criminality. In the bourgeois imaginary, vagrants epitomized everything subhuman: they wandered like animals or savages and did not have that most basic of human attributes, a carefully ordered home. Even Hill, in 1868, had called the 'incompetent' class only 'semi-criminal' to distinguish it from the real criminal class 'of vagrants'. Having established the Central Employment Agency in 1871, he began to appreciate that a part of the vagrant population included industrious country folk 'on the tramp', forced to uproot themselves and look for work in the city. These he dubbed 'wayfarers', not vagrants, and insisted on more considerate treatment for them in the casual wards of workhouses.[71] More importantly, he began to feel that a clearer idea of the economic pressures underlying national population movements would lead to more useful solutions.

By the end of the 1860s, Poor Law and employment experts began to think in terms of a 'national' social economy. The fundamental axes of the model were not the rural village and the factory system as in the 1830s but the agricultural districts and the urban jobscape. Given the country–city model, remedies had to be applied at both terminals. Country analysts borrowed from their city cousins to create incentives to keep the agricultural labourer on the land. Proposals for regularizing wages throughout the year included public works in winter, migration to higher-wage agricultural areas, a decasualization scheme (to continue wages during bad weather and illness), profit-sharing farming, and support for labour combinations of all kinds, including the Agricultural Labourers' Union.[72] Shunting traffic in the opposite direction, SSA members like Thomas Webster urged that city paupers be organized into agricultural communities for the reclamation of wastelands. Drawing on a philanthropic tradition stretching back at least to Robert Owen in 1817, these students of social science created yet another point of contact with working-class thinking of the late 1860s although not so close and cordial a point of contact as their positive attitude toward trade unions and co-operatives.[73] For some months it remained an open question whether the Charity Organisation Society (COS) would become an agency for organizing the cultivation of wastelands.

Intimately tied to the Social Science Association, the COS occupied a key position in practical social science at least until the First World War.[74] The COS is conventionally seen as the strict custodian of the 'moral view' of the poor, because it linked poverty to individual character and separated the poor into categories of 'deserving' and 'undeserving' for treatment. Yet the key figures who founded the COS were actually salvaging groups of the poor from the moral rubbish tip by creating an increasingly rounded model of the environmental factors responsible for urban poverty. The wastelands project quickly dropped off the agenda, not due to lack of support but because a separate company aiming to raise capital was deemed a more suitable agency. COS founders did not narrow their view of the causes of poverty; with A.H. Hill as the first Secretary, the employment focus remained. However they assigned the new organization a more limited task, of co-ordinating voluntary and statutory provision for the poor in a locality, in order to attack the old enemies of indiscriminate almsgiving and unconditional doles. They saw themselves as one flank of the large army aiming to 'eradicate pauperism'. Effort now went into organizing the COS as a parish vetting body, devising the system of family casework in the process, to direct applicants to the appropriate agency for their needs.[75] Starting in London, the COS tried to spread its philosophy and methods nationwide by mounting national Conferences in the early 1880s which became regular events from 1890 onward as well as by launching several periodicals, the most important of which, the *Charity Organisation Review*, started in 1885, just as the SSA was collapsing.

The SSA's capacity to provide space for durable perspectives and to produce vigorous institutional offspring helped, paradoxically, to undermine it over time. To dismiss the Association's members as 'the Schoolmen of the nineteenth century' who crusted into obsolescence by the mid-1880s and lost touch with new realities does not adequately describe the complex clutter of the later social science scene, with its residual, dominant and emergent intellectual elements. The next two chapters will explore some key changes but here continuities also need stressing. The SSA type of approach to poverty, which moved in two strategic directions at once, towards increasing environmentalism and increasing fragmentation, still loomed large in early-twentieth century social science. The early work of William Beveridge, for example, like his paper on the 'Problem of the Unemployed', read to the Sociological Society in 1906, rehearsed the arguments of his classic book of 1910 and tried to prove that the 'unemployed problem is industrial and not merely personal'. His typology of the 'industrial causes of distress' bore a striking resemblance to the categories earlier developed by SSA members. Not only did he subdivide the unemployed into familiar groupings, but prescribed familiar treatment for each category on the divide and remedy principle.[76]

179

Previous analysts have diagnosed the decline of the SSA in terms of its increasing irrelevance to a changed political situation marked by the rise of the Liberal Party, which took over and politicized some issues of concern, and the resurgence of socialism.[77] While these developments played a part in hastening its death, the Social Science Association was also devoured by its own progeny. Throughout its career and especially from the late 1860s, the Association spawned specialist conferences and groups which sometimes 'took off' into their own independent existence and long outlived their incubating host. Bodies concerned with pauperism, or as it began to be called, the poverty question or with women's work, illustrate this pattern of growth. From 1871, the SSA ran annual conferences for Poor Law Guardians which then became a Central Committee of Poor Law Conferences in 1877. The COS most spectacularly outlived and outshone its parent. Formed under SSA auspices in 1859, the Society for Promoting the Employment of Women applied for registration under the Companies Act in 1878 and was still operating at the turn of the century. The Ladies' Sanitary Association also enjoyed a vigorous existence until the turn of the century when its amateurs turned professional. The bodies concerned with poverty or health grew vigorously in the ecology of social science which developed in the 1880s: Chapter 8 will explore their function and a new phase of professionalization in a changing social organism. But before the new phase can come under the microscope, a powerful discursive growth requires examination. Not only did the body metaphor affect the depiction of the very poorest social groups and reverse the linguistic rescue of many of the casual poor but it shaped the understanding of society as a whole in ways which remained important well into the twentieth century.

Part III

TWENTIETH-CENTURY CENTURY DIRECTIONS

7

BODY METAPHOR IN SOCIAL SCIENCE, 1850-1930

By the late nineteenth century, organic and evolutionary perspectives had become pervasive in British social science. Historians have observed and contextualized this development in different ways. Intellectual historian John Burrow, for example, has shown how the concern with evolutionary laws which held throughout the whole of the natural and social world produced a vision of a meaningful universe which could fill the vacuum left for some intellectuals by the decline of Utilitarianism and the collapse of Evangelical faith. Historian of science Robert Young has insisted on 'the mutual constitutiveness of scientific and social thought', a process which Engels and other earlier commentators felt demanded a robust exposé:

> The whole Darwinist teaching of the struggle for existence is simply a transference from society to living nature, of Hobbes' doctrine *bellum omnium contra omnes* (war of all against all) and of the bourgeois-economic doctrine of competition, together with Malthus's theory of population. When this conjuror's trick has been performed...the same theories are transferred back again from organic nature into history and it is now claimed that their validity as eternal laws of human society has been proved.[1]

This chapter will also look at some of the same material but from a different angle. Within evolutionary thinking, the focus will fall specifically on key representations, from 1850 onwards, of society as a human or as another organic body. This use of body

183

metaphor figures as a recent variation on an ancient theme. Anthropologists like Mary Douglas have shown how many cultures, at many times and in many places have used an image of the human body to represent an ordered social system. Conversely the same people have used images of the grotesque or dehumanized body to convey social disorder. Rabelais' work, as interpreted by the Soviet critic Bakhtin, explodes with grotesque popular bodies which, with their enormous bulk, huge noses and noisy anuses, challenge official (classical and Christian) ideals of order. Historians of seventeenth-century England will readily remember how conservatives attacked radicals for wanting to deform the body politic into 'a many-headed monster'. Herbert Spencer recognized that 'a perception' positing 'some analogy between the body political and a living individual body, was early reached and has from time to time re-appeared in literature', but only in his time, with the advent of 'physiological science' did the perception become less vague and less fanciful.[2]

In a new development from the 1850s onward, body metaphor became intertwined with a discourse of biology so that figures of speech became transformed into scientific truths. This alchemy biologized social differences and turned social inequalities into natural inequalities. By means of a metaphor which often cast different social groups as different bodily parts, relations of social power involving dominance and subordination, control and being controlled, superiority and inferiority, value and invalidity could be presented as facts, even as laws of nature. The use of body metaphor amounted to more than an interesting intellectual shift. It had very real intellectual consequences in terms of patterning experience and of highlighting or blurring certain features of social life, and it had very real social consequences especially for the poor. Nancy Stepan is right to argue that 'a theory of metaphor is as critical to science as it is to the humanities'.[3] This chapter will explore three versions of body metaphor in British social science and their implications for the construction and treatment of the poor. Finally, I will speculate on why body metaphor should have become so dominant in the bourgeois social science of the period.

THE STATIC PHYSIOLOGICAL BODY IN SANITARY SCIENCE AND IN THE SSA

This version of body metaphor became widespread in the 1850s and drew upon two existing traditions. In one model of the social body, the bourgeois male was held up as the head (of the family and the household as well as of society), and his wife, daughter or sister formed the heart. The working classes, as Dickens savagely noted in *Hard Times*, were often called the hands: political economy writing, like Andrew Ure's *Philosophy of Manufactures*, sometimes characterized operatives as the 'muscular system' of the industrial organism. Increasingly, as Leonore Davidoff and others have shown, domestic servants became associated with the lower parts and back passages of newly remodelled bourgeois houses and with the actual care of these areas of bourgeois bodies.[4] Within the emerging fields of sanitary and of moral science, the representation moved a stage further and the casual poor (in distinction to the true working classes) began to be represented as excrement, as polluting fluid, or as drains. The Reverend Sidney Godolphin Osborne, brother-in-law of the Reverend Charles Kingsley, made perhaps the most extravagant use of caecal imagery in the influential essay on 'Immortal Sewerage', written for *Meliora* in 1853. In the same piece, Osborne used other equally noxious phrases to describe very poor people without fixed homes. He called them 'living nastiness', 'human nuisances', 'moral miasmas', 'immortal refuse', 'draining of civilization', 'festering mass of depraved physical matter', 'deep dirt-pools of social life', 'social drainage', 'cesspool of moral depravity'.[5]

Osborne was working with a model of the social body which concentrated attention on the matter flowing in and out of the lower openings and which drew upon a tradition stemming from Scottish Enlightenment medicine's concern with physiology. From the 1830s onward, public health activists tried to transpose views of organic physiology to the social body with greater or lesser success. Thus Kay-Shuttleworth drew upon views of an organism having a monitoring and regulating sensibility but found that the social body was not as perfectly organized to achieve harmony among its members and hoped that statistical inquiry could supply some of the sensory deficit. His collaborator on Poor Law inquiries, Dr Southwood Smith, developed ideas of physiology as a continual circulation of supply and waste, and extended this view to the vital processes of a healthy city.[6] In the 1840s public health reformers, who were developing sanitary science, highlighted any instances of close proximity between the poor and excrement. Chadwick, a good mirror of metaphoric fashions, described a Glasgow tenement in terms of interlocking courtyards of excrement:

> the first was occupied entirely as a dung receptacle of the most disgusting kind. Beyond this court the second passage led to a second square court, occupied in the same way by its dunghill; and from this court there was yet a third passage leading to a third court, and third dungheap.[7]

By the 1850s, a further slippage had occurred. Observers not only pictured the very poor as living near excrement but actually as excrement. This powerful new representation overlapped with the concept of the perishing and dangerous classes from reformatory science. The Reverends Osborne and Kingsley became active in the Public Health Department of the Social Science Association where discussions added this new representation of the poor as body refuse to the existing view of the urban poor as particularly prone to physical disease and other forms of disorder.

The work of Mary Douglas on *Purity and Danger: An Analysis of Concepts of Pollution and Taboo* can help to illuminate this new representation. She argues that if the body represents ordered society, and its boundaries are protective walls, then the openings of the body as the most vulnerable places can easily become real foci of anxiety. What flows in and out of the openings has tremendous disruptive potential. In Douglas's words:

> The body is a model which can stand for any bounded system. Its boundaries can represent any boundaries which are threatened or precarious....We cannot possibly interpret rituals concerning excreta, breast milk, saliva and the rest unless we are prepared to see in the body a symbol of society, and to see the powers and dangers credited to social structure reproduced in small on the human body.[8]

Douglas provides a perspective to help explain why excrement and prostitution became two issues of obsessive concern in mid-Victorian sanitary and moral science. Both defecation and sex concentrate on lower body openings and both involve the exit and ingress of matter seen as dangerous to social order.

Prostitution, called 'the great social evil' from the mid-1850s onwards, involved a trespass through body openings which threatened social order in several ways. Not only were prostitutes anomalous 'public women' who actually did business with their sex (sacred equipment for motherhood), but they created social confusion by having sexual relations with clients from a higher social class. Dr William Acton rehearsed some further dangers at the Public Health Department of the Social Science Association only to find his medical lobby eventually being confronted by an equally spirited group of women in social science who adopted prostitutes as their special concern (Chapter 5). Acton argued that prostitutes, via their clients, introduced pollution in the form of venereal disease into respectable family dynasties, and when prostitutes married and disappeared back into the ordinary population they bred offspring who further threatened the quality of the national race. The case for the Contagious Diseases Acts, subjecting prostitutes to medical inspection but never troubling their clients, rested on the further claim that prostitutes were contaminating the armed forces on whom the defence of the nation's boundaries depended, or, to draw on body metaphor again, on whom the protection of the body politic relied. Yet in a contradictory way, as Alain Corbin has shown with relation to France, prostitutes also played a kind of useful role by acting as human sewers (putrefying themselves in the process) and draining off excess male sexuality which also diluted middle-class vigour.[9]

Whether pictured as contaminators or drains, prostitutes were being rubbished with body imagery. Josephine Butler, leader of the great crusade against the Contagious Diseases Acts, immediately grasped the connection between linguistic violence and social coercion. In her book *The Constitution Violated*, the title brilliantly embodying the connection between the body physical and the body politic, she repudiated the argument that prostitutes 'ought to be "treated as foul sewers are treated, as physical facts and not as moral agents"'. She continued,

Sewers have neither souls nor civil rights; by admitting into their political theory the idea that any class of human beings whatever may be reduced to the level of an inanimate nuisance for political purposes, these writers have demonstrated...the intimate connection between a growing materialism and the most cruel and oppressive despotism.[10]

There is no need to belabour the point about how the representation of groups of human beings as excrement or as sewers leads to and justifies exceedingly dominative intervention in their lives. Butler pointed to forcible gynaecological examination for prostitutes which she also more sensationally called instrumental rape by speculum. Interestingly, Osborne's essay did not end up calling for the detention of the homeless poor in labour camps, a demand which became fashionable among progressive social scientists at the turn of the twentieth century. Instead he proposed a kind of moral sewerage treatment plant in the form of schools and preaching stations aimed at the poorest groups.[11] Using organic metaphor does not necessarily preclude bringing about significant change by altering the social environment. However some other visions of the social body, which drew on biological imagery, did sometimes make the poor more unalterably unfit.

THE COMPETITIVE SOCIAL BODY IN HISTORICAL MOTION: EUGENICS AND SOCIAL HYGIENE

From a number of directions intellectual currents converged by the 1860s to create a mainstream of thought which set the social body into historical or evolutionary motion. The milestones usually cited include: Auguste Comte asserting the subordination of sociology to biology and accenting the alternation of organic and critical periods in his scheme of world history, Charles Lyell's geological work pointing to eons of continuous natural development rather than special providential intervention by God, Herbert Spencer's enunciation of the law of evolution or the development of natural and social organisms from the simple to the complex; and most importantly, perhaps,

188

the publication of Charles Darwin's *The Origin of Species* in 1859.[12] Historians have grouped much of the thinking which assumed the transferability of evolutionary perspectives between the natural and social world under the general category 'Social Darwinism'. But as Jones's study has shown, Social Darwinism had many varieties, and here I will point to some key features of the social body in the tradition as a whole and then concentrate on the variety of social body that figured in eugenics and social hygiene.

I want to focus on eugenics and social hygiene for a number of reasons. First, eugenics became a latter-day Darwin family hobby: not only did cousin Francis Galton (1822-1911), as gentleman scientist and mathematician, shape its basic emphasis and approach and fund its institutional apparatus, including a laboratory and professorship at London University, but Darwin's sons figured prominently in the Eugenics Education Society founded in 1908.[13] More importantly, eugenics carried one variety of body metaphor into the centre of social debate and into the Sociological Society (see p.233) where it jostled against other versions of the evolutionary social body being developed by progressive Liberal, Geddesite and Fabian sociologists. Indeed the eugenic vision even proved too bleak and non-interventionist both for con-servative meliorists and reformers who integrated eugenics into a field they called social hygiene which aimed to improve both nature and nurture at the same time. Sexologist Havelock Ellis (1859-1939) grandiloquently called social hygiene 'a develop-ment even a transformation, of what was formerly known as social reform'. 'It is the task of this hygiene', he announced, 'not only to make sewers but to re-make love.'[14]

In Social Darwinism more generally considered, populations of organisms took part in a demanding and difficult evolutionary drama where competition, 'struggle for existence', 'survival of the fittest' and 'natural (or artificial) selection of stocks' all featured. Mid-Victorian thinkers moved the more brutal forms of struggle between social organisms into earlier stages of evolution, or exported them geographically away to the colonies. They saw present European civilization being vitalized by vigorous free competition between individual organisms. In Darwin's own narrative about *The Descent of Man* (1871, 1874), the Malthusian imbalance between population growth and food supply had ensured a struggle for existence in early times both in terms of having to work hard to survive where too little food was available and in terms of warring with other tribes for command of the environment. Victory depended upon internal cohesion or, paradoxically, upon the development of 'the social instincts'. Struggle, in one form or another, could never be eliminated:

> Man, like every other animal, has no doubt advanced to his present high condition through a struggle for existence consequent upon his rapid multiplication; and if he is to advance still higher, it is to be feared that he must remain subject to a severe struggle. Otherwise he would sink into indolence, and the more gifted men would not be more successful in the battle of life than the less gifted.[15]

Neither Darwin nor Herbert Spencer put much emphasis on positive breeding policies although both worried about 'interference' with natural selection, particularly in the form of state or charitable aid to the poor, which would enable weaker stocks to survive without much struggle.[16]

Regarded by his contemporaries as the arch-proponent of struggle (he certainly celebrated the 'beneficial results of survival of the fittest'), Herbert Spencer actually underplayed power and conflict in his depiction of capitalist industrial society. Putting his own organic gloss on a romantic picture he shared with other provincial Liberals of the Manchester School, he portrayed industrial society as the most peaceful and co-operative, differentiated and integrated social organism yet evolved, which might even become a worldwide system of alert and intelligent activity. Spencer used the organic analogy to legitimize pure laissez-faire industrial capitalism; paradoxically he embraced the organic metaphor to refuse the vision of society as a 'manufacture'. In a Burkeian way, Spencer argued against purposive intervention in a social process where causes and consequences were complex and incalculable and where 'the social organism cannot be dealt with in any one part without all other parts being influenced in ways which cannot be foreseen': error resulted from regarding society as 'a manufacture; whereas it is a growth'.[17]

Spencer's favourite organic analogy was not so much to the

human body as to rudimentary organisms like the coelenterata which had developed an external system of organs for coping with the environment (food and enemies) and an internal system for 'sustenation'. In his three-stage model of social evolution—from primitive to militant to industrial society—he borrowed features from the coelenterata to characterize the militant phase, basically organized by com-pulsory co-operation for external offence and defence, and the industrial stage organized by means of voluntary co-operation for peaceable reproduction. For Spencer, war and industrial society, like oil and water, did not mix. His model could not make sense of the imperialist drama that began to dominate the late nineteenth-century scene except as a regression from the industrial to the militant phase of evolution, a 'rebarbarization', in his own words.[18]

From the 1890s, however, in the context of growing concern about Britain's chances in international economic and imperialist rivalry, contemporary conflict could not be denied and the key contestants became identified as social and especially as national organisms. Eugenics and social hygiene largely considered the social body coterminous with the nation-state: Social Darwinism could now almost be renamed National Darwinism. Although Galton's first eugenic texts appeared in the 1860s, eugenics really began to catch on from the 1890s and especially during the Boer War when issues of Britain's international viability became very salient. Eugenists saw the nation as composed of stocks or races of inferior or superior kinds and considered that national survival depended on the 'dominant fertility of its fitter stocks'. In the extreme views of Karl Pearson (1857-1936), Galton's crown prince of biometry and the leading academic in the field,

> the scientific view of a nation—is that of an organized whole, kept up to a high pitch of internal efficiency by insuring that its members are substantially recruited from the better stocks and kept up to a high pitch of external efficiency by contest, chiefly by way of war with inferior races, and with equal races by the struggle for trade routes and for sources of raw material and of food supply.[19]

While physical health formed an important part of racial vigour, especially after the shocking statistics about the poor physical

191

state of British army recruits to the Boer War, organizing intelligence provided the real key to the efficiency of the national organism in international survival. For Pearson,

> The nation, however prosperous, however hardy, however big, will fail when it comes to a crisis, when it is suddenly placed in a new environment, unless it has organized brain-power controlling its nervous system right away to the smallest outlying points.

Compared with the tremendous concentration on the openings of the lower body in the static body metaphor, the concentration in the Social and then National Darwinian discourse moved to the strong controlling head. The very poor were redefined to reflect this. 'Immortal sewerage' also became 'feeble-mindedness' or 'mental defect'. The lower parts of the body remained crucially implicated, because reproductive politics played such a central role, but only the individual and the social head would be able to regulate the lower parts of the body to ensure national vigour. Eugenists regarded intelligence or its absence as hereditary. They drew on the bias of their own tradition, especially Galton's rather haphazard research into 'golden families' (including his own) with a high endowment of what he called 'natural genius'. They also made use of the work of biologist August Weismann whose germ plasm theory gained wide acceptance at the same time that Gregor Mendel's genetic experiments were being rediscovered. Given the emphasis on heredity, and anxiety about the unfit multiplying too rapidly (because of low mental capacity coupled with social welfare support), eugenics moved away from the rhetoric of natural selection. Taking its cue instead from the managed breeding of animals, eugenics became obsessed with a positive and negative strategy for the 'rational' selection of stocks. The intelligent classes were urged to reproduce as a form of national service for men as well as for women. Dr C.W. Saleeby, in an article subtitled 'the New Scientific Patriotism' gave a new meaning to dying for one's country when he urged the less fit deliberately to renounce parenthood and allow their family dynasties to die out for the good of the country.[20] If they did not learn to curb their desires they should run the risk of being restrained.

Eugenists increasingly believed that the feeble-minded had a genetic mental defect which prevented them from exercising rational control. This defect could be described in different ways. H.H. Goddard, the widely-read American expert whose Vineland served as a pioneering custodial institution for 'feeble-minded girls', transposed Mendelian genetics from sweet peas to morons. He posited a recessive gene for feeble-mindedness, which produced a moron when present in double strength or created a dull worker type when appearing in combination with a gene for normal intelligence. He started the American hunt for concealed defectives who might appear normal but who carried the double-strength recessive gene which could only be detected by means of intelligence testing.[21] In Britain, all the old occupants of the category 'immortal sewerage' were now moved into the ranks of the 'feeble-minded'. According to Havelock Ellis, 'the association between prostitutes and feeble-mindedness is intimate'. Without a strong organizing head, they could not control their lower parts: 'feeble-minded girls, of fairly high grade, may often be said to be predestined to prostitution, if left to themselves, not because they are vicious, but because they are weak and have little power of resistance'. Ellis widened the net of feeble-mindedness to enmesh criminals and argued that 'closely related to the great feeble-minded class, and from time to time falling into crime, are the inmates of workhouses, tramps and the unemployable'.[22] The idea that these 'kind of people, all tending to be born a little defective' made up tribes of Ishmael who spread feeble-mindedness down the generations caught the imagination of eugenists and of legislators who set up a Royal Commission on the Care and Control of the Feeble-Minded and, in 1913, gave custodial powers to restrain the reproduction of large defective families.[23]

It is tempting to argue that women, within this eugenic version of body metaphor, would be regarded simply as the womb of society. However, to distinguish the superior breeding stock from the feeble-minded, great emphasis was placed on the value of women whose total range of qualities, intelligence included, had reached their highest perfection. Ellis's book on *Social Hygiene* spent much of its time discussing the position of women, an emphasis which needed no apology since

> The breeding of men lies largely in the hands of women. That is why the question of Eugenics is to a great extent one with the woman question. The realization of

eugenics in our social life can only be attained with the realization of the woman movement in its latest and completest phase as an enlightened culture of motherhood, in all that motherhood involves alike on the physical and the psychic sides. Motherhood on the eugenic basis is a deliberate and selective process, calling for the highest intelligence as well as the finest emotional and moral aptitudes, so that all the best energies of a long evolution of womanhood in the paths of modern culture here find their final outlet.[24]

Few women were recorded as taking part in Sociological Society discussions, but a woman who did, Mrs Meredith, now extended the communion of labour idea to eugenics when she reportedly spoke of

the emergence of the conscious woman's movement all over the world (by which she meant the taking by woman of her rightful place beside man in industry, art, science, religion, civil and political life, and last, but not least, in this matter of eugenics), the emergence of this movement coincided with, and was inextricably concerned in the other movement referred to by the lecturer, namely, the superseding of the idea of 'struggle for life' by that of 'mutual aid'....there was, at any rate, one point of view in which the biological and the sociological aspects found themselves fully harmonised, and that was the maternal point of view.[25]

In eugenics and social hygiene traces remained of the bogus analogy between colonial natives, women and workers as all more or less equivalently mentally infantile in terms of brain size; but a more graduated pecking order was also developing. Well-developed, educated women ranked higher than dull male worker types who ranked higher than mental defectives, including prostitutes, criminals and all the supposedly inferior dark races of the empire. Indeed some eugenic research, like that published by Alice Lee in 1902, was discrediting any connection between brain size in women and intelligence.[26]

The eugenic discussion 'of the comparative worth' of the black and white races strikes an historian inhabiting a more egalitarian paradigm as preposterous and offensive. Stephen

Gould has shown, after reanalysing the data of craniologists Samuel Morton and Paul Broca, how unquestioned assumptions about negro inferiority so deeply structured thought that they led to an inadvertent skulduggery, an intellectual cannibalism in the form of unintentional cooking of results. Galton provided a very slipshod example of scientific procedure when he simply asserted, without evidence, that negro averages and deviations were two grades below those of people 'with Anglo Saxon qualities', that there were virtually no superior types among negroes, few potential merchant types, but, invoking an earlier version of the category of feeblemindedness, that the incidence of 'half-witted men is very large'. To back this up, he referred to unnamed books about negro servants in America and his own first-hand experience in Africa: 'the mistakes the negroes made in their own matters were so childish, stupid, and simpleton-like, as frequently to make me ashamed of my own species'.[27]

In biometrics, the statistical distribution of ability in relation to class received more emphasis than the genetic mechanisms for producing embarrassments, workers or morons. From the time of the pioneering work of Adolphe Quételet in the 1830s, statistical regularities carried huge plausibility as genuine laws of nature. If one graph was good, two were better. Galton, in his famous Huxley lecture of 1901, superimposed Charles Booth's classification of the London poor onto his already existing standard deviation curve of natural ability (from *Hereditary Genius*, 1869) and found that the true working class, Booth's Class E, were fixed at the mediocre mean, while the intellectual classes formed the small fraction off the superior end of the curve and, in satisfying symmetry, those with the least 'civic worth', or Booth's classes A and B, composed the small faction at the lower end. The assumption that the biological and social hierarchy coincided pretty well was supported by further research like later-notorious Cyril Burt's testing of children from a state school and from the Dragon School in Oxford in 1909, which concluded that 'the superior proficiency at intelligence tests on the part of boys of superior parentage was inborn'; or, at the other end of the social scale, Heron's work of 1910, which concluded that slums were a 'racially selective' environment attracting 'physically inferior' types. As several historians have noted, eugenists turned class into a biological phenomenon.[28]

The eugenic discourse proved more cruel than preceding

languages of denigration. At least with regard to the latter the *perishing* of the perishing and dangerous classes were available for rescue and re-formation however dominative. Similarly the phrase 'immortal sewerage' contained the intimation that this group could be spiritually recycled to remove the sewerage and retain the immortality. Defining the same people as congenital mental defectives deflected attention away from 'improvement' and made it easier to regard them as fit only for custodial care to prevent breeding.

Undiluted eugenic pessimism proved too harsh a dose for many activists in the social science tradition. Social hygiene, with its eugenic component but also its commitment to improving nurture at the same time as nature, received more support. If eugenic improvement involved generations of time, improvement in physical and mental health by means of childcare, diet and housing could be effected immediately.[29] Moreover, by using the word nurture, or environment, rather than talk of changing society or social 'circumstances', the authority of biology could still be invoked. The manifold crisis to be described in more detail later in this chapter and in the next, together with the service-oriented groups who began to have a vested interest in ministering to the crisis, not least the women to be discussed in Chapter 9, redoubled the determination to make an impact now rather than stand by and wait for generations yet unborn. Especially in the localities, continuing on after the First World War, a cluster of local authority and voluntary initiatives accented health.

The marriage between biology and nurture reached a kind of interwar climax in the Peckham Pioneer Health Centre first opened in 1926. Run by two biologists, Drs Scott Williamson and Innes Pearse, the accent was on biological nurture for both the individual and the social body as well as on giving eugenic advice to couples wanting to conceive children. Drawing an analogy with the way in which 'the floating reserves of the maternal body' could improve progeny, they described the centre as 'a social placenta in the living body of society'. In another place they designated the centre as that 'functional zone of mutuality' which linked 'community' with its constituent 'cells'.

In our understanding, 'community' is built up of *homes* linked with *society* through a functional zone of mutuality.

As it grows, in mutuality of synthesis *it determines its own anatomy* and physiology, according to biological law. A community is thus a specific 'organ' of the body of Society and is formed of living and growing cells—the homes of which it is composed.[30]

Designed as a virtual glasshouse both inside and out, the glass in the centre would bring about the interpenetration of biology and society in several ways. The glass would serve as a kind of giant microscopic slide for the scientist: 'the human biologist also requires special "sight" for his field of observation—the family. His new "lens" is the transparency of all boundaries within his field of experiment'. The glass would also function as a giant greenhouse nurturing the member-families who would be able to grow spontaneously, not least by being visible to each other at all times, into community. The centre was deliberately envisioned as being analogous to more traditional focal points of community. Like the church, market place, village green, the centre would provide 'an open forum, with its recesses roofed and warmed in winter, yet open to the sunshine'. By using the language of community the biologists indicated that the Peckham experiment straddled several traditions or shared several overlapping discourses in the interwar period. Besides coming from the social hygiene impulse the centre saw itself as a 'functional, zone of mutuality' and thus as an example of the third type of social body.

THE DYNAMIC AND FUNCTIONAL: NEW LIBERAL AND FABIAN EVOLUTIONARY BODIES

In the same Sociological Society where Galton made an important, stage-managed introduction of eugenics to the educated public, other strains of evolutionary thinking vigorously challenged the idea of a competitive social body. Using different strategies of intellectual attack, New Liberal, Fabian and Geddesite sociologists proposed an increasingly differentiated, co-operative and functional social body as the outcome of a progressive evolutionary process. The Geddes camp attacked biological reductionism, an effective charge from Patrick Geddes and J. Arthur Thomson who were both professors of biology. But they also continued to search for processes which operated both in the organic and the social realm and came to argue (like Prince Kropotkin) that co-operation and sacrifice constituted the true law of all life:

> be it mammal or bird, insect or even worm—all these survivals of the truly fittest, through love and sacrifice, sociability and co-operation simple to complex—need far other prominence than they can possibly receive even by some mildewing attenuation of the classic economic hypothesis of the progress of the species essentially through the internecine struggle among its individuals at the margin of subsistence.[31]

Both in natural and social world, they posited a female anabolic tendency towards constructive nurturing complemented by a male katabolic metabolism which actively consumed energy, and they underlined the value of the anabolic contributions to evolutionary development and to public as well as private life. The Geddes school gave a biological dimension to the feminist idea of the sexual communion of labour.

New Liberal and Fabian sociologists more singlemindedly searched for distinctively human evolution. In 1901, in *Mind in Evolution*, L.T. Hobhouse, Britain's first academic sociologist, whose brand of sociology dominated the subject until the 1950s, drew on animal psychology and homespun experiments with Jack his dog and Tom his cat to clarify the moment at which animal became human and truly human evolution became possible.[32] Both Hobhouse, appointed in 1908 at the London School of Economics and Political Science (LSE) and the founders of that institution, Fabian socialists Beatrice and Sidney Webb, insisted that the suppression of struggle and conflict became one test of progress. Just as the Geddesites wanted to erase classical economics from the Darwinian panorama, so the New Liberals and Fabians wanted both to embrace and reject Herbert Spencer's vision. They retained Spencer's law of increasing differentiation and integration, but roundly refuted what they saw as his celebration of individualism and conflict and his confusion of mere survival with progress. Hobhouse insisted that 'advance in organisation diminishes the oppor-tunities for conflict. In proportion as life is well ordered the struggle for existence is suppressed'. The Webbs wrote '"the survival of the fittest" in an environment unfavourable to progress may—as every biologist knows—mean the survival of the lowest parasite'.[33]

Once into the distinctively human world, when conceiving the social body, Liberal and Fabian sociologists made their contribution to the functionalist perspectives which, as Robert Young argues, came to dominate in the European social sciences around the First World War.[34] Both Hobhouse and the Webbs envisaged the most developed social organism as being highly differentiated, in terms of structure and function, and yet harmoniously integrated. Both put great emphasis on ethical consensus as key cement for holding the 'self-maintaining organism' together. Hobhouse's four criteria of social development included not only efficiency (survival capacity including metabolism and defence) and extent (geographical size and scope of 'the tissue of social relations') but also 'freedom' and 'mutuality'. Using biological language, he depicted more developed societies as having more intense 'metabolism' and needing more 'vital fluid' or 'energy'. Such vitality could only come when social relations allowed the maximum freedom for the full development of individuals, although this very release of energy had to be kept from exploding the whole by a practice of mutuality or 'service to an end in which each who serves participates'.[35]

The Webbs saw the social organism as composed of social organisations which developed from the simple to the complex, whose changing structure and function provided the focus for meticulous historical examination. Although they owed an obvious debt to Spencer, they differed in palpable ways. The Webbs worked empirically, mainly with documentary historical evidence, whereas Spencer's 'idea of a tragedy' in Huxley's famous quip, 'was a deduction killed by a fact'.[36] Their choice of trade unions and local government as key historical experiments and as catalysts of further social growth[37] would have raised Spencer's heckles as would their reliance on 'specialised groups of brain-workers on whom for the most part, the execution of...social purpose will necessarily devolve'.[38] The Webbs's biggest departure from Spencer lay in their unshakeable faith in the effectiveness of purposive human action in the evolutionary process:

The whole of social life, the entire structure and functioning of society consists of human intervention.

199

The essential characteristic of civilised, as distinguished from savage society, is that these interventions are not impulsive but deliberate; for, though some sort of human society may get along upon instinct, civilisation depends upon organised knowledge of sociological facts and of the connections between them.[39]

More uncertain about the scope for social engineering, Hobhouse remained nervous about using the term 'the social organism' which might connote (as it did for the eugenists and arguably for the Webbs), a definite 'central consciousness' locatable in a definite social group carrying out the thinking and directing functions of the social body. He also worried that the term 'social organisation' might leave the impression that structure could be 'intelligently planned for a purpose' at any but the highest social stage.[40] Unlike Spencer, both Hobhouse and the Webbs did not think that evolution immaculately delivered ethics as 'a species of transcendental national physiology'.[41] Hobhouse repeatedly argued the need for the study of social purpose as a vital level of sociology but one that had to be probed with the tools of philosophy. Although he defined his terms so that development, regarded organically (scientifically), coincided with development regarded ideally (ethically), nonetheless, he made it possible to tackle the ethical issues explicitly rather than biologize them beyond the possibility of discussion.[42] He thus opened the way to an interesting study of meanings and values in the context of social structures which has become familiar again now in the area of cultural studies.

Conceiving the developed social body as a functional and harmonious, organic and ethical unity, the New Liberals and Fabians regarded elements which supposedly disrupted the system as dysfunctional or as diseased and pathological. This did not lead to an endorsement of the status quo even if the tendency in Hobhouse's thought, according to Collini, and in functionalism more generally, according to Young, was 'to concentrate on the potential for harmony at the expense of analysing the actuality of conflict'.[43] As functionalists, they had difficulty conceiving of dialectical unities, that is equilibria composed of contradictory forces. Nonetheless, they considered the type of workers involved in the organized and sometimes militant labour movement, for example, as exceedingly functional both on organic and ethical grounds. Once again, however, the very poor found their place in distinctly non-functional processes. No longer portrayed only as sewerage or drains, or as feeble-minded, the casual poor also became casualties of social disease like destitution or unemployment.[44] In some ways, this marked a significant shift because the pathology was no longer located in individual inadequacy but in social processes. Disease did not come from defects of character as in sewerage, or defects in individual heredity as in feeble-mindedness so much as from defects in social organization. The Webbs argued that the best way to deal with disease was by means of prevention, and offered a cluster of administrative solutions, for example, to regularize employment and to provide health measures especially for children.

Yet a depressing sense of *plus ça change* remained. When it came to chronic sufferers, the Webbs displayed frightening enthusiasm for surgical removal or quarantine. Both in 1911 and 1920 they highlighted the indeterminate but morally-inflected category of feeble-mindedness, which they tied in the familiar eugenic way to prostitution and juvenile crime. They urged the need to mount constant detective searches for the problem would not take care of itself:

> Indeed, it may almost be said to be a peculiarity of the congenitally feeble-minded that they will not die of starvation. The girls drop into prostitution and the boys into theft on the least provocation.[45]

The Webbs believed in the need to 'permanently segregate, under reasonably comfortable conditions and firm but kindly control, all the congenitally feeble-minded'. A Lunacy Authority would handle this quarantining while the proposed Ministry of Labour would provide farm colonies for retraining the unemployed for whom the Labour Exchanges could not find work, and run Reformatory Detention Colonies for the morally recalcitrant who had court convictions (for vagrancy or for neglecting to maintain their families).[46] Although the Webbs also addressed the problem, it is interesting that Hobhouse would not let the issue of feeble-mindedness and poverty go by without at the same time focusing on wealth: 'financially communities are much more encumbered with the charges of functionless wealth than with those of functionless poverty'. Spotting a real issue of power here, he observed, 'we might eliminate the feeble-minded, but who will ever eliminate the too strong-minded?' When it came to their comparative power to affect the actual organic unity, 'one per cent of feeble-minded in a population is a weight that can be borne,' whereas a mere handful of supermen, perhaps a single one with his satellites, may wreck a civilisation.'[47]

THE ATTRACTION OF BODY METAPHOR

One thing is clear about the visions of the social body discussed so far. They all put the head on top and gave it controlling importance over other parts of the body. The social head-ship might be centralized as in eugenics, or, as in the case of the New Liberal vision, diffused among many developed individuals.[48] By positioning the body this way, they joined a long dualistic tradition in Western culture, especially in Judaeo-Christianity and in philosophy and science, which separated the soul and mind from the body and which privileged spirit and later intelligence and ethical consciousness over the rest of the body. In Christian tradition, the soul formed the bit of the divine that humanity shared with God, while the physical body was connected downward with the animals in the great chain of being.[49] In philosophy and science, Cartesian rationality asserted about human being: 'I think, therefore I am.'[50] The separation sometimes moved further into an opposition between soul/mind versus body so that the best body was visualized as a disembodied body, all spirit or intellect liberated from its distracting and detracting organic container.

It is not surprising that the early nineteenth-century British middle class working hard to form its collective and individual identities should find a place somewhere within this tradition. As Chapter 3 indicated, the middle class defined itself in relation to its construction of social groups above and below. By contrast to the landed interest, the middle class stressed its serious Christian discipline, its renunciation of bodily indulgence in wanton drink and sex, its superior intelligence and energy, and as Michel Foucault noted, its commitment to physical vigour in the family—its red blood compared with effete aristocratic blue blood—on which national vitality later was thought to depend. In 1908, nurse M.E. Loane clearly expressed this sense of the middle class as a tonic to the social body when she found it difficult to say whether, as a nation, we owe most to the members of the middle classes who have risen above their station, to those who have maintained themselves in it, or to those who have intermarried with wage-earners, lending them fresh health, and strength and vigour.[51]

Looking down instead of up, the middle classes also represented the working classes as unhealthy on many levels. Chapter 3 has already spotlighted how the physical body figured in a wide-ranging middle-class concept of disorder which linked organic disease, the disorganization of urban space, moral degeneration and political disorder.

Besides figuring in analytical frameworks, the body also became a personal arena of challenge. Middle-class men had to live out a new identity and continually attempted to divide, classify, order and discipline their own lives in myriad ways which included separating the public from the private, the street from the home, men from women, children from adults and so on. But the decisive test of self-discipline, Leonore Davidoff argues, was a man's battle with his own body and especially for control over his sexuality.[52] Reverend Charles Kingsley, Reverend Osborne's brother-in-law, provides an interesting case here. Not only were the clergy masters of the arts of persuasion in the business of conversion such that we can expect to find them commanding the largest number of rhetorical strategies. But, in Kingsley, the boundaries between his conscious and unconscious seem to have been poorly patrolled with the result that he 'could never distinguish dreams from imagination, imagination from waking impression, and was often thought to be romancing when I was relating a real impression'.[53] Kingsley was obsessed with personal cleanliness: 'if I have a spot on my clothes', he confided to J.M. Ludlow, 'I am conscious of nothing else the whole day long.' He constructed his world around polarities which appeared as clearly in his social science as in his fantasy tales like *The Water-Babies*. Filth and cleanliness, black and white, evil and good, vice and virtue, sexuality and purity, women and ladies, were some of the deeply-connected opposites in the shared bourgeois imaginary. In *The Water-Babies*, Tom the sooty, black foul-mouthed, chimney sweep must be drowned, cleansed (indeed baptized) in the sea of the great nurturing mother (Mrs Doasyouwouldbedoneby) to be worthy of joining immaculately pure, blond, white young Ellie in heaven. In a famous lecture to Bristol working men on washing, Reverend Kingsley implied an equivalence between the sacrament of Baptism and a daily cold bath.[54] Reverend Kingsley was also obsessed with his own sexuality which he did not deny but tried ingenuously to find ways to cleanse. Recently-discovered letters to his fiancée Fanny Grenville reveal intimate details of his sexual longing and his attempts to contain and sanctify these thrilling but dangerous desires. Self-mortification was supposed to purify him for pleasure:

> Tomorrow I fast, not entirely but as much as I can without tiring myself. Only to acquire self-control and keep under that happy body, to which God has permitted of late such exceeding liberty and bliss.[55]

Other middle-class people tried to control the threatening side of their natures by a process which resembles what psychoanalysts call splitting and projection. Followers of Melanie Klein see splitting and projection as a normal mode of defence in young infants but as a regressive posture in adults.[56] I would like to consider the process not as infantile but as integral to the identity formation of the Victorian middle-class individual and to the formation of the class as a collective group. It is the kind of process which can help to account for the phobic intensity of the feeling and language surrounding sexuality and bodily 'dirt'. Middle-class men and women seemed to take the feelings that they found threatening or intolerable in themselves and unconsciously projected them outward, assigning them to other class, national or racial groups. The sexuality refused by the middle class was deposited into other social groups like the working class piled into incestuous beds, Irish people likened to animals and black people seen as lascivious savages. These inferior but magnetic Others carried a heavy part of the 'white man's burden', the qualities he could not or would not consciously face in himself. Class consciousness and the class unconscious reinforced each other and the resulting structures of the whole imaginary (encompassing conscious and unconscious mental landscapes) remained very durable.

Yet the strategy of splitting and projection never fully succeeds because people cannot banish what actually form parts of themselves. As Stallybrass and White have argued, the feelings refused and repressed in the self become demonized and unclean and yet the focus of obsessive attention and a key constituent of fantasy and longing: repugnant yet fascinating, reviled but deeply desired.[57] An individual or a cultural type prone to splitting creates a world of continuous threat and terror because the ongoing menace has not only to do with people outside but with a constant campaign to defend against what is always there in the self and what is unconsciously desired to make the self whole. This kind of perspective seems to provide a helpful way to account for the magnitude of danger attached to the low social types submerged into categories like the perishing and dangerous classes and immortal sewerage who had no real social power. Stallybrass and White ask us not to be surprised that capitalism locates 'its most powerful *symbolic* repertoires at the borders, margins and edges (one could add openings), rather than at the accepted centres of the social body'.[58]

If the body formed such an integral part of the class unconscious as well as of middle-class consciousness and became such a strategic battleground for individual bourgeois men it is not surprising that the body should become an enduring part of social science from above. It is tantalizing to speculate about how the psychic tendency towards splitting and projection might also have reinforced analytical patterns in the scientific habits of professional men. The new specialized sciences like sanitary, reformatory and moral science developed by the older professions at the midcentury period tended to split the poor into different fragments, and sometimes accented different causes, but certainly devised different remedies for the pathology of each splintered group. Division of the subject went hand in hand with division of professional labour: divide and remedy became the operative golden rule. This analytic habit of dividing, separating, classifying and prescribing different remedies for each category pervaded the Social Science Association. A psychic penchant towards splitting might have reinforced the intellectual impetus towards dividing and remedying social subjects. However, this argument must not be pushed too far. This chapter has shown how intellectual effort was also moving in the opposite direction towards methodological holism. But interestingly, whether the movement went towards fragmentation or unification, it was related to the body or expressed in body metaphor. The favourite image for depicting a high-level integrated organism was a human body where sexuality, lower instinctual behaviour and mental defect were being controlled by the intelligent (and ethically conscious) head.

BODY METAPHOR AND THE PROFESSIONAL CLASSES

From the mid-nineteenth century onward, those who used body metaphor in social analysis tended increasingly to assign the role of the head to the professional classes. Indeed a recurrent pattern appeared, which was a tendency to biologize the indispensability or superiority of the educated classes at crisis moments in class relations when professional people were working hard to legitimate themselves, sometimes against the real or imagined threat of their possible expropriation. The model of the static social body came into widespread use in the wake of the revolutionary crisis of 1848. As Chapter 4 has already argued, the older learned professions used the panic to try, finally, to detach themselves from the old landed order, to find their place at the forefront of the middle class and to establish their expert knowledges as indispensable to the diagnosis and treatment of social pathology. In this period, the commitment to recycling 'immortal sewerage' by means of public health, reformatory penology and redemptive education, became a crucial signifier of social service. The heads that would regulate the lower body apertures and flows were the professional men who created and dominated these new sciences. Josephine Butler recognized the connection between the new experts, rapidly making their way into the civil service, and the language of 'immortal sewerage', when she wrote in 1871 about

> the coercive and oppressive politics which such materialists, though frequently professing radicalism, will readily adopt, merely transferring the power of the deprivation of civil and human rights from the hands of a monarch or a hereditary aristocracy into those of official experts who will be the elect of a fully enfranchised people, and therefore more dangerously confided in by the people.[59]

The eugenic discourse originated in the crisis of social relations around the 1867 Reform Act. Having first ventilated his ideas in a paper in 1865, Galton published his *Hereditary Genius* in 1869, in the context of the anxious discussion about giving the vote to some working men. How to safeguard social order, or what could seem very much the same thing, how to safeguard your own social kind, and ensure them against the extinction of their social role, became a real concern. Galton met the challenge by renaming the educated classes together with the landed social establishment as biologically superior stocks necessary for the survival of the fittest. His roll-call of genius appears slightly eccentric now but matched almost exactly with those groups that John Gray had dismissed, in his 1825 *Lecture on Human Happiness*, as socially nonproductive and largely useless as well. Galton's inventory of ability and Gray's hitlist included judges, statesmen, English Peers, military commanders and divines.[60] Gray would have allowed literary men, men of science, poets, musicians and painters a bit of usefulness to the extent that they educated, healed and amused the majority of the population. But Gray, unlike Galton, would not have recognized any special merit in senior classicists of Cambridge University for example. Galton designated Oxbridge graduates as the cream of the natural ability group, a sentiment echoed in 1906 by the pioneer social psychologist William McDougall, when he confidently announced that 'we have now well-nigh perfected the social ladder' and urged that the Oxbridge elite which he called 'the emerged tenth' (in contrast to the 'submerged tenth', another popular name for the 'residuum') who had passed into high civil service posts by way of competitive examination, should be given higher salaries so they could marry earlier and get on with breeding their superior stock.[61]

By the turn of the twentieth century, when the political agenda was being articulated in terms of national efficiency or deterioration, a wide range of professional people found a privileged place in body discourse.[62] Public health professionals, for example, inclined towards social hygiene which gave them an important role in improving the vitality of the race. Pure eugenics, according to Searle, especially attracted academics.[63] Thus Liverpool University's first Professor of Social Science, Alexander Carr-Saunders, also held the Presidency of the Eugenics Education Society for many years. Another academic direction in which eugenics moved was towards social psychology pioneered by Galton's associate McDougall and by surgeon and neurologist Wilfred Trotter. This new science put crowd psychology at the middle of its concerns and largely biologized the age-old concept of the mob, arguing that the crowd had a 'herd instinct' or collective characteristics different from its individual members, and that the crowd manifested animal behaviour like marked irrationality and potential for violence.[64] This biologization of the crowd took place in a political setting around 1908 where earnest Liberals were becoming disillusioned with democratic 'machine' politics and where the growing scale both of the working-class movement and of suffragette action presaged the possibility of social worlds turning upside down.[65] So far this chapter has made reference mainly to the international dimensions of the turn-of-the-century national crisis. Unless the internal class crisis and scale of movement coming from below is brought into the picture, the response coming from the Liberal and Fabian sociologists cannot be adequately understood. This, together with the role of old and new professionals in social science, is the subject of the next chapter.

8

NATIONAL CRISIS AND PROFESSIONALIZING SOCIAL SCIENCE, 1890-1920

This chapter will track a second wave of professionalization. The first wave had involved the older professions establishing a beachhead in social science inside and outside the Social Science Association. The second wave brought these educated professionals and a rapidly expanding lower stratum of professionals together in a concerted effort to serve the nation in a period of perceived crisis. The last chapter noted the fears, from the 1870s onwards, about Britain's relative decline compared with strong international rivals, which shook middle-class confidence in an unprecedented way. As disruptive was the internal class crisis. From the 1880s, the 'residuum' increasingly inspired guilt and fear, especially when they spilled out of the East End to demonstrate and riot; their poverty, monitored in a new round of local surveys, became a preoccupation for persons of intellect and property. The surging growth of organized working-class movements also made the sanguine optimism of the Social Science Association less possible for those looking on from above.

The scale and dynamism of the labour movement required attention and, in the end, containment. Trade unionism was expanding, becoming more militant and reaching to the unskilled as well as the skilled. The co-operative movement was growing vigorously to the point in 1905 where it could boast two million members and the Co-operative Wholesale Society as one of the biggest businesses in the world; it talked not of the British commonwealth but of creating the Co-operative Commonwealth. Socialism revived and gathered increasing momentum from the early 1880s onwards. Ethical socialists made a devastating attack on the capitalist industrial system, targeting not only its inefficiency but its immorality and selfishness, thus occupying the moral high ground which the British middle class had customarily considered its own.[1] This 'New Life' socialism attracted some of the new professionals while a number of the older professional middle class also flirted with the labour movement until the mid-1890s. The social and political situation was extremely fluid for a time and both socialism and Liberalism contained several rival projects. From above and from below, a scramble for socialism took place every bit as frantic as the scramble for Africa.[2] In one kind of socialism and labour practice coming from below, a large number of working people seemed to be producing social forms which could dispense with capitalist and some professional social roles and allow for a large degree of self-activity and self-governance.

At the same time, some of the progressive middle class responded to the social crisis by creating political alternatives, like New Liberalism, and more acceptable strands of socialism, like Fabian collectivism. Advanced Liberals and Fabians also created analytical alternatives, like sociology, and paid attention to training experts to undertake social science and service work. Victor Branford, the financial mainstay of the Sociological Society, disclosed a kind of sibling rivalry between sociology and socialism for the same discursive territory when he told the story of the university professor of philosophy who came to join the Society because he had been 'converted to sociology, believing sociology to be socialism, a confusion which he pointed out was far from confined to universities or philosophers'.[3] Sociology and social science became ways of jumping on the bandwagon of progress steaming in the direction of social justice for all, yet retaining a position in the driver's seat for educated and trained middle-class professionals. As in other countries, social science became part of strategies for containing certain kinds of socialism and other working-class energies bubbling up from below. After exploring the social background of social science activists, this chapter will examine three areas growing rapidly in the period—professional training in social science, social survey work and unifying sociology—before finally probing some socialist and working-class responses to these kinds of initiatives.

LIBERALS AND FABIANS IN
SOCIAL SCIENCE

However much they quarrelled with each other, the dominant voices in social science before the First World War came from the same social matrix. The men tended to be university graduates who had often studied under the inspiring T.H. Green at Oxford and then carried his social imperatives into the city where they moved into the orbit of committed social servants like Canon Barnett of Toynbee Hall. They often married like-minded women, some of whom had also received university educations. A conspicuous number of married couples became active in social service alongside the more familiar single social mothers. For example, after finishing Oxford, Bernard Bosanquet (1848-1923) settled in London. As a man of independent means, he pursued his interest in philosophy and taught the subject to working men while also taking an active part in the educational side of the COS. In 1894, he married Helen Dendy (1860-1925), who had studied at Cambridge, and was now serving as the paid secretary of the Shoreditch District Committee of the COS. Once married, she continued her COS work unpaid and later edited the *Charity Organisation Review*.[4] However gender-divided their marital labour (see Chapter 10), these couples felt that marriage, rather than being antithetical to, might even provide a more perfect vehicle for social service. Sidney Webb (1859-1947) impressed Beatrice Potter (1858-1943) when he promised 'to subordinate even our affection for each other to one single purpose to serve our people'.[5] Not university educated, Sidney entered the Civil Service by way of the new competitive examinations and went on to read for the bar before he married handsome, independently wealthy, home-educated Beatrice. Their wedding rings were inscribed *pro bonum publico*.

During the 1880s, this social group became deeply concerned with poverty, however they defined it, and were committed to a life of service to grapple with 'the social problem' as they termed it. Beatrice, in her remarkable autobiography, *My Apprenticeship*, identified a widespread 'class-consciousness of sin':

a growing uneasiness, amounting to conviction, that the industrial organisation, which had yielded rent, interest

211

and profits on a stupendous scale, had failed to provide a decent livelihood and tolerable conditions for a majority of the inhabitants of Great Britain.[6]

She pointed to the collapse of Christian belief, the persistence of intense but now free-floating ethical energy, and the resulting switch from God-service to man-service. Many middle-class progressives in the social science world did suffer a more or less painful crisis of faith and transfer their sense of social duty into social study and social reform which they felt would lead to a fuller life for the majority. To name but a few: Beatrice herself, the Bosanquets, L. T. Hobhouse, Patrick Geddes, J. A. Hobson (the New Liberal 'economic heretic') and Alfred Marshall (the pioneer of professional economics). The Ethical Movement attracted many of these activist intellectuals and helped to shift the bourgeois discourse about morality beyond the old obsession with individual rectitude to a concern with social ethics not only in terms of the duties attaching to given social roles but the ethical value of the very roles themselves.[7]

However, not everyone experienced a crisis of Christian faith. Canon Augustus Barnett and his wife Henrietta epitomized the kind of social Christianity which attracted advanced Liberals (and was also being practised in another variant in the Labour Church), which had a serious concern with social sin ('sin in the sense of missing the best') and social redemption, and which inspired the same dedication to social service. The commitment of the Barnetts to salvation through the sharing of education and culture, their attempts to recruit university men into this service, and their example of Settlement life at Toynbee Hall (which had no religious tests) as a real way of living among the poor, all made Christianity a comfortable spiritual home where many of the progressive middle class could still continue to live. Many of the key players in the social science story in this period, Clement Attlee, William Beveridge, Hubert Llewellyn Smith, E. J. Urwick, began their active social service while in residence at Toynbee Hall.[8]

During the 1880s, the COS version of scientific philanthropy provided a common starting point for advanced Liberals of the period even if many left it sooner or later. For example, the Barnetts worked within the COS from its inception until 1895 when they created a sensation in the charity world by leaving its

212

Central Committee on the grounds that its opposition to state action and its obsession with individual thrift had ossified a living gospel into 'laws that will never grow'. Beatrice Webb, too having decided that 'the most hopeful form of social service was the craft of a social investigator', began her study of the London poor as a COS visitor in Soho in 1883. From 1886 she assisted Charles Booth with his survey into London Life and Labour and then moved on again to study the co-operative movement and follow a more 'socialist' path.[9]

Beatrice did not take these turnings alone. Many advanced Liberals moved closer to the labour movement during and after the 1889 dock strike. Paradoxically the strike experience did much to defuse the fantasy that the residuum posed a revolutionary threat by showing how trade unions could absorb large numbers of the underemployed into 'the ranks of working men'. Llewellyn Smith insisted that it had become possible to separate 'the treatment of social disease and the radically different question', to which he would devote himself at the Board of Trade, 'of the claims of Labour'.[10] By the mid-1890s, such people perceived capitalism as a diseased organism and the Liberal Party as on the brink of collapse. Advanced minds set about searching for a collectivist philosophy and experimented with new political alignments and groupings like the 'New Party'. Operating within an organic metaphor, they looked for fresher and healthier growths emerging from the womb of existing institutions which could now be consciously nurtured. In Sidney Webb's words,

> the necessity of the constant growth and development of the social organism has become axiomatic. No philosopher now looks for anything but the gradual evolution of the new order from the old without breach of continuity or abrupt change of the entire social tissue at any point during the process.[11]

The labour movement provided a possible growing point. Sidney and Beatrice did their first piece of collaborative work on the *History of Trade Unionism*, published in 1894, to be followed soon after by *Industrial Democracy* in 1897. L. T. Hobhouse brought out his study of *The Labour Movement* in 1893 which, like the Webbian blueprint for democracy, proposed a new balance between trade unions, co-operative organizations and state agency. But the Liberal and Fabian pendulum never swung any closer to labour.

Instead, one result of this period of searching and experiment was the creation of a discursive field which shunted labour thinking and activity offside, or rather gave it a place on board a much bigger national omnibus. The organic social metaphor played a strategic role (which will be considered later in the chapter) as did overlapping discourses which designated the key collective as the nation or, more often in Liberal and Fabian circles, the community or the state philosophically considered, or the modern democratic state. The accompanying emphasis on the 'citizen' giving service to this collective, or to a smaller institution within it, also served to devalue the role of the 'producers', still a favoured name labour activists gave to themselves. These new discourses became dominant among the professional classes around the Boer War as part of the obsessive concern with the deterioration of the national body. The new vocabulary did not signify a wholesale shift in middle-class sensibility from individualism to collectivism, from philanthropy to state action, from less to more adequate analyses of poverty and other social problems. As Collini has argued, in his sharp dissection of educated political debate in the decades before the First World War, individualists and collectivists all accepted some form of the state, just as all were concerned with developing individual character and committed to an ideal of service.[12] In social science circles it should be added, all came out in favour of training experts to engage in social analysis and to perform social service. They were unified by yet another factor, that all could look equally suspicious from a working-class point of view.

Taking those convenient couples, the Bosanquets and the Webbs to mark out fairly contrasting poles of the advanced intellectual spectrum, it is illuminating to see how both came from such different directions to the same point of actively creating the institutional machinery for the training of professionals. For the Bosanquets and for their colleague, Professor E. J. Urwick, the director of the first School of Sociology and Social Economics, the state was an ethical society where the 'citizen-conception' prevailed. Every citizen would perform service in a range of institutions, such as the family, the neighbourhood, class (or industry) and the nation-state. Citizens would cultivate a sharp awareness of which forms of these collectivities would most contribute to the common good and try to bring these forms into being. Thus true citizens (including disenfranchised women) would mould the selfish and divisive family into the ethical family which would function and see itself as a 'nursery of citizenship'.[13] For the Bosanquets, the family became the shaping key institution (see Chapter 10) although the labour movement in 'the most sensitive part of the social organism' also crucially demonstrated the working-class capacity for independence and altruism.

The more conventional state machinery would move in harmony with the citizen-conception only to the extent that it allowed space for the most ethical forms of institutions to grow. This often meant that the state had to refrain from hijacking citizen duties but instead encourage people to serve in a vital range of voluntary collectivities. Above all, the Bosanquets reacted suspiciously to any state measures, whether old-age pensions or free school meals, which they feared might deprive the family of its awesome responsibilities. At the same time they were prepared to support state action which they felt would energize the family or catalyze participation. State elementary education would ensure a certain rudiment of citizen-training. Public Health and Poor Law agencies were acceptable not only as safety nets against starvation and death. Attached to them, and to the voluntary agencies, the Bosanquets envisioned an army of trained, salaried social workers who would monitor the very poor family 'with a view to its restoration to independent citizenship'.[14]

At the other end of the spectrum, the Webbs paradoxically had much more time for the state and much less time for the casual poor. They began by studying the labour movement and examined the belly of the supposed monster for signs of new social growth. Trade unions might appear threatening because workers were 'forming within the state, a spontaneous democracy of their own'. But careful analysis revealed that trade unions had grown from simple and homogeneous to complex and differentiated organisms, with a vital function devolving more and more on professional experts'.[15] In their vision of *Industrial Democracy*, the Webbs gave the formal state predominance in a new constitutional ecology. Trade unions and professional associations would protect people in their capacity as producers, co-operatives would safeguard people as consumers but only the municipal and national state could take the overview of the common good and represent the interests of all in their overriding capacity as citizens. However, the state would first need to be transformed by putting trained experts in control. 'Above all', wrote Beatrice, 'we want the ordinary citizen to feel that reforming society is no light matter and must be undertaken by experts especially trained for the purpose.' Trained voluntary workers would also have a place in pushing people up a higher ladder, 'constantly raising the standard of civilised conduct and physical health' above the state-enforced national minimum.[16]

The Webbs and the Bosanquets assigned training a high priority on the social science agenda. The Webbs wanted the LSE to train the experts on whom social reform and the future of the state would depend. From 1888 onward, the Bosanquets took part in initiatives which developed eventually in 1902 into the London School of Sociology and Social Economics, another institution for training people wanting to engage in social or public work. Helen Bosanquet argued that there existed

> branches of administrative work where the lack of experience is so dangerous to the community that it may well be questioned whether for a time at any rate it may not be necessary to have the trained and professional expert as administrator.[17]

However reluctantly the bride walked into the marriage parlour, the merger in 1912 between the School of Sociology, which was suffering from financial problems, and the LSE, which received government grants, went off relatively smoothly given any supposed incompatibility of individualists and collectivists.

SOCIAL SCIENCE AND PROFESSIONAL 'TRAINING'

The calls for training arose in the context of an explosion of middle-class salaried and voluntary occupations. The earlier Social Science Association had started at a time when the older or learned professions were assuming their modern form. Its preoccupations were largely shaped by these high civil servants, lawyers, doctors and ministers, backed up by women emancipating themselves through social work and to a lesser extent by reform-minded politicians, captains of industry and activists in

216

working-class movements. As practitioners of social science, they often remained amateurs in the sense that they received no formal training and usually gave their service on a part-time and unpaid basis. Now, increasingly in connection with the deepening social crisis, a rapid expansion took place of salaried jobs, particularly in local government and the civil service and in fields to do with health and cultural production or, to put it another way, with the creation and communication of knowledge and common sense largely to the working class. Such jobs included teaching and lecturing, writing and journalism, social work and administration, while many of the new government jobs also dealt with the lives of labour and the poor.

It is important to remember that many of the women who became full-time social workers remained unpaid volunteers and would not show up in the census statistics.[18] Also not clearly reflected in the statistics in Table 8.1 (p.218), contemporaries noted the increase of scientific and especially of managerial personnel in industry following upon the separation of ownership and administration made possible by the advent of limited liability. As a closely related development, qualifying associations and training courses came into existence to put the new occupations on a professional basis.[19]

Liberals of all stripes (from the Bosanquets to Hobhouse) together with the Fabians and other middle-class socialists attached utmost significance to the formation of this new stratum of professionals and to their qualifying associations. The Fabians were the first to theorize what they variously called the 'nouvelle couche sociale', 'the intellectual proletariat' or 'the professional proletariat' and what has subsequently come to be called the professional-managerial class (PMC). The Fabians saw this group as possessing property in the form of ability which earned rent just as capital received surplus value and land collected rent; the Fabians created a new trinity in the doctrine of the three rents. While in command of indispensable administrative and scientific skills, the intellectual proletariat received salaries, just as manual workers got wages, and did not have the same essential interests as profit-making capitalists. Moreover their professional associa-tions expressed their commitment to a service rather than a pecuniary ideal, which might be blinkered at the moment but could be expanded into a commitment to 'the good of the community as a whole'. The fact that the Fabian

217

Table 8.1 Selected Male and Female Professions, 1881–1911

Occupation	MALES					FEMALES				
	1881	1891	1901	1911	% Increase	1881	1891	1901	1911	% Increase
Clergy, ministers, priests	33,486	36,800	39,656	40,142	19.9	0	0	0	3	
Preachers, mission workers &c	2,965	5,119	5,293	4,972	67.7	1,660	4,194	4,803	5,955	258.7
Monks, nuns, sisters of charity	?	?	239	302	26.4	3,795	4,678	6,219	7,555	99.0
Barristers and solicitors	17,386	19,978	20,998	21,380	23.0	0	0	0	0	
Law clerks	24,502	27,374	34,066	34,106	39.2	100	166	567	2,159	2,059.0
Physicians and surgeons	15,091	18,936	22,486	24,553	62.7	25	101	212	477	1,808.0
Dentists & assistants	3,583	4,628	5,169	7,424	107.2	0	345	140	250	
Midwives, nurses & other medical	7,964	4,088	4,360	5,287	-33.6	37,885	53,944	68,629	86,970	129.6
Teaching (all grades)	46,074	50,628	58,075	68,670	49.0	122,846	144,393	171,670	183,298	49.2
Authors, journalists &c	5,644	7,485	9,811	12,030	113.1	467	787	1,249	1,756	276.0
Scientific pursuits	1,186	1,920	3,176	6,246	426.6	14	42	66	145	953.7
Service: hospital, institution, benevolent	4,270	6,952	10,653	17,394	307.4	11,526	15,501	26,341	41,639	261.3
Local government (excluding police)	17,968	19,765	26,444	13,030* / 41,620	204.2	3,017	5,165	10,426	17,831* / 1,606	544.2
Civil Service officers and clerks, excluding Post office telegraphers	46,132	69,574	100,339 / 57,864	136,569 / 75,356**	196.0	4,353	9,875	16,074 / 1,762	25,445 / 3,411**	484.5
Employed population *(thousands)*	7,759	8,806	10,157	11,456	47.6	3,403	3,946	4,172	4,831	42.0
Total population *(thousands)*	12,640	14,053	15,729	17,446	38.0	13,335	14,950	16,799	18,625	39.7

*Local government Poor Law
**Post Office related

Source: Census of England and Wales, 1911, vol. 10, Occupations, pt. 1, pp. 540–1, HMSO, 1014

membership mostly came from this group seemed further proof of its availability for transformation. The necessary widening of vision would come about by means of the kind of training that the Fabians aimed to provide in the London School of Economics which they saw as 'a national institution for administrative science' to become part of a teaching university in 'the metropolis of the empire'.[20]

The chorus of demand for training swelled with other voices. New legislation began to require training: for example, the Local Government Act of 1888 made training compulsory for Medical Officers and their teams of Sanitary Inspectors. Social workers in scientific philanthropy, even, perhaps especially, women who had received higher education, also began to call for training. Professionalization provided a hopeful answer to the persistent question of how to give dignity to the life-long public work of the single woman. The women's settlement movement became particularly vocal. Although the first wardens like Miss Gruner of the Women's University Settlement in London and Lillias Hamilton of the Victoria Women's Settlement in Liverpool actively resisted training, their successors Margaret Sewell and Elizabeth Macadam played key roles in getting social science institutionalized. In 1893 Sewell set up the first one-year course at the Women's University Settlement in which included lectures from the Bosanquets.[21] In 1896 she joined forces with the COS and with the National Union of Women Workers, a proto-professional association for social workers in many fields, to create the initiative which became the School of Sociology and Social Economics, setting the pattern for courses in other localities.

Wherever the call came from, the courses of training which carried the names 'sociology', 'social science' or 'social economics' were often devised by people like the Webbs and Bosanquets who had large plans for intellectual and social transformation. Their vision of training moved far beyond the current vocational definition of the term and, as a result, got caught up in several interesting paradoxes. It is a truism of sociological literature on professionalization that key steps in the process involve demarcation and specialization, for example, in identifying a specialized task, designing a specialized body of knowledge to be mastered by extensive training, and protecting the task and knowledge from 'unqualified' interlopers.[22] But the pioneer training courses in social science aimed to go in the opposite direction and offer the most comprehensive possible social education to skill people who wished to enter social or public work and administration in order to tackle the social crisis in an informed way.

In his inaugural address, E. J. Urwick, the director of the new School of Sociology, described a daunting and far-from-specialized task when he argued that 'practitioners working in a definite field for the betterment of social life' ought to have more authority than could emanate from their good will or devoted work. Drawing an analogy with the medical profession, he insisted that authority rested on 'firm connection with the body of scientific knowledge' but that social work still stayed stuck in the 'rule of thumb stage, like the barber-surgeons of old'. Authority or 'the power to inspire confidence' had to rest on intellectual capital, which basically meant 'a recognised and sufficient training'. The field of sociology or social science, as they were often interchangeably called, provided the relevant science on which to ground the training of students preparing to 'give not money, but one's best self' in response to 'the new interpretation of the nation's need—to get not only a livelihood, but also life'.

The curriculum Urwick had in mind matched in essentials the sociology that Hobhouse was developing and expounding in the Sociological Society at about the same time. The subject would embrace the processes of social evolution, social philosophy to clarify social ends, social economics to reveal the framework of economic necessity and psychology to elucidate the processes on which character development depended.[23] The actual reading lists provided a sampler of Oxford 'greats' from Plato and Aristotle to T.H. Green in political philosophy, J. S. Mill and Alfred Marshall in economics, Reverend Chalmers and Octavia Hill on welfare. As important, half the course involved practical work to gain experience in a range of social institutions, first the COS and the Poor Law, then local government more generally and voluntary work unconnected with poor relief.[24] That appetite existed for items on this rather heavy menu is evidenced by the way the courses filled up and by the fact that all sorts and conditions of new professionals tried to get crumbs from the academic table. Once the Liverpool School of Social Science and Training for Social Work came into existence in

1906, it was besieged by requests for short courses from bodies like St Aidan's Theological College, the Queen Victoria District Nursing Association, the Liverpool Technical College of Domestic Science, the Poor-Law Examination Board and workers 'engaged in the Social work of the churches and missions'.[25]

While the curricula of the new programmes tried to work in an interdisciplinary way against the specializing tendencies usually involved in professionalization, demarcation certainly took place on another level. The impetus behind training came from people who wanted to create skilled full-time social and public workers who could ginger into being unlimited numbers of fully-developed, fully-participating citizens. But the very fact of associating social science or sociology with an educational programme created a new divisive wedge. In the social science tradition up to this point, social science had embraced social ethics, social analysis and especially social action and many sorts and conditions of people with very varied levels of education, from unschooled working people to university graduates, had quarrelled over these important issues. Once legitimate social science acquired a new attribute, namely a course of training leading to a qualification, its practitioners became restricted to the kinds of people likely to become students; the fact that many of the early courses awarded diplomas as a postgraduate qualification further restricted the catchment. Social science, which aimed to service a democracy, also functioned to create new expert elites.

The new professions in women's social science, particularly in the health field, became deeply tangled in this paradox of undemocratic class displacement. As soon as training became a requirement, usually as the result of legislation, women from a higher social class tended to replace working-class men and women doing an earlier version of a caring task. This pattern had already become apparent in teaching and nursing where trained personnel were not stepping into a vacuum and creating a new occupation but rather challenging pre-existing forms of an activity. In the old unreformed days, domiciliary nursing had been a skill sometimes handed down from working-class mother to daughter, while hospital nursing was sometimes reserved for needy widows in military hospitals or paupers in workhouse infirmaries. Similarly teaching in dame schools provided a form of domestic employment for working-class women who were

221

respected by the communities who sustained them. Insistence on training functioned to cut out just such people who looked ignorant from above but were held in high esteem by their own class.[26]

In the wake of the Boer War, new legislation and training for health professionals accelerated this class displacement. The motherly working-class sanitary visitor of Ellen Ranyard's day gave way to 'a gentlewoman with special training' once health visiting became a municipal service in Manchester and London in 1908 and once Ministry circulars from 1909 onwards laid down training qualifications for the job.[27] The Midwives Act of 1902 which assured a place for female midwives but required them to sit examinations for State Certificates and which established a regulatory body, the Central Midwives Board, eventually led to one type of woman replacing another in the job. In 1911, 83 per cent of declared midwives were married or widowed and 70 per cent over 45 years old: by 1931, the comparable figures were 52 per cent and 48 per cent. Younger, trained, single women from the higher classes were making inroads into a job previously done by older working-class wives and widows. Women in the social science world actively supported this trend: in 1881 the Ladies' Sanitary Association and the Matron's Aid or Trained Midwife's Registration Society had 'earnestly' urged

> more women of a higher social class to adopt the practice of midwifery....If more women of education and cultivation would join to raise the tone of this calling, they would unquestionably confer incalculable blessings upon their country-women while...securing for themselves a remunerative employment which is pre-eminently woman's.[28]

Mrs Mabel Layton of the Women's Co-operative Guild made it painfully clear how the kinds of conditions laid down by the 1902 Act could inhibit even the most determined poor woman. Having moved into nursing from laundressing by accident, she quickly found that she had a real gift for the work and became a skilled midwife on the job with the help of neighbourhood doctors. Even before the 1902 Act she had wanted to take a hospital training but the cost, £30 pounds or more, and a period of three months away from home proved impossible conditions. Later she 'began to save to get the training I longed for. I scraped and saved, twisted and turned clothes, even went so far as to turn an overcoat for my husband.' But when she had accumulated enough money, the local doctor refused to sign necessary papers saying that she 'knew more than the hospital would teach me and that I could not be spared from the neighbourhood for three months'. When the new Act came into force, she took but failed the Examination: 'I was always a little nervous when writing or answering questions, and when I had to do both in a room full of doctors, I felt I should not make a better job of another exam.' Although she received 'bona fide' status, a category which enabled the experienced but untrained to continue legally to practise, she felt humiliated. 'I have never', she confessed, 'let anyone see my certificate.'[29]

The pattern of class replacement mainly involved women but did result in the extrusion of some working-class men although many more men probably feared competition than actually faced it. Making a preemptive strike in 1879, the Chief Inspector of Factories had argued that women would be out of place in the public factory or courtroom which stood 'so opposite to the sphere of her good work in the hospital, the school or the home'. Male Inspectors nervously awaited the 1891 Factories and Workshop Act and the findings of the Royal Commission on Labour which included on its staff four Lady Assistant Commissioners. One outcome was the formation from 1893 of a small band of young Lady Inspectors with training qualifications who were given specific responsibility for trades which employed a preponderance of women. Well-equipped working-class investigators like Sarah Reddish were not considered for the posts. The Lady Factory Inspectors met with some hostility as did women in the Poor Law and Sanitary Inspectorates from male colleagues who tended to be of lower social status. Here male fears proved largely unfounded, but in philanthropic agencies, like the COS, trained women social workers did eventually replace the paid enquiry agents who were mainly working-class males.[30]

NATIONAL CRISIS AND SOCIAL SURVEY

The displacement of old practices by new professionals also became increasingly apparent in social survey work. The growing sense of national crisis gave tremendous impetus to social investigation of all kinds and, in turn, key social surveys generated influential understandings of the crisis if they did not actually create the sense of crisis itself. The best-known example, Charles Booth's survey of *Life and Labour of the People in London*, begun in 1886 and finally reaching seventeen volumes, put the problem of poverty into the centre of the national discussion where it exerted a magnetic pull on social study and service. For the first time in some forty years, he revived the practice of citizens undertaking a voluntary survey of working-class households in a local area (although, in fact, he got his information mostly second hand from new state employees, the School Board Visitors, about households with children). As the Unitarian owner of a Liverpool shipping company who kept his business going while he immersed himself in the London survey, Booth had an intellectual cousinship as well as family ties to some of the provincial businessmen who had founded the earlier statistical societies and created the social survey in the first place. But this time the scale of the enterprise had escalated.

Now the laboratory encompassed the whole of London, which had replaced Manchester as the symbolic city of the age, not least because it lay at the heart of the empire. Soon after Charles Booth began to publish his findings in 1889, General Booth of the Salvation Army produced *In Darkest England and the Way Out* which began with an elaborate analogy showing that minutes away from Westminster lay the East End of London as 'dark' and 'savage' as any interior part of Africa. Historians dispute his motives, but by taking a poverty census, Charles Booth aimed partly to use the scientific detachment of the middle-class investigator to modulate two kinds of influential but, to him, hysterical voices in the culture: moralism and socialism.[31] To Booth, Reverend Mearn's tract, *The Bitter Cry of Outcast London* (1883), epitomized the moral panic about the residuum of East London. Coming just after the 1885-6 riots of the unemployed who had marched out of the East London to demonstrate in Trafalgar Sqare, H.D. Hyndman's assertion that 25 per cent of East-Enders were living in extreme poverty, seemed, to Booth, a prime example of socialist sensationalism. In fact Booth's survey produced an even darker picture, estimating that 30.7 per cent of Londoners lived in poverty. Quaker chocolate manufacturer Seebohm Rowntree investigated York during 1899, a year of exceptional prosperity, and came up with comparable figures of 27.84 per cent below the poverty line. By the time his *Poverty: A Study of Town Life* had gone through four editions in two years, the Boer War alarm about the physical deterioration of army recruits had reached its height. National efficiency had become an obsession.

Both investigators provided people 'of intellect and property' with credible evidence that poverty was a feature of urban life largely beyond the control of the poor. The poverty lines they supposedly pioneered were problematic and more convincing perhaps to social groups other than the poor, because these lines rested on criteria which the poor would not always prioritize as part of their own well-being. In fact Booth's poverty line, set at an arbitrary weekly wage of 18-21 shillings was nearly as impressionistic as Mayhew's, and in Booth's typology of the poor, class A was not an income category at all but a depository for moral refuse, containing a 'savage semi-criminal class of people' to be 'harried out of existence'; yet another incarnation of the old perishing and dangerous classes. Rowntree, drawing on the new science of nutrition and the concern with national efficiency, set his poverty line at the lowest budget necessary to keep a family in a state of 'merely physical efficiency'. He vividly conveyed the draconian nature of this line and how it allowed nothing for expenditure that working people would see as a vital part of their culture or that middle-class people would consider a necessary part of citizenship:

> let us clearly understand what 'merely physical efficiency' means. A family living upon the scale allowed for in this estimate must never spend a penny on railway fare or omnibus. They must never go into the country unless they walk. They must never purchase a halfpenny newspaper or spend a penny to buy a ticket for a popular concert. They must write no letters to absent children, for they cannot afford to pay the postage. They must never contribute anything to their church or chapel, or give any help to a neighbour which costs them money. They cannot save, nor can they join sick club or Trade Union, because they cannot pay the necessary subscriptions. The children must have no pocket money for dolls, marbles, or sweets. The father must smoke no tobacco, and must drink no beer. The mother must

never buy any pretty clothes for herself or for her children, the character of the family wardrobe as for the family diet being governed by the regulation, 'Nothing must be bought but that which is absolutely necessary for the maintenance of physical health, and what is bought must be of the plainest and most economical description.' Should a child fall ill, it must be attended by the parish doctor; should it die, it must be buried by the parish. Finally, the wage-earner must never be absent from his work for a single day. If any of these conditions are broken, the extra expenditure involved is met, *and can only be met*, by limiting the diet; or, in other words, by sacrificing physical efficiency.[32]

The exclusion of 'soft' cultural criteria, the thoroughness of their survey (Booth even published a poverty map of the whole of London) and their neutral tone of voice all enhanced, if not their scientificity, certainly their plausibility in educated political debate. They showed convincingly that more than half of the people beneath the poverty line, regardless of personal habits, earned less than subsistence wages. By adding the dynamic of a poverty cycle, and arguing that nearly every working-class family would experience poverty at some phase in their lives, Rowntree darkened the picture still further. This survey work strengthened the feeling that poverty could not be moralized away.

Neither Booth nor Rowntree used sampling techniques, or 'the representative method' as it was then called, partly because both still shared the older mentality which saw completeness as commanding knowledge and as thorough social service directed towards the welfare of a local *civitas*. But the sense of national crisis which their work helped to fuel precisely facilitated this breakthrough in technique. Rowntree, as E. P. Hennock has shown, wished to use York as a pointer to the national picture but his assertion about 'the startling probability that from 25 to 30 per cent of the town populations of the United Kingdom are living in poverty' failed to convince the civil servants on the Interdepartmental Committee on Physical Deterioration (1904), one of the most influential enquiries for setting the parameters of the social debate after the Boer War.[33] Displacing the old-style local patriots, a professional group of state and academic statisticians developed the methods which made international as well as internal comparisons possible. State statistics had a long history in Britain, but the new sense of national crisis accelerated the professionalization of statistics and breakthroughs in technique. The role of the government statistician, as Desrosières argues, appeared in many countries at this time and the issues about the representative method were thrashed out from 1895 onward in the International Statistical Institute (founded 1883) by figures like A.N. Kiaer, head of the Norwegian Statistical Service, and C.D. Wright of the US Department of Labour.[34]

In Britain, key figures, like Hubert Llewellyn Smith (1864-1945) of the Board of Trade and A.L. Bowley (1869-1957) at the LSE, were not simply technicians but typical pioneer pro-fessionals of this period: at once technically competent but also deeply committed to social service. Llewellyn Smith had specialized in mathematics at Oxford, and on graduation became a lecturer for the University Extension Delegacy. He lived for some years in Toynbee Hall and elsewhere in East London and helped both Booth with his enquiries and Ben Tillett with the 1889 dock strike. When he became Controller-General of Statistics at the Board of Trade in 1903, he found machinery for monitoring data about labour already in place: in 1886 not only had Booth begun his enquiries but parliament had set up a service of labour statistics and this had grown into a Labour Department by 1893. With the advent of Llewellyn Smith, who was later promoted to Permanent Secretary to the Board of Trade, the Department hired skilled statisticians and set to work devising a retail price index (1903), a wages and hours census (1906) and an index of some 100 towns in the UK which made possible a comparison between wages, rents and prices with foreign countries like Germany, France, Belgium and the USA. The government statisticians did not use sampling techniques but rather developed index numbers to express the range of variation between cities. The Board of Trade work added to the growing deluge of facts being poured out by experts from various government departments and inspectorates.[35]

The nationalization of concern, expressed in the preoccupation with national efficiency and an emerging welfare state which would ensure national minimum standards rather than provide the nationalized deterrence of the Poor Law, also opened the way for the use of sampling techniques in order to produce a nationwide picture of working-class conditions. A.L.

Bowley's studies in 1912-13 of 5 per cent of working-class households in Reading, Northampton, Warrington and Stanley, published as *Livelihood and Poverty* (1915), marked out the new direction. Had he not fallen under Alfred Marshall's influence and begun applying statistics to social issues while studying mathematics at Cambridge, Bowley might have remained a school teacher. Thanks to Marshall, Bowley was appointed in 1895 to take charge of statistics at the newly-founded LSE which he did on a part-time basis, supplementing his income with lecturing at University College Reading, until, in 1919, the University of London created a full-time chair in the subject which he occupied until 1936. His importance to the argument here is twofold. First, he developed techniques of random sampling and used the mathematics of probability and standard deviation tests to calculate the margin of error, which facilitated quick and relatively cheap comparative local studies (which could then be matched against government indices to find their place in a national picture).[36] Second, his academic status (like Karl Pearson's at London University) became a driving force for professionalizing statistics.

Prospective social investigators increasingly received a specialist training at university and then went into jobs either in academia or in the civil service to carry on their survey work. All-important national survey work could only be the province of these kinds of professionals given their mathematical expertise and access to large-scale funding. The development of the new statistical posts put the local 'amateur' who carried out a survey of his, or increasingly her, own locality into a different and eventually more subordinate position. I say 'eventually' because during the interwar period, academics attempted a communion of labour with volunteers (who often turned out to be other social service professionals) which still dignified to some extent the contribution of the local citizenry. Thus the famous Merseyside Survey undertaken by the Liverpool University Department of Social Science between 1929 and 1934, on the lines developed by Bowley's London Survey, got funding from the American Rockefeller Foundation as well as from Lord Leverhulme, and was directed by D. Caradog Jones, a trained mathematician. Caradog Jones had on his small staff two statisticians who later went into the civil service, a third who became a member of parliament and a Miss J. E. McCrindell, who liaised with voluntary bodies important for providing 'raw material' especially on infant welfare and household budgets.[37] The balance of power in the co-operation between professional and voluntary effort was swinging towards the professionals who established the agenda for research, although it did not swing fully in this direction until the 1950s.

GEDDES AND THE
CIVIC SURVEY MOVEMENT

Even the survey work which remained most intimately tied to the local community had difficulty disentangling itself from the increasingly strong professional embrace. Some of the most interesting survey work of the prewar period seemed to challenge expertism but also be swept into movements towards greater professionalization, to open democratic directions for development and yet to be deflected from following them. The Civics movement, inspired by Patrick Geddes, which had an American analogue in the Social Survey Movement, and which explicitly used the words 'social survey' for the first time, provides an interesting case in point.[38] Geddes (1854-1932) occupied a central place in the social science world of his time. Coming to sociology from biology, he had studied biology with Huxley and later held the chair in Botany at University College, Dundee. Before the First World War his vision catalyzed local activity in places as far apart as Edinburgh, Dumfermline and Dundee on the one hand and Lambeth, Woolwich and Chelsea on the other. Not only did his Edinburgh Summer Schools of Science and Art act as magnets attracting academics as eminent as William James of Harvard and Charles Zueblin of the University of Chicago, but his wealthy friends Victor Branford and J. Martin White financed new institutional machinery to promote sociology as a discipline, underwriting the Sociological Society (1903) and professorships at the LSE and the newly organized University of London.[39]

Geddes and his wife Anna followed the well-trodden path of late-nineteenth century seekers. They both recanted a fierce Presbyterianism and searched for replacement religions. He joined the Positivist fold for a time. She committed herself to a religion of service to the poor inspired by the work of Octavia Hill and Josephine Butler. Living in an ordinary Edinburgh tenement, they started to develop their vision of sociology as civic science. They created a kind of apotheosis of the mid-century focus on the *civitas*, envisioning the city-state more than the nation-state as the proper venue of citizenship. Sweeping aside some later-Victorian commonplaces of political debate, 'we have done with arguments concerning "the Individual and the State"', claiming that they had moved 'beyond the abstract sociology of the schools—Positivist, Socialist, or other—with their vague discussion of "society" and its "members"', Geddes made a takeover bid for the most resonant recent rhetoric: 'we have reached the definite conception in which all these schools have been lacking—that of Cities and Citizenship'.[40] Rather than see the city only as social pathology in the way usual for late-Victorian social investigators, they argued their kinship with a noble tradition stemming from the ancient Greek *polis* and envisioned a revitalized city providing the suitable medium for the fullest possible human life.

Geddes finally established his headquarters, in the aptly-named 'Outlook Tower', a watchtower positioned high above the city with commanding views. He repudiated any power relation attaching to such 'supervision', claiming that he was adopting Aristotle's ideal of a city that could be seen in its entirety all at once.[41] His cognitive ambition was breathtaking: he arranged the exhibits to be no less than an 'index-museum' to the universe (including the planetary motions), as seen from this point of view in Edinburgh. The top storey with its camera obscura offered a panorama of the region which displayed 'the characteristic qualities of modern painting'; below this came a floor analysing the same prospect from the viewpoints of different specialized sciences; further below, an exhibition of Edinburgh past, present and future, then a lower storey allotted to Scotland, another to Britain, then one to the history and potential of European cities and finally the ground-floor was allocated to the Oriental civilizations and to the general study of Man. Also installed in the Tower, a Civic Business-room undertook practical work, like improving slums or erecting university halls of residence in poorer districts. 'The watchword and endeavour' of this watchtower was 'Civic Survey for Civic Service'.[42] Called 'a Civic Observatory and Laboratory', this 'Encylopaedia Civica' was innovative—even Cubist—in its idea of comprehension, aiming to represent all perspectives on a subject and all different possible futures, as well as allowing for a dynamic element of ever-changing exhibits since understanding would always be changing. Not surprisingly some of the Geddes exhibits, like the Edinburgh room at the Town Planning Exhibition of 1910, could feel like a 'torture chamber' to people with other ideas of order:

> the merest hotch-potch—picture postcards—newspaper cuttings—crude old woodcuts, strange diagrams—archaeological reconstructions...many of them not even framed—shocking want of respect![43]

Transformed by the magic of Geddes's patter they became 'romantic visions' which unsettled common sense.

The 'synoptic vision' which inclusively tried to see everything from all angles went together with another of Geddes' strongest impulses, which tried to recruit everyone to this way of seeing. Indeed he felt that those previously excluded from public municipal life like workers and women, artists and school-children would be most responsive to civic science. Geddes had earlier written a pamphlet *Every Man his Own Art Critic*, now he tried to universalize the process of social survey: 'the essential matter for all of us is to become more and more of surveyors ourselves'.[44] Or, as his disciple Branford put it 'the aspiration—every citizen his own sociologist'. In theory, as did the American Social Survey Movement, Geddes (and the Civics Committee of the Sociological Society) tried to stimulate 'ordinary citizens' to undertake complex investigations of their own communities, extending Le Play's categories of Place, Work and Folk (their eugenicized translation of lieu, travail, famille) to include ecological and historical surveys as well as a 'Social Survey proper' of the present condition of the people, 'their occupation and real wages, their family budget and culture-level'.[45] The next step involved mounting a local exhibition which made extensive use of visual aids like pictures and maps to display the survey results and graphically to bring past, present and future possibilities into relationship, as the necessary preliminary to action. The idea, as in the American counterpart, was to study social problems and energize the locality into civic awareness and action.

Both aimed to catalyse community self-study and transformation. But who composed the community? Whatever the democratic potential of his ambition, Geddes became increasingly involved with the emerging profession of town planning, which took shape rapidly after the 1909 Town Planning Act, thanks to the endowment of chairs in the universities of Liverpool, Birmingham and London, and to the incorporation of the Town Planning Institute in 1914.[46] Increasingly his most responsive audience became town planners, local authorities, teachers and 'leading citizens'. In America the pattern shaped up somewhat differently but the equation of 'the community' mainly with professional people was similar. Local leaders would invite the Russell Sage Foundation to send in academic experts to organize a social survey, which would be carried out with local, volunteer, middle-class help. Ernest Burgess of Chicago exposed something of the power relations implicit in this work which undercut some of its democratic ambition when he asserted that

> community self-study under expert direction is democracy being at school to the social scientist. The social survey is to the community what the demonstration station is to the farmer.[47]

Before the First World War the social survey increasingly began to legitimate the claims of certain professionals to special expertise—academics and social workers in the United States and town planners in Britain—while confirming the service credentials of other emergent professionals whose volunteeer labour in civics constituted a clear work of social service.

The saddest outcome occurred when the work of professionals with deep democratic aspiration was ultimately experienced as oppressive and hateful by the very people whose lives they set out to enhance. Raymond Unwin started as a socialist disciple of Geddes and William Morris, but moved up quickly in the developing profession of town planning and finally became Chief Technical Officer for Building and Town Planning at the Ministry of Health in the interwar period. To the extent that he obeyed his paymasters, he ended up helping to create just those dormitory Council estates which were the farthest remove possible from his own community vision.[48] However, the community self-study impulse did not disappear. When other varieties of social science evacuated the Sociological Society, the Geddesites remained and, from their postwar base of the Institute of Sociology, Le Play House and the *Sociological Review*, continued to catalyze civic survey work and increasingly to recruit women and schoolchildren into the enterprise.[49]

UNIFYING SOCIOLOGY:
A NEW SPECIALISM?

In the context of rampant professionalization which included the growth of a professional managerial class, the association of social science with training some of the new recruits, professionalization in social survey work and in neighbouring intellectual disciplines (see Chapter 10), it comes as no surprise that sociology should also make attempts to set up professional machinery. The Sociological Society, founded in 1903, moved in this direction and aimed to develop sociological theory, run a journal which came to be called the *Sociological Review* and promote sociological studies especially in higher education where Britain lagged far behind Germany, France and America.[50] The Society deliberately chose the term 'sociology' rather than social science, partly to mark out their distance from the limits on theory imposed by the meliorists of the Social Science Association, and partly to signify the concern with social evolution and proclaim a descent, however quarrelsome, from Comte and from Spencer.[51]

Sociology now became a favoured way of naming the total scope of the social science project, which, from the 1820s, had encompassed 'not only a Science, but a Philosophy and an Art, as dealing not only with the facts and conditions of social life but with its ideals and the means of their realisation'.[52] Applied sociology preoccupied most of the main groups which came together to form the Society, especially Geddes and his backers, the eugenics fraction and Liberal intellectuals ranging from C.S. Loch (of the COS) and E.J. Urwick to J.A. Hobson and L.T. Hobhouse. Despite the Society's commitment to sociology as a unifying discipline, tensions riddled the sociological movement. Eugenics largely moved out in 1908, the same year that Hobhouse became the first academic sociologist and concentrated more on developing theory. He increasingly diverged from the Society's strong orientation towards action and, in 1912, resigned from the editorship of the *Sociological Review*. His species of sociology turned out to be rather still-born with few progeny: few other universities established sociology departments until the 1950s and even within the LSE, his programme lost out to a friendly competitor, the more praxis-orientated Department of Social Science and Social Administration (see

Chapter 10). Despite its unifying ambition, sociology turned out to be yet another fragment in the intellectual jigsaw rather than the ordering principle of the whole.

Nevertheless Society members proposed sociology as the unifying discipline and used the organic metaphor to challenge two 'mechanical' means of co-ordinating the work of scientific specialists. They refused to think of unification as mere co-ordination or, in Hobhouse's words, as 'a mere synthesis of the social sciences consisting in a mechanical juxtaposition of their results'. Instead sociology would supply the

> vitalising principle that runs through all social investigation nourishing and nourished by it in turn, stimulating inquiry, correlating results, exhibiting the life of the whole in the parts and returning from the study of the parts to a fuller comprehension of the whole.[53]

Sociology also attacked the analytical tendency, embodied in the Social Science Association, to divide and remedy social subjects. The midcentury idea of 'unification' had consisted of co-ordinating the work of the new specialist fields, being developed by professional men and feminist women, without challenging any of their boundaries. For many reasons including a commitment to personal service which tried to safeguard the individuality of the individual or at least the variety of human types, the principle of classifying into many sub-groups, each of which would receive different treatment, typified the approach of meliorist social science.

Hobson felt especially irritated by the 'piecemeal' habit of mind which resulted in seeing the unemployed question as 'a hundred different questions...to be solved by a hundred different little local remedies.' He complained that

> The method is really not scientific but the reverse. It attempts to treat a unified organic subject by a piecemeal inorganic method. Its collection of facts never attempt to go behind concrete phenomena into the wider movements of industrial life, so as to find out what maladjustment of the larger economic forces is really represented in unemployment.[54]

Both Hobson and the Fabians argued that unemployment was 'a disease of the industrial structure', for Hobson endemic to an economic system which suffered from a basic 'mal-distribution of consuming power'; for the Webbs resulting from laissez-faire anarchy. Both called for a central dynamic which could bring consuming power into continuing balance with productive power. Hobson felt that massive taxation of unearned incomes, militant trade union action and government direction of social investment could bring about redistribution of wealth. The Webbs relied more on the state to use its own productive and sub-contracting powers to create more jobs and thus more effective consuming power.[55]

The organic analogy proved useful in challenging both academic and activist specialization. As importantly, it also functioned to displace class consciousness. Once again, and perhaps more effectively than ever before, professional people invoked the organic metaphor at a time of class crisis when their own role needed buttressing and forces coming from below needed deflecting. When making the case for training, Urwick emphasized that 'nature is always slow' and chided socialism for sometimes trying 'to develop the organism by machinery, forgetting that growth can only come through vital processes'.[56] Geddes proposed the perspective of the civic evolutionary drama unfolding over eons of time as a way of 'transcending' the standpoint 'of either the capitalist or the labour class'.[57] New Liberals targeted Marxism (made flesh in the Social Democratic Federation and later in the Plebs League) as 'mechanical' socialism. According to Hobhouse, Marxism provided 'false economic analysis which attributes all value to labour' which led on to a mistaken politics premised on 'a class war, resting on a clear-cut distinction of classes which does not exist.' Instead of class cleavage, both New Liberals and Fabians stressed the increasing class differentiation and functional interdependence of the modern social organism. The Webbs dissected the process whereby trade unions had become differentiated organisms with workers increasingly relying on elected representatives and trained officials to inform their judgement and carry out their will:

> Though the workmen started with a deeply-rooted conviction that 'one man was as good as another,' and that democracy meant an 'equal and identical' sharing of the duties of government, as well as of its advantages, they have been forced to devolve more and more of

'their own business' on a specially selected and specially trained class of professional experts.[58]

The new sociologists insisted that sociology encompassed social ethics, analysis and action, the levels of concern in the evaluative tradition of social science since the time of the early socialists. Yet on every level, the sociologists were creating approaches and analyses which displaced the ideas and practices of the early socialists and much of the labour movement of their own time. For an ethic of class mutuality, they substituted one of inter-class or community service. On and off the record, the Webbs came increasingly to rely on educated or trained experts as the carriers not only of science but of the service ethic. In the year they founded the LSE, Beatrice wrote 'we had turned our hopes from propaganda to education from the working-class to the middle-class' and then spelled out how

> we staked our hopes on the organized working-class, served and guided, it is true by an elite of unassuming experts who would make no claim to superior social status, but would content themselves with exercising the power inherent in superior knowledge and longer administrative experience.[59]

Victor Branford, in more grandiose mood, spoke of how the universities would equip an

> *elite* of youths and maidens...with a culture deliberately chosen to adjust personal vocation to civic service, so that the social heritage thus transmitted becomes a harmony that unites instead of a thousand discords that sever.[60]

While Hobhouse accused Fabianism (which he called 'official socialism') of creating yet another form of oppression where 'all men and women are either "experts" or puppets', New Liberals were also displacing working-class effort. Hobhouse ever-fond of capturing and remaking resonant language, used the word 'mutuality' to name the concept of service. He created an acceptable version of socialism, which might best be called service socialism: 'It seems to me', he wrote in 1924,

> that there is possible a distinctive kind of Socialism, viz. one based not on Trade Unions but on the community and social service....the Liberal Party might teach Labour true Social-ism in the point of view of the community as a whole.[61]

The phrase 'service to the community' resonated in social science circles until the Second World War. Clement Attlee, Toynbee Hall settler and later Labour prime minister, set the tone immediately after the First World War by inviting working people to participate in social science. In his book *The Social Worker*, 1920, which launched a series called 'the Social Service Library', he celebrated organized working-class self-help but absorbed it into a larger vision. In a final chapter called 'The Social Service of the Working Classes', for example, the co-operative movement no longer signified wide-ranging mutual aid between social brothers and sisters from cradle to grave but a way of 'making trade into a service to the community rather than a source of profit to the individual'.[62]

SOME SOCIALIST AND WORKING-CLASS RESPONSES

How did socialists react to the sociological project, with its service ethic, its organic functionalism, its increasing reliance on experts? The answer has to be complex, not least because socialism was now more diverse than in the early nineteenth century when a nationwide movement had cast its whole analysis and praxis as social science. In the late nineteenth century, many socialist and co-operative groupings no longer gave social science or even the authority of science such a central place. The enthusiasm with which the professional middle classes had annexed social science made the term problematic for some working people, just as the term political economy had become problematic in the earlier socialist period. Rather than consider only the minority of self-professed scientific socialists, this section will explore the discursive fields that socialists and others occupied but no longer so insistently called scientific. To chart this terrain, I will briefly signpost three varieties of discourse in the period up to the end of the First World War: (1) the moral economy of ethical socialism (2) the 'practical socialism' of the co-operative movement and (3) the contested organicism of some leaders in the Independent Labour Party and their Marxist antagonists in the Social Democratic Federation. Finally, I will make a preliminary probe into the vast human territory which lies beyond organized social movements.

The language of moral economy which dignified the role of

the producers was still resonant in late nineteenth-century socialism and largely incompatible with the analyses of the new sociology. Body metaphor figured in a long-standing way in the works of two of the most popular socialist writers, William Morris (1834-96), author of lectures on socialism and *News from Nowhere* between 1887 and 1893 and Robert Blatchford (1851-1943), editor of *The Clarion* newspaper and author of the bestseller, *Merrie England* (1894). They both identified workers as 'the real organic part of society' meaning the vital, as against the parasitic classes, the useful classes contrasted with the useless.[63] In some ways their language recalls Gray's *Lecture on Human Happiness* of 1825. They called the workers 'the real producers' of all useful things in contrast to the capitalists who were practitioners of competition, or as Morris more bluntly put it, perpetual war. While health featured more prominently than sixty years before, and formed an essential part of a 'decent' or 'worthy' life, it could not be achieved in a physical or in a psychological sense, as 'ease of mind', in a situation of 'mere toiling to live, that we may live to toil'. To remedy the social problem, the true producers had to take power of all kinds into their own hands. In Blatchford's words, again using formulae well rehearsed in the 1820s:

> we want the fruits of labour for those who produce them.
> This issue is not an issue between Liberals and Tories, it
> is an issue between Labourers and Capitalists.[64]

Within capitalism, interdependence of classes certainly existed but it was the interdependence of groups whose interests deeply conflicted; this unity rested on contradiction.

For Morris the central task was to create a longing for 'practical equality' in every sphere of cultural production, from art and knowledge to the economy and government. The trained experts towards whom the Webbs looked with confidence, Morris regarded with concern:

> a new middle class to act as a buffer between the
> proletariat and their direct and obvious masters; the only
> hope of the bourgeois for retarding the advance of
> socialism lies in this device.[65]

Morris worried that the Fabian proposals for 'business-like administration in the interests of the public' would work to uphold the society of inequality 'in a somewhat shorn condition, maybe, but a safe one'.[66] The professional class was problematic. Like Gray before him, Morris insisted that the 'professional people of our society' might work hard but 'do not produce' and, as a result, 'consume out of all proportion to their due share'. At present they largely aligned themselves with the capitalists, indeed lawyers and the military were simply 'parasites of property'.[67] The issue of the professionals could only be resolved within a social framework where common ownership and a longing for equality provided a setting for a new collective determination of what were human needs and what constituted useful work to service these.

Not the sharp contours of current conflict, but the vision of fellowship and peace, of beauty and pleasure, that could lie beyond caught the imagination of local socialists. Morris deliberately tried to educate desire so that people would long for socialism with 'the unreasonable passion of a lover'. With Hannah Mitchell, who regarded the socialist movement as her university, he succeeded:

> Perhaps we were not quite sound on economics as our Marxian friends took care to remind us, but we realized the injustice and ugliness of the present system. We had enough imagination to visualize the greater possibility for beauty and culture in a more justly ordered state. If our conception of Socialism owed more to Morris than to Marx, we were none the less sincere.[68]

In the 1880s and 1890s, much of the activity of ethical socialism revolved around 'making socialists', that is, enabling people to live as socialists in the culture of the movement, for example in the Clarion Clubs, where Mitchell and her husband courted. Whatever the shortcomings as a strategy for challenging large constellations of power, this dress rehearsal for socialist life for a time effectively enlisted desire.

Co-operators used a different vocabulary, insisting that their 'practical socialism' both offered the chance to live a new kind of citizenship and to confront capitalism and the 'servile state' with the Co-operative Commonwealth. They used some of the same keywords favoured by New Liberals and Fabians, like citizen and service, but changed the meanings by placing them within a different organizational framework. Compared with either the

Fabian vision of the modern industrial state, largely run by civil servants or the Liberal idea of service within the nation-state and smaller collectivities, the co-operators saw their service as activity within the co-operative movement, which not only embraced activities from cradle to grave, but would eventually expand to become the Co-operative Commonwealth pushing capitalism into the margins. Peter Gurney's illuminating discussion of co-operative discourse provides clear illustrations of the contrast. In 1898, Holyoake was making the distinction between the education necessary for state citizenship and the 'formation of the co-operative mind', essential to 'social citizenship'.[69] The Women's Co-operative Guild staked its claim to both kinds of citizenship. Organizer Sarah Reddish insisted that both men and women had family duties and that both should also be 'interested in the science of government, taking a share in the larger family of the store, the municipality and the State'.[70] Central to the concept of the Co-operative Commonwealth was its ability to service the known needs of its members:

> the people, the real State, shall own and work all concerns and industry for the common good, when there shall be none of all our many needs that we shall not produce for ourselves.[71]

This kind of self-provision, whatever its shortcomings as far as including the poorest in its numbers, could not come about by means of state action from above:

> True social reform will not be brought about by the mere machinery of government, or by the regimentation, inspection, and classification of its citizens by the State, but by the conscious efforts of self-reliant citizens united in their democratically-governed associations.[72]

Co-operative ideologues envisioned a time when the spread and scale of co-operative commercial and cultural undertakings would not only displace capitalism but also replace the existing state.

The socialists who came closest to the sociologists were some leaders of the Independent Labour Party in the period after the Boer War. Most notably, later prime minister, J. Ramsay MacDonald (1866-1937) in his *Socialism and Society*, 1905, used organic metaphor to move in several directions at once: to validate his parliamentary socialist strategy, to critique other socialist approaches and to build bridges, not least discursive bridges, to potential Liberal supporters. Organic metaphor tended to appeal to socialists who wanted to inflate the role of the state at the expense of the producers. He visualized society as an organism, 'a vital relationship between organs, not a bodily form containing these organs' and proposed the state as the central organ:

> Some organ must enable other organs and the mass of society to communicate impressions and experiences to a receiving centre, must carry from that centre impulses leading to action, must originate on its own initiative organic movements calculated to bring some benefit or pleasure to the organism. This is the Socialist view of the political organ on its legislative and administrative sides. It gathers up experience, carries it to a centre which decides corresponding movements, and then carries back to the parts affected the impulse of action.[73]

Seeing in this way allowed for an attack on socialisms predicated on class-based strategies, whether these emphasized class struggle and violent 'rupture' or hoped to proceed through the peaceful conduct of working-class associations: the 'vital fact is not that conflict, but rather the steady subordination of all function and sectional interests to the living needs of the whole community'. His invitation to Liberals to join the movement was issued with scientific guarantees

> that each new stage in evolution retains all that was vital in the old and sheds all that was dead....Socialism, the stage which follows Liberalism, retains everything of permanent value that was in Liberalism.[74]

MacDonald's later works less emphatically used organic analogy but talked more about the state as the representation of 'the community as a whole'. Yet for all the similarities to sociological analysis, there were still significant tensions. Despite the absence of a Morris-type awareness of the way in which the state could act to shore up capitalist society, nonetheless, as David Howell points out, ILP leaders were still resistant to Fabian expertism and insisted on the motive power of the moral conviction and informed opinion of the vast majority of 'the people'.[75]

241

MacDonald's organicism partly served, like the New liberal variant, as a scientific stick with which to beat Marxism. He received cheers from *Labour Leader* for an attack which 'kills two fallacies with one weapon—the fallacies of individualism and Marxism'. He also got jeers in the Social Democratic Federation paper *Justice* from Marxist Max Beer who accused him of 'Bourgeois Socialism' and 'Biological Sociology'.[76] The SDF, which occupied a relatively small space on the socialist map in this period, most insistently called its analyses scientific. Beer derided two schools of biological sociology, one depending on body analogy, and drawing inspiration from Comte and Spencer (he placed MacDonald here) and another school, attaching itself to Darwin, emphasizing struggle between races and leading largely to imperialist politics. Nonetheless other Marxists aligned more enthusiastically with Darwin but confined his authority to the natural world. In the words of Edward Aveling,

> as the teaching of Darwin won and revolutionised the world of thought in so called natural science, so surely the teaching of Marx is winning and will revolutionise the world of thought in social science.[77]

Yet, however diverse its different strands, however wide its geographical spread, and however ambitious the breadth of human life it embraced, socialism still existed within organized movements. The biggest challenge to the historian is to get beyond the organized working class and tap the reservoir of sensibility of working people who never joined an organization, in order to sample their reaction to the middle-class professional social scientific offensive. This is notoriously the hardest area in which to take soundings. But one extraordinary text from the period does afford glimpses into what George Eliot called 'the roar on the other side of silence' and raises profound and disturbing considerations. Stephen Reynolds, a university-educated journalist, went to live and work with the Woolley brothers who were Devon fisherman. Together, in 1911, they produced a book entitled *Seems So! A Working-Class View of Politics*. This text is saturated with a sense of class difference so deep that it undercuts surface disagreements among the political parties including Labour. To the fishermen, the differences and quarrels which seemed so divisive to middle-class intellectuals before the First World War, were nearly invisible from the point of view of the poor.

Put bluntly, from the fishermen's perspective, individualists and collectivists seemed united in scientifically harassing the poor and trying to reshape them into another class mould. Reynolds and the Woolleys named this process as cultural imperialism: 'the imperialistic attitude, which regards the poor, sub-consciously if not consciously, as a kind of subject race, to be made efficient not so much for the benefit of themselves as for that of the dominant classes, is common enough'.[78] They identified most of the linguistic techniques of denigration which made way for this roughshod renovation: likening the poor to animals, to savages, to children. In a brilliant observation, they insisted that without the real recognition of cultural difference, the social reform from above felt reformatory to those below.

> Reforms are needed badly enough in many directions, but it should always be borne in mind that what seems reform to the giver may be reformatory to the recipient. That which dissatisfies the poor man in his own life is not, as a rule, what horrifies the legislating onlooker. And it cannot be denied that the poor man knows his own life better than any one else can know it for him.[79]

Lest it be thought these were socialists talking, Reynolds and the Woolley brothers attacked theoretical socialism and especially collectivism saying that

> the theoretical aspects of Socialism do not appeal to them (working people) and they resent as much as ever any State interference in their private lives. Bureaucrats they mistrust: a chill Fabian efficiency has no attractions for them. What they want is fair play between man and man.[80]

Of all the varieties of socialist, the Fabians appeared the most frightening: 'in the intellectual field, we admire with a shiver the boundless self-confidence of a Fabian Society in the direction of knowing what is good for people and managing them to their own advantage'. The *Seems So* reaction to the Royal Commission on the Poor Laws, where Helen Bosanquet headed the Majority and the Webbs wrote the Minority Report, could be summed up as a plague on both your (work)houses. They felt that 'both Majority and Minority treat the poor too much as inferiors'. Moreover, they articulated a deep class rift over inspection, so

243

strategic for over 100 years to social science from above, so abhorrent from below:

> the general schemes of both majority and minority are dependent on inspection for their proper working. No sooner does the Commission come to handgrips with poverty itself than out pops an inspector, like a Jack-in-the-box. And not only that; voluntary charity is to be thoroughly reorganized and put on an inquisitorial basis. In the sweat of thy brow, and under the eyes of inspectors, shalt thou eat thy bread!...Inspection means the judgment of one class by the standards of another; the teaching of people how to live under circumstances of which the teachers have had no personal experience. If carried through, it means also the forcing of the ideals of one class on another class, and nothing is so demoralizing as that.[81]

State action embodying this kind of attitude offered no acceptable answer to social questions: in the vernacular of the Woolleys,

> The laws they passes for the poor up to Parliament only chucks 'ee into the hands of the policeman, an' 'spectors, an' lawyers, an' such-like—out o' the frying-pan into the fire—an' then they raises taxes on the little you have got for to keep thic lot going. Us don't want their kindness of that sort. Us'd rather muddle on our own old way.[82]

The work of the Woolleys and Reynolds gives a glimpse of the deep reservoir of resentment that has lain in wait for experts and professionals who have wanted to impose their own cultural codes. These voices from below raise central questions about the social tendency of the professional managerial class and the sciences they have developed, issues which are still in dispute. In more recent times, analysts like Harold Perkins have seen the growing prominence of professionals in possession of what has variously been called human, educational, cultural or intellectual capital heralding a new post-industrial era in which old-style class society (a binary model with a small ruling class exploiting a large underclass) gives way to a professional society, open in principle to the advancement of everyone, promising a just reward for every useful service. Perkins also argues that in reality, development has moved towards parallel hierarchies which contend with each other, for example, professions in the business sphere and in the civil service fighting it out during the 1980s.[83]

By contrast, socialist analysts and activists, like the Ehrenreichs, have emphasized the amount of conflict and attempted control which has often historically characterized the relations between the professional classes and the working class. Reynolds and the Woolleys would probably have agreed more with this school of interpretation. Despite the anomalous position of the professional-managerial class and however much they have asserted their independence and commitment to service, their role has often been to sustain 'the reproduction of capitalist culture and capitalist class relations' not least by moving in and taking over where working people had earlier operated their own cultural forms.[84] Yet the situation remains contradictory. The position of the PMC is unfixed and professional people have also been a continuing source of progressive movement. The Ehrenreichs recognize that no project to democratize cultural production can hope to be effective in the future without co-operation and alliances between workers of hand and brain. But working together has to start with realistic assessments, in their words, of the 'tensions and differences which tend to separate working and middle class people into different universes so that we might, at least within the context of a socialist movement, try to overcome them'.[85]

Always sensitive to strategies of denigration, Stephen Reynolds also made the point that the poor man 'is treated like a child badly brought up by its parents, a child very wronged and very naughty'. Perhaps it was the women who were active in social science, to whom I shall now return, who brought the art of treating the poor as children to its perfection. Reynolds and the Woolley brothers expected nothing different from the other gender of 'the likes o' they' in a 'Suffragette House of Lords'.[86] Were Reynolds and the Woolleys right?

9

WOMEN'S SOCIAL SCIENCE AND SOCIAL WORK, 1890-1920

'We began on the crest of a wave of national social self-consciousness', recalled Margaret Sewell, warden of the Women's University Settlement and pioneer of social work training.[1] Women's social science surged forward on the tide of crisis partly because many male observers turned a social searchlight onto motherhood. Anna Davin has reviewed the ranks of unintended allies who included imperialists like Major General Sir Frederick Maurice KCB, Fabian socialists like Sidney Webb, eugenists like Dr Caleb Saleeby and public health professionals like Arthur Newsholme.[2] They all placed a heavy responsibility for the health and vitality of the British race squarely on the shoulders of working-class mothers. Women's social science, already built around a discourse of motherhood, also helped to set the national agenda and benefited from it. In the new context of national crisis, with body metaphor so salient, women could present motherhood of all kinds as strategic to the survival of the nation. Motherhood helped to justify the increasing political activity of women: suffragists often demanded citizenship in order to bring maternal qualities into public life and also to enlist the state to protect mothers.[3] Motherhood helped to legitimize the emergent caring professions: without social work mothering there was little chance that poor women would become proper mothers. In the context of the national obsession with motherhood, this chapter will explore developments in women's professionalization and the growing complexity of social motherhood and social science.

246

WOMEN'S PROFESSIONALIZATION

The very words 'social work' and 'social worker' came into increasing use from the 1880s to denote work with the poor and to designate the people, usually the women, doing it. To some extent this was the old scientific philanthropy or practical social science decked out in new linguistic dress. The types of philanthropy pioneered in the midcentury continued as main and growing branches of social work: work in residential institutions or in clubs with young women and children, in model housing as managers and rent collectors, in hospital and district nursing, in systematic visiting of the homes of the poor, in Poor Law institutions with 'children of the state' and in Charity Organisation Society casework. But increasingly social work accommodated the whole spectrum of social reform views, including some forms of socialism, just so long as personal service to individual working people remained a feature. Attlee defined social work as 'the expression of the desire for social justice, for freedom and beauty and for the better apportionment of all the things that make up a good life'.[4] He made room in social work for prophets as well as social thinkers.

The numbers of women involved on a regular basis in social work increased, whether or not they received salaries, and the accent on training and 'careers' was new.[5] By the First World War, professional and qualifying associations had appeared in many women's occupations, particularly in the health field.[6] Social workers concerned with 'helping and caring for Women and Girls' organized into local groups and then, from 1890 affiliated to the National Union of Women Workers (NUWW), which held a peripatetic annual Conference reminiscent of the Social Science Association,[7] and helped to set rolling the training programmes for social workers which gained momentum in this period. The state entered the field of women's professional work on a new scale, and created new paid positions for women. By 1908, Clara Collet, the pioneer woman investigator at the Board of Trade, could sit down to a second annual dinner of thirty-five women Inspectors and Investigators from various government departments. The state also increasingly licensed and co-opted the existing work of women, for example in midwifery, district nursing and health visiting.

By the First World War, women's professionalization was

moving fast, but in certain predictable grooves. Although they attacked the citadel, the Fabian Women's Group did not make much headway into the centres of power in the public sphere: the higher echelons of government, civil service, law, banking and business remained largely closed to women. To the extent that women cracked the higher grades of the civil service, they held posts dealing with women or juveniles which included supervising other women workers. In medicine, the only educated profession to admit women in numbers, the patients of lady doctors tended to be women and children. The Sex Disqualification (Removal) Act of 1919 theoretically opened a new line of advance but departments of state like the Treasury simply sidestepped the law which became a 'dead letter' for women civil servants in the 1920s.[8] The Fabian women dreamed of 'an end to dependence' and the start of real freedom to choose a sphere of work. But that freedom was often constrained by the conceptions of social motherhood and of the sexual communion of labour (Chapter 5), developed by women, ratified by professional men and buttressed by the state, which structured much of women's professionalization.[9] Some women professionals positively welcomed this constraint. Cecile Matheson, active in the NUWW, investigator of *Women's Work and Wages* and later Warden of the Birmingham Women's Settlement, recommended the new university training for social work in terms of women needing

> in their work an interest that shall appeal to heart and imagination as well as to intellect and business capacity, also the middle aged worker who is without home ties of her own tends to grow weary of life and to seek to crush maternal emotions which seem to exist but give her pain.[10]

She pointed to 'the group of employments that might fitly be called the "social service" with its central salaried posts in various philanthropic undertakings'.

The first step in the professionalization process, in some sociological models (see p.219), involves the definition of a job that needs full-time attention, the delineation of core tasks and the designation of special knowledge which can only be acquired through training. What many women professionals saw as the tasks to be done or the task they were permitted to do involved bringing their womanly qualities into the public sphere. The job might involve facilitating childbirth (so that even single women could take part in birth). It might involve attending to adequate childrearing, paying special attention to education and health, and extend into guiding and protecting adolescents or, indeed, women of any age. Professional social motherhood could now be even more cavalier about overriding biological parenthood than its midcentury precursor. To a more intangible quality of moral maternity could now be added much more tangible certificates and diplomas signifying special training and scientific knowledge in a situation where legislation made it increasingly easy to remove children, once assessed as being in moral danger, into an institutional home. Miss Poole, launching a discussion on 'The Classification of Homes', a staple topic in the NUWW, warned 'that amongst many zealous workers there is not the respect for the parental tie that there ought to be'.[11]

In the period between 1880 and 1920 and indeed far beyond, educated, often professionalizing women, dominated women's social science. Yet their focus of concern or subject matter was often poorer women. Social science staged a fascinating theatre of encounter between women of different social classes, a social drama which posed crucial questions about the extent to which social difference undercut sisterhood. To add to the complexity, women's social science was not a simple single story. With such a groundswell of approval, motherhood inevitably became a contested concept, even within the field of women's social science, never mind at the boundary lines with man-made policy (sometimes created by what was called 'the masculine State'[12]).

The rest of this chapter will spotlight three different groups who help to illuminate the complexity of social science and social motherhood at the time. The cast of characters will be, first, the Women's University Settlement in Southwark to lead into a discussion of scientific social work, second the Fabian Women's Group which can exemplify a variety of scientific socialism and, third, providing a contrast to both, the Women's Co-operative Guild and especially the social settlement they ran at the People's Store in Sunderland on Coronation Street. In this period, women's groups undertaking systematic investigations and engaging in practical social science proliferated and other organizations particularly from the industrial wing of the women's movement, for example the Women's Industrial Council, could stand in for some of the groups I have chosen.

But my three cases usefully represent different approaches to social science and the Fabian Women's Group is doubly interesting because it was concerned both with women as waged workers and as housewives. I will again refer to the disciplining, protecting and empowering faces of social motherhood to finger the texture of relations with the poor and as a way of pointing to incompatible attitudes which also informed constructions of sisterhood and womanhood in this period. While I argue that one attitude appeared more prominently in the work of some groups, I am not suggesting that each group of women displayed only one aspect: the real situation was more complex. Thus some members of the Women's University Settlement, which frequently used a disciplining discourse, helped the local Women's Co-operative Guild, which I present as an empowering organization.[13] However, it is useful to distinguish between basically divergent attitudes to bring out more clearly the tensions which existed and could, in some cases, even undermine the most precious aims and cherished hopes of the social investigators and social workers themselves.

THE WOMEN'S UNIVERSITY SETTLEMENT AND SCIENTIFIC SOCIAL WORK: THE DISCOURSE OF THE DISCIPLINING MOTHER

Part of the dominant strain in the ecology of women's social science, the Women's University Settlement (WUS) carried on the older traditions of scientific philanthropy and yet pioneered the professionalization of this kind of work. The Settlement served as a depot where older routes intersected and new departures began. It did not start much activity of its own but rather supplied personnel to other agencies. Because it worked so closely with other groups sharing the same assumptions, WUS provides a convenient window onto a whole cluster of initiatives. WUS was intimately allied with the Charity Organisation Society and was even asked to become the local COS in 1891; Helen Bosanquet occasionally resided there before her marriage. WUS was closely connected with the housing initiatives of Octavia Hill who sat for more than ten years on the WUS Executive. The most influential warden of WUS, Cambridge-educated Margaret

Sewell (1851-1937), acted as the unofficial spokeswoman for the whole women's settlement movement.[14]

Following in the footsteps of Toynbee Hall for men, the Women's University Settlement opened in 1887 in a poor district of Southwark and set the model for most of the later women's houses all over the country. By 1920, at least thirteen settlements in London involved women and settlements were also operating in Birmingham, Bristol, Chesterfield, Liverpool, Manchester, Middlesborough, Stoke-on-Trent, Dundee and Belfast. WUS provided a surrogate home and family for women graduates and students who undertook the service of the poor, 'especially of the women and children' in the neighbourhood.[15] The men's settlements often served as stepping stones to political careers. George Lansbury facetiously observed that

> men who went into training under the Barnetts...could always be sure of advancement of their own interests and the interests of the poor were best served by leaving E. London to stew in its own juice while they became members of parliament, cabinet ministers, civil servants.[16]

Few such openings beckoned women. Rather the settlements provided a pathway mainly to a professionalized version of themselves in scientific social work.

As the last chapter showed, the women's settlements played a key role all around the country in getting training programmes started, usually in connection with a local university. The early phases of training involved the further development of a midcentury version of social science. Now the feminine dimensions of human life were to move beyond being simply necessary to complete the picture and achieve a full communion of labour. They were to occupy a place at the centre of social knowledge. Whatever the culminating discipline was called— whether social science, social economics, sociology or any combination of these—women's special nature and concerns would have a key role to play. Helen Bosanquet wrote an early textbook entitled *The Strength of the People: A Study in Social Economics* (1902). Drawing upon new trends in analytic and experimental psychology (Stout, James and Lloyd Morgan), she stressed the difference between animals, driven by instinct, and the human capacity to build up habits of being guided by conscious interests or rational purpose. In her analysis, as

251

indeed in much sociology of the period, personal service and self-sacrifice in larger collectivities, traits usually associated with women, were identified as the rational purpose most distinctive of humanity at its highest level of development. Bosanquet argued that the family, which was already seen as the natural location of women and their most appropriate intellectual concern, was also a key analytical element in social economics.

Throughout her life, she continued to develop the argument that unless the family were brought into focus, all social analysis would be distorted, all disciplines would be inaccurate and all social action would fail. Even the sciences of the public sphere needed to encompass the family. However distasteful it might feel to connect economics with 'that consecrated corner' of 'disinterested services, of mute affection, of intercourse which brings pleasure and not merely profit', it was precisely these 'disinterested affections of family life' which gave the greatest motive to economic activity and the first experience of altruistic habit: 'the easiest and most natural means of emancipation from the narrow cycle of the lower life'. The vaunted male egotists at the centre of old-style Utilitarian science, with their thirst for more power and wealth were dismissed as 'degenerate specimens'.[17] The family was also strategic for political science: indeed 'ultimately the State itself must always be moulded by the Family, since it is in the Family that the citizen is made'.[18] The feminine concern for the practical was to be enshrined in a science which was to be immediately relevant to real life: Bosanquet's social economics was to be an 'applied science'.[19] This became a real point of tension with the male-controlled universities (see Chapter 10).

Scientific social work tended to accept present institutions in an improved form as the highest stage of social development. Thus the theoretical part of training consisted of Bosanquet-type analysis centring on the importance of character and on the ethicized institutions which would produce its highest development. The family was never really interrogated. A patriarchal form was assumed, containing a provider-father and a home-based dependent mother. Mothers were so firmly forced into the world of nature that they were evoked with the imagery of sunshine nurturing plants (the 'child crop' in this nursery). Not usually prone to purple passages, Bosanquet launched into a lyrical lullaby about the need for mother-love in infancy and beyond:

as the child grows older, this sun of love, which shines alike on the just and the unjust, is no less necessary to enable it to develop its highest qualities, to open out into blossom and fruit.[20]

Bosanquet frowned upon mothers working for money either inside or outside the home and considered motherhood a full-time if not a life-long occupation.[21] Gender division marked the culture that men and women settlers brought to the East End. Men settlers shared art and intellect with the poor while women settlers participated in 'the analogy suggested between our culture of fruit and flowers and the community's culture of its children'.

The practical side of training involved becoming oriented to the map of statutory and voluntary agencies in the parish.[22] In this ecology, the role of social workers was, in nurse M.E. Loane's already-quoted words, 'the completion of family and neighbourhood life'.[23] They functioned as social mothers whose service— indeed self-sacrifice—provided the necessary catalyst for proper working-class family life. Bosanquet inflated the service of social workers at the expense of poor people's sacrifice:

> The unceasing sacrifice of patiently unintelligent women and selfishly unintelligent men is of little use to the community. It does not rise to the level of self-sacrifice, for there is seldom anything voluntary about it; it is submission to the brute forces round them.[24]

In a chapter called 'the Remedy', she urged the adoption of 'the aggressive method' used some 80 years earlier by the Reverend Thomas Chalmers which involved refusing relief from above and 'insisting on claims to mutual helpfulness which the natural ties of a family imposed on its members. Nay, he even went so far as to insist that such a claim existed between neighbours'.[25] A curious paradox this—making social workers necessary to coerce into being the ordinary kinship and neighbourhood networks which were already there, and on which the poor had always relied in order to survive. In Bosanquet's preliminary textbook, the social worker appeared in the guise of a disciplining mother.

The stance of the disciplining or even the punishing mother was already conspicuous in the scientific philanthropy tradition. I am certainly not arguing that the upper-class women brought hostile feelings to their work. This would be to iron flat a very complex tissue of experience, which included among its strands the tremendous courage to step beyond conventional bourgeois expectations into public work and take up residence in new-style collegiate families, where deep and enduring friendship formed one of the patterns among women social workers themselves. Social workers also wished to extend friendship to the poor. Having heard Canon Barnett speak about East-enders needing friendship more than money, Miss Patterson decided, 'I want to go and be their friend: I know they are drunkards and a worse class of people than I have ever seen, but I would try so hard to help them if only Papa and Mamma will let me'.[26] And serve them she did for the rest of her life. Compassion for the sufferings of the poor, respect for their heroic coping in situations of immense difficulty, liking and learning from one another, disdain for amateur do-gooders who prescribed nostrums irrelevant to material realities, despair at the inadequacy of the social worker's help—these feelings all formed part of the rich emotional mixture involved in inter-class contact. Moreover some social workers saw their effort as preparing poorer women for citizenship. In an angry letter to novelist and settlement activist, Mrs Humphrey Ward, Helen Bosanquet argued the case for votes for poor women (even the 'slatterns' on the streetcorner), to bring them dignity (not least in the eyes of men), to give them 'an interest in matters outside the narrow round of their daily toil' and 'to contribute an element of experience to our political deliberations which no other class can adequately represent'.[27]

But the dominant discourses of scientific social work assumed authority as well as compassion. Settlers often described themselves in a cosy language of neighbourliness: they moved into an area to become neighbours to the poor and thereby create a neighbourhood. But settlement was also built into a more explicit language of cultural imperialism which accented neighbourhood in a harsher way. For Attlee the very word 'settlement' assumed the presence of dangerous, sub-human Others and a practice of imperialism at home equivalent to that in the colonies abroad:

the very name 'Settlement' suggests that...when they were started, the lives of the working classes were something apart from the rest of the nation, so far apart, indeed, that to visit them was like entering a foreign and possibly savage territory where a fort was to be erected, from which expeditions could be sent to get in touch with the natives.[28]

Alice Hodson of the Lady Margaret Hall Settlement used imperialist imagery to depict the ideal women's settlement warden as an authoritarian but benevolent colonial governor and also a domineering yet loving mother capable (unlike men) of bringing about change in a peaceful and harmonious way:

> If someone were wanted to take entire charge of a newly conquered territory, how well she would fill the post! She could teach the natives all things necessary for their moral and physical well-being: design their houses, lay out their gardens, and teach them how to sew and to cook. She would use the resources of the land for their general edification, and without any commotion or disturbance would soon make the place into a self-respecting, well-doing colony.[29]

As Vicinus has so perceptively noted, the imperialist metaphor was helpful to upper-class women. Service in the empire and emigration to the colonies promised adventure, freedom, space and power to men. Women could also find a kind of 'freedom by "emigrating" to the East end'.[30] The conflation of a colonial governor with a strong mother pointed to the kind of stance settlement women could take in relation to poor women.

The disciplining tradition of social work contained many forms of educative surveillance, making continuous survey possible. Octavia Hill's housing managers aimed not only to oversee housing complexes and give owners a modest return on their capital, but to use the weekly visit to collect the rents as an opportunity to instil habits of order in the tenants. 'Punctual payment is enforced', Canon Barnett explained, 'chiefly because of the element of order and regularity it introduces into families, the cause of whose trouble is generally disorder.'[31] Standing her ground in the face of an encroaching municipal sector, Hill insisted that 'the poor and less disciplined, above all, need trained ladies as managers in their dwellings'. Ellen Chase, an American student of Hill's, was certain that the re-formation of tenants would come through the power of friendship creating 'an enlarged family'. But she also acknowledged the reality of another kind of power: 'we were allowed to govern our little domain as we liked and make of it what we could.'[32] Eviction was the ultimate threat, although evidence from Beatrice Webb's domain, the Katherine Buildings, where she collected rents for a time, suggests that tenants voted with their feet and that those who remained were a self-selected group.[33]

Charity Organisation Society practice could easily move a step further from discipline to punishment. The COS regarded indiscriminate almsgiving as one of the most powerful causes of urban pauperism, not least because it demoralized the poor, made them dependent on outside agencies for survival and encouraged them to develop skills of deception to exploit the welfare system. As an example, Sewell pointed to an enterprising woman who arranged to receive help from the Anglican clergy of her own parish, from Sisters of another parish, from a Roman Catholic priest and from a Chapel milk charity. She then had the impudence to apply to the local COS for relief as well![34] The COS aimed to give assistance only where it would enable cases, usually families, to become self-supporting. From the COS viewpoint, family casework, that is careful investigation together with follow-up inspection, was needed to discriminate between what were first called the 'deserving' and 'undeserving', but later called the 'helpable' and the 'unhelpable poor'. Whatever the subjects of scrutiny were called, the basic COS concern with classifying people on the divide and remedy principle and the obsession with exposing frauds could easily lead to a basic suspicion of all applicants.[35] Since the COS also aimed to co-ordinate voluntary and state activity, they shunted the unhelpable poor in the direction of the hated Poor Law authorities. The dissonance between the gentle rhetoric of love and the harsh reality of action struck Beatrice Webb who insisted that

> The one door opened by these 'friends of the poor' to all those they were unable to help privately, deserving as well as undeserving, was that of the workhouse with its penal discipline 'according to the principles of 1834'. Thus, well-to-do men and women of goodwill who had gone out to offer personal service and friendship to the dwellers in the slums, found themselves transformed into a body of amateur detectives, in some cases initiating prosecutions of persons they thought to be impostors,

and arousing more suspicion and hatred than the recognised officers of the law.[36]

The punitive stance often took its psychic toll on the social workers themselves. The COS provided a harsh discourse which was in constant tension with some of the more generous feelings of the social workers. Trained by means of lectures and an apprenticeship in the COS, Alice Hodson found COS attitudes 'really up-to-date and scientific' but 'a little paralysing'. Leaving aside her difficulties about interrogating 'a proud sensitive man' which made her 'feel hot and cold all over', or her inhibitions about visiting the poor 'when you really have no particular reason for going to see them', she found the Committee meetings

> sometimes very depressing, for there is often such a stoney-hearted, cold-blooded feeling about their way of doing things. I sympathize with the member who said that when he hung his hat up outside the door he could not help saying, to himself, 'Those who enter here leave hope outside'. I do indeed leave hope, and sometimes courage too, outside.[37]

Giving nothing at all in a situation of crying need felt brutal to many social workers, as well as to the poor themselves. Withholding seemed to contradict Christian injunctions to charity as a mode, in Beatrice Webb's already quoted words, of entering into 'communion with the supreme spirit of love at work in the universe'. Hodson felt this tension and sometimes dealt with it, like many other social workers did, by allowing generosity to override discrimination, by giving the forbidden doles and be damned.[38] But at other times resolutions became more contorted indicating the harsh directions into which the COS pushed people of good will. Hodson had just been reading the life of St Francis and the subversive thought struck her that 'according to his teaching efforts to make people thrifty are a mistake'. She also pondered 'strong definite language in the Bible about taking no thought for the morrow, and not being anxious about food and clothing'. But, in the end, she decided that 'the only way to carry out that command is to be really thrifty. How can a reasonable person be justified in taking not thought for the morrow, unless he has done all he can do to prepare for it'.[39] Only bread which had been diligently saved could be cast upon the waters!

Not surprisingly social workers themselves strained at the COS bit and tried to break out of it before the First World War. The Guild of Help movement, started in Bradford in 1904, and the Personal Service Society, laid emphasis not only on the importance of friendly visiting, but on co-operating with the whole range of local authorities and not simply the Poor Law. The wider pattern of co-operation became dominant after the First World War and was also expressed in the proliferation of local Councils of Social Service, composed of representatives from both the voluntary and government sectors. Instead of privileging the discourse of social motherhood as the language of relations between women of different classes, voluntary agencies now appealed 'to common citizenship', either under-lining service to the municipality or to the 'organized community'. They managed to attract a 'different class of visitor', according to Dorothy Keeling of Liverpool, 'from the lower income groups. We thus felt that we established a rather new tradition in the history of social work'.[40] Nonetheless, social inequalities remained largely intact. Perhaps Margaret Llewelyn Davies of the Women's Co-operative Guild came nearest the truth when she acknowledged that 'promiscuous giving produces evils' but refused to be 'reconciled to any suppression of the compassionate instincts'. The real solution she felt was not the 'negative and estranging politics' of the COS but 'deeper sacrifices than have yet been made, a change in life's conditions, when the odious words "rich" and "poor" will be wiped out of our vocabulary'.[41] The kind of social sacrifice she proposed, which amounted to a voluntary social revolution, was incon-ceivable to many women of good will.

THE FABIAN WOMEN'S GROUP:
PROTECTIVE MOTHERHOOD
UNDERCUTTING SISTERHOOD?

The protective face of social mothering was most visible among women from the middle class or gentry who saw poor women as victims of systems or forces beyond their control. The notion of 'reform' involved here had less to do with remaking individual character and more to do with remaking legal, political and even economic systems. But the question of who was to think and act for whom was still very problematic and advocacy tended to

258

outweigh any commitment to agency for poor women. Protective mothers could be exceedingly sensitive to sex oppression and extremely admiring and supportive of their poorer 'sisters'. Yet at the same time they could continue to infantilize the poor by failing to see poor women as capable of acting for themselves or by not thinking very much about how to skill poor women to become historical agents in their own right (or write!). In a similar case today, Chandra Mohanty has pointed up how third world women feel oppressed by the tendency of their metropolitan sisters to see them as 'victims' and to think and act on their behalf, which recasts the old cultural imperialism into a new feminist shape.[42]

Continuing from the mid-Victorian period and developing into the field of moral welfare, protective mothers had been concerned with prostitutes as the exemplary female victims of manifold systems of oppression, not least the oppression of male sex. By the late-nineteenth and early-twentieth century women researchers were also placing working-class wives and mothers at the centre of the investigative stage although all the issues opened up by focusing on them also allowed for discussion, often in a coded rather than explicit way, of experiences also shared by women from other social groups.[43] Thus if prostitution was the only permitted subject area in which to express fears of sexual danger, so a focus on the economic and legal traps which constrained poor wives also had their analogues elsewhere. Nor was male violence a one-class affair. It is worth keeping in mind that a protective discourse about poor women, of which male authority clearly approved, also opened up a space for exploring gender problems common to women of all classes and for trying to forge the conceptual underpinnings of a pan-social sisterhood.

The Fabian Women's Group made the major attempt in the period to theorize the possibilities of a united women's movement across the divides of class. It was a socialist grouping with a unifying ambition, but I will argue that debilitating tensions remained between its analysis and its political practice. By adopting a protective stance in its practical politics with poor women, it could reproduce some of the very inequalities it was trying to remove. While such a discrepancy is most striking in a socialist movement explicitly aiming for equality, it also featured in other interclass groups where professional women predominated. Organized in 1908, initially by a small group of women most of whom had suffered imprisonment for their suffragette actions, the Fabian Women's Group quickly grew to 200 paying members within the year. Composed of intellectual and professional women, including the lower status but rapidly proliferating teachers, clerks, secretaries, writers and journalists, the group also managed to involve in its activities if not attract into membership many prominent women from labour and socialist movements.[44] Traffic moved in the other direction too when Fabian women took active roles in other groups, for example, Barbara Hutchins in the Women's Industrial Council (1894-c.1917) which also aimed to 'organize special and systematic inquiry into the conditions of working women' and Dr Ethel Bentham in the Women's Labour League, formed in 1906 to work for labour representation and for women's social interests in their neighbourhoods.[45] Beatrice Webb played little part in the Fabian Women's Group.

Like the earlier Owenite socialists, the members of the Fabian Women's Group were determined not to allow the class issue to conceal gender oppression. 'Socialists must recognize', they insisted, 'that women's economic revolt is not merely against the enslaving economic control of the capitalist state, but against the enslaving economic control of the husband.'[46] They were committed to economic independence for women of every type whether married, single, mother, childless, young or old. This central concern structured their social scientific work because 'the greatest stumbling block we found in our way was that women themselves have not studied the question scientifically in their own interests. The available material is presented by the male investigator with his own unavoidable sex bias.'[47] So, for example, Ellen Smith undertook to test one of the strongest arguments for paying women lower wages for the same work, namely that they were usually dependent on their husbands and had no dependents of their own. Her questionnaire-based research found that over 51 per cent of the respondents wholly or partially supported dependents.[48] The Fabian Women's Group is rightly remembered for an impressive series of study groups, social investigations and analytic works illuminating the economic position of women.

The Fabian women started with a map of the research that needed to be done and embarked on study groups first on the

Disabilities of Women as Workers (1909) and then on the Disabilities of Mothers as Workers (1910).[49] In both enquiries they toppled a number of pillars of conventional wisdom about sexual difference like the idea that women were incapacitated by menstruation or menopause, made mad by uterine or ovarian disorders or that women were significantly weaker or less intellectual than men.[50] Yet they embraced some other sacred cows, especially motherhood. Entering fully into the spirit of the times they asserted that the only feature distinguishing women from men was their capacity for motherhood: thus maternality became the essence of femininity. They also connected motherhood directly with service to the nation. Childbearing, declared gynaecologist Dr Ethel Vaughan-Sawyer in a typical effusion, 'is the supreme service which she alone can render to the State of which she is a member, and is on a par with the primary duty of the adult male to defend his country against invasion'. Women's special task in citizenship was 'race-production'.[51]

While the Fabian women upheld maternity as the key point of sexual difference with men, they also felt strongly that some women had 'no natural aptitude for the rearing of children' and that all women needed a release from childcare into other productive work. 'The normal woman', according to Mabel Atkinson, 'like the normal man, desires a mate and a child, but she does not therefore desire nothing else.' The Fabian women were contesting the idea that motherhood was virtually a life-sentence a view held by many male observers and by most women in the scientific philanthropy tradition. Instead the Fabians were keen to explore modes of collectivizing housework and the possibility of having children looked after in nurseries by trained professionals, indeed people like themselves.[52]

The real challenge became to combine motherhood and economic independence. Around 1914, a number of writings appeared which analysed the historical class divisions within the women's movement and the potential for greater unification. Here the women broke new intellectual ground: 'the economic history of this country from the point of view of the workers, to say nothing of the women workers, has yet to be written'.[53] Mabel Atkinson, later a lecturer in political economy in London University, argued that before the industrial revolution 'the household was, as a general rule, the unit of industry and women worked in it as members of the family for the production of exchange as well as of use values'. During the industrial revolution women from different classes experienced the separation of household and workplace very differently: 'parasitism became the fate of middle class women, ruthless exploitation that of the working class women'. Single women of the middle-class struggled for entry into the competitive male arena of the public sphere and eschewed marriage. Working-class women, by contrast, were brutally thrust into economic competition where they weakened the position of their menfolk. As a result two groups of oppressed women from two different historical experiences wanted seemingly opposite things and were inclined to incompatible strategies:

> among working women there is less sex consciousness. Evolving social enthusiasm tends to run rather into the channel of labour revolt in general than into a specific revolution against the conditions alleged to be due to sex differences. The working woman feels her solidarity with the men of her class rather than their antagonism to her. These facts explain the relative lukewarmness of working class women in the distinctly feminist movement.[54]

However, now the times were changing and both sections of the 'women's movement' were moving closer together. Working women were finding that the masculine state and the male working class could collude to ignore them, blatantly the case with the National Insurance Act. Middle-class women now yearned for a life which combined work and motherhood, not one that forced a choice between the two. Analysis had revealed the ground for a more united sisterhood. But the practical politics of protection were perhaps in tension with solidarity or possibly not adequate foundations on which to build the unity the Fabian women sought. How did the Fabian women relate to poor women?

Early in its life, the group received funds 'to study the effect on mother and child of sufficient nourishment before and after birth'. Under the direction of Maud Pember Reeves, they changed the terms of reference and instead of distributing food and monitoring its effects, they carried out a painstaking, five-year long investigation of the weekly budgets of some forty families with an income of *Round About a Pound a Week* (the title of their study published in 1912 and 1913). Although the Bermondsey mothers were 'curiously efficient' at mental arithmetic, the idea of keeping a written budget was largely alien to them. Pember Reeves recounted the difficulties in teaching the women to do budgets, a skill she did not think would be particularly useful to them once the enquiry had finished. She produced the most sustained dialogue in this connection and, by savouring the comedy of the situation, made the actors seem faintly ridiculous, for example when reporting how children played scribe with a prolix attention to the stories within which the mothers remembered their expenditure.[55] Despite its being 'extremely humiliating' to eight women, Pember Reeves disclosed the fact of their illiteracy probably thinking that the book would never reach them. The study supplied perceptive chapters, peppered with remarks from the Bermondsey women, about the kinds of issues which especially preoccupied investigators from above like housing, sleeping accommodation, facilities for cooking and washing, etc. This information both educated reformers and supplied grist for their political mills.

Pember Reeves and her Fabian colleagues showed their great admiration for these poor women being able to manage at all in the circumstances but also a sense of the women being ground down by the material pressures:

> That the diet of the poorer London children is insufficient, unscientific, and utterly unsatisfactory is horribly true. But that the real cause of this state of things is the ignorance or indifference of their mothers is untrue. What person or body of people, however educated and expert, could maintain a working man in physical efficiency and rear healthy children on the amount of money which is all these same mothers have to deal with? It would be an impossible problem if set to trained and expert people. How much more an impossible problem when set to the saddened, weakened, over burdened wives of London labourers?[56]

The investigators constructed poor women as active if oppressed in the private sphere but in need of advocacy in the public sphere. In the final two chapters which analysed causes and remedies Pember Reeves gave the housewives little to say. She had fenced them out earlier by an assumption that their horizons were too limited to be of use: 'the same surroundings with a little more money a little more security and a little less to do, was about the best their imaginations could grasp'.[57]

This silencing led to a strange outcome. The Fabian investigators ended up by calling for more state intervention and especially for a 'Department of Public Guardianship', making the assumption that parents 'would be only too glad to take advantage of its advice'. Yet Pember Reeves was aware that the poor mother's

> experience of State guardianship of her children may be that Public authority, without troubling as to whether or not fulfilment be in her power, forces further duties and responsibilities on to her shoulders in respect of those children through the threatened medium of the police, with all the horrors of prison in the background.[58]

The Fabian women diagnosed the problem of the state in terms of its being a 'masculine state' to be remedied by votes for women. Not all working people were equally confident that the feminized state would make the difference and class tensions often remained even where women worked together in the women's suffrage campaign.[59]

Of course poorer women appreciated the support they received from the active and articulate Fabian women on issues like legislative protection of women's work and state endowment of motherhood. Without detracting from the committed activity of the Fabian women, it would be possible to characterize their approach as containing tensions between advocacy and empowerment. Working-class women rarely helped to set the agenda in most of the investigative, analytic or policy work produced by the Fabian Women's Group. Rather advocates usually spoke on their behalf, a relationship which always makes the kind of unity envisioned by Atkinson difficult to achieve. However much unifying categories, like women workers or sisterhood or even citizenship, may be employed, like the contested concept of motherhood, these categories can also express inequality, especially where some women workers supervise others, or where some sisters are considered big siblings with authority and others regarded as poor little sisters to be looked after, or where some women citizens have the vote while others are kept waiting.[60]

Professional expertise, unless handled with care, could also result in some women disempowering others. For the Women's Industrial Council enquiry into Married Women's Work, Hutchins wrote up the investigations carried out by ex-shopworker and later Labour cabinet minister, Margaret Bondfield, who betrayed her lack of confidence when discussing her Yorkshire research:

> I learned a lot about home life in the woollen textiles, but it was not the sort of information that could be much use as the basis of enquiry. I realized how unfitted I was for the task, which could be much better done by health visitors and properly trained investigators.[61]

Why was she unfitted? Only because of growing conventions about agendas of significant questions and the presumption that newly-established training was needed to carry them out. Some Fabian women regretted the tendency to represent poor women rather than help them to represent themselves. Thus Dr Ethel Bentham, who gave evidence for the Women's Labour League to the Royal Commission on Divorce and Matrimonial Causes, observed that

> my experience, which naturally coloured the whole, is that of a single woman and a middle class woman looking on, however sympathetically and with whatever comprehension, still from outside....the conviction that we could bring to the Commission and to the public cannot be as weighty as that which must come from the utterances of those who know of their own knowledge, and tell us in English that may halt but leaves us in no doubt of their meaning, that some of the very foundations of society are rotten beneath their feet.[62]

THE WOMEN'S CO-OPERATIVE GUILD:
THE DISCOURSE OF
THE EMPOWERING MOTHER?

The dialogue of the dominating mother and the deficient or defenceless daughter may have been important in negotiations over gender roles with middle-class men. But, arguably, it created unfavourable conditions for the growth of another kind of family: a sisterhood among women of different classes. To use the language of motherhood again, from the point of view of the poor, what was needed was a social mother who could let children go and recognize them as fully grown adults who were separate and different from herself, who could be active agents in shaping their own fate and who could organize independently from her. What was needed was not a disciplining or a protecting mother but an empowering mother. Then, as now, this good mother was hard to find. However, Margaret Llewelyn Davies (1861-1944), of the Women's Co-operative Guild, seems to have been one of the exceptional people. After attending Queen's College, of which her father was principal, and Girton College which her Aunt founded, she followed a familiar path into voluntary social work in the Marylebone neighbourhood. But she then took a different turning when she became active in the Women's Guild which reached out to the constituency that was the most notoriously difficult to organize: married working-class women based at home.

Davies served as the General Secretary of the Guild between 1889 and 1921 and proved an inspired organiser. Not only was she committed to helping women develop the skills for self-organisation and active citizenship in a democracy but she worked hard to open public space where poor women could speak for themselves. Whenever she was asked to testify to state inquiries, she immediately asked Guild members for their own statements which she submitted instead. Their evidence to the Royal Commission on Divorce created a sensation because it was unprecedented. In an argument about whether evidence from the Church of England's Mothers' Union should be taken more seriously, she grounded credibility on self-representation, insisting that 'the views of a self-governing organisation of workers are more representative of working-class opinion than those of any working-class body managed by another class'.[63]

The politics of self-representation shaped Davies's investigative practice. For the survey on maternity experiences, she thought it would be 'valuable to allow the women to tell their own story in their own way'. Writing to 600 Guild officials. She arguably led the witnesses by asking them not only to answer five simple statistical questions (about number of children, stillbirths, miscarriages etc.) but to say what they have felt about the difficulty of taking care, the ignorance that has prevailed on the conditions of pregnancy and how these conditions result in lack of health and energy, meaning that a woman cannot do justice to herself or give her best to her husband and children.[64]

But the 400 replies, of which 160 were reproduced in *Maternity: Letters from Working Women*, made many spirited proposals for remedial action and brought out themes not covered by this guidance, some of which ended up at the centre of Davies's analysis. Thus Davies identified insufficient wages as the major cause of problems and indicated that relations between husband and wife could exacerbate or alleviate difficulties.

Working-class women experienced Davies as immensely supportive, as local testimonials on the occasion of her retirement showed. From Enfield, Eleanor Hood remembered how it was the sight of Davies's face, the veritable vision of the empowering mother, which encouraged her to speak in public for the first time:

> I was almost frightened to death, but when I stood up to speak I saw your face in the audience, and the different expressions that passed over it were an inspiration to me, when you smiled or clapped I went on with a fresh heart, and when you congratulated me at the end, I made up my mind to do all I could to merit your confidence in me. And I am not the only one who has to thank you for showing them what they are capable of doing, over and over again.[65]

When given the chance to speak in their own voices, poor women made clear that they preferred a setting where they came together as adult equals. The experience of being infantilized into obedient daughters by putative mothers from another class was irksome. A Guildswoman made a revealing comparison between the Guild and the Mothers' Meetings, run by the parish and the Ladies' Sanitary Association:

> I used for a short time to attend a Mothers' Meeting, and did so more from a point of duty than anything, but after joining the Guild I did not feel to have the patience to listen to the simple childish tales that were read at the former, and did not like to feel we had no voice in its

control. There is such a different feeling in speaking of trial and troubles to Guilders (where they are real) than to speak to the Ladies of the Mothers' Meeting. You know that they (the Guilders) have a fellow feeling being all on an equality.[66]

Arguably this Guilder could have been an unusual woman who enjoyed holding branch office and making the fullest use of the chance to be an active citizen within the movement. What of women who had less energy to give to the Guild?

The Women's Co-operative Guild was keen to bring co-operation to the very poor and devised the idea of a Social Settlement connected to a People's Store to help with the task. The chief 'experiment' located in Coronation Street, Sunderland, got coverage in the co-operative and the national press and in various journals like *The Hospital*, which ran an article about it entitled 'Modern Sociology' and 'A Slum Experiment'.[67] Both in its activities and the quality of relationship between the settlers and the local women, Coronation Street makes an interesting counterpoint with the Women's University Settlement and with the Fabian Women's Group. Davies first envisaged the project to a large extent within the familiar social work mould. Speaking of the need for a 'co-operative colony' and even a 'colonial committee' to run it, she went on to detail the services it could provide including 'all the various aides to thrift' and rent collecting 'on the plan of Miss Octavia Hill', which she had also cited to meet the objections of male co-operators that the majority of slum dwellers were 'a very worthless class of people'. With the help of Mrs Abbott and in the face of grumbles from the Co-operative Union who wanted to save the money, Davies carried out a survey of several local areas for information about poverty and shopping in the winter of 1902. Besides using informants from the co-operative movement, she relied heavily on state inspectors, especially Lady Sanitary Inspectors and School Attendance Officers, to take her into poor homes. In York she also de-briefed Rowntree and his secretary at some length.[68]

But the idea of a co-operative store as the centre of the project, the democratic thrust of the Guild and the movement as a whole, and the personality of Davies herself as the main settler in Sunderland led to interesting transformations of the settlement experience. There was a clearer recognition of the material and cultural conditions of the life of the poor, and the store enabled a new kind of connection with these realities. Rather than giving good advice on cooking and feeding, as other types of social workers tended to do—advice which was sometimes laughably irrelevant to the practicalities of preparing food in poor homes where storage space and cooking stoves were usually absent—the Coronation Street Store supplied an appetizing cooked meat counter. So popular was this facility, that the People's Store Butchery department in March 1903 actually had the lowest working expenses and highest profits per pound of sales and generated a 'divi' bigger than anywhere else in town.[69]

Because of the store, a different relationship with street life, so often a point of cultural clash between social workers and the poor, became possible. Vicinus has highlighted the paradoxical process whereby women social workers increased their own freedom of movement in the streets while pursuing activities which took the poor off the streets. With the blessing of the 'Store Ladies', the poor absorbed the store into their street culture, making it a part of the street spectacle and a backdrop for the playing of the scene. The store, which was specially built with large windows and brilliantly lit until very late at night, was

> as good as a Christmas tree for the small children out of the neighbouring alleys. The bright electric light makes our corner such a capital place for games in the evening, and besides there is the chance of seeing visitors go in and out, or having a talk with the 'missus from the desk'. A small escort will sometimes trot beside us up the street when there is anything specially important, or confidential to say. 'We do like having the store here', said one of them.[70]

The eyecatching displays of 'ticing' food and notices especially at holiday time provided a focus for 'a kind of outdoor club for the neighbourhood'. The genuine delight that Davies took in the children (she lovingly jotted snippets of their conversation into an exercise book) paid dividends with their parents. Children crowded in to join the penny bank which had over 2,000 members by the beginning of 1904. At first, they would make three or four transactions a day—perhaps playing with it nearly as a game or perhaps directing the multiple monetary tran-sactions of a day to flow through a formal agency. The children then often brought their parents in (or instances where this happened were publicized): for example the little girl who drew out a shilling and 'gave her mother sixpence to help her join the store'.[71]

In a style very different from that of other social work strategies, the resident ladies actually created space, beyond the usual meetings of the shareholders of the store, for poor women to express what they wanted. At holiday times like Easter Tuesday, Davies and her co-worker invited the nearest women neighbours to take tea in the little hall festooned with spring flowers. From twenty-six families, twenty women came with babies, and, after a song with a chorus from a neighbour, 'we had a talk about all the ways in which the store and the hall could be of use'. The women made many suggestions, among them that the store could sell coal and oil, that a summer outing would be nice, that children should be put out to skilled trades.[72] As was usual in women's social work, poor mothers were a special concern but here, besides setting up a Guild branch which met on Wednesday evenings, and mounting lectures on family health by Dr Bertha Webb, settlement activity was informed by the sense of the women having very little opportunity for public enjoyment. 'The women don't manage to get out "holidaying"', wrote Davies when giving the account of the Easter tea, 'and they seemed to appreciate this little change, and being "waited upon".' The Tuesday night party, which packed out the hall, had been virtually taken over by mothers as the only activity, including Guild meetings, to which they could bring their babies: 'sometimes it might almost be called a baby show'.[73]

The store ladies targeted adolescent girls, another usual focus of the work of the social mother, and set up a Co-operative League for young women which met on Thursday evenings. It supplied the usual dose of talks on health and beauty; Yet there were differences here too, like trips to visit the Leaguers at work. By focusing on the working parts of their lives, the store ladies did something to address the anomaly of considering grown wage-earners as 'girls', a kind of infantilization which was sometimes resented elsewhere. Margaret McMillan's ill-fated singing class came to a climax when the 'girls' (aged 15 to 30 plus), sobered by rumours about wage reductions, enquired into Margaret's situation and turned the motherhood tables:

kindness, a motherly kindness and deep concern burned in their eyes and made a warm atmosphere. I was in the arms of Whitechapel.

But the girls went on to advise her to 'chuck it':

These here lessons o'yorn ain't no good to us. You are so comical with yer books and yer singin'. What d'ye tike us for? Kids? Babies in Harms, hey?...Them people as come abaht a-'elping of us with 'ymns, and jawin' us, and a-getting up tea-fights—well—their buns is alright, but they ain't got the 'ang of us, see?[74]

Despite its success, in autumn 1904 the Coronation Street Settlement closed under pressure from the Sunderland Co-operative Society. For some time a large faction had both resisted special treatment for any co-op store, especially when this meant extra expenditure, and expressed suspicion of 'settlement' as a mode of work tainted by philanthropy. In the end, it would seem an alliance between equality and parsimony combined to defeat a strategy of positive discrimination. Some democratic men of the movement, wanting an equality of treatment here and now, came into conflict with the women of the Guild who insisted that special treatment was needed precisely in order to move towards a situation of greater equality at a future time for the very poor.[75] The store continued without the accompanying cultural activities and survived beyond the days of Davies's retirement: she referred to the whole episode of the settlement in her speech accepting the Freedom of the Guild. Until 1921 she played the role of secretary extraordinary, of empowering mother, not within the context of a settlement but for the Guild itself.

SOCIAL SCIENCE AND
CULTURAL DIFFERENCE

Then as now, deep class differences could undermine the effective practice of social science and social work. Thorny class problems also created a difficult soil for the growth of a woman's culture or of a new kind of family of sisterhood among women across the class divide. Scientific social workers, particularly those in the visiting agencies, became more aware than ever before of the class chasms they had to cross. Yet even some of the most sensitive among them could not finally embrace cultural difference without thinking it cultural inferiority. An anthropologist by instinct, visiting nurse M.E. Loane edged very close to an appreciation of cultural difference on a key issue of concern, morality:

> in the real essentials of morality, they (the poor) are, as a whole, far more advanced than is generally believed, but they range the list of human virtues in a different order from that commonly adopted by the more educated classes. Generosity ranks far above justice, sympathy before truth, love before chastity, a pliant and obliging disposition before a rigidly honest one. [76]

But in the end she drew back: 'in brief', she concluded, 'the less admixture of intellect required for the practise of any virtue, the higher it stands in popular estimation'. Since she prized intellect, her verdict seemed devaluing—the poor were loving but not very intelligent. Looking more closely at her juxtaposition of virtues, she really seemed to be saying that the poor valued a kind of loving which did not involve withholding. Compared with the middle-class idea of the place of love, the poor did not feel that values like justice, truth, chastity or honesty should impede or override uninhibited giving.

The class difference over moral values jeopardized social work. The cultural clash over honesty was a fundamental problem in social investigation. Equally difficult was the simple fact of class distance and mutual suspicion. Social investigators, rent collectors and district nurses continually argued that they were in a special position to see the objective picture because they had no charity to give or because they were part of the daily material needs of the poor (for housing and health). The fact that Beatrice Webb could group the rent collector with the School Attendance Officer as part of 'the normal machinery' of their lives indicated just how little she really saw from the point of view of the poor.[77] 'N-spectres' like the Attendance Officer (the 'punishment man') were often anathema to the poor, something voluntary visitors and career social workers continually puzzled about. Always a sensitive observer, Loane noticed this 'horror of inspectors' and its consequences. Often the poor were torn between dislike for an abuse and dislike for inspectors and just as often allowed hatred of inspectors to prevail and the abuse to go unreported. For example, child abuse was frowned upon and yet the poor also feared the N-Spectre from the 'Cruelty Society' (the National Society for the Prevention of Cruelty to Children), and suspicion lingered even while, according to Behlmer, the poor became increasingly willing to enlist 'the cruelty man' into their own efforts to maintain neighbourhood standards.[78] The army of inspectors entering the houses of the poor increased in this period as did the ranks of volunteer visitors and career social workers. It is really no surprise that the poor should smudge any clear dividing line between different categories of visitor and treat the whole collective plague with suspicion and reserve. Working-class women closed class ranks and created real problems for social workers that Loane shrewdly identified. The poor suspected the motives of other classes and would tend to confide in their own kind, thus thwarting mutual confidence and affection. 'Class barriers', wrote Loane,

> are firmly erected and closely guarded by the poor. Any working man's wife would more readily confide her private affairs to a neighbour with whom she has had bitter, year-long quarrels, than she would to the kindest and most discreet of nurses or district visitors.[79]

In turn the more disciplining social workers suspected the motives of the poor. The new recognition that different classes attached a different degree of importance to honesty threw question marks over the value of interview and of statistics of any kind. Unfortunately some of the investigators reached their most profound insights while sharply on the lookout for frauds, and went on to berate the character of the poor rather than to interrogate the process of the interclass interview itself. Investigators stumbled upon the truth that the skill of the poor and relatively powerless was to play to different audiences and to tell them what they wanted to hear, consciously or unconsciously acting out what they felt were their interrogator's expectations of them. A complex drama of interaction took place that would have to be untangled before the 'facts' could be got straight. Partly, the poor were displaying their good manners; courtesy dictated an obliging disposition. Thus the Fabian investigators initially found a

> consensus that the strange lady would probably like to sit in a draught and, if complimented on her knowledge of the value of fresh air and open windows, she might

repeat in a weary manner commonplaces on the subject which had obviously been picked up from a nurse, doctor or sanitary inspector.[80]

Partly the ability of the poor to adapt to the audience enabled them to gain any advantage in a situation basically stacked against them. The advantage might simply be protection against further inquisition or it might be some kind of a dole. Helen Bosanquet was exasperated at the way the poor regarded religious visitors as 'natural prey'. Equally struck by their capacity to shift into different languages, she described how once

> I went to receive applications for relief in a parish room connected with one of our churches. I used to see the same people afterwards in a different place and capacity, and was astonished at their completely different tone and bearing. In the first instance I was regarded as a professional 'sister', and their talk was interlarded with pious ejaculations and enumerations of the classes and services and mothers' meetings which they attended, and I seldom got any real intercourse with them until I gave them an appointment to meet me at another address.[81]

When coupled with reticence especially about wages and expenditure, the interview, which had never really been questioned in social survey technique before, became problematic. Loane came to feel that direct questions were not so quick a route to information as circuitous chat, double checking with neighbours and keen observation on regular visits.[82]

Hardly ever recognized or acknowledged, the psyche of the women investigators coloured what they saw. The whole East End experience exhilarated and frightened the social workers and challenged their deepest tolerances and taboos. They expressed their own sense of mental vertigo, of balance at risk in descriptions of street life which assaulted all their senses. Helen Bosanquet observed how a

> walk down one of these street during the busy hours of the evening *bewilders* every sense; the uncertain flare of the kerosene over the stalls mingles with the steadier blaze of innumerable gas-jets to *dazzle* the eyes, the hoarse shouts of costers and shopmen rising above the chatter, laughter, and wrangling of the crowd *deafen* the

ears; while pungent odours, amongst which fried fish is always the strongest, *assail* the nostrils on every hand until we turn for relief to the quiet and darkness of some deserted side street (italics added).[83]

Dirt, that powerful symbol of matter out of place, of rampant disorder in the middle-class sensibility, seemed to lurk and penetrate everywhere. Hodson felt that dirt even 'deposited itself in the innermost recesses of your being' and described her bath as a kind of daily purification ritual.[84]

Occasionally, very occasionally, scientific workers glimpsed the truth that what they saw and what they found repugnant in the slums had as much to do with their own sensibility and their own mood as with any objective reality. Beatrice Webb during her rent collecting stint, at a time of relative personal calm, noticed the light-heartedness of the poor and more often felt 'envy than pity' about them. When she felt stressed, it was the disorder of the slums which stood out: 'when overtired, the tenants haunt me with their wretched, disorderly lives.' A year after her father's sudden and then lingering breakdown in health, which required her daily and anxious attendance upon him, her mood became despondent and the social work appeared hopeless:

> this East End life, with its dirt, drunkenness and immorality, absence of co-operation or common interests, saddens me and weighs down my spirit. I could not live down here; I should lose all heart and become worthless as a worker. And practical work does not satisfy me; it seems like walking on shifting sand, with the forlorn hope that the impress of one's steps will be lasting, and guide others across the desert....Social intercourse brings out, and springs from, the worst qualities in East London; as a society it is an ever-increasing and ever-decomposing mass; the huge mass smothering the small centres containing within them the seeds of social life and growth.

Just how efforts sank to nothing was epitomized by the Katherine buildings, where all the influence of the lady collectors was undermined by an undertow of filth:

The meeting-places, there is something grotesquely

coarse in this, are the water closets! Boys and girls crowd on the landings—they are the only lighted places in the buildings—to gamble and flirt. The lady collectors are an altogether superficial thing. Undoubtedly their gentleness and kindness brings light into many homes: but what are they in face of this collective brutality, heaped up together in infectious contact; adding to each other's dirt, physical and moral?[86]

The sense that both the social workers and the poor were sinking into a mire 'from which there was no rising', was one way of describing the failure of some of the social work project.

Perhaps the most tragic incompatibilities of all were class differences over the expression of love. Social workers were deeply determined to give their love to the poor. But their class ways of communicating respect and friendship did not always carry the intended message to ears tuned by a different culture. Thus Octavia Hill, like many visitors, stressed the need for treating the poor with the same

courtesy as I should show towards my other personal friends; there would be no interference, no entering their rooms uninvited, no offer of money or the necessaries of life. But when occasion presented itself, I should give them any help I could, such as I might offer without insult to other friends, sympathy in their distresses, advice, help and counsel in their difficulties, introductions that might be of use to them, a lent book when unable to work; a bunch of flowers brought on purpose.[87]

Unfortunately these impeccable manners were being carried into a culture where continual exchange of material necessities was precisely the currency of friendship. Attlee was unusual in appreciating the rationality of gift-giving compared with saving: 'openhandedness and generosity are the admired virtues', acting as a social insurance policy which guaranteed that you would be helped in turn when your time of need arrived.[88] Poor people could not understand how social workers could withhold and still say they were friends, although the poor also got used to these strange class ways. According to Hodson, 'the ideal visiting lady, is, in the opinion of the inhabitants, one who takes with her a large purse, and a book of relief tickets...professionals are not expected to give'.[89]

276

The loving advice proffered sometimes clashed with existing cultural practices which made good sense within the material context of the lives of the poor. Although social workers were contemptuous of unrealistic advice about cooking, in the key area of infant care they still stressed the discipline of separation and regular schedules and criticized continual cuddling, demand feeding, irregular bedtimes and custom of sleeping in the parental bed. Ironically these practices, which were perfectly rational in overcrowded dwelling spaces where infant distress could be a sharp irritant, now get expert approval for being especially nurturing.[90] To make the offer of friendship yet more problematic, individual personality was sometimes in tension with repeated declarations of intent to love. The most extreme example of this kind of character was Octavia Hill, who, despite her effusive writing about love, was a domineering person, 'often dictatorial in manner'.[91] With the poor she simply stood firm, indeed sometimes totally silent, until they capitulated to her will. Her inflexibility in a culture valuing 'a pliant and obliging disposition' could not be experienced as friendly, although her provision of housing in good repair and of odd jobs to do that repair could be appreciated.

As often as not, increased class contact aggravated rather than reduced mutual incomprehension. It is a tragic myth to assume that interaction with others inevitably leads to greater understanding. Much depends on the extent to which you are really willing to respect others on their own terms rather than diminish them on yours. As poor women became recalcitrant, social workers sometimes became demoralized and shrill. Looking back over twenty years, Louisa Twining, for example, concluded that some of her work had been a failure, which she blamed on the insanity and heredity of the poor. She gave the example of a discharged prisoner 'so steeped in crime and vice...that goodness seemed to surprise her, especially with regard to truthfulness. Thus one day she said to a companion, as a proof of almost supernatural virtue, "Miss T. wouldn't tell a lie to save her own sister".'[92] This seems less an example of horrendous crime and vice than another instance of the clash of two cultural codes. Here was the middle-class social worker with her self-sacrificial commitment to God the Father who enjoined truth, honesty and rectitude above sympathy and who enabled her to move in the public sphere alongside men. And here was the poor woman committed above all honesty to human sisters.

Twining was perhaps an extreme example, an old lady from an earlier era; just as Emmeline Pethwick was very young when she noted how a working girl would choose loyalty to pals over 'the supreme importance of getting her own soul saved' or telling the truth.[93] As this chapter has shown, there were also more sensitive attempts to create interclass understanding in this period, and after the First World War a more generous rhetoric appealing for 'common citizenship' became pervasive. Even Margaret Sewell, pressed by younger colleagues during the War, began to envision the day when 'social work will no longer carry the meaning it does today--the work of one class as such for another as such'.[94] But to secure such an outcome, continual and respectful attention will always have to be paid to cultural difference. Otherwise the most paradoxical results are possible. Women in this and an earlier period offered to humanize and moralize cruel and heartless masculine systems of science and the state. But some of these women could participate in the creation of yet more systems, probably just as cruel and heartless, in the name of motherhood and love.

10

UNIVERSITY CHALLENGE
Twentieth-Century Signposts

During the twentieth century, universities and the state have become the key institutional players in the social science story. Signs of this direction of development appeared early. The 1902 Education Act, for example, provoked widespread opposition from the labour movement because, by abolishing directly-elected local Education Committees, it seemed to close an important channel for influence from below and leave the state in control of a key area of cultural production. At the same time, and partly as a technocratic response to the national crisis, civic 'redbrick' universities and municipal polytechnics proliferated.[1] Compared with the nineteenth century, when working-class movements and informally-educated women made pioneer contributions to action-oriented social knowledge, the relative space for cultural production from below was contracting. But there have been gains as well as losses. The new institutional ecology did not suddenly arrive ready-made. It developed through complex processes of class and gender contest and negotiation. This chapter will signpost some key episodes involving universities and the state, first in relation to working-class intellect, and then mediating the entry of 'social science' into the academic curriculum where it came to occupy a gendered place in intellectual hierarchies. Finally, contests over objectivity, inside and outside universities, will be tracked in order to chart some possible ways out of current dilemmas.

UNIVERSITIES AND WORKING-CLASS INTELLECTUAL PRODUCTION

During the mid-nineteenth century, as already noted, both Cambridge and Oxford had created a University Extension service partly to make a 'national' canon of knowledge accessible to newly-enfranchised working men. However thirsty for knowledge, working men seemed to drink from these founts of cultural wisdom only when they could claim the services in some sense as their own, as, for example, when the local organizing committee was under working-class control. In the later part of the nineteenth century, more graduates arrived to labour in the educational vineyard particularly around the settlement movement which gave central importance to sharing university culture with the people. For example, Bernard Bosanquet founded a night school called the London School of Ethics and Social Philosophy which first met at Toynbee Hall in 1886, then made and broke relations with University Extension, and finally in 1899 tried unsuccessfully to get adopted by the University of London. It managed to attract not so much working-class students as Board School teachers.[2]

Finding a form for an education which could have an Oxbridge content but still be under enough working-class control to attract working-class students was the achievement of the Workers' Educational Association (WEA). The brainchild of Albert Mansbridge (1876-1952), a clerk in the Whitechapel warehouse of the Co-operative Wholesale Society, the idea of the WEA was incubated in the neighbouring cultural nursery of Toynbee Hall. The WEA's characteristic features—the local organizing secretary and the self-governing tutorial class taught by a university don—gave working-class students the kind of control which in some places could easily lead to huge departures from the establishment curriculum and to bold intellectual innovation. It was held as a point of principle that 'each student is a teacher, and each teacher is a student'.[3] R.H. Tawney's pathbreaking work in economic and social history grew out of the agenda set by his tutorial classes at Longton and Rochdale.

Yet different visions of the task of education jostled against each other in this partnership. Not Mansbridge so much as some of his co-operative comrades and later WEA activists wanted an education in social science which would provide really useful knowledge for class emancipation. The orthodox university view revolved around the task of giving an 'impartial' liberal education and also incorporating a labour leadership into an existing culture of power:

> It has always been the privilege of the older Universities (though, of course, not to the exclusion of the new) to train men for all departments of political life and public administration....The Trade Union secretary and the 'Labour member' need an Oxford education as much, and will use it to as good ends as the civil servant or the barrister. It seems to us that it would involve a grave loss both to Oxford and to English political life were the close association which has existed between the University and the world of affairs to be broken or impaired on the accession of new classes to power.[4]

Such declarations fed the suspicions of some labour activists. ILP Leader Ramsay MacDonald insisted 'you cannot recreate Oxford by an infusion of working men....Oxford will assimilate them, not they Oxford'. Even in the co-operative movement, the role of the university provoked contention. The secretary of the Oxford Co-operative Society asked in 1910, 'is the educational teaching of the Universities—in social science, i.c., history, economics and political science—in line with the emancipation of labour, viz., the abolition of private trading and the substitution by co-operation?.'[5]

The fracas around Ruskin College at Oxford partly produced the acrimony of the debate. Founded by an American socialist millionaire in 1899, Ruskin offered a curriculum in the social sciences to working-class students. After two years, the American money dried up and problems began. A mutual flirtation between the college and the university ended with the Ruskin principal Dennis Hird being dismissed and his special subject, sociology, being replaced, at the university's insistence, by a course on temperance. Even though later adjustments gave the college more autonomous control over its affairs, student critics felt that the University 'still retained its hold on the education'.[6] The critics, who had been maturing their ideas in *Das Capital* reading groups, formed themselves in 1903 into the Plebs League, the name inspired by the American socialist

Daniel de Leon's tract on class struggle in the ancient world. They responded to the harassment of Hird with a student strike in 1909 which ended in a secession and the founding of a rival Central Labour College in Oxford. Their magazine *The Pleb*, carried a 'Declaration of Working-class Independence in Education'. Nearly ten years later, in the wake of the Russian Revolution, the Plebs made this strong statement about their task as workmen in the production of education and knowledge:

> The League takes its stand on the fact of the class-struggle; it asserts that the Labour movement has its basis in the antagonism of interests existing between Capital and Labour—this being the central, fundamental factor in present-day society. It accordingly insists that the education with which the Labour Movement is concerned must be based on a recognition of this antagonism. It urges that this antagonism of economic interests is inevitably translated into an antagonism of ideas—most apparent in those very studies, roughly to be described as the 'social sciences', in which Labour is primarily interested. It believes that 'impartiality' in such subjects is impossible, that the mere attempt to realize it betokens a failure to grasp the root facts of social development; and, further, that even were it attainable, it is obviously not the concern of the working-class movement. Education, in the view of the Plebs League, is necessarily propaganda; the only question being; What kind of propaganda? Propaganda based upon the ideas of the ruling class, taught in the Universities which express its class outlook upon society; or propaganda based upon the point of view of the working class, and designed to equip the workers for their struggle against capitalism and capitalist ideology?[7]

The Plebs's initiative took hold, with considerable trades union support, especially in the mining areas of South Wales and among railway men.

So impressive was their waging of cultural war, that the 1917 Royal Commission of Enquiry into Industrial Unrest in their Report on Wales spotlighted the work of the Central Labour College in the valleys and prescribed an antidote very much in the flavour of the period, recommending the University as the centre of the life of the community, gathering to itself its aspirations and hopes, fulfilling its deepest needs and ever shaping it to nobler purposes....In Wales every industrial centre should have its university class in close contact with the life and culture of the University.[8]

The Central Labour College initiative spread rapidly, with local groups federating into the National Council of Labour Colleges in 1922 and with activity peaking in 1925-6. These developments took place under the watchful eyes of local education inspectors and the Department of Education which channelled funds, under the Fisher Education Act of 1918, both to the universities and the WEA partly in order to strengthen a strategy of counter-attraction. The Central Labour College, despite its popularity, foundered on the barrier of finance, and finally closed when trade union funds dried up after the defeat of the General Strike. From 1926 onward, the NCLC (which finally disbanded in 1964) increasingly changed into a body providing training for trade unionists. Marxist education became less universally accessible as it became increasingly confined to Communist Party branches.[9]

This episode of educational conflict taught some lessons. Independent education relying only on working-class funding was, as usual, difficult to sustain on any real scale. The more stable alternative was a cluster of providers which included the state, the universities (17 had extra-mural departments by 1939) and the WEA, the body which safeguarded room for working-class and student influence. This became the dominant configuration in the interwar period and was not without its tensions over which party should prevail in the balance of power. Different patterns emerged in different localities; thus in Leeds the WEA prevailed while in Hull the University predominated. The WEA was no tame government puppet: indeed as Brian Simon has observed, more Marxism was being taught in the WEA by the 1940s and 1950s than in the NCLC and some of the most important socialist intellectual work of recent years has come from people teaching in the WEA matrix. For example, Raymond Williams was working with the WEA in Sussex when he wrote *Culture and Society* (1958) and E.P. Thompson produced *The Making of the English Working Class* (1963) while a Leeds extra-mural tutor. Nonetheless, the Second World War marked an important turning point which repositioned the whole adult education effort. Many interwar activists like George Thompson, the socialist WEA organizer for Yorkshire, saw adult study equipping workers to service their class not to escape from it: 'we don't want our children to remove from one class to another. We want them to stay where they are.'[10]

The educational ladder became a reality after the Second World War. The 1944 Education Act, which established free secondary education, together with special university grants for returning servicemen, and later, in 1960, mandatory maintenance grants for all students, helped produce a important shift in the relations between class, the state and the production of knowledge. The welfare state always contained rival technocratic and egalitarian projects, and over the following fifty years it became clear that that the hopes for equality of opportunity were not being realized. Monitoring in the 1950s revealed that while access to grammar schools increased, the sifting process tended to move to a later stage, with working-class children dropping out before the sixth form or university entrance. Professor A.H. Halsey, the expert in the field, spoke of how 'statistics of inequality of educational opportunity became popular knowledge and turned access to the universities into an almost commonplace criterion of distributive justice'. But even the university expansion of the 1960s, in Halsey's words, 'kept pace with the growth of the service or professional and managerial classes', but did not involve a fundamental change in the class composition of university student bodies.[11] The best and brightest did climb the educational ladder, but not the class as a whole.

The continual monitoring of educational opportunity points to two further significant changes involving class and the production of knowledge. Halsey, who became Director of the Oxford Department of Social Administration Studies in 1962, was himself a representative of the new social group, from working- and lower-middle class backgrounds, that later came to dominate in social science and sociology as a result of the wartime changes. The son of a skilled worker, Halsey only came to the LSE as a result of the grants available to ex-servicemen; his prewar career had been as a public health inspector, just the kind of new professional discussed in Chapter 8. The Professor of Social Administration at the LSE, Richard Titmuss, who never attended University but called himself 'a student of society', had also worked as an inspector—for an insurance company—before becoming involved in wartime work for the government. He argued that wartime exigency had helped to push the egalitarian project along, since both the military and civilian populations would only accept wartime discipline in return for a promise of greater equality for citizens in the long run.[12] Thus members of a new social group took over social science research in their capacity as educated experts even if many were committed to a redistribution of social opportunity.

Moreover the postwar welfare state relied on social science research to an unprecedented degree, needing a constant flow of information to target redistributive projects, to monitor their progress and, as a strategy of winning consent, to keep the citizenry informed even when targets were not being met. Not only did the state, particularly when a Labour government was in power, take over the finance of universities and expand its financial support for academic social science research, but elaborated its own research apparatus. The Government Social Survey presents an interesting case because it brought together the various institutional strands of social science research. After a shaky wartime start, the Social Survey was put on a more stable footing in 1941 by the appointment of a new director with a background in commercial market research, Louis Moss, who proceeded to work under the eyes of a Scientific Advisory Panel that included academics. This convergence[13] signalled the development of a formidable research community.

The large presence of universities and the state in the social science field and the formal possibility that working-class scholars can train to become experts within it, have changed the amount of authority that outside groups and older modes of producing knowledge can exert. For example, although still the source of impressive innovation, 'adult' or 'workers" or 'women's' education, do not now carry a sense of transformative social potential, but exist more as adjuncts to 'proper', that is, government-financed, university, education. This process of displacement and demotion has been going on for a long time. It has already been noted in the nineteenth-century medical field where courses of training and state licensing discredited previous knowledges and practices. The state also effectively killed the popular working-class private elementary schools both by branding their education as inefficient or worse and by refusing them the power to issue the leaving certificates necessary for pupils to get a job. The initiatives of the Central Labour College not only withered for lack of funds but were smothered by law which aided the rival agencies. Part of the process of displacement and devaluation has been the tendency to brand outsider knowledges as unscientific. Immersed in founding the LSE to train experts with a scientific perspective, Beatrice Webb derided socialist working men as

> especially afflicted with the theological temperament—the implicit faith in a certain creed which has been 'revealed'; to them by a sort of inner light. 'Why is it that I, a poor ignorant man,' said Hobart, one of the ILP to me yesterday, 'have perceived "the truth" whilst educated men with leisure and brains are still adhering to the old errors'.[14]

In the end this kind of Fabian attitude made working-class thinking appear amateurish and partisan. But it would be a great disservice to allow the apparently finished result to conceal the process of marginalization and to mask active attempts to create the impression that less powerful or less academic groups do not have the capacity to produce and distribute their own knowledge.

Paradoxically, the old radical slogan that 'knowledge is power' has become increasingly true in the divisions of labour which characterize late twentieth-century cultural production. An educated or trained minority of salaried brainworkers, whether they work in industry, in education, in the civil service, in the social services or in what have come to be called the cultural industries, design ('preconceptualize') the orthodoxies and systems within which the majority live at work or after work. In the current modes of producing scientific knowledge the same kind of division of labour exists. Whether in state departments, private think tanks or in universities, a minority actively define the problems for investigation, design the research strategies, reach the conclusions and market the results while a large majority of support and housekeeping staff, including most of the women involved, carry out instructions from above at every stage. Like women and ethnic minorities, most working people have found themselves not expelled from the dominant processes of producing scientific knowledge so much as demoted to a more subordinate place within them. Even if the possibilities for constructing viable outside alternatives have shrunk compared with 150 years ago, nonetheless, as Mike Hales's praxis has demonstrated, there always remains space for creating solidarities and understandings even 'in and against' the huge cultural enterprises that dominate the present scene.[15]

UNIVERSITIES AND GENDERED SOCIAL SCIENCE

The last chapter revealed how professionalization was a gendered affair and how the conception of social motherhood still powerfully shaped the course of women's professionalization. The twin concept of the sexual communion of labour, originating in the mid-nineteenth century, also survived and helped to structure the entry of social science into academia. While the communion idea made co-operation between men and women indispensable to the advancement of science, the form of that co-operation usually involved an imbalance of power which derived from the specifics of gender division. Endowed with a capacity for intuition and love, for practical work and attention to detail, women's nature supposedly gave them an affinity for work with individuals or small family groups. By contrast, the more wide-ranging intellect of men justified their command over intellectual production and over large institutions. In practice, this meant that while women certainly expanded their social role and achieved a notable degree of relative autonomy in most social science fields, men usually exercised the ultimate intellectual and institutional power.

During the mid-nineteenth century, the distribution of work in sanitary science provided a significant case in point. Here medical men kept control of the production of knowledge, preparing the lectures that the lady supervisors attended and the tracts which the sanitary visitors distributed. One of the male theoreticians of the communion of labour idea, the Reverend F. D. Maurice, when recommending a college to train women to work alongside professional men, insisted that the male doctor must be in control of knowledge: 'he must determine absolutely

287

what they (women) see and what they shall do. He must fix the amount of knowledge in physiology or pathology they will hear, or ought to hear.'[16] Nonetheless women managed to retain a significant area of autonomy. Following the pattern set by Ellen Ranyard and her Biblewoman Marion, ladies became 'superintendants' who dealt with financial affairs, presided over mothers' meetings and hired and supervised 'kind, good, motherly' working-class women who did the actual visiting work.[17] This amounted to a paradoxical situation where women used dominance in a wage labour relationship to protect themselves from gender subordination. However, in the end, this version of dominance and autonomy disappeared when the sanitary visitors finally professionalized into health visitors in the first decade of the twentieth century. Not only did middle-class women take the new training courses and replace working-class women but the visitors became organizationally responsible to the Medical Officer of Health, almost invariably a man.

By the late nineteenth century the pervasive communion of labour principle even shaped the marital partnerships of couples committed to social science. Although a formidable intellect herself, with first-class honours in the Moral Sciences Tripos and the author of many books and articles, Helen Bosanquet actually undertook the practical work of visiting the poor. Her philosopher husband Bernard, who found this part of the work 'uncongenial' and simply 'did not know what to say', stayed in the Charity Organisation Society central office developing the intellectual underpinnings of its work.[18] While Fabian Women's Group activist, Mrs Maud Pember Reeves went out and about collecting budgets from Bermondsey housewives, Mr Pember Reeves spent time in Houghton Street running the London School of Economics. In Oxford, the wives of the dons whose work professionalized fields like philosophy and history, highly-educated women like Mrs T. H. Green, Mrs H. A. L. Fisher, Mrs Arnold Toynbee, Mrs H. A. Prichard and Mrs A. D. Lindsay busied themselves with nearly full-time social work in familiar agencies like the Ladies' Health Committee, the Charity Organisation Society and the Poor Law Guardians.[19]

A similar situation existed in Cambridge where Mrs Alfred Marshall presided over the COS and became active in the Women's University Settlement while Professor Marshall pioneered modern economics. Mary Marshall (1850-1944) did not start off this way. A pioneer student at Newnham College Cambridge, as Mary Paley she had studied under Marshall, taken up a post as a lecturer in economics and co-authored Marshall's first book, *The Economics of Industry* (1879). Once they married, however, she moved more into the communion of labour mode. Although she continued teaching economics at Newnham, her first priority was servicing her husband to the point of effacing herself. John Maynard Keynes remembered that she never

> discoursed on an economic topic with a visitor, or even took part in the everlasting economic talks of Balliol Croft. For the serious discussion she would leave the dining-room to the men, or the visitor would go upstairs to the study, and the most ignorant Miss could not have pretended less than she to academic attainment.[20]

The communion of labour formula had an impact on the gendering of social science research in terms of the choice of subject and expected use of results if not so clearly on the research methods employed. Marshall was well-known for obstructing the passage of women at Cambridge but was perhaps operating more along communion of labour lines. He was certain that the proper study for woman was womankind and many women intellectuals agreed, but not all. He advised Beatrice Webb:

> if you devote yourself to a study of your own sex as an industrial factor, your name will be a household word two hundred years hence: if you write a history of Co-operation it will be superseded or ignored in a year or two.[21]

She responded not only by studying the co-operative movement but, in partnership with Sidney Webb, the history of that most masculine of labour forms, trade unions. Nonetheless, she never freed herself from gendered ideas of intellectual work. She thought documents the most 'indispensable' instruments of discovery while more feminine personal observation and interview, at which she excelled, she rated as less important. According to the Webbs, the woman

> is specially well-adapted for sociological inquiry; not merely because she is accustomed silently to watch

motives, but also because she gains access and confidence which are instinctively refused to possible commercial competitors or political opponents.[22]

Beyond the Webbs, there was no clearcut consensus that some research methods were particularly feminine or even feminist. The last chapter showed how women used methods ranging from quantitative or qualitative questionnaires to face-to-face interviews. Some Fabians, like Mabel Atkinson and Barbara Hutchins, pursued historical research which has always been useful for disrupting common sense by showing that times have existed when the dominant paradigms differed. What was more agreed was the idea that research would lead directly to action, the necessary result, within the communion of labour formula, of women's passionate caring and practical bent. L.T. Hobhouse spoke of the similarity between his wife and her friend Sybella, wife of Victor Brandford:

> They shared the direct practicality in the sense of values in the things closely affecting human happiness and misery, which is perhaps the most important corrective that women's minds bring to bear on the more abstract and legalistic methods on which men are wont to judge public affairs. To both the idea of redeeming human beings from misery and squalor was no external interest that might be taken up and dropped and taken up again as occasion served, but a passion which was an integral part of the personality and endured to the end.[23]

In the end, the communion of labour pattern shaped the academic career of social science as a field of study. Pre-academic social science, whether practised by women or men, automatically involved considerations of social purpose and social action. Depending upon the variety of social science, the proposed agenda for action could range from large-scale revolutionary change (as in early socialist science) to more limited casework with individuals and family groups (the COS emphasis). But practical application, often carefully informed by theory, formed a key part of the social science remit. It would not be quite true to say that in Britain the social sciences developing inside the universities followed the American pattern of presenting themselves, by the 1890s, as militantly detached: the British situation varied from discipline to discipline and from university to university. Certain social science disciplines like history, from the 1860s onwards, followed in German footsteps, eschewed the moral prophecy that once had been part of the role of the man of letters and emphasized the methodical use of documents to build up arguments.[24] By contrast, philosophy as being developed by T. H. Green and then carried on by a distinguished line of Masters of Balliol, like A. L. Smith and A. D. Lindsay, gave social ethics a central place and demanded rigorous discussions of social purpose as a key task of the discipline.[25] Nonetheless, even the scholars who saw the rationale of their disciplines in terms of social relevance seemed nervous about actually absorbing practical training into the university world.

The first conference between the COS and university representatives, held in 1902 to explore the possibility of mutual relations, exposed mutual tensions. Professor Marshall started the day with a talk on 'Economic Teaching at the Universities in Relation to Public Well-being' and the meeting then considered COS resolutions which called for training in 'social science and economics, with special reference to social obligation and administration' and for harnessing university teaching to this task.[26] Although COS activists, like G.T. Pilcher, argued that 'sound theory was only sound practice conscious of itself, and sound practice must be consciously based on sound theory', the economists present wanted to keep theory and practice apart. Friendly academics like Professor Chapman from Owens College Manchester and Professor Foxwell then at Cambridge thought it 'imperative that the teaching of the Universities should be free from any suspicion of bias in controversial matters'.[27] Once graduated, students could find principles of action outside and gain 'practical acquaintance with social problems'. The economists effortlessly equated the practical with the partisan although some, like Foxwell, knew full well that ideological leanings shaped theory just as heavily. They did however also point to University Extension (a less authoritative intellectual space?) as an appropriate setting where the desired teaching could take place. Reservations moved in both directions. While the academics warned about the dangers of harbouring partisan subjects, some activists also wished to keep their distance, complaining that universities were 'amateurish' in social questions.[28] As a result, with the backing of the Women's University Settlement and the National Union of Women Workers, the COS decided to open the independent School of Sociology and Social Economics, discussed in Chapter 8, where both theory and practice could become part of the curriculum. As José Harris insists, this kind of initiative transcended the supposed divide in British sociology between philosophical and empirical traditions, because 'courses were quite deliberately geared to a synthesis of praxis and general theory, with, if anything, an intellectual bias towards the latter'.[29]

How did such a heady intellectual brew come to be perceived as an academic mixture particularly suited to the ladies? From the first, observers noted that women had more appetite for training than men. Speaking of social settlements, Urwick observed

> that the training idea is likely to occupy a much more important place in a women's settlement than in a men's. In the latter (this, by the way, is very dangerous ground) there is possibly less need for specific training. I do not know whether this is due to the constant discussion of theory and practice in social, political and charitable matters, or to a more general familiarity with economic principles, or to more arrogant self-confidence among the men.[30]

For men, a liberal university education with residence in a social settlement could provide training enough, especially since they often moved on to become influential civil servants and Liberal or Labour politicians. This pattern persisted despite Beatrice Webb wanting to entice these male reformers into the LSE so that they could start, 'behaving towards their profession as the great civil engineer, lawyer or medical man behaves. In political life the standard of natural ability is remarkably high, the standard of acquirements ludicrously low'.[31]

Schools of Sociology, Social Science or Social Study proliferated in the first decades of the twentieth century, in places like London, Liverpool, Birmingham, Bristol, Leeds, Manchester, Oxford, Glasgow and Edinburgh, often in association with University Extension.[32] Because these programmes largely attracted women students wishing to train in social administration and social work, academic social science began to be docketed as a woman's subject. The wartime state solidified this association by generating an increasing demand for women social workers, especially for welfare supervisors to oversee women workers in the munitions industry, and by catalysing efforts to expand and co-ordinate social work training. In 1917, the Home Office sponsored a conference which resulted in a Joint University Council for Social Studies, with Elizabeth Macadam as Secretary. Even the choice of Macadam might have further cemented the gender connection: Macadam had served as Warden of the Victoria Women's Settlement and then taught in the Social Science programme at Liverpool University.[33]

Soon after the War, the universities began to absorb social science into the curriculum proper but on the communion of labour pattern. Although more women taught and studied in these departments than elsewhere in the universities, men tended to occupy the senior positions in social science and social administration. Macadam may have become Liverpool's first salaried university lecturer in Social Work in 1911 but the newly-established Charles Booth Chair of Social Science went to a man in 1923. When Professor Carr-Saunders left in 1937 to become Director of the LSE, Mary Stocks (the Vice Chancellor's widow) was tipped as a strong candidate but T.S. Simey got the chair in 1939.[34] In these Departments of Social Science, practical social work had less status than social policy. Eventually, in the 1950s, some Social Science Departments themselves became the practical and less esteemed side of theoretical sociology just as household or domestic science became the lower status women's area of science and home economics the Cinderella sister to real economics both in Britain and America.[35] Interestingly, women found space to move in economic history, particularly at the co-educational LSE, just as women today seem to have a wide berth in the history of science, both borderline fields which disrupt disciplinary paradigms.

In the short run, the 'women's' subjects proved very successful. The LSE Department of Social Science and Social Administration was popularly known as 'Urwick's Harem'.[36] At the LSE, practical subjects did not link so closely to women as elsewhere since it aimed to be a 'national institution for administrative science', not least to please vital paymasters like the army and the railway companies who sent their personnel for training. Nonetheless, the Social Science Department had a much larger complement of women tutors than the Sociology programme.[37] The Ratan Tata Department of Social Science, as it was renamed in 1917 after the Indian industrialist who was its chief benefactor, proved so buoyant in terms of earning grant and student income that it threatened to swamp the other LSE programmes. Only the collapse of the Tata fortunes in the depression of the early 1920s led to the demotion of the Department into a poor relation to the Faculty of Commerce, which could rely, paradoxically, on government grants. Ending up in an uneasy relationship with the Sociology Department, Social Science continued to boast distinguished male professors of social administration like Titmuss and Brian Abel-Smith, while women in the more junior posts tended to preside over social work.

A similar story about going from riches to rags can be told about King's College for Women at London University which set up a Department of Household and Social Science in 1908. The Department had a lifelong fairy Godfather in John Atkins, a highly-connected physician with a concern about infant mortality, who attracted such lavish funding to the Department that it threatened to become the whole of the college.[38] The Royal Commission on the University of London in 1913 even recommended that the Department be left in total occupation of the College site in Kensington, a gesture of state interference which provoked the resignation of Reverend Headlam as Principal of King's. The Department offered an innovative and interdisciplinary course, bridging the natural and social science divide: not only did students learn physics, chemistry, biology and physiology but economics (taught by Fabian Mabel Atkinson) and household administration.[39] Nonetheless, the Department went into financial crisis after the First World War, when donations and student income dried up.[40] It managed to continue and even received a Royal Charter as Queen Elizabeth College in 1953, partly in recognition of its pioneering work in nutrition and microbiology. But plagued by financial difficulties, it finally came full circle, re-merging with King's College in 1986, and lost any separate gender or curricular identity.[41]

The entry of social science into academia and the development of the university social sciences took an inordinately long time. This process, which never moved smoothly in one direction, together with the eventual absorption of most of the voluntary agencies into the welfare state, removed or demoted some areas of relative autonomy for women. While it is true that the Director of the School of Sociology and Social Economics was a man, nevertheless the sponsoring bodies of the School, the Women's University Settlement and the National Union of Women Workers, had women in positions of command, while the Charity Organisation Society placed women in paid positions. Once the LSE had incorporated the School of Sociology, Urwick still held the directorship but the original sponsoring bodies no longer had a role. They eventually disappeared or became unrecognizably transformed. The Women's University Settlement is a prime example. After the Second World War, the voluntary Settlement became a Community Centre run by the local Council. In 1959, for the first time in its history and every time a vacancy occurred thereafter, the warden's job went to a man.[42]

Within the university world, women's role so far may be summed up as increasing presence but as responsibility without power. Particularly as a result of university expansion in the 1960s, women students are now reaching near parity with men, although the class and racial composition of the student body has not significantly altered in the older universities. The faculty picture is less balanced. The aggregate statistics for 1993-4 show that women comprised only 23 per cent of academic staff in the older universities and clustered at the lower end of the career ladder: 19.5 per cent of women were on temporary contracts, 68 per cent were lecturers, 10 per cent senior lecturers and only 2.5 per cent professors, while the comparable figures for men were 8 per cent, 56.2 per cent, 22.5 per cent and 13.3 per cent.[43] Not surprisingly, struggles over equal opportunities issues are lively at the moment. Since the upsurge of the women's movement in the 1970s issues about gender perspectives in the production of knowledge, as in the mid-nineteenth century, have again tried to pose challenges to dominant paradigms. The discipline of women's or gender or feminist studies has this disruptive intent. A growing discussion on the science question within feminism has contributed to rethinking central concepts of objectivity in science in a way which makes conceptual room for knowledges from outside academia to intrude into the ivory tower.

UNIVERSITY SOCIAL SCIENCE AND CONTESTS OVER OBJECTIVITY

Both social science and the social sciences took a long time to get established in universities. Writing in 1935 in the *Encyclopaedia of the Social Sciences*, E.M. Burns pointed to the 'lateness of their inclusion' and noted that even

> today, except in London, the social sciences occupy the smallest, least popular, and least well-endowed position among all the subjects at the different universities.[44]

Since histories often trace the successful steps that disciplines took to gain university status, it is a good idea to pause and consider what really amounted to stumbling and erratic progress. As historians have noted before, when compared with other countries, the British case appears singular and peculiar. Both in the United States and Germany, departments of sociology, never mind departments housing the other more expected subjects like economics, had become firmly established by the First World War. In Britain, economics had the most elaborated professional machinery, thanks to Marshall's efforts, in terms of learned societies and journals, like the British Economic Association and the *Economic Journal*, both founded in 1890, but professorships existed only in Cambridge, London University, Glasgow, Birmingham, Leeds, Bristol and Liverpool before the First World War. Until the 1950s few sociology degrees were available outside London University and, although social science programmes were widespread, only Liverpool and London had fully-fledged Departments. Resistances to the development of academic social science proved strong and protracted. Some of these resistances also need to be understood as positive impulses in alternative directions which might still offer useful resources for journeys away from what became the mainline track. The issue of whether social science or the social sciences should be largely academic activities involved contests over the social connection and social utility of social science in which three main practices of objectivity figured and are still taking an active part.

The idea of objectivity as detachment, which has become dominant (although powerfully challenged) since the 1950s, remained recessive in the social sciences in Britain up until the

Second World War. Feminist analysis has made sharp observations on this understanding of objectivity in relation to the physical and natural sciences, which illuminate the social sciences as well. The detached version of objective science assumes a neutral and value-free practice where a disinterested observer methodically pursues answers to questions or tests hypotheses with empirical evidence. The dignified version of this science tries to seal itself off from society. Issues about the social origins or social impact of scientific activity, about the social fingerprinting of questions or the social application of results do not figure, indeed become tabooed because they supposedly contaminate the objectivity of the process. The project, however, is not quite so bland or hermetically sealed as this description might suggest. Donna Haraway identifies this enterprise with the Starship Enterprise in a genre of travel literature where the scientist stars as a fearless adventurer into the unknown (who dares 'to boldly go where no man has gone before') seeking truth regardless of obstacle or hardship: 'science as heroic quest and as erotic technique applied to the body of nature are utterly conventional figures'.[45] The heroic myth still attracts entrants into the scientific professions even though it sharply contradicts the reality. In the real world, powerful and highly interested parties fund research for utilitarian reasons and the gap between discovery and social application narrows every minute. Sandra Harding reminds us that a fifty-year gap separated Faraday's discovery of electric current and Edison's construction of the first power station: by contrast recent research into lasers barely reached completion before engineers began to use it in designing new weapons and telephone systems.[46]

In Britain the ideal of detached objectivity became prevalent during the nineteenth century in the physical rather than the social sciences as part of the process of professionalization. Scientists energetically tried to gain professional status by detaching themselves from practical work which they equated with commercial profit-making activity. For example, in 1844 Lyon Playfair, who worked as a chemist in the Manchester cotton industry, castigated

> people who saw no need for investigating laws which
> may after all lead to no practical end. Such are the men

297

who can only see beauty in the infinity of the divine
wisdom when it shows how to cheapen the yard of calico
by a diminution of labour.[47]

In typical mid-nineteenth century fashion, Playfair juxtaposed a
service ethic to the profit motive, and argued that science should
perform public service and be funded by a neutral party like the
state. Following his own advice, he made his living as a new-style
state servant working on a series of investigative commissions
and then held a post in the Government School of Mines. The
same antipathy to being tarred by a commercial or industrial
brush led to another strategy which involved staking out pure
scientific research as the profession's particular concern without
any considerations about social service intruding. This
orientation became materially possible when the ancient and
many of the redbrick universities incorporated the natural
sciences on this very basis. Even in Owens College Manchester,
possibly the most closely tied to a local industrial base, the
commitment to pure scientific research remained influential.[48] At
Oxford and Cambridge a non-utilitarian bias in the natural
sciences harmonized with the ideal of a liberal (non-vocational)
education and fit well with the attempt of the ancient
Universities to re-form themselves into research as well as
teaching institutions and use these dual tasks to define the work
of the professional academic.

The ideal of detached objectivity did not take hold in the
social sciences in Britain until much later. Both in Germany and
in the United States, a commitment to detachment came earlier
partly as a strategy to protect academics from the very real threat
of persecution and victimization for their political views. The
apolitical stance developed by many academics under the Kaiser
Reich continued during the short-lived Weimar period
particularly as the economic crisis of the 1920s deepened. In the
USA, as Mary Furner has shown, momentum in two directions
stopped dead in the mid-1880s at a moment of explosive class
conflict. The American Social Science Association virtually
abandoned its attempt to create a practical social science
curriculum for university students wanting to become reforming
social workers or civil servants. At the same time key
practitioners of ethical economics, like Henry Carter Adams,
Richard T. Ely, J. R. Commons, who concentrated on welfare

issues and relations between capital, labour and the state, lost their academic jobs for expressing sympathy with trade unions. Partly for protection, professional colleagues (like Professor Seligman of Columbia University in New York) and groups (like the American Economics Association) began developing a concept of scientific enquiry which rejected any normative discussion of social purpose or any involvement in active politics.[49]

This self-denying ordinance lapsed to some extent during the 'Progressive Era' between 1890 and 1920. University research serviced social action moving in different directions: Columbia sociology was connected with the world of the COS while Wisconsin research under the inspiration of Commons supported a use of the state to equalize the power of industrial contestants (by means, for example, of minimum wage and protective legislation). Nonetheless many academics remained cautious about associating research with reform. Professor Albion Small, who headed the University of Chicago's Sociology Department, founded in 1902 as the first in the country, and who demoted the practical side and effectively shunted women off into a new Department of social work, confided in 1895 that

> there is so much misapprehension of Sociology as a science of reform that although I hope to take up reform movements years hence, I am now going off in my lectures into transcendental philosophy so as to be as far as possible from these reform movements and thus establish the scientific character of my department.[50]

In America, the pendulum swung decisively to the notion of detached science after the Russian Revolution and postwar red scare and witch-hunt. Detached objectivity became the watchword for work funded by large foundations like Ford and Carnegie, who had been rebuked in 1915 for sponsoring science on the other side of the class war to fight labour, and who now began to work through more anodyne bodies like the American Council of Learned Societies (founded 1919) and the Social Science Research Council (founded 1924).[51]

In Britain educated professionals did not have any comparable threat of victimization hanging over their heads. British professionals had closer (often family) relations with the landed or industrial interest and had easier access to power in

299

government and the civil service than did their US or European counterparts. Both Haskell and Goldman argue that the very lack of political influence spurred the professionalization of American social science and accelerated its movement into a university setting, while Abrams lamented that the opposite situation in Britain operated as a brake on the emergence of the professional sociologist and impeded the development of sociology as an academic discipline. 'Perhaps', Abrams speculated,

> sociology was built slowly in Britain for the obverse of the reasons that the welfare state has been built slowly in America. At the best of times the social scientist is likely to be caught in the cross-fire of a concern to develop his science and a concern to promote social action. Potential British social scientists experiencing this dilemma found themselves in an almost unique situation: government and party politics were open to them, the universities were closed. It is hardly surprising that they succumbed readily to the lure of administrative opportunity.[52]

To pry the university doors open, Abrams argued, sociology would have needed to prove that its integrating perspective amounted to more than intellectual eclecticism and to tone down the attacks of pioneers like Geddes on 'impractical academicism' which did not endear the subject to potential university hosts. As previous chapters have shown, the British professional ideal involved a social service ethic which broadened the scope of non-academic social science and moulded a concern with social purpose and action into its essential contours. The service ethic also created a tradition of socially relevant social sciences within universities which remained powerfully active at least until the 1950s and involved a second variety of objectivity.

A notion of objective science for reform (however various and incompatible the blueprints for reform) might even be called the dominant British tradition until the 1950s. Within this second type of objectivity, which had no qualms about setting socially relevant questions and assuming that results should influence policy and action, a further contest took place about whose eyes could see most truly and whose intelligence could lead most rationally to reform. This variety of objectivity often featured in a context where the educated classes addressed social problems or crises which involved working-class power. By the later nineteenth century the working classes, particularly in their disciplined movements, had become an entrenched and recognized part of the citizenry, but were seen as myopic by progressive science from above. Progressive social science basically offered to provide trained experts, equipped with corrective spectacles, which would facilitate either larger (long-range) or more mobile vision indispensable for the constructive exercise of power. Social scientists in this period often employed this optical imagery. In Frankfurt and then at the LSE, Karl Mannheim developed the sociology of knowledge which argued that all knowledge was socially rooted and therefore that most social groups had only partial vision—except for the 'socially unattached intellectuals' who could move among and above the partial perspectives and navigate 'all contradictory points of view'.[53]

Professor Marshall had already developed a kind of English analogue when he pointed to the importance of professional economists, or a training in economics, in an age of working-class power

> that may be a great good if well guided. But it may work grave injury to them, as well as to the rest of the nation, if guided by unscrupulous and ambitious men or even by unselfish enthusiasts with a narrow range of vision.[54]

University study would skill economists to see from other men's points of view and, from this mobile (ad)vantage point, develop the most rational analyses and policies:

> again the general thoughts of a University, especially when aided by the social training of Oxford and Cambridge, strengthen that use of the imagination which says to a man—put yourself in his place....the young man who has studied both sides of labour questions in the frank and impartial atmosphere of a great University is often able to throw himself into the point of view of the working man and to act as interpreter between them and persons of his own class with larger experience than his own. This is of special importance now that power has passed into the hands of the working classes.[55]

For over one hundred years proponents of social science had been searching for and arguing about the social groups with the most objective gaze. Social science from above tended to associate clarity of vision with some criterion of neutrality which did not preclude social action or indeed sweeping reform. Jeremy Bentham, who was obsessed with optical imagery, felt that the 'transparent management principle' operated best when the manager was made visible and accountable to multiple sets of observing eyes. His later disciples, like Edwin Chadwick, increasingly identified such managers with new-type state officials freed from dependence on parliamentary politicians and without vested interests either in the capital or the labour camp. Professional men of the midcentury identified themselves as the most suitable candidates to take over the scientific mantle of objectivity because their ethic of service transcended vested interest. The twentieth-century social scientists modified the professional ideal to take in university or higher education which they assumed to be impartial and which not only produced an independent wide-ranging view but a power of vision which could encompass and evaluate what other people saw. These trained graduates would then enter the professions, politics and public administration (Marshall was also keen for them to become businessmen) where they could act as guides for the more blind energies of working-class might.

Graduates could remain academics and still engage in service until the 1950s in many places. The Social Science Department of the University of Liverpool exemplified this patrician practice of epistemology and duty. The Department had begun as a School of Social Science which was a university adjunct and also connected to the social work community in the city. In 1917, it became a University Department proper, thanks partly to arguing its vital role in postwar reconstruction and its capacity to analyse 'the social condition of England...one field of knowledge which the Universities have left practically untilled'.[56] The first Professor of Social Science, Carr-Saunders, was a model East-End settler; after Eton and Magdalen he moved to Toynbee Hall, served on the local Council and Board of Guardians, and became active in the WEA and the Working Men's College. Under Carr-Saunders, the Department launched the Merseyside Survey, using Bowley's methods to explore the realities of family poverty, the industrial conditions that created mass unemployment and, finally, patterns of working-class leisure and culture. This fifteen year long project amounted to the Department's clearest indication of its commitment to serving the locality as a brains trust.

The Department, its personnel and its friends were an integral part of the characteristic cluster of organizations that made up interwar social praxis. The Liverpool Council of Social Service, replicated in many cities, was perhaps the exemplary body, composed of representatives from statutory and voluntary agencies as well as the university who all aimed to work together in order to service the locality. However, service and citizenship should not be confused with mutual support and self-representation: the civic practice of service to the community tended to come from above.[57] After the Second World War and even into the 1960s when the phenomenal expansion of sociology as a discipline began to take place (28 new departments and 30 new chairs founded within a decade), Liverpool still tried to steer the old course against clear winds of change and fluttering banners proclaiming professional neutrality. To Professor T. S. Simey, value-free sociology really meant 'free of local commitment'.[58]

The coming of the postwar welfare state provided the setting for the expansion of social research and for the transfer of the intellectual baton to sociologists from the new 'lower class' social group represented by A. H. Halsey (see p.284). To some extent their new equation of professionalism with value neutrality and their concentration on method was partly an attempt to dislodge patrician styles of service. To dispose of one style of service, they underplayed all activist postures, although, in reality, they could probably be seen as substituting a new version of objective science for reform. Committed to the redistributive project and Labour supporters on the whole, their choice of subjects for research, like enquiries into inequality in education, remained politically relevant. And yet, paradoxically, their professionalism and methodological leanings, for example their reliance on statistical expertise, did not always invite the majority of the people into the science-making process.[59] The new sociologists also made their brainpower available to government on an unprecedented scale: Halsey, for example, advised Labour education minister Crossland on the changeover to comprehensive secondary schools and Tory prime minister Margaret Thatcher about nursery education.

The interdependence and interpenetration of academic and state research increased especially during the periods of Labour government after 1964. An important milestone in 1965 was the establishment of the Social Science Research Council, the key state funding body for postgraduate training and academic research which survived a Thatcherite onslaught in 1982, signalling not only the effectiveness of resistance campaigns but the utility of this kind of agency to a modern state, regardless of which political party holds power. The state also expanded its own research capacity to feed the insatiable appetite of what is now being called its 'knowledge base', necessary not only to discharge its functions but to legitimize its actions as being scientifically informed.[60] The Government Social Survey ran a continuous Household Expenditure inquiry and completed over 600 ad hoc surveys during its first forty years of existence; to this prodigious output has to be added the masses of statistics being compiled by individual government departments. In this climate, resistances lingering on from the first decade of the twentieth century gave way; sampling techniques, for example, were now routinely used, and the state itself became the source of methodological developments.[61] The postwar penumbra of research organizations has serviced a version of objectivity which emphasises technical competence and has tended to provide the tools for social engineers within accepted present frameworks.

This configuration was disrupted by challenges from the left and from the right. The socialist and feminist intellectual revolt of the 1960s and 1970s demanded transformative analysis and praxis. This momentum in turn was stalled by Conservative attacks on universities in general in the 1980s and larger than average cuts in sociology, now identified in right-wing fantasy as the revolutionary subject. The tendency of monetarism to see activities which do not produce value (profits) as valueless led to huge cutbacks in the civil and 'caring' services so integrally connected to the history of social science.[62] A crisis is also an opportunity; the Chinese ideogram for crisis contains both the idea of danger and of possibility. Many of the patterns welding science to service have been shattered but this may be the moment to begin making new patterns in terms of vision and action. So far this chapter has looked at visions of science from above especially those which assert a special disengaged capacity for an overview. As working people themselves sometimes suggested, mobile vision might be all well and good but detached retinas do not often see clearly, especially when they try to focus another person's reality. Recently feminist scholars from the natural and social sciences have been discussing a third practice of objectivity which locates knowledge in fields of social force. One position in the debate, which some earlier socialists shared, inverts the idea of paramount authority and privileges the view from below.[63] A second, and more useful approach, dissolves the idea of paramount authority altogether. Haraway, a biologist by training, with a special interest in primates (including humans), points to the urgent need to think in terms of a metaphor of embodied vision, which sees vision as part of the sensory system of animate creatures, not as the free-floating mind's eye. This leads directly to the central insight that all vision, no matter how vastly aided by the new visualizing technologies, which can photograph, for example, star wars or cell wars, actively and only partially construct a reality:

> The 'eyes' made available in modern technological sciences shatter any idea of passive vision; these prosthetic devices show us that all eyes, including our own organic ones, are active perceptual systems building in translations and specific ways of seeing, that is, ways of life. There is no unmediated photograph or passive camera obscura in scientific accounts of bodies and machines; there are only highly specific visual possibilities, each with a wonderfully detailed, active, partial way of organizing the world.[64]

We are left with the perception that all vision is partial and socially situated, an insight which has analytical, ethical and political consequences.

This kind of feminist objectivity does not amount to relativism, which is the linked opposite to the idea of neutral unitary scientific truth. Relativism, like the belief in unitary truth, involves an insensitivity to social positioning and power and leads to a general feeling that all perspectives are equally possible to adopt and have equal status and validity. By contrast, objectivity as partial and situated knowledge, perhaps a better term would be relational knowledge, calls for a deep sensitivity to power and to the ways in which different knowledges dignify or disempower groups of people in concrete social situations.

This kind of insight leads away from unthinking attempts to represent others, and towards efforts to achieve more mutual understanding and if possible co-operative action, exploring what Haraway calls 'the possibility of webs of connections called solidarity in politics and shared conversations in epistemology'.[65]

Throughout this book, I have tried to visualize social science as social practice, and show how pre-academic social science, though divided and riven, saw itself as socially influenced and practically important. The much-used slogan 'knowledge is power' and the search for 'really useful knowledge' underline this clear concern. I have also become repeatedly aware of how deep social differences have real epistemological ramifications. To quote William Blake, without tidying up his gendered language: 'as a man is so he sees'. From the vantage point of their different social positions and life experiences, people looking at the same society even in the same place in the same period of years often simply saw different problems as being the most urgent. Where the early statisticians and social investigators highlighted physical disease and social disorder in filthy crammed cities, the early socialists saw oppressive power relations, particularly in the social relations of economic production and in the family, as the real problem. Where women from more powerful classes worried deeply about the absence of adequate parenting and about 'friendless girls' among the poor, poor women practised their own version of parenting and surrounded themselves by people they considered supportive friends. Even where people used the same legitimating language, and spoke in terms of happiness or citizenship, they often accented these terms in different, even incompatible, ways.

An awareness of the perceptual differences that arise from cultural diversity leads to a difficult area of ethical concern. One of the sad lessons of this book seems to be that social science from above has often acted as a variety of cultural imperialism. The habit of seeing difference as deficiency has existed from the beginning of the social science tradition and has received institutional buttressing ever since. At the beginning of the tradition, working people could more easily articulate their own science as against versions of science being imposed upon them from above. This intellectual confidence of less powerful people became gradually undermined by professional men and women wanting and needing to gain the monopoly over social science and by large outside agencies and particularly the state taking over fields like education where the production of knoweldge took place. Higher education, one of the dominant preserves of social science, has remained doggedly exclusive despite admitting, particularly since the 1960s, a minority of the most able students from 'lower' social groups. Academics have not often argued for a version of science which safeguards the authenticity of the voice and experience of people unlike ourselves. Indeed we are caught in a contradiction created by a narrow idea of professionalism which rests our own legitimacy on the authority of our special training and special insight if not any longer on our social service to the community at large. The superiority of our training and vision which supposedly assure the legitimacy of our careers also mark us off from the rest of humanity. The foundation of our own material positions rests on excluding not including others in the active pursuit of our intellectual work.

Having spent so much time unravelling the complex ties between social location and social knowledge it would be unrealistic to end with a sermon on correct thought. Nonetheless several commandments strike me as essential for people who still see the most important role of a science project or indeed of intellectual work to enlarge human freedom. Liberation cannot involve cultural imperialism. We must always try to keep analytic space open for people who are 'being studied' to appear as active agents (even if not the most powerful forces) in social life. In contemporary history, a more daunting challenge invites us to develop practices of social study which allow room for people to speak for themselves and thus to represent themselves. This involves the task of dissolving boundaries between university and non-university knowledges and between professional and non-professional forms of speech, at the same time as constructing forums for co-operative exploration where hierarchy is dismantled. There have been gestures in this kind of direction in many scattered places from the 1970s onwards. In the heyday of the women's liberation movement, mutual improvement societies reappeared which brought together university and non-university women and which incubated some of the most impressive feminist studies.[66] In sociology at present, feminists are exploring methods which give the subjects of study a more active part in the research process.[67] Movements like the Federation of Worker Writers and Community Publishers have made it possible for the writing of working people to reach print and have begun to formulate new standards of 'literary merit' or cultural value based on this practice.[68] Inevitably this kind of 'conversation in epistemology' leads to recognition of perceptual differences that arise from social positioning and inequality. An awareness of the interpenetration of knowledge and power must be built into any practice of social science which yearns after a freer life for the majority of people. In Haraway's words, rational knowledge must come to be understood as 'power-sensitive conversation' so that science does not represent the search for closure and final truth but the concern with 'that which is contestable and contested'.[69]

NOTES AND REFERENCES

PREFACE AND ACKNOWLEDGMENTS

1. E. Janes [Yeo], 'The Quest for the New Moral World: Changing Patterns of Owenite Thought, 1817–1870', MA thesis, University of Wisconsin, 1963; E. Yeo, 'Social Science and Social Change: A Social History of Some Aspects of Social Science and Social Investigation in Britain, 1830–1890', PhD thesis, University of Sussex, 1972.
2. The group I worked with is QueenSpark whose publications are available from 11 Jew Street, Brighton BN1 1UT. Together with other local groups we formed the Federation of Worker Writers and Community Publishers; the work of this movement and its battles with the Arts Council over definitions of 'literature' and 'literary merit' are recounted in P. Maguire *et al.*, *The Republic of Letters: Working-class Writing and Local Publishing*, Comedia Publishing Group, London, 1982.

INTRODUCTION

1. National Association for the Promotion of Social Science (NAPSS), *Trans.*, 1857, p.26; *Northern Star*, 10 Nov. 1838.
2. For useful ideas on historical categories, see E.P. Thompson, 'The Poverty of Theory', in *The Poverty of Theory and Other Essays*, Merlin, London, 1978, pp.237–8; also D. Riley, *'Am I that Name?' Feminism and the Category of 'Women' in History*, Macmillan, London, 1988, pp.1–2.
3. A.H. Halsey (ed.), *Traditions of Social Policy: Essays in Honour of Violet Butler*, Oxford, Blackwell, 1976, p.viii; J. Bernard, 'Re-viewing the Impact of Women's Studies on Sociology', in C. Farnham (ed.), *The Impact of Feminist Research in the Academy*, University of Indiana Press, Bloomington, 1987, p.197.
4. W.B. Gallie, 'Essentially Contested Concepts', *Proceedings of the Aristotelian Society*, vol.LVI (1955–6), p.198, urges attention to the

historical development of appraisive concepts; also his *Philosophy and the Historical Understanding*, Chatto and Windus, London, 1964, ch.8; A. McIntyre, 'The Essential Contestability of Some Social Concepts', *Ethics*, vol.LXXXIV (1973), p.7. S. Collini, *Liberalism and Sociology: L.T. Hobhouse and Political Argument in England, 1880–1914*, Cambridge University Press, Cambridge, 1979, p.15 discusses individualism and collectivism as contested concepts.

5. Riley, *Am I that Name?*, ch.1; J. Scott, 'Deconstructing Equality-versus-Difference: or, the Uses of Poststructuralist Theory for Feminism', *Feminist Studies*, vol.14 (1988).

6. Studies of plebian political economy include N. Thompson, *The People's Science: The Popular Political Economy of Exploitation and Crisis,1816–1834*, Cambridge University Press, Cambridge, 1985; G. Claeys, *Machinery, Money and the Millennium: From Moral Economy to Socialism, 1815–60*, Polity, Cambridge, 1987.

7. The intellectual history work of my Sussex colleagues, John Burrow, Stefan Collini and Donald Winch stands out as pathbreaking: e.g., J.W. Burrow, *Evolution and Society: A Study of Victorian Social Theory*, Cambridge University Press, Cambridge, 1966, Collini's *Liberalism* and their joint opus, *That Noble Science of Politics: A Study in Nineteenth-Century Intellectual History*, Cambridge University Press, Cambridge, 1983, Prologue. From sociology too, there have been recent attempts to disrupt the canonical view which sometimes only partly succeed because, while considering present day social movements and the making of new knowledges, they still concentrate on 'great' theorists in the past albeit giving them a political agenda, e.g., S. Seidman, *Contested Knowledge: Social Theory in the Postmodern Era*, Blackwell, Oxford, 1994.

8. Although confined to educated men, the best study of the interplay between social thought and social organization remains P. Abrams, *The Origins of British Sociology: 1834–1914*, University of Chicago Press, Chicago, 1968. Of course the work of 'great' thinkers also bears the mark of social fingerprinting: see e.g., J.D.Y. Peel, *Herbert Spencer, The Evolution of a Sociologist*, Heinemann, London, 1971 and A. Desmond and J. Moore, *Darwin*, Penguin, London, 1992, which place these theorists into social context.

9. E.P. Thompson, *The Making of the English Working Class*, Pelican, Harmondsworth, 1968, p.939. For his more extended discussion of the dialectics of class formation, see *Poverty*, p.238.

10. L. Davidoff and C. Hall, *Family Fortunes: Men and Women of the English Middle Class, 1780–1850*, Hutchinson, London, 1987, p.13.

11. For an excellent discussion of the mutual dependence of the categories 'woman' and 'social', see Riley, *Am I that Name?*, ch.3.

12. Unfortunately S. Collini, *Public Moralists: Political Thought and Intellectual Life in Britain 1850–1930*, Clarendon, Oxford, 1991, pp.3, 29, marginalizes women although he places Mill at the centre of discussion. W. LePenies, *Between Literature and Science: The Rise of Sociology*, Cambridge University Press, Cambridge, 1988, p.14 talks of the 'secret history' of the significant role in modern social science

played by women like Taylor and Beatrice Webb (pp.112ff.).
13. For early anthropology see G. Stocking Jr., *Victorian Anthropology*, Free Press, New York, 1987, ch.7; for later developments, S. Feuchtwang, 'The Discipline and its Sponsors', in T. Asad (ed.), *Anthropology and the Colonial Encounter*, Ithaca Press, London, 1973.
14. Alison Twells explores this movement in '"Let Us Begin Well At Home": Class, "Race" and Christian Motherhood in the Writing of Hannah Kilham (1774–1832)' to appear in E. Janes Yeo (ed.), *Radical Femininity: Women's Self-Representation in Nineteenth and Twentieth Century Social Movements*. For the same imagery of darkness and light applied to Africa see J. and J. Comaroff, 'Through the Looking–glass: Colonial Encounters of the First Kind', *Journal of Historical Sociology*, vol.I (1988), pp.10, 23.
15. G. Jones, *Social Darwinism and English Thought: The Interaction Between Biological and Social Theory*, Harvester, Brighton, 1980, p.158.
16. R. Williams' ideas on language and his discussion of social production are most clearly developed in *Marxism and Literature*, Oxford University Press, Oxford, 1977, parts I and II. For M. Foucault, *The Order of Things: an Archaelogy of the Human Sciences: An Archaeology of the Human Sciences*, Tavistock, London, 1970 and his *Power/Knowledge. Selected Interviews and Other Writings 1972–77*, ed. C. Gordon, Harvester, Brighton, 1980, ch.5. J. Weeks, 'Foucault for Historians', *History Workshop*, no.14 (Autumn 1982), provides a clear account of his concerns. Terry Eagleton's discussion of a renewed study of rhetoric as the way out of a poststructural relativist morass is helpful: *Literary Theory: An Introduction*, Basil Blackwell, Oxford, 1983, pp.205–6, 210. For the issue of language in feminist movements and scholarship, see D. Cameron, *Feminism and Linguistic Theory*, Macmillan, 1985, intro.
17. See Scott, 'Deconstructing', pp.35–6 for a clear exposition of Foucault's ideas on discourse.
18. H. Bosanquet, *The Strength of the People: A Study in Social Economics*, Macmillan, London, 1902, p.330.
19. R. Williams, *Politics and Letters: Interviews with New Left Review*, Verso, London, 1981, pp.135–6; also Williams, *Marxism*, pp.108ff., for his discussion of contested hegemony.
20. V.N. Voloshinov, *Marxism and the Philosophy of Language*, 1929, trans. L. Matejka and I. Titunik, Harvard University Press, Cambridge, Mass., 1986, p.23.
21. M. Llewelyn Davies, 'Women and Citizenship', *Co-operative News*, 29 Oct. 1904; *The Women's Co-operative Guild*, Kirby Lonsdale, 1904, p.151. I owe these references to Gill Scott whose chapter '"As a War-horse to the Beat of Drums": Representations of Working-class Femininity in the Women's Co-operative Guild 1880s to World War Two' will appear in the forthcoming volume *Radical Femininity*.
22. E.P. Thompson, 'An Open Letter to Leszek Kolakowski', in *Poverty*, pp.144–5.
23. For a discussion of how incorporation in cultural process changes

both host and guest, see E. and S. Yeo (eds), *Popular Culture and Class Conflict, 1590–1914: Explorations in the History of Labour and Leisure*, Harvester, Brighton, 1981, p.141; chs. 5 and 10 discuss class contest and cultural form.

24. These phrases all come from D. Haraway, 'Situated Knowledges: The Science Question in Feminism and the Privilege of Partial Perspective', in *Simians, Cyborgs, and Women: The Reinvention of Nature*, Free Association Books, London, 1991, pp.190, 191, 196. S. Harding, *The Science Question in Feminism*, Cornell University Press, Ithaca, 1986 gives a useful account of feminist approaches to the history of science to that date; for her position now, *Whose Science? Whose Knowledge? Thinking from Women's Lives*, Open University Press, Milton Keynes, 1991. See too H. Rose, *Love, Power and Knowledge: Towards a Feminist Transformation of the Sciences*, Polity, Oxford, 1994.

1 SOCIAL SCIENCE FROM ABOVE

1. Robert Owen, for example, focused on the industrial revolution and the 'manufacturing system, which has already essentially altered the relative condition of all classes in Britain' and which 'cannot fail to force a greater change in human affairs than has been effected by all the previous revolutions which have agitated the world', *Birmingham Co-operative Herald*, 19 Sept. 1829. The Reverend Robert Vaughan spoke in urban terms of 'the great social revolution' which was creating 'the age of great cities' and saw the key class contest as the 'struggle between the feudal and the civic, as generally represented by the landlord and the mercantile class': *The Age of Great Cities or Modern Society Viewed in its Relation to Intelligence, Morals and Religion*, 1843, Irish University Press reprint, Shannon, 1971, p.1. However, most urban investigators would have stressed a crisis in relations between rich and poor in large towns, see ch.3 below.

2. Hannah to Martha More, 20 Mar. 1790, in William Roberts (ed.), *Memoirs of the Life and Correspondence of Mrs. Hannah More*, 2nd edn, Seeley and Burnside, London, 1834, vol.II, p.225.

3. Frances Lady Shelley quoted in E.P. Thompson, *The Making of the English Working Class*, p.60, who insists that policing the poor was the real project.

4. T. Bernard, 'Preliminary Address to the Public', in *The Reports of the Society for Bettering the Condition and Increasing the Comforts of the Poor* (hereafter SBCP, *Reports*), vol.I, T. Becket, London, 1797, pp.i–iii. Bernard, the son of the Governor of the Massachusetts Bay colony, made a considerable fortune as a practising barrister and by marrying heiress Margaret Adair. He left the law to take up philanthropy in which his wife was also active. His account of the founding of the Bettering Society is reprinted in T. Bernard, *Pleasure and Pain 1780–1818*, ed. J. Bernard Baker, John Murray, London, 1930, pp.53ff. My thanks to F.R. Prochaska for his unpub-

lished paper 'To Help the Poor to Help Themselves: The Philanthropy of Sir Thomas Bernard, 1795–1818'. For the emergence of new-type philanthropy in the 1780s, see D. Andrew, *Philanthropy and Police: London Charity in the Eighteenth Century*, Princeton University Press, Princeton, 1989.

5. For Malthus's disruption of previous views of the harmony of man and nature, see R. Young, *Darwin's Metaphor: Nature's Place in Victorian Culture*, Cambridge University Press, Cambridge, 1985, ch.1; for his challenge to ideas of duty to the poor, see G. Claeys, *Machinery*, p.20; for development of his views, D. Winch, *Malthus*, Oxford University Press, Oxford, 1987. The full references for works cited in this paragraph are: the Reverend T. Malthus, *An Essay on the Principles of Population*, 1798, Penguin edn, Harmondsworth, 1970; J. Bentham, 'Tracts on the Poor Laws and Pauper Management', 1797ff., *Works*, ed. J. Bowring, William Tait, Edinburgh, 1843, vol.VIII; W. Wilberforce, *A Practical View of the Prevailing Religious System of Professed Christians in the Higher and Middle Classes in this Country Contrasted with Real Christianity*, T. Cadell Junior and W. Davies, London, 1797; T. Gisborne, *An Enquiry into the Duties of the Female Sex*, T. Cadell Junior and W. Davies, London, 1797, a companion to his *Enquiries in the Duties of Men in the Higher and Middle Class of Society*, 1794 which reached a 4th edn in 1797. In *The State of the Poor*, 3 vols, 1797, Cass reprint, London, 1966, Eden followed the example set by Sir John Sinclair, *The Statistical Account of Scotland*, 21 vols, William Creech, Edinburgh, 1791–9.

6. E.P. Thompson, 'Eighteenth–century English Society: Class Struggle without Class?', *Social History*, vol.III (May 1978), p.150. For the role of 'mercy', D. Hay, 'Property, Authority and the Criminal Law', in Hay *et al.* (eds), *Albion's Fatal Tree*, Allen Lane, London, 1975, p.62. Claeys, Machinery, ch.1, pp.187ff., explores Christian rights of the poor and stewardship duties of the rich, and E.P. Thompson provides an extended discussion of 'moral economy' in *Customs in Common*, Penguin, London, 1991, ch.V. B. Webb, *My Apprenticeship*, Longmans, Green, London [1926], p.198, for her view of charity. For SBCP use of negative words, *Reports*, vol.I, p.iv, vol.III, 1802, pp.2–4, 9 for rejection of 'noxious' natural rights theory or 'occult and abstruse investigations'; ibid., p.11 deplores concern with 'motive' of the donor rather than effect on 'the object', the poor recipient.

7. R. and S. Wilberforce, *The Life of William Wilberforce*, John Murray, London, 1838, pp.194–5. T. Bernard, *Spurinna or the Comforts of Old Age*, Longman, Hurst, Rees, Orme and Brown, London, 1816, p.93, for the importance of 'a regular habit of Self Examination', kindness to dependents and attention to the poor. Copying Benjamin Franklin's idea, Unitarian Harriet Martineau also tabulated her day's 'virtues and vices', H. Martineau, *Autobiography*, Smith, Elder, London, 1877, vol.I, p.25. For the Evangelicals and revolution, V. Kiernan, 'Evangelicalism and the French Revolution', in *Past and Present*, no.I (1952) and C. Hall, 'The Early Formation

of the Victorian Domestic Ideology', in S. Burman (ed.), *Fit Work for Women*, Croom Helm, London, 1979.

8. Max Weber, *The Protestant Ethic and the Spirit of Capitalism* (1920), trans. Talcott Parsons (1930), Unwin University Books, London, 1968, pp.26–7, 110, 115–18.

9. Bernard's list, SBCP, *Reports*, vol.III, p.9; vol.I, p.viii for remarks on service. The Reverend Venn wanted children to become 'industrious, frugal, sober and moderate, faithful and obedient' and to grow into 'useful servants, good husbands, and careful masters of a family', quoted in M. Hennell, *John Venn and the Clapham Sect*, Lutterworth, London, 1958, p.136. More assured the Bishop of Bath and Wells that her aim was 'to train up the lower classes in habits of industry and piety', letter dated 1801, *Memoirs*, vol.III, p.133.

10. Society for Bettering the Condition of the Poor at Clapham, *Rules and Regulations*, 2nd edn, London, 1805, pp.29, 26. T. Bernard, 'Extract from an Account of a Society for Bettering the Condition of the Poor at Clapham', SBCP, *Reports*, vol.II, 1800, pp.343ff.

11. J. Bentham, *Works*, vol.VIII, p.416. For Bernard and SBCP, *Reports*, vol.V, 1808, pp.10–11, vol.I, pp.417–18 also for the preoccupation with lowering the poor rates; SBCP Clapham, *Rules*, pp.27, 31.

12. Ibid, pp.3–5, 11, 27.

13. H. More to the Reverend J. Newton, 15 Sept. 1796, *Memoirs*, vol.II, pp.465–6; also Martha More, *Mendip Annals: or a Narrative of the Charitable Labours of Hannah and Martha More in their Neighbourhood, Being the Journal of Martha More*, ed. A. Roberts, James Nisbet, London, 1859, p.78. For her methodical approach to reconstructing village culture, J. McLeish, *Evangelical Religion and Popular Education*, Methuen, London, 1969, pp.57ff.; More to Wilberforce, 1791, *Memoirs*, vol.II, pp.300ff., T. Bernard, 'Extract from an Account of the Mendip Schools', SBCP, *Reports*, vol.II, pp.303ff.

14. See Hall, 'Early Formation' for the best discussion of early Evangelicals and separate spheres and R. Furneaux, *William Wilberforce*, Hamish Hamilton, London, 1974, pp.166–8 for Wilberforce's relations with his wife. For Enlightenment writing on sexual difference, J. Rendall, *The Origins of Modern Feminism: Women in Britain, France and the US 1780-1860*, Macmillan, London, 1985, pp.13–17; for reproductive medicine, see T. Laqueur, 'Orgasm, Generation, and the Politics of Reproductive Biology', in C. Gallagher and T. Laqueur (eds), *The Making of the Modern Body: Sexuality and Society in the Nineteenth Century*, University of California Press, Berkeley, 1987.

15. L. Davidoff and C. Hall, *Family Fortunes: Men and Women of the English Middle Class, 1780–1850*, Hutchinson, London, 1987.

16. H. More, *Coelebs in Search of a Wife*, 5th edn, Seeley and Burnside, London, 1809, vol.II, p.20.

17. C. Cappe, *Thoughts on the Desirableness and Utility of Ladies Visiting the Female Wards of Hospitals and Lunatic Asylums*, London, 1816, p.376;

S. Trimmer, *The Oeconomy of Charity; or an Address to Ladies concerning Sunday–Schools; The Establishment of Schools of Industry under Female Inspection; and the Distribution of Voluntary Benefactions*, T. Longman, London, 1787, pp.21, 15; For Evangelical women and philanthropy, Hall, 'Early Formation', p.28; A. Summers, 'A Home Away from Home—Women's Philanthropic Work in the Nineteenth Century', in Burman, *Fit Work*, pp.36–9; F.R. Prochaska, *Women and Philanthropy in Nineteenth–Century England*, Clarendon Press, Oxford, 1980, intro., part 2; Rendall, Origins, pp. 262ff.; D. Thompson, 'Women, Work and Politics in Nineteenth-century England: The Problem of Authority', in J. Rendall (ed.), *Equal or Different: Women's Politics, 1800–1914*, Basil Blackwell, Oxford, 1987, pp.71–4.

18. For her defence in the Blagdon controversy, see More to the Bishop of Bath and Wells, 1801, *Memoirs*, vol.III, pp.133–5; McLeish, *Evangelical*, p.62.

19. M. Hopkins, *Hannah More and her Circle*, Longmans, Green, New York, 1947 gives a lively picture of her more worldly years.

20. M. More, *Mendip*, pp.82, 86. More to Wilberforce, 1791, *Memoirs*, vol.II, p.305.

21. Hellfire warnings: M. More, *Mendip*, p.109; 'The Sunday School', in *The Works of Hannah More*, Henry G. Bohn, London, 1853, p.188

22. H. More to Mrs Carter, 1 Oct. 1789; reply from Carter, 1789; More to a Friend, Jan. 1792, *Memoirs*, vol.II, pp.178, 180, 311; M. More, *Mendip*, pp.16, 23.

23. Ibid., p.62.

24. Quoted in Hennell, *Venn*, p.114; H. More, journal entry 19 Jan. 1794, *Memoirs*, vol.II, p.415; also Wilberforces, *Wilberforce*, vol.I, p.342: 'the fraternal spirit of Revolutionary France...threatened our own population with the infection of her leprous touch'. For localized doctors' use of this imagery in the late eighteenth century, see F. Mort, *Dangerous Sexualities: Medico-Moral Politics in England since 1830*, Routledge and Kegan Paul, London, 1987, pp.22ff.

25. Bernard, 'Extract from an Account of the Ladies' Committee for Promoting the Education and Employment of the Female Poor', SBCP, *Reports*, vol.IV, 1805, p.186. Mort, *Dangerous Sexualities*, p.32 on hygenics.

26. M. More, *Mendip*, pp.107, 149, 163.

27. H. More to a Friend, 1792, *Memoirs*, vol.II, p.318; More to Wilberforce, 1791, ibid., p.302, for an account of how mothers initially demanded that children be paid to come to school and worried that the Mores would 'acquire a power over them (the children) and send them beyond the sea'.

28. M. More, *Mendip*, pp.65, 107; for the same situation in York, C. Cappe, *An Account of Two Charity Schools for the Education of Girls: and of a Female Friendly Society in York*, William Blanchard, York, 1800, pp.71, 96.

29. SBCP, *Reports*, vol.IV, Appendix, pp.65; 122ff. for the aims and activity of the Ladies' Committee; pp.141ff. for the survey questionnaire

and vol.V, 1808, Appendix, pp.23–4 for its distribution. For the explosion in the number of benevolent organizations and women's part in them, F. Brown, *Fathers of the Victorians: The Age of Wilberforce*, Cambridge University Press, Cambridge, 1961, ch.9; F.R. Prochaska, 'Women in English Philanthropy 1790–1830', *International Review of Social History*, vol.XIX (1974), pp.428–31 and his *Women and Philanthropy*, p.109.

30. Thompson's *Making of the English Working Class* gives the classic account of Working-class consciousness in this period while A. Briggs, 'The Language of "Class" in Early-Nineteenth Century England', in Briggs and J. Saville (eds), *Essays in Labour History*, vol.I, Macmillan, London, 1967, pp.54–60, as well as his 'Middle–class Consciousness in English Politics, 1780–1846', *Past and Present*, no.9 (1956), gives a good picture of bourgeois consciousness.

31. A. Ferguson, *Essay on the History of Civil Society*, 1767, ed. Duncan Forbes, Edinburgh University Press, Edinburgh, 1966, p.122. For overviews of the Scottish project, G. Bryson, *Man and Society: The Scottish Inquiry of the Eighteenth Century*, Princeton University Press, Princeton, 1945; N. Phillipson, 'The Scottish Enlightenment' in R. Porter and M. Teich (eds), *The Enlightenment in National Context*, Cambridge University Press, Cambridge, 1981, pp.19–40; Collini, *Noble Science*, ch.1.

32. [James Mill], *A Fragment on Mackintosh*, Baldwin and Craddock, London, 1835, p.149, Bentham in 1795 quoted by E. Halévy, *The Growth of Philosophic Radicalism* (1928), Faber and Faber, London, 1952 edn, p.188; T. Paine, *Rights of Man, Being an Answer to Mr Burke's Attack on the French Revolution*, 1791–2, Penguin, Harmondsworth, 1969, pp.63–4.

33. C. Everett, *Jeremy Bentham*, Weidenfeld & Nicolson, London, 1966, pp.22, 35, 44, 76ff. and J. Semple, *A Study of the Panopticon Penitentiary*, Clarendon Press, Oxford, 1993.

34. J. Bentham, *An Introduction to the Principles of Morals and Legislation*, 2nd edn, Pickering, London, 1823, vol.I, p.1: the first edition was printed in 1780 but not published until 1789. For T.B. Macaulay, contestable concepts, 'which cannot be circumscribed by precise definitions', included 'power, happiness, misery, pain, pleasure, motives, objects of desire', 'Mill's Essay on Government: Utilitarian Logic and Politics', 1829, reprinted in J. Lively and J. Rees (eds), *Utilitarian Logic and Politics*, Clarendon Press, Oxford, 1978, p.107

35. J. Bentham, *Theory of Legislation*, trans. from E. Dumont by R. Hildreth, 8th edn, Kegan Paul, Trench, Trübner, 1894, p.120. L. Boralevi, *Bentham and the Oppressed*, Walter de Gruyter, Berlin, 1984, p.97; p.107 for the indigent.

36. James Mill, 'An Essay on Government', 1819, reprinted in Lively, *Utilitarian*, pp.69, 93–4. J. Dinwiddy, *Bentham*, Oxford University Press, Oxford, 1989; p.82, for Bentham's postwar support for manhood suffrage with a literacy qualification.

37. Macaulay, quoted in Collini, *Noble Science*, p.101; ch.3 covers the

dispute as does Lively, *Utilitarian*, 'Intro.' which reprints the main contributions to it. Ibid., pp.126–7 for Macaulay's views on induction and motivation.

38. J.S. Mill, *Autobiography*, 1873, Penguin, London, 1989, pp.93–4. Collini, *Noble Science*, ch.2 gives a good account of the emergence of political economy; also Winch, *Malthus*, ch.6, for the disputes between Malthus and Ricardo on the analysis of postwar distress and the desirable directions of economic growth

39. Mill, *Autobiography*, p.106. For the best picture of the personnel and activity of the Philosophic Radicals, see J. Hamburger, *Intellectuals in Politics: John Stuart Mill and the Philosophic Radicals*, Yale University Press, New Haven, 1965, ch.1. Chairs were also created in political economy in Oxford (1825), Cambridge (1828), King's College London (1831).

40. J. Mill, *A Fragment on Mackintosh*, p.278. For attitudes to women's suffrage, Boralevi, *Bentham*, ch.1; Mill, *Autobiography*, p.93; Mill, 'Essay on Government', p.79. J.S. Mill, 'On the Definition of Political Economy and on the Method of Investigation Proper to it', *Westminster Review*, vol.XXVI (1836), pp.134–5, placed within the remit of 'morals or ethics', the study of 'the feelings called forth in a human being by other individual human or intelligent beings as such; namely, the *affections*, the *conscience*, or feeling of duty, and the love of *approbation*'.

41. W. Pare, *An Address Delivered at the Opening of the Birmingham Co-operative Society*, 17 Nov. 1828, Birmingham Co-op. Society, Birmingham, n.d., p.8. Security was also discussed by the Co-operative economists in terms of individual security (each worker receiving the value he had created) and social security (the community as a whole appropriating the collective fruits of its labour): W. Thompson, in *An Inquiry into the Principles of the Distribution of Wealth Most Conducive to Human Happiness*, 1824, Kelley reprint, New York, 1963, pp.78, 384ff.

42. Young in 'Darwin's Metaphor', pp.31–9 analyses Malthus and Chalmers (see p.67); also Boyd Hilton, *Age of Atonement: The Influence of Evangelicalism on Social and Economic Thought, 1795–1865*, Clarendon Press, Oxford, 1988.

43. Martineau, *Autobiography*, vol.I, p.170; pp.120, 164, 173 for family encouragement and permission; pp.160–1, 171 for her 'calling' to do the project. For two and a half years, the political economy tales became a week-long wonder of disciplined production, pp.193–4; R. Webb, *Harriet Martineau: A Radical Victorian*, Columbia University Press, New York, 1960, pp.116–17. M. Walters, 'The Rights and Wrongs of Women: Mary Wollstonecraft, Harriet Martineau, Simone de Beauvoir' in A. Oakley and J. Mitchell (eds), *The Rights and Wrongs of Women*, Penguin, Harmondsworth, 1976, perceptively discusses her in relation to gender issues. For provincial Unitarian beliefs and gendered culture, see pp.66ff. below.

44. 'Miss Martineau's *Monthly Novels*', *Quarterly Review*, vol.XLIX (1833), p.151. J. Newton, 'Engendering History for the Middle

Class: Sex and Political Economy in the *Edinburgh Review*', in L. Shires (ed.), *Rewriting the Victorians*, Routledge, London, 1992, p.8 on gatekeeping role.

45. [W. Empson], 'Illustrations of Political Economy. Mrs. Marcet—Miss Martineau', *Edinburgh Review*, vol.LVII (1833), p.3; 'Mrs Loudon's *Philanthropic Economy*', *Westminster Review*, vol.XXIII (1835), p.2 and 'John Hopkins on Political Economy', ibid., vol.XXII (1835), p.3 for the view that Marcet was about to 'present Political Economy to the world under the figure of a decent matron, freed from the dirt and ignominy with which cribbed and narrowed notions of utility have besmirched her comely brow'.

46. Empson, 'Illustrations', p.62. J.S Mill to T. Carlyle, 11, 12 Apr. 1833, in *Earlier Letters*, ed. F. Mineka, *Works*, vol.XII, University of Toronto Press, Toronto, 1963, p.152 in which he also felt that the system had work to do of a destroying kind after which it would expire. [T. Lister], 'Mrs. Gore's, Women as They Are', *Edinburgh Review*, vol.LI (1830), p.445 for novel-writing as perhaps something 'women do better than men'; Martineau, *Autobiography*, vol.I, p.169, II, p.1, for James Mill's views.

47. Empson, 'Illustrations', pp.38, 11.

48. J. Mill, 'Essay', p.93; Briggs, 'Middle-class Consciousness' and 'Language of "Class"', pp.54–60. K. Marx and F. Engels, *The German Ideology*, Part I, C.J. Arthur, ed. Lawrence and Wishart, London, 1974, pp.65–6 for a new class's claim to universality. For new standards of public and private probity compared with fashionable aristocratic masculinity, Davidoff, *Family*, pp.21–2; for convenience of keeping virtue at home, B. Taylor, *Eve and the New Jerusalem: Socialism and Feminism in the Nineteenth Century*, Virago, London, 1983, p.126.

49. Riley, *Am I that Name?*, ch.3.

50. S. Lewis, *Woman's Mission*, 2nd edn, John W. Parker, London, 1839, p.129. For Scottish Enlightenment views on the family and on maternal education, Rendall, *Origins*, pp.23, 27; also her 'Vice and Commerce: Women in the Making of Adam Smith's Political Economy' in E. Kennedy and S. Mendus (eds), *Women in Western Political Philosophy*, Wheatsheaf, Brighton, 1987, pp.71–2.

51. L. Barrow, *Independent Spirits: Spiritualism and English Plebeians, 1850–1910*, Routledge and Kegan Paul, London, 1986, p.146. For stimulating discussions of 'experience' as an historical category, R. Williams, *Keywords: A Vocabulary of Culture and Society*, Fontana, London, 1983, also the entry for 'science'. Thompson, 'Poverty of Theory', pp.199–200.

52. J. Bentham, *Works*, vol.VIII, p.416.

53. W. Cooke Taylor, *The Natural History of Society in the Barbarous and Civilized State: An Essay Towards Discovering the Origin and Course of Human Improvement*, Longman, Orme, London, 1840, vol.II, p.261. This work was dedicated to Archbishop Whately. W. Cooke Taylor, *Notes of a Tour in the Manufacturing Districts of Lancashire*, 1841, Cass Reprint, London, 1968; *Factories and the Factory System, from*

Parliamentary Documents and Personal Observations, Jeremiah How, London, 1844.

54. Collini, *Noble Science*, pp.103, also 111–12.

55. C.F. Bahmueller, *The National Charity Company: Jeremy Bentham's Silent Revolution*, University of California Press, Berkeley, 1981, pp.74–5; For Rickman's motivation, M. Cullen, *The Statistical Movement in Early Victorian Britain*, Harvester, Hassocks, 1975, pp.12–13.

56. Quoted in Bahmueller, *National*, p.158; the discussion here draws on pp.59, 188, 254 n. 116; ch.3 deals with the Panopticon; P. Corrigan and D. Sayer, *The Great Arch: English State Formation as Cultural Revolution*, Basil Blackwell, Oxford, 1985, p.156. M. Foucault, *Discipline and Punish: The Birth of the Prison*, trans A. Sheridan, Allen Lane, London, 1977, in the chapter on 'Panopticism', pp.201ff., explored the power relationship resulting from the feeling of being under constant surveillance by unseen eyes.

57. T. Bernard, 'Extract of an Account of the Introduction of Straw Platting at Avebury', SBCP, *Reports*, vol.IV, pp.91–3; the Reverend Glass, 'Extract from an Account of a Village Shop at Greenford', ibid., vol.III, p.62; More to Wilberforce, 1801, *Memoirs*, vol.III, p.151.

58. T. Bernard, *The New School; Being an Attempt to Illustrate its Principles, Detail, and Advantages*, London, 1809, pp.17–18. 21; the Appendix compares the Bell with the Lancaster system which Bernard also favours. Financed by Bernard, with the Bishop of Durham as patron, the Barrington School was run by Dr Bell himself. For Utilitarian support of Lancastrian Schools, Collini, *Noble Science*, p.95.

59. T. Bernard, 'Extract from an Account of the Institution for Applying Science to the Common Purposes of Life, so far as it may be Expected to Affect the Poor', SBCP, *Reports*, vol.II, pp.205–14; also a Cork and a Dublin Society existed, vol.V, 1808, Appendix, p.150. For technology in Panopticon, Everett, *Bentham*, pp.72–3. For arterial drainage, S.E. Finer, *The Life and Times of Sir Edwin Chadwick*, Methuen, London, 1952, pp.222–4.

60. Bentham quoted in Bahmueller, *National*, p.188; also pp.6, 157, 187 for views on public and private managements.

61. For artificial harmonization of interests, see Halévy, *Philosophical Radicalism*, p.36 and Finer, *Chadwick*, pp.15, 24–6. Dinwiddy, *Bentham*, p.11 for sinister interests.

62. Thompson, *The Making of the English Working Class*, pp.860–1.

2 SOCIAL SCIENCE FROM BELOW

1. *Poor Man's Guardian* quoted in R. Johnson, '"Really Useful Knowledge": Radical Education and Working-class Culture 1790–1848', in J. Clarke *et al.*, *Working-class Culture: Studies in History and Theory*, Hutchinson, London, 1979, pp.78–9 which gives an excellent account of oppositional practice in education.

2. New Moral World (henceforth NMW), 12 Jan. 1837.

3. E. Yeo, 'Christianity in Chartist Struggle 1838–42', *Past and Present*, no. 91 (1981) pp.110–13, *passim* and 'Chartist Religious Belief and the Theology of Liberation', in J. Obelkevich *et al.* (eds), *Disciplines of Faith: Studies in Religion, Politics and Patriarchy*, Routledge and Kegan Paul, London, 1987, pp.410–21. Thompson, *The Making of the English Working Class*, pp.86–96 discusses the radical constitutionalism of the 1790s; also H. Cunningham, 'The Language of Patriotism, 1750–1914', *History Workshop*, no.12 (Autumn 1981) and J.A. Epstein, *The Lion of Freedom: Feargus O'Connor and the Chartist Movement, 1832–42*, Croom Helm, London, 1982. *Northern Star*, 28 Aug. 1841, for making every man his own lecturer to prevent 'a mere system of lectureship'.

4. E.T. Craig, 'Socialism in England: Historical Reminiscences', in *American Socialist*, Oneida, New York, 24 Jan. 1878; in the *Lancashire Co-operator*, 11 Jun. 1831, Craig insisted that Owenite doctrine provided 'the principles of Social Science'.

5. This complex movement went through several phases and changes of name. Between 1829 and 1834, it contained Co-operative retail and producer societies usually committed to a communitarian future, Equitable Labour Exchanges operating a labour value currency and the Grand National Consolidated Trades Union whose defeat ended this phase. In 1835, the movement regrouped as the Association of All Classes of All Nations (AACAN), then added a National Community Friendly Society (NCFS) to raise funds and finally merged the two bodies into the Universal Community Friendly Society of Rational Religionists. In the post-1834 period, adherents frequently called themselves socialists but, with the advent of the Rochdale pioneers (1844) and the collapse of the Queenwood Community (1845), the name co-operation again came to the fore. J.F.C. Harrison, *Robert Owen and the Owenites in England and America*, Routledge and Kegan Paul, London, 1969, 'Anatomy of a Movement'.

6. W. Thompson, *Distribution*, p.viii. For the Owenite contribution to language, A. Bestor, 'The Evolution of the Socialist Vocabulary', *Journal of the History of Ideas*, vol.IX (1948), pp.277–80. For studies of the term, see my 'Social Science', pp.45–6. L. Goldman, 'The Origins of British "Social Science": Political Economy, Natural Science and Statistics, 1830–1835', The Historical Journal, vol.XXVI (1983), p.606 argues that term and concept of a science of society, are 'intrinsically associated with the early nineteenth-century French Positivist tradition' which came into English discussion via J.S. Mill in 1836; but G. Claeys insists on another separate development of an Owenite configuration which Mill knew well not least because he debated against Thompson in 1825: '"Individualism", "Socialism" and "Social Science": Further Notes on a Process of Conceptual Formation, 1800–1850', *Journal of the History of Ideas*, vol.47 (1986), p.88–9.

7. Quoted by N. Thompson, *People's Science*, pp.153; 152ff. for the counterattack from the political economists.

8. For 'co-operative' and 'competitive economists', *Birmingham Co-operative Herald*, 1 Jun., 1 Sept. 1829; *Lancashire and Yorkshire Co-operator*, 29 Oct. 1831. 'Moral economy' featured in J. Watts, *The Facts and Fictions of Political Economists*, Manchester, Abel Heywood, 1842, pp.iv, 14, 15; 'social economy' in *Political Magazine*, ed. W. Carpenter, Sept. 1831, p.19.

9. W. Hawkes Smith, *The Errors of the Social System—being an Essay on Wasted, Unproductive and Redundant Labour*, Longman, London, 1834, pp.9–10. Hawkes Smith held office on the local and national levels of the movement and took part in every Birmingham Co-operative project during his lifetime: see my 'Social Science', pp.21–5.

10. W. Hawkes Smith, *Letters on the State and Prospects of Society*, Birmingham, reprinted from the *Philanthropist* newspaper, 1838, p.6; *Letters on Social Science*, Flindell, Birmingham, 1839, pp.9, 11–12.

11 J.S. Mill, 'On the Definition of Political Economy', quoted in 'Social Science versus Political Economy', *NMW*, 19 Nov. 1836 where the other arguments of this paragraph also occur. The same critique was still alive and well in J. Hole, *Lectures on Social Science and Organization of Labour*, John Chapman, London, 1851, p.26. Mill proposed that pure mental philosophy would consider the laws of man as an individual; that morals or ethics would study the feelings which came into play in relation to other individual beings; the wealth pursuing dimensions would concern political economy and finally feelings generated by living in an aggregation of human beings for a common purpose/s would come under the remit of 'social economy' or the 'science of politics' or 'the social science'.

12. *NMW*, 26 Nov. 1836, 28 Jan. 1837.

13. *Lancashire and Yorkshire Co-operator*, Apr. 1832.

14. For later views about social ethics as part of sociology, L.T. Hobhouse, 'Editorial', *Sociological Review*, vol.I (1908), p.5. 'Sociology', *Encyclopaedia of Religion and Ethics*, vol.XI (1920), p.656.

15. *Midland Representative*, 9 Jul. 1831. In R. Owen, *Lectures on the Rational System of Society: Derived Soley from Nature and Experience*, London, 1841, p.2, he broke the first part into two stressing 'the Science of the overwhelming Influence which humanly-devised External Circumstances may be made to have over Human Nature'.

16. Some socialists explicitly saw the task as reuniting male and female qualities in every human being. Goodwyn Barmby argued to be a true 'Socialist, every man must possess the woman-power as well as the man-power, and the woman must possess the man-power as well as the woman-power. Both must be equilibriated beings': quoted in Taylor, *Eve*, p.178.

17. R. Owen, *Book of the New Moral World*, 1844, Kelley reprint, New York, 1970, Part VI, p.48; C. Bray, *The Philosophy of Necessity*, 1841, Longman, Orme, Brown, Green and Longmans, vol.II, pp.435–6.

18. Taylor, *Eve*, pp.136ff. and 184ff. gives a robust account of the holy war.

19. The Reverend F. Close, *A Sermon Addressed to the Female Chartists of Cheltenham...August 25, 1839*, Hamilton Adams, London, 1839, p.14, also pp.3–4, 8, for arguments in this paragraph.
20. Ibid., pp.14, 17.
21. Quoted in Taylor, *Eve*, p.135; for Emma's story, pp.130–56.
22. *The Pioneer*, 8 Feb. 1834. My thanks to Helen Rogers for this reference.
23. C. Bray, *Phases of Opinion and Experience During a Long Life*, Longmans Green, London, 1884, pp.64–5; Pare was president of the First Birmingham Co-operative Society, edited two local Owenite journals and held office in the AACAN and NCFS. After being sacked as Registrar because of his socialism, his farewell dinner was attended by some 70 leading citizens: R.G. Garnett, 'William Pare: a Non-Rochdale Pioneer', *Co-operative Review* (May 1964), p.149, *Birmingham Journal*, 22 Sept., 5 Nov. 1832.
24. Hawkes Smith, *NMW*, 31 Dec, 1836; State, p.11; *Midland Representative*, 25 Jun. 1831.
25. G.J. Holyoake, *Sixty Years of an Agitator's Life*, 3rd edn, Fisher Unwin, London, 1893, vol.I, pp.10, 20–5.
26. G.J. Holyoake, *Secularism, the Practical Philosophy of the People*, London, 1854, p.3. His intellectual odyssey is tracked in J. McCabe, *The Life and Letters of G.J. Holyoake*, Watts, London, 1908, vol.I, p.28. Craig also moved from piety through phrenology to socialism: *American Socialist*, 6 Dec. 1877.
27. For phrenology see R. Cooter, *The Cultural Meaning of Popular Science: Phrenology and the Organisation of Consent in Nineteenth-century Britain*, Cambridge University Press, Cambridge, 1984.
28. *The Reasoner*, ed. G.J. Holyoake, 28 Oct. 1857; *Self Help by the People*, Trübner, London, 1857, p.7; Holyoake, *Sixty*, vol.I, pp.143, 148, 160 for his martyrdom over remark that in community people could erect as many churches as they pleased but he thought it bad political economy to spend in this way, given the poverty of the people.
29. *Birmingham Co-operative Herald*, 1 Sept. 1829; 1 Oct. 1829, for Owen's statement; J. Watts, *Metaphysical Parallels in Juxtaposition For and Against the Existence of God*, Watson, London [1842], p.5.
30. Ripponden quoted in Thompson, *The Making of the English Working Class*, p.873.
31. W. Thompson, *Distribution*, pp.166, 423. M. Beer, A *History of British Socialism*, Allen and Unwin, London, 1948 edn, part II, pp.189–99 for the political economists.
32. John Gray, *A Lecture on Human Happiness*, 1825, London School of Economics reprint, London, 1931, pp.69–70, 15 for this discussion; Claeys, *Machinery*, ch.5 looks at Gray's ideas.
33. *The Pioneer*, 8 Feb. 1834, p.191; Gray, *Lecture*, pp.18–19.
34. R. Owen, 'Address Delivered...August 21, 1817', in *The Life of Robert Owen*, vol.IA., 1857–8, Cass reprint, London, 1967, p.111; *Birmingham Co-operative Herald*, 1 Jul. 1829.
35. *Birmingham Co-operative Herald*, 1 Jun. 1829.
36. Gray, *Lecture*, pp.61–4 made the fullest analysis of competition which

had great resonance in areas with non–mechanized industries: Birmingham Labour Exchange Gazette, 2, 9 Feb. 1833. Hawkes Smith made the machinery arguments in Birmingham insisting that this would be the scenario of the future: *Midland Representative*, 10 Dec. 1831.

37. Quoted in Thompson, *The Making of the English Working Class*, p.873. The *Midland Representative*, 14 Apr. 1832, insisted that 'the middle class are like all other men—the creatures of circumstance. Their characters are formed by institutions, and their relative position in society to the other classes....It is not men, then, but institutions that are in fault and consequently the remedy lies not in abusing the men, but in reforming the institutions'.

38. W. Thompson, *Appeal of One Half the Human Race, Women, Against the Pretensions of the Other Half Men, to Retain them in Political, and thence in Civil and Domestic Slavery*, 1825, Virago reprint, London, 1983, p.67.

39. *The Co-operative Magazine and Monthly Herald*, vol.I (Aug. 1826), p.257.

40. R. Owen, *Lectures on the Marriages of the Priesthood in the Old Immoral World*, Leeds, 1840, p.30.

41. Taylor, *Eve*, discusses these fears on pp.206ff., and how women socialist lecturers responded, pp.212–16.

42. Hawkes Smith, *Social Science*, pp.11–12.

43. *Crisis*, 6 Jul., 21 Sept., 12 Oct. 1833, for classes in the London Social Community.

44. I discuss these problems in 'Culture and Constraint in Working-class Movements', in Yeos, *Popular*, p.167. For a concrete example of choosing the present over the future in Manchester, *NMW*, 23 May 1840.

45. For contest in London, Thompson, *The Making of the English Working Class*, pp.817–18, also I. Prothero, *Artisans and Politics in Early Nineteenth-century London: John Gast and his Times*, Dawson, Folkestone, 1979, pp.195–203; for a debate with the SDUK, *Birmingham Journal*, 30 Jun., 14, 28 Jul. 1832.

46. Besides Craig, who left the area to manage the Ralahine estate in Ireland, this group included plumber James Rigby, radical publisher and bookseller Abel Heywood, fustian cutter then journalist Lloyd Jones, and Robert Cooper, a clerk. They were not only active in Owenism, where Cooper became a social missionary and Rigby deputy governor of the Queenwood community, but in other movements of the period including the campaign for an unstamped press, the Ten Hours movement and trade unions. Later Jones moved into Christian socialism and Cooper into secularism and suffrage politics. Fustian cutter, then clerk, Rowland Detroisier, was taken up by the Benthamite circle in London where he worked as a lecturer and died young: G. Williams, *Rowland Detroisier, a Working Class Infidel, 1800–1834*, Borthwick Papers, no.28, York, 1965. For Rigby: *Northern Star*, 1 Jan. 1842; Heywood: W. Axon, *The Mayor of Manchester and His Slanderers*, Manchester, 1877; Jones: P. Redfern,

The New History of the CWS, London, Dent, 1938, p.580; Cooper: *Dictionary of Labour Biography*, vol.II, pp.103ff.

47. Practical provision can be traced through the *Lancashire Co-operator*, 11 Jun.–20 Aug. 1831 continuing as the *Lancashire and Yorkshire Co-operator*, Sept. 1831–Apr. 1832.
48. See my 'Culture', pp.160–3 for Working-class halls.
49. Ibid., pp.172ff., more fully analyses middle-class response.
50. *Crisis*, 19 Oct. 1833; Johnson, 'Really Useful', p.94 traces the acceptance of state education; see my 'Culture', pp.164–5 for financial difficulties of sustaining Halls of Science.
51. P. Gurney, 'The Making of Co-operative Culture in England, 1870–1918', Univ. of Sussex PhD thesis, 1989, ch.2; Holyoake's comment in *Co-operative News*, 7 Mar. 1874.
52. *Lancashire and Yorkshire Co-operator*, Jul. 1832, pp.2–3.
53. *NMW*, 17 Dec. 1836, also Joseph Smith in ibid., 12 Nov. 1836.
54. J.F. Bray, *Labour's Wrong and Labour's Remedy; or the Age of Might and the Age of Right*, 1839, LSE reprint, London, 1931; H. McCormac, *On the Best Means of Improving the Moral and Physical Condition of the Working Classes*, Longman, London, 1830, pp.5–6.
55. *NMW*, 21 May 1842; also *Northern Star*, 23 May 1840, whole front page for Co-operative statistics; ibid., 19 Nov. 1842 for appeal to trade unions for statistics since those 'got up by the Government authorities and capitalists cannot often be depended upon, where the interests of the working men are concerned'. P. Gosden, *Self-Help: Voluntary Associations in the Nineteenth Century*, Batsford, London, 1973, pp.52–3 for friendly societies developing considerable actuarial skill long before commercial life insurance companies became interested in a working-class market.
56. For this enquiry, *Birmingham Journal*, 21 Jul., 15, 22 Sept., 1832.
57. *NMW*, 24 Febuary 1838; Smith, State, p.45.

3 MIDDLE-CLASS SOCIAL SURVEY AND URBAN SOCIAL DISORDER

1. 'Fourth Annual Report', *Journal of the Statistical Society of London* (hereafter JSSL) vol.I (1839), p.8. For earlier statistics, Cullen, *Statistical*, 'Prelude'. Sinclair's definition was embraced by most early nineteenth–century statisticians, e.g., J. Cleland, 'An Account of the Former and Present State of Glasgow', *Glasgow and Clydesdale Statistical Society Transactions*, Glasgow, 1836, p.52.
2. B. Heywood, 'Address... 1832', in *Addresses Delivered at the Manchester Mechanics' Institution*, London, 1843, p.60 also p.56 for concern with cholera.
3. Davidoff, *Family*, p.21.
4. J. Kay-Shuttleworth, *The Moral and Physical Condition of the Working Classes Employed in the Cotton Manufacture in Manchester*, 2nd edn, 1832, Cass reprint, London, 1970, pp.8,10. When Kay married Lady Janet Shuttleworth in 1842, to placate her family he attached her name to his: Janet Shuttleworth to James Kay, 2 Feb. 1842,

no.257, Kay-Shuttleworth Papers, John Rylands University Library of Manchester. I shall refer to him throughout as Kay-Shuttleworth.

5. R. Richardson, *Death, Dissection and the Destitute*, London, Routledge and Kegan Paul, London, 1987, chs 1 and 2.

6. R. Morris, *Cholera 1832: The Social Response to an Epidemic*, Croom Helm, London, 1976, pp.101–8; Rev. W. Hanna, *Memoirs of Thomas Chalmers*, Thomas Constable, Edinburgh, 1854, vol.II, p.249.

7. Kay-Shuttleworth, *Moral*, p.13.

8. The view of O.R. McGregor, 'Social Research and Social Policy in the Nineteenth Century', *British Journal of Sociology*, vol.VIII (1957), p.147. Mort argues a convergence of medicine and Evangelicalism in a medico-moral alliance: *Dangerous Sexualities*, pp.30–2.

9. Gaskell is a shadowy figure who treated Working-class patients and tried to implement plans for cottage gardens for weavers and schemes for reclaiming wastelands: *Prospects of Industry*, Smith, Elder, London, 1835. His *Artisans and Machinery: The Moral and Physical Condition of the Manufacturing Population Considered with Reference to Mechanical Substitutes for Human Labour*, 1836, Cass reprint, London, 1968, expanded *The Manufacturing Population*, Baldwin and Cradock, London, 1833 where his famous analysis of the changing countryside also appeared. McCormac (1800–86), a prominent local citizen, served in five institutions which dealt with the poor including the Fever Hospital, and managed to interest the Belfast House of Industry in a quasi-Owenite plan for creating employment for paupers. See H. McCormac, *A Plan for the Relief of the Unemployed Poor*, Belfast, 1830; entry in the *Dictionary of National Biography* (hereafter DNB).

10. McCormac, *An Appeal on Behalf of the Poor*, Archer, Hudgson and Jellett, Belfast, 1830, pp.3–6, 11–15; Gaskell, *Artisans*, pp.11–58.

11. See F. Smith, *The Life and Work of Sir James Kay-Shuttleworth*, Murray, London, 1932.

12. Kay-Shuttleworth, *Moral*, pp.77–8, 90–1.

13. Ibid., p.8. He made some of his most explicit use of body metaphor when speaking of moral disease: pp.62, 63 where he prescribed the proper treatment of the social body by 'the cultivation of religion and morality' to be added to political economy's calculations about wealth.

14. Ibid., pp.12, 43.

15. Ibid., pp.32, 21. See too M. Poovey, 'Curing the "Social Body" in 1832: James Phillips Kay and the Irish in Manchester', *Gender and History*, vol.V (1993).

16. Quotes from Kay-Shuttleworth, *Moral*, pp.112, 77, 9.

17. Societies were also mooted in Barnsley, Doncaster, Gateshead, Halifax, Leicester, Nottingham, Portsmouth, the Potteries, Sheffield, Tavistock and Tonbridge: Cullen, *Statistical*, p.119; chs 6–9 for the provincial societies. Membership lists are most continuously available for Manchester and Bristol, appended to the *Annual Reports*, and in London's annual *List of Fellows*. The *Proceedings of the Liverpool Statisical Society*, Liverpool, 1838 included a membership list as did

the *Constitution and Regulations of the Glasgow and Clydesdale Statistical Society*, Glasgow, 1836. The activists of the other groups can be identified from passing reports in *JSSL* and in the records of the Literary and Philosophical Institutions of which they sometimes formed a section.

18. S. Greg, *Two Letters to Leonard Horner on the Capabilities of the Factory System*, London, 1840, p.16. These letters, for private circulation, were dated Jan. 1835 and Mar. 1838. For the Manchester Society, T.S. Ashton, *Economic and Social Investigations in Manchester, 1833–1933*, King, London, 1934; also D. Elesh, 'The Manchester Statistical Society' in A. Oberschall (ed.), *The Establishment of Empirical Sociology: Studies in Continuity, Discontinuity and Institutionalisation*, Harper and Row, New York, 1972.

19. B. to P. Heywood, Letter d. 20 Sept. 1847, in T. Heywood, *A Memoir of Sir Benjamin Heywood*, Manchester, n.d., p.122.

20. E. Gaskell, *The Letters of Mrs. Gaskell*, J. Chapple and A. Pollard, (eds.), Manchester University Press, Manchester, 1966, letter to Eliza Fox [1850], no.68, p.106. W. Gérin, *Elizabeth Gaskell, A Biography*, Clarendon Press, Oxford, 1976, pp.48, 52, 62.

21. T. Chalmers, *On the Sufficiency of the Parochial System, without a Poor Rate, for a Right Management of the Poor*, Glasgow, William Collins, 1841, pp.110, 106, 115; Hanna, *Chalmers*, vol.I, pp.506ff. Ch.9 below for Helen Bosanquet's debt to Chalmers; also N. Masterman, *Chalmers on Charity*, Constable, London, 1900 and *Dr. Chalmers and the Poor Laws*, Douglas, Edinburgh, 1911.

22. J.H. Thom, *A Spiritual Faith*, 'Memorial Preface' by J. Martineau, Longmans, London, 1898, p.15. Rev. Carpenter of the Bristol Society edited J. Tuckerman, *Christian Service to the Poor in Cities, Unconnected with any Religious Denomination*, Philp and Evans, Bristol, 1839. For influence on Independent chapels, Kay-Shuttleworth, *Moral*, p.67.

23. *JSSL*, vol.I (1839), p.551. Also see the lengthy statement of aims in Bristol Statistical Society, *Proceedings of the Second Annual Meeting*, Bristol, 1838, p.9.

24. 'Report upon the Condition of the Town of Leeds and of its Inhabitants' by a Statistical Committee of the Town Council, *JSSL*, vol.II (1839). Leeds Town Council Minutes, 9 Nov. 1838, p.466, Leeds Central Library.

25. The classification comprised statistics covering 'the great purposes of mankind in society': appropriation, production, instruction, protection, consumption and enjoyment: London Statistical Society, 'Sixth Annual Report', *JSSL*, vol.III (1840), pp.4–5, 6. There were 2,000 copies of the mammoth questionnaire circulated but only a few replies received: London Statistical Society, *First Series of Questions Circulated by the Statistical Society of London*, London, 1836; J. Bonar and H.W. Macrosty, *Annals of the Royal Statistical Society, 1834–1934*, The Society, London, 1934, pp.31, 36.

26. *Report of a Committee of the Manchester Statistical Society on the Condition of the Working Classes in an Extensive Manufacturing District in 1834,*

1835 and 1836, James Ridgway and Son, London, 1838, p.5; C.B. Fripp, 'Report of an Inquiry into the Condition of the Working Classes of the City of Bristol', in Bristol Statistical Society, *Proceedings of the Third Annual Meeting*, Bristol, 1839, p.10; 'Report to the Council of the Statistical Society of London from a Committee of its Fellows appointed to make an Investigation into the State of the Poorer Classes in St. George's in the East', in *JSSL*, vol.XI (1848), p.193.

27. Manchester, *Extensive Manufacturing District*, p.4; Kay to Chalmers, Manchester Appendix, item 4.

28. D. Rowe, 'The Chartist Convention and the Regions', *Economic History Review*, 2nd series, vol. xxii (1969), pp.58–9, 71–2 gives the 1839 questionnaire and analyses the 23 returns; for the replies, British Library, Add. Ms. 34,245B, Miscellaneous Papers of the Chartist General Convention, fols 276–311.

29. W. Langton, Tables Showing the number of Churches, Chapels and Sunday Schools in Manchester and District (paper 1834–5 session), Manchester Appendix; 'Report upon...Leeds', *JSSL*, vol.II (1839), pp.415–16; Bristol Statistical Society, 'Church Accommodation', *Proceedings of the Fifth Annual Meeting*, Bristol, 1841, pp.13–16; Rev. Wyatt–Edgell, 'Moral Statistics of the Parishes of St. James, St. George, and St. Anne Soho in the City of Westminster, *JSSL*, vol.I (1839), pp.479–81.

30. These demands in Manchester Statistical Society, *On the State of Education in the Borough of Manchester in 1834*, London, 1835, pp.5, 7–12; Ibid., 2nd edn revised, London, 1837, p.v; *On the State of Education in the Borough of Salford in 1835*, London, 1836, p.13; *Report of a Committee of the Manchester Statistical Society on the State of Education in the Borough of Liverpool in 1835–6*, London, 1836, pp. 40, 43.

31. For resistance to give information on friendly societies, Bristol, *Second Annual Meeting*, p.10. Notice of socialist activity in B. Heywood, 'Condition of Irlams O'the Height', 11 Feb. 1835 in Manchester Appendix, item 24 and *Education...Manchester in 1834*, p.32; *Education...Salford*, pp.28, 30.

32. A. Alison, *Some Account of My Life and Writings: An Autobiography*, W. Blackwood and Sons, Edinburgh, 1883, vol.I, p.379; J. Cleland, 'Account of Glasgow', p.35.

33. London Statistical Society, 'Fourth Annual Report', *JSSL*, vol.I (1839), p.2. J. Boyle, 'Account of Strikes in the Potteries in the Years 1834 and 1836', ibid., pp.37–45; H. Ashworth, *Inquiry into the Origin, Progress and Results of the Strike of the Operative Cotton Spinners of Preston from Oct. 1836 to Feb. 1837*, Manchester, 1838.

34. For bourgeois ordering, L. Davidoff, 'Class and Gender in Victorian England', in J. Newton *et al.* (eds), *Sex and Class in Women's History*, Routledge and Kegan Paul, London, 1983, p.27; Stallybrass, *Transgression*, p.50. For reluctance to give information on numbers of beds and people, Manchester, *Extensive Manufacturing District*, p.14; Bristol, *Second Annual Meeting*, p.10.

35. Quotes from Bristol, *Third Annual Meeting*, pp.7–9.
36. See note 30 above for education surveys.
37. T. Carlyle, 'Chartism', 1839, in *Works*, Ashburton edn, London, 1883, p.262.
38. Bristol, *Third Annual Meeting*, p.7.
39. C.R. Baird, 'Observations on the Poorest Class of Operatives in Glasgow', *JSSL*, vol.I (1839), p.171; J. Heywood, 'Report of an Inquiry Conducted from House to House into the State of 176 Families in Miles Platting...in 1837', ibid., pp.34–6; W. Felkin, *Remarks upon the Importance of an Inquiry into the Amount and Appropriation of Wages by the Working Classes*, Hamilton, London, 1837.
40. 'Report upon...Leeds', *JSSL*, vol.II (1839); *Northern Star*, 6, 13 Feb. 1841, for Chartist involvement and emphasis on inequality of provision for rich and poor wards of Leeds.
41. H. Ashworth, 'Statistics of the Present Depression of Trade at Bolton: Showing the Mode in which it affects the Different Classes of a Manufacturing Population', *JSSL*, vol.V (1842), p.77; W. Neild, 'Comparative Statement of the Income and Expenditure of Certain Families of the Working Classes in Manchester and Dukinfield, in the Years 1836 and 1841', ibid., vol IV (1841), pp.321–2, 334. J. Finch Jr., *Statistics of Vauxhall Ward (Liverpool), Showing the Actual Condition of More than Five Thousand Families*, Walmsley, Liverpool, 1842, pp.11–15, 35.
42. 'Report...on Parishes of...Westminister', *JSSL*, vol.III (1840), pp.17–18; C.R. Weld, 'On the Condition of the Working Classes in the Inner Ward of St. George's Parish, Hanover Square', ibid., vol.VI (1843), pp.117–18; 'Report of a Committee...of the Statistical Society of London...to Investigate the State of Inhabitants and their Dwellings in Church Lane, St. Giles', ibid., vol.XI (1848), p.17.
43. 'St. George's in the East', ibid., pp.193; 200–1 for tables of trades and wages, 206–7 for earnings of single women by trades, 208–9 for rents.
44. The London Society distributed copies of the Leeds report and said that other boroughs had pledged to make the same kind of survey at Census time: 'Sixth Annual Report', *JSSL*, vol.III (1840), 'Seventh Annual Report', vol.IV (1841), p.71, 'Eighth Annual Report', vol.V (1842), p.89.
45. For, example, John Cleland, having made his own census of Glasgow in 1819, ran the official census of 1831; Dr Duncan, head of the uncompleted survey of the Liverpool working classes, later became the Health of Towns Commission informant.
46. Corrigan, *Great Arch*, pp.124–5, 134–5.
47. Finer, *Chadwick*, pp.2–3.
48. E. Chadwick to Bishop Blomfield, 16 Dec. 1844, Chadwick Papers, item 2181, copybook VI, p.63.
49. Finer, *Chadwick*, pp.15ff. Philip Corrigan has the clearest idea of how Chadwick's programme acted to take the state out of politics and make it appear, routine, normal, natural and neutral, *Great Arch*, p.123.

50. E. Chadwick, 'The Development of Statesmanship as a Science by the Investigation of the Phenomena of State Necessities', in B. Richardson (ed.), *A Review of the Works of E. Chadwick*, 1887, Dawson Reprint, London, 1965, vol.1, pp.133, 137; also the idea that the larger the number of witnesses, the more error tended to be cancelled out: *The Poor Law Report of 1834*, ed. S. and E. Checkland, Penguin, Harmondsworth, 1974, pp.71–2.

51. Factories Inquiry Commission, *First Report of the Central Board, Parl. Sess.*, vol.XX, 1833, p.68. Chadwick Papers, item 72 on the civil service; for corruption of vestry officers, E. Chadwick, 'The New Poor Law', *Edinburgh Review*, vol.LXIII (1836), p.524; also Finer, *Chadwick*, pp.78–9.

52. Corrigan, *Great Arch*, p.159 says the majority of the new–type state servants after 1832 were doctors and lawyers; also his 'State Formation and Moral Regulation in Nineteenth-Century Britain: Sociological investigations', University of Durham, PhD thesis, 1977, for more details about the social composition of this group.

53. S.E. Finer, 'The Transmission of Benthamite Ideas 1820–1850', in G. Sutherland (ed.), *Studies in the Growth of Nineteenth-century Government*, Routledge and Kegan Paul, London, 1972, pp.23–5.

54. 'Instruction Concerning the Reception of the Royal Commission' in C. Driver, *Tory Radical: The Life of Richard Oastler*, Oxford University Press, Oxford, 1964, App. C. For early examples of Working-class suspicion of inspectors, Finer, *Chadwick*, p.62; for twentieth-century instances see chs 8 and 9 below.

55. E. Chadwick, *Report on the Sanitary Condition of the Labouring Population of Great Britain*, 1842, ed. M. Flinn, Edinburgh University Press reprint, 1965, intro. for timing.

56. Ibid., p.413. For the tenacity of miasmatic theory of disease, see Charles E. Rosenberg, 'Florence Nightingale on Contagion: The Hospital as Moral Universe', in C. Rosenberg (ed.), *Healing and History*, Dawson, New York, 1979, pp.112, 117.

57. *Lancashire and Yorkshire Co-operator*, Apr. 1832.

58. J. Salt, 'Isaac Ironside and Education in the Sheffield Region in the First Half of the Nineteenth Century', Univ. of Sheffield MA thesis, 1960, pp.147–9, 157ff., tells the Sheffield story; J. Toulmin Smith, *Local Self-Government and Centralization*, John Chapman, London, 1851, made Chadwick's version of public health and civil service bureaucracy a particular target, pp.158ff., 303–4, 346–7.

59. Chadwick, *Sanitary Condition*, pp.307, 299, 334–5 for quotes in this paragraph.

60. Ibid., p.98.

61. 'Examinations Taken By Mr. Spencer. B.2. Western District', *Reports from Commissioners, Factories, Parl. Sess.*, vol.XX, 1833, pp.22–5. My thanks to Sophie Hamilton for drawing my attention to the questionnaire.

62. *Reports from Commissioners, Children's Employment, Mines, Parl. Sess.*, vol.XVI, 1842, p.181.

63. S. Hamilton, 'Images of Femininity in the Royal Commissions', in

Yeo, *Radical Femininity* (forthcoming) quoting 'Evidence Collected by S.S. Scriven', Mary Barrett, witness no.72, *Reports from Commissioners,...Mines, Parl. Sess.*, vol.XVII, 1842, p.122; vol.XV, 1842, p.26 for shortened version of testimony in 'First Report of the Commissioners'.

64. 'Report by Charles Barham M.D....Cornwall and Devon', ibid., p.806.

65. 'First Report of the Commissioners', ibid., vol.XV, p.35.

66. For the background of the survey and for Mayhew's life, see E.P. Thompson, 'Mayhew and the *Morning Chronicle*', in H. Mayhew, *The Unknown Mayhew: Selections from the Morning Chronicle, Labour and the Poor*, ed. E.P. Thompson and E. Yeo, Merlin, London, 1971. Provincial surveys included *Inquiry into the Condition of the Poor of Newcastle-upon-Tyne from the Newcastle Chronicle*, Newcastle, 1850 and 'The Condition of the Working Classes of Edinburgh and Leith', appearing in the *Edinburgh News*, 25 Sept. 1852 to 29 Jul. 1854.

67. Letter I, 19 Oct. 1849 quoted in E. Yeo, 'Mayhew as a Social Investigator', *Unknown Mayhew*, p.54; pp.55–60 for a more extended analysis of his method of studying a trade.

68. Letter V, *Morning Chronicle*, 2 Nov. 1849, reprinted in *The Morning Chronicle Survey of Labour and the Poor: The Metropolitan Districts*, Caliban, Firle, 1980, vol.I, p.104.

69. Ibid., p.99.

70. Letters IX and X, 16 and 20 Nov. 1849, *Unknown Mayhew*, pp.152–3, 159–60.

71. Yeo, 'Mayhew', p.71.

72. Letter IV, 30 Oct. 1849, quoted ibid., p.83.

73. Letter XXV, 11 Jan. 1850, *Morning Chronicle Survey*, vol.II, p.290.

74. Thompson, 'Mayhew', pp.32–4.

75. Letter XXXI, 31 Jan. 1850, *Morning Chronicle Survey*, vol.III, p.97.

76. Ibid., p.98.

77. *London Labour and the London Poor*, Mayhew, London, 1851, vol.I, p.3. Contemporary anthropological influences included the work of Dr J.C. Prichard of the Bristol Statistical Society (also president of the Ethnological Society), whose *Natural History of Mankind* started from the Enlightenment idea of social stages, that is, hunting, herding and civil society, arguing that different skull formations attached to each. Dr Andrew Smith's work on 'The Origin and History of the Bushmen', *Philosophical Magazine*, vol.IX (1831) argued that more settled tribes were often surrounded by wandering tribes. Conflating the two, Mayhew borrowed the idea of social stages but said they could coexist even in a civilized society.

78. Letter XII, 27 Nov. 1849, *Morning Chronicle Survey*, vol.II, p.1.

79. *London Labour*, 1851, vol.I, pp.20–1.

80. Stallybrass, *Transgression*, ch.3.

81. Thus the Rev. T. Beames, author of the first analytic study of urban slums, admired Mayhew's work, but picked out only those parts which related to housing: *The Rookeries of London: Past, Present and Prospective*, 1852, Cass reprint, London, 1970, pp.39, 79ff. Mary

Carpenter, *the* authority on juvenile delinquency, took quick and angry notice only of Mayhew's work on ragged schools: *Reformatory Schools for the Children of the Perishing and Dangerous Classes, and for Juvenile Offenders*, 1851, Woburn reprint, London, 1968, p.126.

82. The Manchester Society was saved by an influx largely of doctors and lawyers who replaced systematic social surveys with the practice of an expert giving a paper on his special field. Compared with 24 surveys commissioned by the business plutocrats in the earlier years, only two education surveys were carried out in the Society's name between 1842 and 1880, although occasionally individual members, like Salford coroner D. Chadwick, made virtuoso surveys on their own: Manchester Statistical Society *Trans*, 1861–2; 1865–6 for the failure of a project to prepare local statistics for the Social Science Congress.

4 PROFESSIONAL MEN, SCIENCE AND SERVICE

1. The following statistics are taken from H.J. Perkin, 'Middle-Class Education and Employment in the Nineteenth Century: A Critical Note', in *Economic Hisstory Review*, vol.XIV (1961–2), p.128, 'Table 2. Selected Male Professions, England & Wales, 1851–81':

	1851	*1861*	*1871*	*1881*	*Percentage Increase 1851–81*
Law	32.2	33.7	38.7	43.6	35.4
Medicine	34.0	36.1	41.2	45.1	32.7
Literature & Science	1.9	3.1	6.3	8.0	321.1
Education	28.0	32.9	36.0	51.5	83.9
Religion	30.1	35.5	39.5	43.9	45.8
Administration	49.7	60.6	67.7	72.6	46.1
Employed Male Population	5,875.8	6,518.4	7,250.3	8,108.3	38.0
Total Population	17,927.6	20,066.2	22,712.3	25,974.4	44.9

Perkin gives a useful warning that Census figures in this period would tend to underestimate the numbers actually practising medicine or law, p.128.

2. For cultural and intellectual capital, see H. Perkin, *The Rise of Professional Society*, Routledge, London, 1989 pp.6–10. Also G. Becker, *Human Capital: A Theoretical and Empirical Analysis with Special Reference to Education*, 3rd edn, University of Chicago Press, 1993. For Marxist work, see B. and J. Ehrenreich, 'The Professional-Managerial Class', 1976, which was republished with critical responses in P. Walker (ed.), *Between Labour and Capital*, Harvester, Hassocks, 1979.

3. For the eighteenth–century client relationship of clergy and solicitors to the aristocracy, see E.P. Thompson, 'Class Struggle?', p.142; for critiques of the clergy, see my 'Christianity', pp.126–8; for physicians and the landed interest, N. and J. Parry, *The Rise of the Medical Profession*, Croom Helm, London, 1976, p.105, also I. Waddington, *The Medical Profession in the Industrial Revolution*, Gill and Macmillan, Dublin, 1984, pp.2–4; for the reputation of doctors as grave-robbers, Richardson, *Death*, part III; Chadwick to Blomfield, 16 Dec. 1844 for Loudon; for unreformed ancient universities, S. Rothblatt, *The Revolution of the Dons. Cambridge and Society in Victorian England*, Faber and Faber, London, 1968, pp.17, 187–8.

4. F. Myers, 'George Eliot', *Essays: Modern*, London, Macmillan, 1883, p.269, describing a conversation with her.

5. G. Trevelyan evidence to Playfair Commission (1875) quoted in Corrigan, *Great Arch*, p.159.

6. Chadwick to J. Kay-Shuttleworth, 15 Jul. 1844, quoted in Finer, *Chadwick*, p.157; pp.157ff., for distrust of curative medicine.

7. Quoted in R. Lambert, *Sir John Simon, 1816–1904 and English Social Administration*, Macgibbon, London, 1963, pp.217 note, 227, 229; also 215, 266 for contrast with Chadwick.

8. Quoted in ibid., p.150.

9. Ibid., pp.114–15, 130ff.

10. The *DNB* gives an account of his life.

11. S. Powers, 'The Diffusion of Sanitary Knowledge', NAPSS *Trans.*, 1860, p.714; Lankester lectured 'On Water' in the Ladies' Sanitary Association series on Physiology.

12. Quoted in Lambert, *Simon*, p.153.

13. H. McCormac, *Moral-Sanatory Economy*, Belfast, 1853, p.115. Eight of the twelve chapters were titled 'Physical training', 'Clothing', 'Food', 'Drink', 'Air', 'Drainage', 'Prevention of disease'.

14. D. Gorham, 'Victorian Reform as a Family Business: the Hill Family', in A. Wohl (ed.), *The Victorian Family: Structure and Stresses*, Croom Helm, London, 1978, pp.139–40.

15. For Attwoodite views, F. Hill, *The National Distress, with its Remedies, Real and Imaginary*, Longman, London, 1830, p.6; R. and F. Davenport Hill, *The Recorder of Birmingham*, London, 1878, p.200. For the Political Union, F. Hill, *An Autobiography of Fifty Years in Times of Reform*, Constance Hill (ed.), R. Bentley and Son, London, 1894, pp.18, 44, 76; Gorham, 'Hill Family', p.132. For views on Owen, Hills, *Recorder*, pp.87, 378ff.; R. Hill, *Home Colonies: Sketch of a Plan for the Gradual Extinction of Pauperism and for the Diminution of Crime*, Simpkin and Marshall, London, 1832; F. Hill, *Autobiography*, p.104.

16. Gorham, 'Hill Family', pp.126ff.

17. F. Hill, *National Distress*, pp.44–9.

18. F. Hill, *Autobiography*, pp.115, 114; Hills, *Recorder*, p.16.

19. Ibid., p.155.

20. Select Committee on Criminal and Destitute Juveniles, Minutes of Evidence, *Reports from Committees, Parl. Sess.*, vol.VIII, 1852, pp.34–5.

21. *Authorized Report of the First Provincial Meeting of the National*

Reformatory Union, London, 1856, p.87.

22. *Ragged School Shoe Black Society, its Origin, Operations and Present Condition*, London, 1854, pp.14–15; J.R. Fowler, 'Street Occupations', *NAPSS Trans.*, 1862, p.490–1.

23. H. Byerley Thomson, *The Choice of a Profession*, London, 1857, p.5; A.V. Dicey, 'Legal Etiquette', *Fortnightly Review*, n.s., vol.II (1867), p.177, n.1. For Mayhew's view of professional men as the 'aristocracy of intellect', see *The Great World of London*, London, 1856, part II, pp.64–9. Perkin, *Professional Society*, p.83 discusses other mid-century observations, e.g., by Marx and M. Arnold, about a divided middle class.

24. Perkin, ibid., p.9 stresses the generalizing potential of the professional ideal; for socialist versions, see ch.8 below.

25. For fuller accounts of developments within the medical profession, W.L. Burn, *Age of Equipoise: A Study of the mid-Victorian Generation*, Allen and Unwin, London, 1964, pp.204ff.; Parrys, *Rise*, chs. 6–7; Waddington, *Medical*, chs. 4–7; M. Jeanne Peterson, *The Medical Profession in Mid-Victorian London*, University of California Press, Berkeley, 1978. For the legal profession, A.M. Carr-Saunders and P.A. Wilson, *The Professions*, 1933, Frank Cass reprint, London, 1964, pp.26, 45–8; R. Cocks, *The Foundations of the Modern Bar*, Sweet and Maxwell, London, 1983.

26. For points in the following two paragraphs, see Manchester Medico-Ethical Association, *Rules and By-Laws*, 3rd edn, Manchester, 1862, p.6; *18th Annual Report*, 1865–6, pp.5, 15–16. Waddington, *Medical*, pp.154–5, calls attention to earlier books anticipating the medico-ethical movement; for the legal profession, see Carr-Saunders, *Professions*, p.19; *Rules and Regulations of the Manchester Law Association, Established 12 Dec. 1838*, Manchester, 1839.

27. *British Medical Journal*, 12 Sept. 1857; also *Lancet*, 28 Aug. 1858, 7 Jun. 1862. *The Law Magazine and Law Review* repeatedly tried to point out how lawyers could lend their expertise to help social reformers in every Department of the Social Science Association, e.g., Nov. 1858, pp.158, 169, 173; Feb. 1860, p.403. 28. F. Hill, *Autobiography*, p.314.

29. W. Armytage, *Civic Universities: Aspects of a British Tradition*, Ernest Benn, London, 1956, pp.171 for medical school pressure, 173–4 for London; also H. Hale Bellot, *University College London, 1826–1926*, University of London Press, London, 1929, p.144ff. T. Kelly, *For Advancement of Learning: The University of Liverpool, 1881–1981*, Liverpool University Press, Liverpool, 1981, pp.24–8 for medical education, p.44 for 1848 town meeting. E. Fiddes, *Chapters in the History of Owens College and of Manchester University, 1851–1914*, Manchester University Press, 1937, p.21 for original plan incorporating a medical school.

30. M. Pattison, *Suggestions on Academical Organisation with Especial Reference to Oxford*, Emonston and Douglas, Edinburgh, 1868, p.327, 154, 24. P. Dodd has the sharpest perception of this bid for national hegemony, 'Englishness and the National Culture' in R.

Colls and Dodd (eds), *Englishness: Politics and Culture 1880–1920*, Croom Helm, London, 1986, pp.3–4. University reform and the development of the academic profession is studied in T. Heyck, *The Transformation of Intellectual Life in Victorian England*, Croom Helm, London, 1982, ch.6 and in A. Engel, *From Clergyman to Don: The Rise of the Academic Profession in Nineteenth-century Oxford*, Clarendon Press, Oxford, 1983; also see Perkin, *Rise*, p.86.

31. For idea of a clerisy as part of university reform, see Kent, *Brains and Numbers: Elitism, Comtism, and Democracy in Mid–Victorian England*, University of Toronto Press, Toronto, 1978, ch.1; also Heyck, *Transformation*, pp.170–1, discusses the reformation of the public schools and their adoption of the Christian service ethic developed by Dr Thomas Arnold at Rugby.

32. For Cambridge, see Rothblatt, *Revolution*, pp.143–80.

33. The quotes in this paragraph come from M. Richter's brilliant study of *The Politics of Conscience: T.H. Green and His Age*, Weidenfeld and Nicolson, London, 1964, pp.130, 195, 297, 317, 345. Green's influence (pp.293, 13) reached its height after his death with the publication of his work and the appearance of Mrs Humphrey Ward's novel *Robert Ellsmere* (1888), whose character Dr Grey was modelled on Green. Several key figures to be discussed in ch.8 below came under his spell.

34. However, the 938,000 new voters nearly doubled the electorate. For University figures backing reform, *Essays on Reform*, 1867, B. Crick (ed.), Oxford University Press reprint, Oxford, 1967; see too Kent, *Brains*, ch.3, also Harvie, *The Lights of Liberalism: University Liberals and the Challenge of Democracy*, Allen Lane, London, 1976.

35. R.G. Moulton of Cambridge quoted by J.F.C. Harrison, *Learning and living, 1790–1960: A Study in the History of the English Adult Education Movement*, Routledge and Kegan Paul, London, 1961, p.227; pp.220ff. for the University Extension movement.

36. For civil service reform, see G. Wallas, *Human Nature in Politics*, Archibald Constable, 1908, pp.251–6; E. Chadwick, 'Competitive Examination', in Richardson, *Chadwick*, vol.I, p.338.

37. C.P.B. Bosanquet, *London: Some Account of its Growth, Charitable Agencies and Wants*, Hatchard, London, 1868, pp.168, 151; E. Denison, 16 Oct. 1866, in *Letters and Other Writings*, ed. B. Leighton, Richard Bentley and Son, London, 1872, p.18. Bosanquet was the son of a north country landowner and half brother of philosopher Bernard Bosanquet, student of T.H. Green and later key figure in the Charity Organisation Society. Denison was the son of the Bishop of Salisbury while Hill was the son of the lord of the manor at Grissonhall, Norfolk.

38. Denison, 2 Sept. 1867, *Letters*, p.49.

39. T. Huxley, 'On the Physical Basis of Life', *Fortnightly Review*, vol.XI (1869); H. Martineau, *Autobiography*, vol.I, 371ff.; Webb, *Martineau*, p.306; Mill, *Autobiography*, pp.163–4.

40. C. Kent, *Brains*, p.178, n. 8 gives an interesting occupational breakdown of 83 British Comtists into 16 academics, 13 lawyers, 10

higher civil servants, 10 in business, 6 workers, 2 engineers, 19 of no determined occupation.

41. A. Comte, *A General View of Positivism*, trans. J.H. Bridges, Trübner, London, 1865, p.136; F. Harrison, *Order and Progress*, 1875, Harvester reprint, Hassocks, 1975, pp.151–2.

42. F. Harrison, *Autobiographic Memoirs*, Macmillan, London, 1911, vol.I, p.248. Contact was not easy: ibid., pp.266–7 for 'repulsive' characteristics of infidel halls; M. Vogeler, *Frederic Harrison: The Vocations of a Positivist*, Clarendon Press, Oxford, 1984, p.57 for his dislike of *Bee-Hive* soirées.

43. Rev. J.R. Green reviewing *Essays on Reform* in *Saturday Review*, vol.XXIII (1867), p.439. Harrison, *Order*, p.274 acknowledged the gap between skilled and unskilled workers.

44. R. Harrison, *Before the Socialists: Studies in Labour and Politics 1861–1881*, Routledge, London, 1965, ch.VI.

45. Harrison, *Memoirs*, vol.I, pp.248, 265; E. Gaskell to W. Robson [c. Feb. 1850], Gaskell, *Letters*, p.105.

46. Rev. F.D. Maurice, 'Plan of a Female College for the Help of the Rich and Poor', in *Lectures to Ladies on Practical Subjects*, 3rd edn revised, Macmillan, Cambridge, 1857, p.24.

47. Maurice to Ludlow, 24 Nov. 1849, in J.F. Maurice, *The Life of Frederick Denison Maurice, Chiefly Told in His Own Letters*, 4th edn, London, 1885, vol.II, pp.26–7.

48. Maurice to Kingsley, 2 Jan. 1850, ibid., p.32. For the band of brothers, N.C. Masterman, *John Malcolm Ludlow: The Builder of Christian Socialism*, Cambridge University Press, Cambridge, 1963, pp.74ff.

49. O. Brose, *Church and Parliament: The Re-shaping of the Church of England 1828–1860*, Stanford University Press, Palo Alto, 1959, pp.94ff., 198ff. For slur on Blomfield, O. Chadwick, *The Victorian Church*, pt. I, Adam and Charles Black, London, 1966, p.133.

50. Ibid., p.331; p.549 for Maurice's 'martyrdom'.

51. B. Lambert, *Sermons and Lectures*, ed. R. Bayne with a Memoir by J. De Montmorency, Henry Richardson, Greenwich, 1902, p.24 for his work on statutory bodies in the parish which he deemed 'a sphere of usefulness which thoroughly justified my position as an East-end vicar'.

52. S. Godolphin Osborne, 'Immortal Sewerage', in *Meliora: or Better Times to Come*, ed. Viscount Ingestre, John W. Parker and Son, London, 2nd series, 1853, p.17. See *DNB* for his life.

53. Osborne, 'Immortal Sewerage', ibid., pp.14–15.

54. B. Lambert, *Pauperism: Seven Sermons Preached at St. Mark's Whitechapel, and One Preached before the University of Oxford, with a Preface on the Work and Position of Clergy in Poor Districts*, Southeran, London, 1871, p.19; (W. Rathbone) A Man of Business, *Social Duties Considered with Reference to the Organisation of Effort in Works of Benevolence and Public Utility*, London, 1867, p.5.

55. C. Kingsley, 'The Massacre of the Innocents: A Speech in Behalf of the Ladies' Sanitary Association...1859', in *Sanitary and Social Lectures and Essays*, Macmillan, London, 1892, pp.226–7.

56. Although later F. Harrison's most notorious statement was 'The Emancipation of Women', *Fortnightly Review*, vol.L (1891), p.445; Vogeler, *Harrison*, p.90 for wife Ethel's agreement.

57. NAPSS *Sess.*, 1872–3, p.422 and Mill, *Autobiography*, pp.178–9 for reception of works.

58. In 1830, Mill, a rising clerk under his father in the East India Company, met Taylor, already married and the mother of two children. He fell in love with her at a time when he was still reconstituting himself from a breakdown in 1826. Although Taylor tried a short separation from her husband, she remained within her marriage for the next twenty years, while her 'intellectual and spiritual intimacy' with Mill developed. After her husband's death, she married Mill in 1851. For Mill-Taylor, Rossi, 'Sentiment', pp.6, 27; 40–1 suggests that her position as a married woman made it difficult to sign the *Political Economy* jointly. F. Hayek, *John Stuart Mill and Harriet Taylor: Their Friendship and Subsequent Marriage*, University of Chicago Press, Chicago, 1951.

59. Mill, *Autobiography*, pp. 187, 175–7, 132–3, 159. The *Logic*, started in 1837, contained his views on the provisional nature of political economy: *On the Logic of the Moral Sciences: A System of Logic, Book VI*, 1843, Bobbs–Merrill reprint, Indianapolis, 1965, p.90.

60. Mill, *Autobiography*, pp.187–8, 146–9.

61. Ibid., pp.178–9, 186–7; J.S. Mill to Harriet Taylor, 19, 21 Feb., 21 Mar. 1849, in *The Later Letters of John Stuart Mill*, 1849–73, ed. F. Mineka and D. Lindley, *Works*, vol.XIV, University of Toronto Press, Toron-to, 1972, pp.8–9, 11, 19. J.S. Mill, *Principles of Political Economy with Some of their Applications to Social Philosophy*, Sir John Lubbock's Hundred Books edn, Routledge, London, 1891, pp. 499–502. G. Claeys, 'Justice, Independence, and Industrial Democracy: The Development of John Stuart Mill's Views on Socialism', *Journal of Politics*, vol.49 (1987), usefully tracks the development of Mill's thinking but underplays Taylor.

62. G.J. Holyoake, *John Stuart Mill: as Some of the Working Classes Knew Him*, Trübner, London, 1873, p.3. Holyoake's gratitude was also personal: Mill lent him sums of money and helped his son get an entrée into the Longman publishing house, Letters d. 26 Mar. 1856, 25 Mar. 1871, Mill-Taylor Papers, items I/35–36, II/170–1.

5 SOCIAL MOTHERS AND SOCIAL SCIENCE

1. 'Queen Bees or Working Bees?', Review of a paper read by Bessie Rayner Parkes to the NAPSS, *Saturday Review*, 12 Nov. 1859. For the best discussion of the surplus woman 'problem', see M. Vicinus, *Independent Women: Work and Community for Single Women 1850–1920*, Virago, London, 1985, ch.1.

2. [W.R. Greg], 'Why are Women Redundant?', *National Review*, vol.XIV (1862) pp. 446, 452. For the legal status of women, see L. Holcombe, *Wives and Property: Reform of the Married Women's Property Law in Nineteenth Century England*, Basil Blackwell, Oxford, 1983.

3. For Langham place as a cultural centre, see J. Rendall,'"A Moral Engine"? Feminism, Liberalism and the *English Woman's Journal*', in *Equal or Different: Women's Politics 1800–1914*, Basil Blackwell, Oxford, 1987, pp.112–18; P. Levine, *Victorian Feminism: 1850–1900*, Florida State University, Tallahassee, 1987, p.15; R. Strachey, *The Cause: A Short History of the Women's Movement in Great Britain*, 1928, Virago reprint, London, 1978, chs 4 and 5. The fullest study remains unpublished: D. Worzala, 'The Langham Place Circle: the Beginnings of the Organized Women's Movement in England, 1854–70', University of Wisconsin PhD thesis, 1982.

4. Comte had declared: 'biological analysis presents the female sex, in the human species especially, as constitutionally in a state of perpetual infancy in comparison with the other; and therefore more remote, in all important respects, from the ideal type of the race. Sociology will prove that the equality of the sexes, of which so much is said, is incompatible with all social existence, by showing that each sex has special and permanent functions which it must fulfill in the natural economy of the human family': *The Positive Philosophy of Auguste Comte*, trans. and condensed by H. Martineau, Trübner, London, 2nd edn, 1875, vol.II, p.112. C. Eagle Russett, *Sexual Science: The Victorian Construction of Womanhood*, Harvard University Press, Cambridge, Mass., 1989, pp.40–2, 93, 149 for Spencer and Darwin.

5. F.P. Cobbe, 'Social Science Congresses and Women's Part in Them', *Macmillan's Magazine* (Dec. 1861), p.90. For her biography, see *The Life of Frances Power Cobbe*, by herself, 2 vols, Houghton Mifflin, Boston, 1894.

6. M. Carpenter, 'Women's Work in the Reformatory Movement', *English Woman's Journal*, vol.I (1858), pp.289–90. For her life, J.E. Carpenter, *The Life and Work of Mary Carpenter*, 1879, Patterson Smith reprint, Montclair, 1974; J. Manton, *Mary Carpenter and the Children of the Streets*, Heinemann, London, 1976; H. Shupf, 'Single Women and Social Reform: The Case of Mary Carpenter', *Victorian Studies*, vol.XVII (1974).

7. Carpenter, 'Women's Work', pp.291–2.

8. Quotes from E. Moberly Bell, *Octavia Hill: A Biography*, Constable, London, 1942, pp.27, 26, 101; for a perceptive and sympathetic portrait, see J. Lewis, *Women and Social Action in Victorian and Edwardian England*, Edward Elgar, Aldershot, 1991, ch.1.

9. Carpenter, *Reformatory*, pp.38, 68. M. Carpenter, 'Ragged and Industrial Schools', NAPSS Trans., 1858, p.307; 'On Certified Industrial Schools and their Principle and Actual Operation', ibid., 1859. This view became the common sense among men as well, cf. J. Hubback, 'Prevention of Crime', ibid., 1858, p.345.

10. See Florence Hill (M.D.'s daughter), *Children of the State: the Training of Juvenile Paupers*, Macmillan, London, 1868; also see review in *Englishwoman's Review*, no.VII (Apr. 1868), pp.452–6. Louisa Twining, 'Object and Aims of the Workhouse Visiting Society', NAPSS *Trans.*, 1858, p.666; Ellen Woodcock and Sarah Atkinson,

ibid., 1861, pp.646, 651; M. Carpenter, 'What Shall We Do With Our Pauper Children', ibid, p.688. These views were also the conventional wisdom among men in the field, e.g., W.R. Lloyd, 'Workhouse Schools and Parish Apprentices', ibid., 1858, p.661; E. Denison, 'Some Remedies for Metropolitan Pauperism', in *Letters*, p.206. Poor Law Inspector E.C. Tufnell argued that girls especially needed small schools on the 'family system': Letter to Louisa Twining, 18 May 1860, Twining Papers, item 27B, Fawcett Library.

11. J. Butler (ed.), *Woman's Work and Woman's Culture*, London Macmillan, 1869, pp.xxviii, xxv.

12. Rylands quoted in G.W. and L.A. Johnson (eds), *Josephine Butler: an Autobiographical Memoir*, Hamilton and Kent, London, 1909, p.112.

13. E.g., barrister J.R. Fowler, 'Home Influences on the Children of the Dangerous Classes', NAPSS *Trans.*, 1861, p.456; for a later version, A. Maddison, *Hints on Rescue Work: A Handbook for Missionaries, Superintendents of Homes, Committees, Clergy and Others*, Reformatory and Refuge Union, London, 1898, 2nd edn, 1914, pp.12–13 which gives an interesting glossary of terms including 'Home', 'Matron' and rejects 'penitent','penitentiary'.

14. For Boucherett, *English Woman's Journal*, vol.IV (1860) p.394; Sarah Austin complained that Shirreff's mothering was wasted on ungrateful daughters: Shirreff provided 'a clean and comfortable home, the decencies of life, maternal care and kindness, and many other excellent things—for which they have not the slightest taste or desire. What they like and will have is liberty, liberty to be rude and filthy, to eat garbage, to dress in tawdry rags, to pig together and to live dissolutely. It goes to my heart to think of that charming, gifted creature bestowing her life so': quoted in A. Jameson, *Letters and Friendships (1812–1860)*, ed. Mrs S. Erskine, Fisher Unwin, London, 1915, p.167.

15. See her NAPSS paper 'The Preventative Branch of the Bristol Female Mission', *English Woman's Journal*, vol.VI (1861), p.147 which ran two Homes for learners who had 'no adequate guardianship...their parents being dead or absent, unwilling or unable to attend to them'.

16. For controversy over sisterhoods, *Englishwoman's Review*, no.I (Oct. 1866), pp.54–60, no.II (Jan. 1867), pp.99–103; for range of religous communities, Vicinus, *Independent Women*, ch.2 and passim for Homes in other branches of social work.

17. B. Bodichon, *Women and Work*, Bosworth and Harrison, London, 1857, pp.15, 36; E. Davies, *The Higher Education of Women*, 1866, AMS reprint, New York, 1973, p.110; also H. Taylor, 'Enfranchisement of Women', 1851, in J.S. Mill, *The Subjection of Women etc.*, Virago reprint, London, 1983, pp.17–18.

18. A. Jameson, *Sisters of Charity and the Communion of Labour: Two Lectures on the Social Employment of Women*, Longman, Brown, Green, Longmans & Roberts, London, 1859.

19. Cobbe, 'Social Science', p.92; also J. Butler's similar statement in *Women's Work*, p.xxxvii. Emily Davies objected to the 'dual theory'

but she seemed to be targeting the conventional Ruskinian idea of complementarity which kept women in the home rather than the feminist reworking of the concept which gave women public mobility: Davies, *Higher*, pp.16, 178–80.

20. Shaftesbury, NAPSS *Trans.*, 1859, p.10; Northcote, ibid., 1869, p.24.
21. C. Biggs, 'Women's Share in Social Science', *Englishwoman's Review*, no.X (Jan. 1869), p.89, 'The Debt Women Owe to the Social Science Association', n.s., no.CLVII (May 1886), p.196 for appreciations. For Craig, K. McCrone, 'The National Association for the Promotion of Social Science and the Advancement of Victorian Women', *Atlantis*, vol.VIII (1982), pp.42–3, n.22.
22. *Saturday Review*, 14 Jun. 1862.
23. B. Bodichon, 'On the Extension of the Suffrage to Women' received a two–line mention in NAPSS *Trans.*, 1866, p.794 whereas 'Mr Hare's Electoral System' and subsequent discussion occupied pp.202–8, 268–76. McCrone, 'NAPSS', for support of feminist initiatives.
24. Cobbe, 'Social Science', pp.83–4, 91; Mill, *Logic*, Book VI, ch.10.
25. Hastings, NAPSS *Trans.*, 1857, p.xxi; Richson sermon in Manchester *Guardian*, 4 Oct. 1866.
26. B.R. Parkes, 'What Can Educated Women Do?', *English Woman's Journal*, vol.IV (1860), p.297. 27. 'The Workhouse Visiting Society', *English Woman's Journal*, vol.I (1858) pp.386, 388; Cobbe also spoke of the 'dry bones' of the Poor Law over which 'the flesh and blood of warm free charity should clothe the whole, else it is but a grim and hideous image', *Englishwoman's Review*, No.III (Apr. 1867), p.163. For Twining, see K. McCrone, 'Feminism and Philanthropy in Victorian England: The Case of Louisa Twining', *Canadian Historical Papers* (1976); also L. Twining, *Recollections of Life and Work*, Edward Arnold, London, 1893.
28. For Twining's experience of resistance, *Recollections*, p.113; 165 for her desire to operate on 'the communion of labour' pattern. For Lady Stephen's difficulties, *Englishwoman's Review*, no.II (Jan. 1867), pp.107–9.
29. Rev. F.D. Maurice, *Lectures to Ladies*, p.16.
30. Bodichon, *Women*, p.51; Davies, *Higher*, p.91.
31. For gynaecology's discovery of female diseases like 'Nymphomania, Erotomania, Uteromania (later subdivided into Andromania, Clitoromania, Hypatomania) and Ovarian Madness' see A. Owen, 'Subversive Spirit: Women and Nineteenth Century Spiritualism', Univ. of Sussex PhD thesis, 1987, pp.213ff.; for medicine as a key buttress of sexual division, L. Duffin, 'The Conspicuous Consumptive: Woman as an Invalid', in S. Delamont and L. Duffin (eds), *The Nineteenth-century Woman: Her Cultural and Physical World*, Croom Helm, London, 1978, pp.27, 31–6. For Cobbe's experiences with doctors, *Life*, vol.I, pp.310–13, and her attack on their definition of femininity and their role in vivisection: vol.II, pp.542, 577. For mutual hostility of feminists and doctors, B. Harrison, 'Women's Health and the Women's Movement in Britain: 1840–

1940', in C. Webster (ed.), *Biology, Medicine and Society*, 1840–1940, Cambridge University Press, Cambridge, 1981, pp.28ff.

32. Anderson's 1866 NAPSS remarks were later developed into an article in *Macmillans Magazine* (Apr. 1867); M. Vicinus and B. Nergaard, *Ever Yours: Florence Nightingale, Selected Letters*, Virago, London 1989, p.276 for defence of nurses' status.

33. Dr E.H. Sieveking, 'On Dispensaries and Allied Institutions', in Maurice, *Lectures to Ladies*, p.116.

34. W.C. Dowling, 'The Ladies' Sanitary Association and the Origins of the Health Visiting Service', Univ. of London MA thesis (1963) gives the best account of this body in all its phases.

35. *Lancet*, 19 Apr. 1862.

36. O. Hill, 'District Visiting', *Our Common Land*, Macmillan, London, 1877, p.25.

37. Rev. J.S. Brewer, 'Workhouse Visiting', in Maurice, *Lectures to Ladies*, p.301.

38. Ibid., pp.13, 14, 17.

39. For Ladies' Conferences, NAPSS *Trans.*, 1869, pp.xxvii, 609–10; 1870, pp.xxxv, 547–66. For the women's meeting against the C.D. Acts, *Englishwoman's Review*, n.s., no.IV (Oct. 1870), p.302 which also covered the Ladies' Conference. J. Walkowitz, *Prostitution and Victorian Society: Women, Class and the State*, Cambridge University Press, Cambridge, 1980 gives the best account of the views and campaigns for and against the Acts.

40. *Leeds Mercury*, 24 Dec. 1870.

41. *Saturday Review*, 12 Apr. 1862.

42. Quoted in S. Chitty, *The Beast and the Monk: A Life of Charles Kinglsey*, Hodder and Stoughton, London. 1974, p.254.

43. Davies, *Higher*, pp.22–3, 81, 165, 167, 86; Butler quoted in B. Caine, *Victorian Feminists*, Oxford University Press, Oxford, 1992, p.95 in a useful chapter on Davies.

44. Lewis, *Women in England*, pp.88–97 for a discussion of equal rights feminism and social maternalism; O. Banks, *Faces of Feminism: A Study of Feminism as a Social Movement*, Martin Robertson, Oxford, 1981, pp.6–8 for a different typology of Equal Rights, Evangelical and Socialist Feminism, which I agree with Jane Lewis maternal feminism undercuts. Karen Offen in 'Liberty, Equality and Justice for Women: The Theory and Practice of Feminism in Nineteenth-century Europe' in R. Bridenthal *et al.* (eds), *Becoming Visible: Women in European History*, 2nd edn, Houghton Mifflin, Boston, 1987, pp.338–9, distinguishes between individualist and relational feminism and sees the latter, which places women essentially in family relations especially with men and children, as the dominant historical form in Europe; see too her 'Defining Feminism: A Comparative Historical Perspective', *Signs*, vol.XIV (1988). Scott, 'Deconstructing', pp.38–48, rejects any binary opposition between equality and difference and makes the most useful interpretation both for analysis and action.

45. M. Wollstonecraft, *A Vindication of the Rights of Woman*, 1792,

Penguin, London, 1992, pp.263, 264 for maternal citizenship, pp.80–1, 108–9, 125, for shared human nature.

46. Ch.2 above.
47. For her early life, S. Herstein, *A Mid-Victorian Feminist: Barbara Leigh Smith Bodichon*, Yale Universitiy Press, New Haven, 1985. ch.1; H. Burton, *Barbara Bodichon, 1827–1891*, London, John Murray, 1949, p.36.
48. M. Lowndes (Bessie's daughter), *I too have Lived in Arcadia*, Macmillan, London, 1941, p.74.
49. Strachey, *The Cause*, pp.71ff., ch.6. Also, J. Rendall, 'Friendship and Politics: Barbara Leigh Smith Bodichon and Bessie Rayner Parkes', in S. Mendus and J. Rendall (eds), *Sexuality and Subordination: Interdisciplinary Studies of Gender in the Nineteenth Century*, Routledge, London, 1989 for their early friendship and activity.
50. Rendall 'Moral Engine', pp.122, 127–8, 135; also B.R. Parkes's articles like 'The Ladies' Sanitary Association' and 'On the Best Means of Forming Local Sanitary Associations' in *English Woman's Journal*, vol.III (1859), vol.IV (1860).
51. Burton, *Bodichon*, pp.96, 138.
52. Ibid., pp.207ff.; Herstein, *Bodichon*, pp.184ff.; Rendall, 'Moral Engine', p.114, for her relations with Jameson.
53. Lowndes, *Arcadia*, pp.33, 53.
54. M.E. Loane, *An Englishman's Castle*, Edward Arnold, London 1909, p.231.
55. E. Chase, *Tenant Friends in Old Deptford*, Williams and Norgate, London, 1929, p.21.
56. W. Acton, *Prostitution Considered in its Moral, Social and Sanitary Aspects*, 2nd edn, 1870, Cass reprint, London, 1972. p.166. For good historical work on splitting, see especially L. Davidoff, 'Class and Gender in Victorian Britain', in J. Newton et al. (eds), *Sex and Class in Women's History*, Routledge and Kegan Paul, London, 1983, pp.21–3 and Stallybrass, *Transgression*, ch.4.
57. Nightingale, *Ever Yours*, pp.3–4.
58. Johnsons, *Butler*, pp.58–9; J. Carpenter, *Carpenter*, pp.138, 33.
59. Cobbe, *Life*, vol.I, p.88, vol.II, p.359.
60. M.E. Loane, *The Queen's Poor: Life as They Find it in Town and Country*, Edward Arnold, London, 1905, p.196.
61. J. Butler, *The Duty of Women in Relation to Our Great Social Evil...25 Nov. 1870*, p.7, Fawcett Library.
62. J. Butler, *A Letter to the Mothers of England: Commended also to the Attention of Fathers, Ministers of Religion and Legislators* [1881], p.3, Fawcett Library.
63. J. Butler, *The Lady of Shunem*, Horace Marshall, London [1894], p.91; *Duty*, pp.5–6.
64. J. Butler, *Reminiscences of a Great Crusade*, new edn, Horace Marshall, London, 1911, p.42.
65. J. Butler to Henry Wilson, 22 Apr. 1875, Butler Collection, Fawcett Library.
66. Carpenter, 'Women's Work', p.293.

67. C. Bynum, 'Jesus as Mother and Abbot as Mother: Some Themes in Twelfth-Century Cistercian Writing', *Jesus as Mother: Studies in the Spirituality of the High Middle Ages*, University of California Press, Berkeley, 1982.

68. *Annual Report*, 1900 also 1864, quoted in F. Finnegan, *Poverty and Prostitution: A Study of Victorian Prostitutes in York*, Cambridge University Press, Cambridge, 1979, pp.210, 202.

69. Ibid., p.191.

70. Ibid., p.174.

71. For renaming, 'A House of Mercy', *English Woman's Journal*, vol.I (1858) p.17.

72. Finnegan, *Poverty*, pp.179, 204; for discipline problems, pp.193–7. The same pattern of inmates leaving existed in Brighton in the Albion Hill Home, *Annual Report*, 1890, 1910, 1911, Brighton Reference Library. My thanks to Olivia Bennett for drawing my attention to this material.

73. For aims and work of these bodies, National Reformatory Union, *Authorized Report*, pp.v–vii, 11; Reformatory and Refuge Union, 'Objects', in *First Annual Report*, 1857; also *A Handbook on the Formation, Objects, Management and Results of Existing Reformatories, Refuges and Industrial Schools*, London, 1860; *Reformatory and Refuge Journal*, London, 1861–65; *Conference of Managers and Superintendents of Reformatory and Industrial Institutions*, London, 1869.

6 THE SOCIAL SCIENCE ASSOCIATION

1. My 'Social Science', chs. 5–8, deals with the SSA at greater length.

2. These bodies are discussed in L. Goldman, 'A Peculiarity of the English? The Social Science Association and the Absence of Sociology in Nineteenth–Century Britain', *Past & Present*, no.114 (1987), pp.150ff.

3. The argument that the SSA embodied the science of successful Liberalism is made by ibid.; Abrams, *Origins*, ch.4 also recognizes its social power while bemoaning its negative contribution to sociological theory. Earlier critiques include B. Rodgers, 'The Social Science Association 1857–1886', *Manchester School of Economic and Social Studies*, vol.XX (1952), p.300.

4. B.R. Parkes, 'Women's Work in Charity', *English Woman's Journal*, vol.III (1859), p.195. K. McCrone, 'NAPSS' has considered women in the Association, while W. Leach, *True Love and Perfect Union: The Feminist Reform of Sex and Society*, Basic Books, New York, 1980, ch.11, looks at women in the American SSA.

5. E. Denison, 'On the Difficulties of Associated Charity', in *Letters*, pp.229–30.

6. *Reasoner*, 3 Jun. 1846.

7. For the slower pace of change, Bray, *Phases*, pp.63, 64, 118; G.J. Holyoake, *Organisation: Not of Arms—But Ideas*, James Watson, London, 1853, p.5; E.T. Craig, *The Irish Land and Labour Question*, Trübner, London, 1893, p.37. For ultimate faith in Community,

Bray, *Philosophy*, 2nd edn, 1863, pp.382–9, 406; Craig in *American Socialist*, 10 Jan. 1878. For Holyoake's repudiation of community, *The History of Co-operation*, Fisher Unwin, London, 1906, vol.II, p.674.

8. W. Pare, *The Claims of Capital and Labour: with a Sketch of Practical Measures for their Conciliation*, Ward and Lock, London, 1854, pp.13, 22, 26.

9. *Cooper's Journal*, 1850, pp.1–2, W. Lovett, *Life and Struggles in Pursuit of Bread, Knowledge and Freedom*, Trübner, London, 1876, pp.324–5. Lovett was the complete London artisan radical although his views on organization and leadership eroded his credibility in the majority Chartist movement. Cooper, a journalist, wrote *The Life of Thomas Cooper*, 1872, Leicester University Press reprint, Leicester, 1971.

10. *Transactions of the Co-operative League, formed Mar. 1852 to Promote the Scientific investigation of the Principles of Co-operative Action, with a View to their Application to Action*, London, 1852, p.1.

11. Hole, *Lectures*, p.ix. Hole, a clerk, edited the journal of the communitarian Leeds Redemption Society. He became active in co-operation and in the Yorkshire Union of Mechanics' Institutes, Harrison, *Learning*, pp.119ff.

12. Gurney, 'Co-operative', chs 2–3.

13. Lovett's 'ABC' started in the *Bee–Hive*, 9 May 1868. Harrison, *Before*, p.226 for Engels' verdict.

14. W. Williams, 'On the Teaching of Social Economy' NAPSS *Trans.*, 1857, pp.512–15; W. Stewart and W. McCann, *The Educational Innovators, 1750–1880*, Macmillan, London, 1867, vol.I, pp.326–41 for Ellis whose version of social science was taught in London, Glasgow and Manchester before being introduced into the curriculum of the London Board Schools by Rosamund Davenport–Hill, where it became a forerunner of civics.

15. L. Jones and J.M. Ludlow, *The Progress of the Working Class 1832–1867*, 1867, Kelley reprint, Clifton, New Jersey, 1973, p.283; the *Bee–Hive*, 14 Oct. 1865. Holyoake complained that Hastings refused a paper with communitarian views, *Reasoner*, 31 Oct. 1858. F. Harrison was very miffed at the exclusion of his paper on the London builders' strike 'to make way for some ideas about the Rights of Women by an American lady of colour': *Memoirs*, vol.I, p.268.

16. A social science periodical press also came into being. The forerunner was the collection of essays edited by Viscount Ingestre, called *Meliora*, which tried to give an overview of the 'division of labour' in the 'social movement of our day. To do good has been a common object; but individuals have marked out, as their own, particular fields of labour': first series, 1852, p.ix. After that, publications proliferated including the *Philanthropist* (1855–61) which changed its name to the *Philanthropist and Social Science Gazette*; *Meliora, a Quarterly Review of Social Science in its Ethical, Economical, Political and Ameliorative Aspects (1858–69)*, the *Social Science Review* (1862–66)

'based on the principles of the National Association' although independent of it and the *Journal of Social Science* (1865–6), the SSA's own journal which became in 1867 a record of its *Sessional Proceedings*.

17. Manchester *Guardian*, 1 Mar. 1866. Reminder of this London generosity prompted Manchester to offer the Assize Courts for the congress sessions.
18. *Lancet*, 15 Jun. 1862.
19. *Manchester Meeting Programme of Arrangements*, Manchester, 1866, p.12; Manchester *Examiner and Times*, 14 Sept. 1866.
20. Lists of Congress attenders are available for Bradford, 1859 (Bradford Central Public Library), Glasgow, 1860 (Mitchell Library), Bristol, 1869 (Bristol Central Library, College Green) and in a pamphlet entitled, NAPSS, *Laws etc. 1866–1881* (Manchester Central Library) which also includes most of the extant membership lists for 1866–7, 1870–1, 1872–5 and 1880–1. Goldsmiths' Library, Senate House, University of London holds the list for 1869–70. The accounts were printed in the annual *Transactions*.
21. *Reasoner*, 6 Jan. 1858. Although Owen at first welcomed the Association (Owen to Brougham, 3 Oct. 1857, Brougham Papers, 10,109), the first Congress disappointed him and he proposed a rival 'Social Science League' to further the communitarian mode of change: *Prospectus for the Social Science League*, Goldsmiths' Library copy, pencilled note by William Pare.
22. Abrams, *Origins*, pp.44, 49–50; Goldman, 'SSA', p. 136.
23. *Daily News*, 26 Sept. 1870, quoted in ibid.
24. For attenders at preliminary meeting, Hastings to Brougham, 1 Aug. 1857, Brougham Papers, 13093; NAPSS *Trans.*, 1857, p.xxvi; J.L. Clifford Smith, *Twentieth-fifth Anniversary: A Manual for the Congress, with a Narrative of Past Labours and Results*, London, 1882, p.3.
25. The Departmental Standing Committees, which more than the governing Council actually determined the intellectual agenda, were named in the membership lists and in the 'Report of the Annual Business Meeting' in the NAPSS *Sessional Proceedings*, which started in 1865. I am basing arguments about their occupations on an analysis of members who served for three or more years during 1866, 1869, 1870, 1872, 1873, 1874 and 1880.
26. NAPSS *Trans.*, 1863, pp.xxxvi–xxxix, note.
27. Ibid., 1857, p.xxv.
28. Ibid., 1867, p.35; also 1869, pp.28–9. Spencer thought the SSA 'absurdly self-titled' and attended only an 1881 meeting on copyright law: Peel, Spencer, p.228; for Mill's participation, apart from serving on the first Committee of the Social Economy Department, see Goldman, 'SSA' pp. 147–8; the Positivists took part in the discussions on trade unionism.
29. Between 1856 and 1867, Lord Stanley gave himself a 'sociological' self-education, studying Spencer, Malthus, Mill, Comte, de Tocqueville and Quételet as well as keeping abreast of the literature of social investigation: Goldman, 'SSA', pp.146–7.

30. R. Warwick, 'The Operation of the Poor Laws', NAPSS *Trans*, 1862, p.757; also G. Carr, ibid., 1858, p.655.
31. Hills, *Recorder*, p.169; Brougham, NAPSS *Trans.*, 1859, p.36.
32 Carpenter, *Reformatory*, p.20.
33. NAPSS *Trans.*, 1860, pp.xxix for Committee on the Census, xxvii–viii for special Committee on the Registration of Births and Deaths; NAPSS *Sess.*, 14 Apr. 1870, p.383 for Resolutions of the Executive Committee about the 1871 Census. For Committee of Inquiry into Trade Societies, P. Rathbone to Brougham, 27 Aug. 1859, Brougham Papers, 21852; NAPSS *Trans.*, 1859, p.660 where the Committee also indicated its intention to give a full airing to the views of the unions to redress the situation where employers had 'better command of the avenues by which public opinion is influenced'; the findings came out as Committee on Trades Societies Appointed by the NAPSS, *Report on Trades Societies and Strikes*, John Parker and Son, London, 1860.
34. *Law Magazine and Law Review*, vol.VIII (Nov. 1859), p.189.
35. NAPSS *Trans.*, 1857, p.xxii.
36. Ibid., 1861, p.xvii–xviii, also ibid., 1868, p.133.
37. NAPSS *Sess.*, 20 Aug. 1868, pp.429–30; Ruskin's questions, pp. 406–7.
38. NAPSS *Trans.*, 1868, pp.114, 115. For Fawcett, see *DNB* entry; L. Goldman (ed.), *The Blind Victorian: Henry Fawcett and British Liberalism*, Cambridge University Press, Cambridge, 1989, chs. by P. Deane and Goldman.
39. D. Rubinstein, *A Different World for Women: The Life of Millicent Garrett Fawcett*, Harvester Wheatsheaf, London, 1991, chs 2 and 3. She was nominated, but not elected, as the first lady member of the Political Economy Club; when widowed, she became the leader of the National Union of Women's Suffrage Societies.
40. J. Thorold Rogers, 'Address', NAPSS *Trans.*, 1883, pp.83ff.; Bonamy Price, 'Address on Economy and Trade', ibid., 1878, pp. 128–30; W. Westgarth, 'The Recent Controversies Upon Economic Method', ibid., 1880, pp.734–5; Ingram's presidential 'Address' in British Association for the Advancement of Science, *Report*, 1878, pp.641–58.
41. At the Bradford Congress (1859), a cluster of papers dealt with the factory system. More often, factories figured more incidentally in standard papers to the Social Economy Department about local trades and industries and here little was said about the factory system as a special way of structuring human relations for production or about the social condition of factory workers. Significantly the Public Health Department rather than Social Economy problematized factory work but only in connection with occupational disease and accidents: see e.g., NAPSS *Trans.*, 1862, pp.670ff.
42. E. Ackroyd, 'On Relations betwixt Employer and Employed under the Factory System', ibid., 1857, p.527; also p.531 and ibid., 1864, p.479 for Ackroyd quotes in this paragraph.
43. For Manchester statisticians and millowners now praising

legislation, E. Potter, 'On the Position of the Cotton Districts', NAPSS *Trans.*, 1863, p.655. H. Ashworth, *Historical Data Chiefly Relating to South Lancashire and the Cotton Manufacture*, Manchester, 1866, (the full version of his Congress paper), p.24; for his acceptance of trade unions, *Report on Trades Societies*, p.606.

44. Rev. Blaikie, 'On the Collisions of Benevolence and Social Law', NAPSS *Trans.*, 1863, p.710.

45. W. Stanley Jevons, 'On Industrial Partnership', *Lectures on Economic Science*, London, 1870, pp.2–3; the NAPSS commissioned these lectures.

46. The Committee on Trade Societies composed of employers, barristers, Christian Socialists and political economists, tried to dispel a popular impression that trade union leaders were rabble-rousing outside agitators arguing that 'their experience is that the leaders are for the most part quite superior to the majority of their fellow-workmen in intelligence and moderation....The leaders of trades societies are known and responsible men. They have the confidence of their own class': *Report on Trades Societies*, p.xv.

47. Jones and Ludlow, *Progress*, pp.3, 271–2 for quotes.

48. Blaikie, 'Collisions', NAPSS *Trans.*, 1863, pp.709–10.

49. *Report on Trades Societies*, pp.600, 602.

50. Ibid., pp.612, 609, 611. Campbell attended as delegate from the Flint Glass Makers of Glasgow.

51. Ibid., pp.xix, xxi, xiii.

52. For the Nottingham Board of Arbitration, with employer and union membership, which fixed wages for 100,000 workers in the hosiery industry of Nottingham, Leicester and Derby, see Mundella, NAPSS *Sess.*, 1867–8, pp.410–12. For NAPSS role in trying to settle the masons' strike, ibid., 1871–2, pp.388–90. For the effort of Pears and Applegarth in the Barnsley powerloom weavers' dispute, ibid., 1872–3, p.420. The Committee was probably disbanded in 1874 owing to lack of funds but individuals continued conciliatory work, ibid., 1873–4, pp.346–7.

53. E.g., John Holmes, 'Facts and Interventions Relating to the West Yorkshire Coal Strike...1858', NAPSS *Trans.*, 1859, p.653; or H. Fawcett, 'The Theory and Tendency of Strikes', ibid., p.639.

54. Meeting on 'Wages and Capital', SSA *Sess.*, 20 Aug. 1868, pp.400–1, 402; a resolution moved by F. Hill asserting harmony of interests was also thrown out at the adjourned meeting, pp.408, 429.

55. Fawcett, 'Address', NAPSS *Trans.*, 1868, p.118; also 'Strikes', ibid., 1859, p.639.

56. J. Holmes, 'The Economic and Moral Advantages of Co-operation in the Provision of Food', ibid., 1857, pp.567–8; 'Industrial Partnership as Carried into Practice by Henry Briggs, Son & Co., at the Whitwood Collieries', NAPSS *Sess*, 14 May 1868, pp.319–20: also T. Hughes, NAPSS *Trans*, 1865, p.533. See too Jevons' eulogy of Briggs, *Lectures on Economic Science*, pp.8–11, 23. However, P. Gurney, 'The Middle-class Embrace: Language, Representation and the Contest over Co-operative Forms in Britain, c.1840–1914, *Victorian Studies*,

vol.37 (1994), pp.259-60, points to the class tensions over co-partnership with Holyoake in 1872 attacking Briggs's anti-unionism.
57. B. Babcock, *The Reversible World: Symbolic Inversion in Art and Society*, Cornell University Press, Ithaca, 1978, p.32; Stallybrass, *Transgression*, pp.5–6, 25.
58. NAPSS *Sess.*, 22 Jun. 1868.
59. J. Symons, *Tactics for the Times as Regards the Treatment of the Dangerous Classes*, London, 1849, p.1.
60. Carpenter, *Reformatory*, p.2.
61. Even Evangelical Lord Shaftesbury could accept the urban environment, with its 'recesses of filth and closely peopled houses' as a shaping factor: 'Address on Public Health', NAPSS *Trans.*, 1858, p.88.
62. On 1867, see R. Harrison, *Before the Socialists*, ch.III. Key texts of the day included, T. Carlyle, 'Shooting Niagara', *Macmillans Magazine* (Aug. 1867); *Essays on Reform*, 1867.
63. M. Arnold, *Culture and Anarchy*, 1869, Cambridge University Press edn, 1963, p.105.
64. Brougham, NAPSS *Trans.*, 1863, p.19; Hill, 'On Co-operation', ibid., 1860, p.753; also Kay-Shuttleworth's fear, not of Working-class organizations, but of 'communism', NAPSS *Sess.*, 20 Aug. 1868, p.396.
65. Stallard in a discussion on outdoor relief, NAPSS *Trans.*, 1868, p.599; also his paper on 'The Necessity for a full enquiry into the Administration of the Poor Laws...', NAPSS *Sess.*, 12 Feb. 1868. Rev. Solly produced statistics showing that while the increase of pauperism in England and Wales between Mar. 1858 and 1867 had been 3%, the increase in London had been 75%; in London alone the increase between Jan. 1867 and 1868 had been 18%: Solly, *Destitute Poor and Criminal Classes. A few Thoughts on how to Deal with the Unemployed Poor of London, and with its 'Roughs' and Criminal Classes*, London, 1868, p.5.
66. Ibid., p.8; NAPSS *Sess.*, 1867–8, p.387; also T. Webster QC, ibid., pp.133–5.
67. A.H. Hill, *Our Unemployed*, NAPSS, London, 1868, pp.7–8. See too his remarks on the paradigm nature of London, 'What Means are Practicable for Checking the Aggregation and Deterioration of Unemployed Labour in Large Towns', NAPSS *Trans.*, 1875, p.657.
68. Denison, 'Some Remedies for Metropolitan Pauperism', 1869, in *Letters*, pp.199–200; Bosanquet, *London*, pp.133–6.
69. Denison, Letter d. 28 Aug, 1867, 'Some Remedies', in *Letters*, pp. 46–7, 195; Hill, *Our Unemployed*, p.7; 'Means for Checking', NAPSS *Trans.*, 1875, p.663.
70. Hill, *Our Unemployed*, pp.11–15, 19–20; 'Means for Checking', NAPSS *Trans.*, 1875, pp.665–6; E.W. Hollond, 'The Labour Market', ibid., 1870, pp.462–3.
71. Hill, *Our Unemployed*, p.8 for his early disgust; *Vagrancy, the Relations of Country Districts to Great Towns, with Suggestions for its more Uniform Treatment, Labour News*, London, 1881, pp.4–5, 6; 'Existing

Impediments to the Circulation of Labour and Suggestions for their Removal', NAPSS *Trans.*, 1872, pp.483–8; 'Means for Checking', ibid., 1875, pp.657–8.

72. Hill said that unions created 'self–reliance, knowledge, and independence, the absence of which make the feckless folk who swell the ranks of our vagrants', *Vagrancy*, p.6.

73. Yet even the call of the Working-class Land and Labour League for 'the State reclaiming the unoccupied lands as a beginning of its nationalisation, and placing the unemployed upon it' could also be supported by some SSA members like Septimus Hansard. For class differences in land schemes, see Harrison, *Before*, pp.212–14.

74. C. Loch Mowat, *The Charity Organisation Society, 1869–1913, its Ideas and Work*, Methuen, London, 1961. Webb, *Apprenticeship*, pp.195ff. H. Bosanquet, *Social Work in London 1869–1912*, 1914, Harvester Reprint, Brighton, 1973.

75. E.C. Price, 'The Origin of the London Charity Organisation Society', *Charity Organisation Review*, vol. VIII (1892), pp.360–3.

76. W.H. Beveridge, 'The Problem of the Unemployed', *Sociological Papers*, 1906 (1907), pp.324–6; Abrams, *Origins*, p.106.

77. Ibid., pp.50–2; Rodgers, 'SSA', p.306 where he also calls members 'Schoolmen'; McGregor, 'Social Research', p.154.

7 BODY METAPHOR IN SOCIAL SCIENCE

1. F. Engels to P. Lavrov, 12–17 Nov. 1875, K. Marx and F. Engels, *Selected Correspondence*, Progress Publishers, Moscow, 2nd edn, 1965, p.302, also p.128 for Marx. R. Young, 'Darwinism is Social', in D. Kohn (ed.), *The Darwinian Heritage*, Princeton University Press, Princeton, 1985, pp.620, 630; Burrow, *Evolution*, p.97. Stocking, *Victorian Anthropology*, p.xiii, has welcomed the broadening of contextual understanding but insisted on the existence and persistence of indigenous ethnological traditions.

2. H. Spencer, 'The Social Organism', 1860, in *The Man Versus The State*, Penguin, Harmondsworth, 1969, pp.198–9. C. Hill, 'The Many–Headed Monster', in *Change and Continuity in Seventeenth-Century England*, London, 1974; H. Bakhtin, *Rabelais and His World*, trans. H. Iswolsky, MIT Press, Cambridge, Mass., 1966; M. Douglas, *Purity and Danger: An Analysis of Concepts of Pollution and Taboo*, Routledge and Kegan Paul, London, 1966.

3. N. Stepan, 'Race and Gender: The Role of Analogy in Science', in D. Goldberg (ed.), *Anatomy of Racism*, University of Minnesota Press, Minneapolis, 1990, p.54 where she explores the presumed identity between women and black 'savages'.

4. L. Davidoff, 'Class and Gender', pp.18–19, 24–7; Stallybrass, *Transgression*, ch.4. A. Ure, *The Philosophy of Manufactures*, Charles Knight, London, 1835, p.55; C. Dickens, *Hard Times*, 1854, ch.10; Peel, *Spencer*, p.172 for Spencer's use of this version of body metaphor.

5. Osborne, 'Immortal Sewerage', pp.7, 9, 10, 11, 12, 14, 16.

6. G. Davison, 'The City as a Natural System. Theories of Urban Society', in D. Fraser and A. Sutcliffe (eds), *The Pursuit of Urban History*, Edward Arnold, London, 1983, pp.361–2 for Southwood Smith; Kay-Shuttleworth, *Moral*, pp.17–18; C. Lawrence, 'The Nervous System and Society in the Scottish Enlightenment', in B. Barnes and S. Shapin (eds), *Natural Order, Historical Studies of Scientific Culture*, Sage, Beverley Hills, 1979, pp.24–7, 31–3; also ch. by R. Cooter, 'The Power of the Body: the Early Nineteenth Century'.

7. Chadwick, *Sanitary Condition*, p.98.

8. Douglas, *Purity*, p.115.

9. Acton, *Prostitution*, pp.27, 76, 246. A. Corbin, 'Commercial Sexuality in Nineteenth–century France: A System of Images and Regulations', in Gallagher, *Modern Body*, p.213.

10. J. Butler, *The Constitution Violated*, Edmonston and Douglas, Edinburgh, 1871, p.176. Interestingly, social purity campaigner Ellice Hopkins turned the metaphorical tables and called men the sewers: 'we women, thank God, have to do with the fountain of sweet waters, clear as crystal, that flows from the throne of God; not with the sewer that flows from the foul imaginations and actions of men': *The Power of Womanhood; or Mothers and Sons*, Wells Gardner, Darton, London, 2nd edn, 1900, p.8.

11. Osborne, 'Immortal Sewerage', pp.14–16. Some proposals for labour camps are discussed in Jones, *Outcast*, pp.303–8.

12. Jones, *Social Darwinism*, pp.xv, 4ff. on biologism before Darwin; also Young, *Darwin's Metaphor*, p.3 for Lyell.

13. For eugenics as an organized movement and for the Darwin family connection, see G.R. Searle, *Eugenics and Politics in Britain, 1900–1914*, Noordhoff, Leyden, 1976, pp.9–10, 12; D. Kevles, *In the Name of Eugenics: Genetics and the Uses of Human Heredity*, Alfred Knopf, New York, 1985, ch.1 for Galton. Also, F. Galton, *Memories of my Life*, Methuen, London, 1908 and K. Pearson, *The Life, Letters and Labours of Francis Galton*, 3 vols, Cambridge University Press, Cambridge, 1914–1930.

14. H. Ellis, *The Task of Social Hygiene*, Constable, London, 1912, pp.1, viii; for the movement, see G. Jones, *Social Hygiene in Twentieth Century Britain*, Croom Helm, London, 1986. Ellis had a vision of a new age that would come via sexual freedom and to hasten this, he trained as a doctor and opened up space for public discussion of this shrouded subject: H. Ellis, *My Life*, London, Heinemann, 1940; S. Rowbotham and J. Weeks, *Socialism and the New Life: The Personal and Sexual Politics of Edward Carpenter and Havelock Ellis*, Pluto, London, 1977, part. 2; P. Grosskurth, *Havelock Ellis: A Biography*, A. Knopf, New York, 1980.

15. C. Darwin, *The Descent of Man and Selection in Relation to Sex*, 1874 edn, John Murray, London, 1901, pp.945–6. For different constructions of Social Darwinism, Young, 'Darwinism', pp.620–1; for Darwin's Mathusianism, Young, *Darwin's Metaphor*, p.2 and ch.2.

16. Darwin, *Descent*, pp.205–6; H. Spencer, *Social Statics*, 1851, reprised

in *Man vs. State*, pp.139ff.

17. Peel discusses the Liberal commerical romanticism, *Spencer*, pp. 193–6. For Spencer's use of organic analogy to underpin the impossibility of effective government action, 'Over-Legislation', *Westminister Review*, vol.LX (1853), p.32 and *Man vs. State*, p.147ff.

18. Ibid., p.209. For his discussion of coelenterata and then the three stages, *The Principles of Sociology*, vol.I, 1876, in *Herbert Spencer: Structure, Function and Evolution*, ed. S. Andreski, Michael Joseph, London, 1971, pp.143ff., 153ff. esp.168–9.

19. K. Pearson, *National Life from the Standpoint of Science*, 2nd edn, Cambridge University Press, Cambridge [1904], pp.46, 17, for both quotes; not all eugenists believed that war was beneficial. Pearson took up the Chair of Applied Mathematics at University College London in 1884 and became Galton Professor of Eugenics in 1911; he founded the journal *Biometrika* in 1901. A sexual seeker, his presence in the Men and Women's Club is explored by J. Walkowitz, *City of Dreadful Delight*, Virago, London, 1994, ch.5; also Kevles, *Eugenics*, ch.2.

20. Saleeby, in *Sociological Papers*, 1904 (1905), p.82.

21. For Goddard and the history of intelligence testing, see S. Gould, *The Mismeasure of Man*, Penguin, Harmondsworth, 1981, pp.158ff.

22. Ellis, *Social Hygiene*, pp.38, 40; also for feeble-minded girls, B. Bosanquet, 'Socialism and Natural Selection', in *Aspects of the Social Problem*, Macmillan, London, 1895, p.302.

23. Ellis, *Social Hygiene*, p.41; Searle, *Eugenics and Politics*, p.30. The authors cited in this paragraph used the American Jukes or Kallikak families as evidence for the inheritance of feeble-mindedness and Goddard touched up photos of the Kallikaks to make them look idiotic: Gould, *Mismeasure*, pp.170, 173; Pearson, *National*, p.101; H. Spencer, *Man vs. State*, p.412 note.

24. Ellis, *Social Hygiene*, pp.46–7.

25. *Sociological Papers*, 1906 (1907), p.188 in discussion about J. Arthur Thomson paper on 'The Sociological Appeal to Biology'; also Mrs Dr Drysdale Vickery and Lady Welby in discussion of Galton's paper on 'Eugenics: its Definition, Scope and Aims', ibid., 1904, pp.60, 76–8.

26. Russett, *Sexual Science*, pp.158, 164–5 for Lee.

27. F. Galton, *Hereditary Genius: An Inquiry into its Laws and Consequences*, 1869, 2nd edn, Macmillan, London, 1892, p.328; also the preface where he urged research into racial fertility, p.xxiv. Young, 'Darwinism', quotes Huxley's 1865 essay 'Emancipation—Black and White', pp.616–17; Jones, *Social Darwinism*, pp.142ff. explores the turn of the twentieth–century discussions.

28. Searle, *Eugenics and Politics*, p.50; B. Norton, 'Psychologists and Class' in C. Webster, *Biology*, p.289; p.306 for Burt's Oxford research, p.313 for uncanny similarity of Burt's statistical findings to Galton's. For Galton, *Hereditary Genius*, pp.22ff.; 'The Possible Improvement of the Human Breed' (the Huxley Lecture), in F. Galton, *Essays in Eugenics*, Eugenics Education Society, London,

1909, pp.8–11, 19–20; D. Heron, 'The Influence of Defective Physique and Unfavourable Home Environment on the Intelligence of School Children' in *Eugenics Laboratory Memoirs*, Dulau, London, VIII (1910), pp.2, 4, 58.

29. Jones, *Social Hygiene*, provides the best picture of these activities.

30. Quotes from I. Pearse and L. Crocker, *The Peckham Experiment: A Study in the Living Structure of Society*, Allen and Unwin, 1943, pp.68, 69, 144, 292. I am indebted to Alison Tuggey for pointing me towards the Peckham Centre.

31. P. Geddes and J. Arthur Thomson, *Evolution*, Williams and Norgate, London, n.d., pp.246–7; Thomson, 'Sociological Appeal', pp.184–5; Geddes and Thomson, *The Evolution of Sex*, London, 1889 and the later *Sex*, Williams and Norgate, 1914, pp.214ff. for evolution, pp.232–4 for communion of labour. For Galton's launch of 'Eugenics: its Definition, Scope and Aims', and the largely sceptical discussion afterward, see *Sociological Papers*, 1904, pp.43–99. Prince Kropotkin's *Mutual Aid*, 1902, was widely read in socialist circles.

32. Collini, *Liberalism*, pp.179ff. ; J. A. Banks, 'The British Sociological Association—the First 15 Years', *Sociology*, vol. I (1967) , p. 2.

33. S. and B. Webb, *The Prevention of Destitution*, 1911, Longmans, Green, London, 1920. This was one of the Webbs' works which was reprinted with no substantial change to relaunch the same discussion after the First World War. L.T. Hobhouse, *Democracy and Reaction*, 1904, Harvester reprint, Brighton, 1972, ch.4, 'Evolution and Sociology', pp.112, 113–16.

34. Young, 'Darwinism', p.622; R. M. Young, 'The Naturalization of Value Systems in the Human Sciences', Open University Course: Science and Belief from Darwin to Einstein, Block VI, *Problems in the Biological and Human Sciences*, Open University Press, 1981, pp.65–110.

35. L.T. Hobhouse, *Social Development: Its Nature and Conditions*, 1924, George Allen and Unwin, 1966, pp.78ff. for biological imagery and four criteria, pp.42ff. for self-maintaining structure; for an earlier version of three criteria before adding mutuality to freedom, see 'Sociology', 1920, in L.T. Hobhouse, *Sociology and Philosophy: A Centenary Collection of Essays and Articles*, LSE and G. Bell, London, 1966, pp.50ff.

36. H. Spencer, *Autobiography*, London, 1904, vol.I, p.467 for Huxley; for Beatrice acknowledging their debt to Spencer, *The Diary of Beatrice Webb*, ed. N. and J. Mackenzie, Virago, London, 1983, vol.II, p.307, 9 Dec. 1903.

37. B. and S. Webb, *Industrial Democracy*, 1897, Longmans, Green, London, 1920, p.xx; also B. and S. Webb, *Prevention*, p.332 for history revealing results of experiment.

38. Ibid., p.334; for trade unions, Webbs, *Industrial Democracy*, p.843.

39. Ibid., p.xxx.

40. Hobhouse, 'Sociology', pp.42–3, 49; *Social Development*, pp.64–5.

41. *Social Statics*, 1851, in Andrewski, *Spencer*, p.234; Young, 'Naturalization', provides an clear discussion of the consequences of the

biologization of ethics, pp.58–9.

42. Hobhouse made many statements about sociology needing to embrace a philosophy as well as a science, e.g., 'Editorial', *Sociological Review*, vol.I (1908), p.5; for the convergence of the two indices of development, see 'Sociology', p.55.
43. Collini, *Liberalism*, p.241; Young, 'Darwinism', p.624,
44. Webbs, *Prevention*, chs. 6, 2.
45. Ibid., p.56; the whole of ch.3 is a critique of pure eugenics urging reform of the 'environment' as well as the race.
46. Ibid., pp.143, 150–1 for labour colonies of different kinds.
47. Hobhouse, *Social Development*, pp.118, 116; pp.111ff. contains an interesting critique of pure eugenics.
48. Jones, *Social Darwinism*, p.41; Spencer, 'Social Organism', *Man vs. State*, p.205 for widely-distributed intelligence.
49. P. Brown, *The Body and Society: Men, Women and Sexual Renunciation in Early Christianity*, Columbia University Press, New York, 1988, pp.432ff.
50. The literature on the mind/body 'problem', a standard issue in philosophy is immense; the feminist critique considers that the real problem is the mentality which defines this as a problem, because it assumes a mind/body split, e.g., Harding, *Science Question*, p.125, ch.6; Haraway, *Simians*, chs 8, 9.
51. M. Loane, *From Their Own Point of View*, Edward Arnold, London, 1908, p.98; M. Foucault, *The History of Sexuality*, vol.I, Penguin, Harmondsworth, 1981, pp.125–6 for concern too with working-class bodies.
52. Davidoff, 'Class and Gender', pp.20–1.
53. Quoted in Chitty, *Beast*, p.27.
54. C. Kingsley, 'Great Cities and their Influence for Good and Evil', 1857, in *Miscellanies*, Parker, London, 1859, vol.II, pp.327, 330; *The Water-Babies: A Fairy Tale for a Land-Baby*, 1863 is most easily available in an abridged children's edition, Puffin Books, 1985.
55. Letter d. 24 Oct. 1843, quoted in Chitty, *Beast*, p.82.
56. The clearest account of Klein's theories about splitting and projection is in H. Segal, *Introduction to the Work of Melanie Klein*, William Heinemann, London, 1964, pp.12–13, 17.
57. Stallybrass, *Transgression*, pp.5, 25, 152.
58. Ibid., p.20; Babcock, *Reversible*, p.32.
59. Butler, *Constitution*, pp.176–7.
60. Galton, *Hereditary*, pp.49–295, containing chapters devoted to these groups together with Oarsmen and Wrestlers of the north country, specimens of fine physical prowess. For Gray, see above, ch.2.
61. Galton, 'Eugenics', p.48 for his working definition of a 'thriving family' as one 'in which the children have gained distinctly superior positions to those who were their class-mates in early life'; also his 'A Eugenic Investigation: Index to the Achievements of near Kinsfolk of some of the Fellows of the Royal Society', *Sociological Papers*, 1904, pp.85–99. W. McDougall, 'A Practicable Eugenic Suggestion', ibid., 1906, pp.64, 65, 72–3.

62. For the national efficiency debate, see e.g., B. Gilbert, *The Evolution of National Insurance in Great Britain: The Origins of the Welfare State*, London, Michael Joseph, 1966; G.R. Searle, *The Quest for National Efficiency*, London, 1970. For the impact on women, A. Davin, 'Imperialism and the Cult of Motherhood', *History Workshop*, no.5 (Spring 1978).

63. G.R. Searle, 'Eugenics and Class', in Webster, *Biology*, pp.223–6, 235. Jones, folding eugenics into social hygiene, argues that eugenics had a wide appeal to local capitalists as well as professionals: *Social Hygiene*, pp.20–1.

64. R. Soffer, *Ethics and Society in England: The Revolution in the Social Sciences, 1870–1914*, University of California Press, 1978, pp.217ff. discusses McDougall and Trotter and other students of crowd psychology.

65. C.F.G. Masterman, *The Condition of England*, Methuen, London, 1909, p.123 conflated 'Mafficking', unemployed demonstrations and 'a spectacle so diverting and yet so foreboding as the "Sieges of St. Stephen's" by the "Suffragettes"', pp.125–36 on crowd electioneering; L.T. Hobhouse, *Democracy*, p.279 for 'mob–mind'.

8 NATIONAL CRISIS AND PROFESSIONALIZING SOCIAL SCIENCE

1. For the quality of Working-class socialism in this period, S. Yeo, 'A New Life: The Religion of Socialism in Britain, 1883–1896', *History Workshop*, no.4 (Autumn, 1977); D. Howell, *British Workers and the Independent Labour Party, 1888–1906*, Manchester University Press, Manchester, 1983, Appendix 1 for useful labour and socialist chronology. For the scale of the Co-operative movement see G.D.H. Cole, *A Century of Co-operation, Co-operative Union*, Manchester [1944], p.371. For trade union growth, H. Clegg, A. Fox and A. Thompson, *A History of British Trade Unions since 1889*, Clarendon Press, Oxford, 1964, vol.I, p.466; for both militancy and destitution seen as a threat, R. Davidson, *Whitehall and the Labour Problem in Late-Victorian and Edwardian Britain: A Study in Official Statistics and Social Control*, Croom Helm, London, 1985, ch.2. For an overall view of this period as one of crisis, M. Langan and B. Schwarz (eds), *Crises in the British State 1880–1930*, Hutchinson, London, 1985.

2. For the multi-class involvement in and competition for socialism, see S. Yeo, 'Notes on Three Socialisms—Collectivism, Statism and Associationism', in C. Levy (ed.), *Socialism and the Intelligentsia*, 1880–1914, Routledge & Kegan Paul, London, 1987; also Levy's ch.5 analysing the class composition of the Independent Labour Party (ILP). For the complexity of Liberalism, P. Clarke, *Liberals and Social Democrats*, Cambridge University Press, Cambridge, 1978.

3. V. Branford, 'The Social, The Socialistic and the Sociological', *Interpretations and Forecasts: A Study of Survivals and Tendencies in Contemporary Society*, Duckworth, London, 1914, p.34. For Fabianism as the socialism of the professional managerial class, E.

Hobsbawm, 'The Fabians Reconsidered' in *Labouring Men: Studies in the History of Labour*, Weidenfeld and Nicolson, London, 1964. Abrams, *Origins*, p.60 argued that before 1914 'many British intellectuals came to see the new sociology and the new liberalism...as theory and practice of a last stand against socialism'; also see Corrigan, *Great Arch*, p.168.

4. For Helen Bosanquet, see J. Lewis, *Women and Social Action*, ch.3 and for Bernard, H. Bosanquet, *Bernard Bosanquet: A Short Account of His Life*, Macmillan, London, 1924. See too A.M. McBriar, *An Edwardian Mixed Doubles: The Bosanquets versus the Webbs. A Study in British Social Policy 1890–1920*, Clarendon Press, Oxford, 1987, ch.1.

5. Quoted in Lewis, *Women and Social Action*, p.123; ch.2 gives a fascinating account of Beatrice's life and work in relation to gender division; also R. Harrison, 'Sidney and Beatrice Webb', in Levy, *Socialism*; *DNB* entry for wedding rings.

6. Webb, *Apprenticeship*, pp.180–2, 143 for class consciousness of sin.

7. For religious crises, see J.A. Hobson and M. Ginsberg, *L.T. Hobhouse: His Life and Work*, Allen and Unwin, London, 1931, p.15; P. Mairet, *Pioneer of Sociology: The Life and Letters of Patrick Geddes*, Lund Humphries, London, 1957, pp.6, 20, 47–8. J.A. Hobson, *Confessions of an Economic Heretic*, 1938, Harvester reprint, Brighton, 1976, pp.20, 56; J.M. Keynes, 'Alfred Marshall, 1842–1924' in *Memorials of Alfred Marshall*, ed. A.C. Pigou, Macmillan, London, 1925, pp.7–8; For the Ethical Movement, I.D. Mackillop, *The British Ethical Societies*, Cambridge University Press, Cambridge, 1986, ch.3; R. Soffer, *Ethics*, pp.180–1. For a clear statement of social ethics applying 'ethical principles to the social structure', Hobhouse, *Democracy*, pp.116–17.

8. H. Barnett, *Canon Barnett, His Life, Work and Friends by his Wife*, John Murray, London, 1918, vol.I, pp.76, 307ff., for social redemption and Toynbee Hall providing 'a simple way in which Oxford men may serve their generation. By sharing their fuller lives and riper thoughts with the poor they will destroy the worst evil of poverty.' For the most recent study of Toynbee Hall, Seth Koven, 'Culture and Poverty: the London Settlement House Movement, 1870–1914', Harvard University PhD thesis, 1987 (forthcoming Routledge).

9. Webb, *Apprenticeship*, pp.150–1, 296ff., 355ff.; Barnett, *Canon Barnett*, vol.II, pp.267–8 for break with COS centre although he remained on the local committee.

10. John Burns, *The Times*, 26 Aug. 1889; H. Llewellyn Smith and V. Nash, *The Story of the Dockers' Strike*, T. Fisher Unwin, London, 1889, p.165; Jones, *Outcast*, ch.17.

11. S. Webb, 'Historic', in *Fabian Essays*, 1889, Allen and Unwin, London, 1962, p.63. For Hobhouse's view of the crisis in the Liberal Party, see *Liberalism*, Home University Library, London, 1911, pp. 219–21. B. Webb diary entries for 20 Jan. and 8 Oct. 1895, *Our Partnership*, ed. B. Drake and M. Cole, Longmans, Green, London,

1948, pp.121, 127–8, indicate widespread discussion about the need for 'a new party' and Hobson, *Confessions*, p.51 described 1896–8 experiments with new alignments of radicals and socialists; see too, Collini, *Liberalism*, p.41. S. and B. Webb, *The History of Trade Unionism*, 1666–1894, Longmans, Green, London, 1894; *Industrial Democracy* and L.T. Hobhouse, *The Labour Movement*, Unwin, London, 1893, p.83, all pointed to wings of the labour movement as growing points although not complete embryos of a society organized in the collective interest. McBriar, *Mixed*, analyses similarities between New Liberals and Fabians, pp.81–3.

12. Collini, *Liberalism*, ch.1; the similarities are also brought out by J. Harris, 'The Webbs, The Charity Organisation Society and the Ratan Tata Foundation: Social Policy from the Perspective of 1912', in M. Bulmer *et al.* (eds), *The Goals of Social Policy*, London, Unwin Hyman, 1989, p.33 and Lewis, *Women and Social Action*, pp.185–6.

13. For citizenship and the state, see B. Bosanquet, 'The Duties of Citizenship', in *Aspects*, pp.9–10; *The Philosophical Theory of the State*, Macmillan, London, 1899, ch.XI, 'Institutions Considered as Ethical Ideas'; E.J. Urwick, *A Philosophy of Social Progress*, Methuen, London, 1912, ch.7: this book was a course of lectures to the School of Sociology. H. Bosanquet, *Strength*, pp.168–9, 314 for labour movement. See too S. Collini, 'Hobhouse, Bosanquet and the State: Philosophical Idealism and Political Argument in England 1880–1918', *Past and Present*, no.72 (1976).

14. B. Bosanquet, 'Charity Organisation and the Majority Report', *International Journal of Ethics*, vol.XX (1910), p.405; 'The Majority Report', *Sociological Review*, vol.II (1909), p.115; 'The Art of Public Assistance', The Royal Commission on the Poor Laws and Relief of Distress...Lectures in Sheffield 1909–10, Bosanquet Papers.

15. Webbs, *Industrial Democracy*, pp.808, 843.

16. Webbs, *Prevention*, pp.252–3, echoing proposals already made in the Minority Report of the Royal Commission on the Poor Laws, 1909; B. Webb, diary entry 22 Sept. 1894, *Partnership*, p.86.

17. Bosanquet, *Strength*, p.322. For Schools of Sociology, H. Bosanquet, *Social Work*, pp.404–5; Bernard felt the merger of the London School of Sociology with the LSE was more of a shotgun wedding, H. Bosanquet, *Bosanquet*, p.54. For the Webbs on the role of the LSE, Webb, *Partnership*, p.145; also Sidney's 1895 memo reprinted in S. Caine, *The History of the Foundation of London School of Economics and Political Science*, LSE, London, 1963, pp.35–6.

18. L. Hubbard estimated 20,000 women as 'paid officials in works of philanthropic usefulness', and 'at least twenty times that number, or about half a million, occupied more or less continuously and semi-professionally in similar works': Hubbard, 'Statistics of Women's Work', in A. Burdett-Coutts (ed.), *Woman's Mission*, Sampson Low, Marston, London, 1893, p.364.

19. G. Millerson, *The Qualifying Associations: A Study in Professionalization*, Routledge, London, 1964, Appendix II, pp.248–9, 256, gives useful lists of the qualifying and professional bodies founded by these

groups between 1880 and 1914. G. Wallas, *Human Nature in Politics*, Archibald Constable, London, 1908, p.267 observed that 'in literature and science as well as in commerce and industry the independent producer is dying out and the official is taking his place'; R.H. Tawney, *The Acquisitive Society*, G. Bell and Sons, London, 1921, ch.X, 'The Position of the Brain Worker', pp.202–3 discusses the emergence of an 'intellectual proletariat to which the scientific and managerial work of industry is increasingly entrusted'.

20. Webb, *Partnership*, pp.101, 364. S. Webb, 'The Rate of Interest and the Laws of Distribution', *Quarterly Journal of Economics*, vol.II (1888), p.208; also Perkins, *Professional Society*, p.132. S. and B. Webb, *A Constitution for the Socialist Commonwealth of Great Britain*, Longmans Green, London, 1920, pp.302–4 for the extension of professional ethics. G. Wallas, who taught political science at the LSE, saw the danger of this group siding with their economic equals and losing Working-class trust, *Human*, pp.265–7.

21. For Sewell, see ch.9 below; for Macadam, who came to Liverpool from WUS, ch.10. For Gruner objections, see Women's University Settlement, Minutes, 26 Nov. 1888, ibid., 13 Jan., 10 Feb., 13 Oct. 1893 for training initiatives.

22. E.g., H.L. Wilensky, 'The Professionalization of Everyone?', *American Journal of Sociology*, vol.LXX (1964), pp.141–5.

23. This paragraph draws on E.J. Urwick, 'Social Education of Yesterday and Today', *Charity Organisation Review*, n.s., vol.XIV (1904), pp.254–5, 262–3.

24. 'Extracts From the Confidential Report of the Social Education Committee of the COS, submitted 8 Jun. 1903' in M. Smith, *Professional Education for Social Work in Britain: An Historical Account*, George Allen and Unwin, London, 1965, pp.50–2; also 'Report of the Sub-committee on the Training of Students, May 22 1902' and T. Blandford, *Syllabus of Lectures on Co-operation in Relation to the Social Condition of the People*, both in WUS Archive.

25. University of Liverpool School of Social Science and of Training for Social Work, *Report of the School for the Session 1911–12*, p.4, Box 826, University of Liverpool Archives.

26. For the unreformed situation in education, see P. Gardner, *The Lost Elementary Schools of Victorian England: The People's Education*, Croom Helm, London, 1984, ch.4; for nursing, B. Abel-Smith, *A History of the Nursing Profession*, Heinemann, London, 1960, p.4; A. Summers, 'The Mysterious, Demise of Sarah Gamp: The Domiciliary Nurse and her Detractors, c. 1830–1860', *Victorian Studies*, vol.32 (1988–9), pp.368, 381; other writers often dismiss pre-Nightingale nurses as drunks and prostitutes: e.g. L. Holcombe, *Victorian Ladies at Work: Middle-Class Working Women in England and Wales, 1850–1914*, Archon, Hamden, Conn., 1973, pp.69–70.

27. Dr Alfred Hill of Birmingham, *Journal of the Royal Sanitary Institution*, vol.XXIV (1903), p.306 where a woman participant at the Bradford Sanitary Congress made the same plea for trained

ladies. For class replacement in health visiting, see Dowling, L.S.A., pp.217, 223, 262. See C. Dyhouse, 'Working-class Mothers and Infant Mortality in England, 1895–1914', in Webster, *Biology*, pp.88ff. and J. Lewis, *The Politics Of Motherhood: Child and Maternal Welfare in England, 1900–1930*, Croom Helm, London, 1980, for growth of health services.

28. Ladies' Sanitary Association, *Thirty–third Annual Report*, 1881, p.22. For developments in midwifery, see Lewis, *Politics*, pp.141ff., statistics on p.145; also J. Donnison, *Midwives and Medical Men*, Heinemann, London, 1977.

29. For Layton's experience, Women's Co-operative Guild, *Life as We Have Known It*, by Co-operative Working Women, 1931, Virago edn, London, 1977, pp.43–6.

30. For male opposition, H. Martindale, *Women Servants of the State, 1870–1938: A History of Women in the Civil Service*, Allen and Unwin, London, 1938, pp.51–2, 55; M. McFeely, *Lady Inspectors: The Campaign for a Better Workplace, 1893–1921*, Basil Blackwell, Oxford, 1988, pp.8–9, 11–12; R. Walton, *Women in Social Work*, Routledge and Kegan Paul, London, 1965, pp.29, 37–9; B. Harrison, 'Women's Health' in Webster, *Biology*, p.56; for gender conflict in public health, see C. Davies, 'The Health Visitor as Mother's Friend: A Woman's Place in Public Health', *Social History of Medicine*, vol.I (1988), pp.50–1. Mowat, *COS*, pp.27–8 for women replacing men.

31. For different readings of Booth's motives, see chapters by K. Bales and E.P. Hennock in M. Bulmer *et al.* (eds), *The Social Survey in Historical Perspective: Britain and the United States 1880–1940*, Cambridge University Press, Cambridge, 1991; also T.S. and M.B. Simey, *Charles Booth Social Scientist*, University Press, Oxford, 1960; R. O'Day and D. Englander, *Mr. Charles Booth's Inquiry: Life and Labour of the People in London Reconsidered*, Hambledon Press, London, 1993.

32. B.S. Rowntree, *Poverty: A Study of Town Life*, 4th edn, Macmillan, London, 1902, pp.133–4, 299–300. My 'Mayhew', pp.88–95, compares Mayhew, Booth and Rowntree.

33. E.P. Hennock, 'The Measurement of Urban Poverty: from the Metropolis to the Nation, 1880–1920', *Economic History Review*, 2nd series, vol.XL (1987), pp.215–16.

34. A. Desrosières, 'The Part in Relation to the Whole: How to Generalise? The Prehistory of Representative Sampling', in Bulmer, *Social Survey*, p.232. Davidson, *Whitehall*, ch.4.

35. H. Llewellyn Smith, *The Board of Trade*, G.P. Putnam's Sons, London, 1928, pp.218–21. Smith became Chief Economic Adviser to the Government between 1919 and 1927: see DNB for his life. Branford enumerated the range of this 'official' work in a history of the 'sociological survey', *Interpretations*, pp.68–9.

36. For Bowley's innovations, see Hennock, 'Measurement', pp.220–3; A.L. Bowley, *Livelihood and Poverty*, Bell, London, 1915; DNB for his life. R. Davidson, 'The Social Survey in Historical Perspective: a Governmental Perspective' in Bulmer, *Social Survey*, pp.363–4

argues that the state was slow to pick up innovative techniques from the voluntary surveys and tended to collect labour not community statistics.

37. D. Caradog Jones, 'Power: A Gift to Ordinary People. The Autobiography of D. Caradog Jones', ch.15, typescript, University of Liverpool Archives, D48/1 (iv); T.S. Simey, 'The School and Department of Social Science, 1904–54', *University of Liverpool Recorder*, no.7 (Jan. 1955), p.6. Caradog Jones had earlier been active in settlement and WEA work as was common for first–generation professionals.

38. M. Bulmer, 'The Decline of the Social Survey Movement and the Rise of American Empirical Sociology', in Bulmer, *Social Survey*, gives a picture of the American case from a different point of view.

39. Mairet, *Geddes*, pp.63–6 for his summer schools, pp.117ff. for vexed story of his association with the Carnegie bequest in Dumferline; see note 7 above for religious odyssey; H. Meller, *Patrick Geddes. Social Evolutionist and City Planner*, Routledge, London, 1990, chs. 4–6.

40. See 1910 Report to Sociological Society reprinted in Geddes, *Cities in Evolution*, 1915, new and revised edn, Williams and Norgate, London, 1949, p.78; P. Geddes, 'A Suggested Plan for a Civic Museum (or Civic Exhibition) and its Associated Studies', *Sociological Papers*, 1906, p.200 for noble civic tradition; for city as pathology, contributions by Ebenezer Howard, J.H. Harley in discussion on Geddes paper 'Civics as Applied Sociology', ibid., 1904, pp.120, 132.

41. Ibid., 1906, p.203.

42. Geddes, *Cities*, pp.96, 114–17.

43. Ibid., xii, xiii.

44. Ibid., pp.157; 86, 122 for role of those previously excluded; Branford, *Interpretations*, p.95.

45. P. Geddes, 'Civics', *Sociological Papers*, 1904, p.116.

46. Geddes, *Cities*, pp.78, 97–8; G.E. Cherry, *The Evolution of British Town Planning*, Leonard Hill Books, Leighton Buzzard, 1974, ch.3 for emergence of the profession.

47. E. Burgess, 'The Social Survey', *American Journal of Sociology*, vol.21 (1915–16), pp.499–500.

48. W.L. Creese (ed.), *The Legacy of Raymond Unwin: A Human Pattern for Planning*, Harvard University Press, Cambridge, Mass., pp.11ff., 74; Cherry, *Evolution*, pp.49, 70–1, 92.

49. D. Farquharson, 'The Dissolution of the Institute of Sociology', *Sociological Review*, n.s., vol.III (1955), pp.167ff.

50. *Sociological Papers*, 1904, pp.284–5; also Abrams, *Origins*, ch.7 and Collini, *Liberalism*, pp.198–208 for the Sociological Society.

51. V. Branford, 'On the Origins and Use of the Word Sociology and on the Relation of Sociology to other Studies and to Practical Problems', *Sociological Papers*, 1904, pp.3–5, 8–9. This paper was circulated with the original statement of intent to form the Society.

52. Hobhouse, 'Editorial', *Sociological Review*, vol.I (1908), p.6; also

Branford, 'Word Sociology', p.15–16.

53. Hobhouse, 'Editorial', p.8; Branford, 'Word Sociology', pp.10–11.

54. J.A. Hobson, *The Problem of the Unemployed: An Enquiry and an Economic Policy*, Methuen, London, 1896, 6th edn, n.d., p.56–7. Hobhouse identified 'the greatest weakness in modern reform movements' as 'the spirit of specialism', *Liberalism*, p.249.

55. Hobson, *Unemployed*, ch.5, 'The Root Cause of Unemployment', and 6, 'The Economy Remedy'; for the Webbs, *Prevention*, p.113. McBriar, *Mixed* shows that there was no love lost between the Webbs and Hobson, p.75, n. 67.

56. Urwick, 'Social Education', p.260; training was often considered an antidote to socialism: e.g. H. Bosanquet had 'seen a strong affection for Socialism die quietly out before experience of good case-work on a background of economic history': 'Methods of Training', 1900, Smith, *Professional Education*, p.88: and the Liverpool University Settlement, *Report*, 1913 (1914), p.6 presented itself as a 'school of social service' which could illuminate 'the frequent labour troubles', concluding 'dreams without insight, theories without substance, are the short road to revolution, not reform'.

57. Geddes, 'Civic Museum', p.214.

58. Webbs, *Industrial Democracy*, p.843; Hobhouse, *Liberalism*, p.167, also *Democracy*, pp.237–8.

59. B. Webb, *Partnership*, pp.92, 97.

60. Branford, *Interpretations*, p.318.

61. Quoted in Collini, *Liberalism*, p.100; in *Democracy*, p.272 he started coupling 'freedom and mutual aid' as discussed in chapter 7; for attacks on the Fabians, ibid., p.228 and *Liberalism*, pp.169–71.

62. C.R. Attlee, *The Social Worker*, G. Bell and Sons, London, 1920, pp.19, 216, 274. E. and S. Yeo, 'On the Uses of "Community" from the Owenites to the Present' in S. Yeo (ed.), *New Views of Co-operation*, Routledge, London, 1988, pp.247; 238–44 for postwar Liberals.

63. W. Morris, 'How We Live and Might Live', 1888, in *Studies in Prose*, etc., ed. G.D.H. Cole, Nonesuch, London, 1974, p.587. For the sense of loss at Morris's death in 1896, see Howell, *ILP*, p.352. First issued in 1894, the sales of *Merrie England* were said to 'have exceeded two million copies' and the book was translated into Welsh, Dutch, German, Swedish, French, Spanish, Hebrew, Danish and Norwegian. After being out of print for 'some years', when the book was reissued in 1908, over 20,000 copies were ordered before the new edition had been publicly announced: R. Blatchford, *Merrie England*, Clarion Press, 1908, p.7.

64. Ibid., p.243; W. Morris, *News from Nowhere*, 1890, ch.17, 'How the Change Came', *Selected Writings and Designs*, ed. A. Briggs, Penguin, Harmondsworth, 1962, pp.273ff.

65. *Commonweal*, Jul. 1885.

66. W. Morris, 'Communism', 1893, *Collected Works*, Longmans, Green, London, 1915, vol.XXIII, pp.267.

67. W. Morris, 'Useful Work versus Useless Toil', in *Selected Writings*, p.120; Morris 'Communism', pp.270ff.

68. H. Mitchell, *The Hard Way Up: The Autobiography of Hannah Mitchell Suffragette and Rebel*, ed. G. Mitchell, Virago, London, 1977, p.116. For Morris on desire, *News*, p.274.

69. G.J. Holyoake, *Essentials of Co-operative Education*, Co-operative Union, Manchester, 1898, p.7. See Gurney, 'Middle-class Embrace', p.269 for term 'practical socialism'.

70. S. Reddish, 'Organiser's Report', Annual Report of the Women's Co-operative Guild, *Co-operative Congress Report*, 1894, p.58; my thanks to Gill Scott for this reference.

71. F. Peachy in *Norwich Co-operative Record*, Aug. 1914; Gurney 'Co-operative', pp.289–90, 313 n. 36, for the strategy of expansion which would marginalize capital and swallow the state.

72. T.W. Mercer in *Plymouth Co-operative Record*, Feb. 1916, quoted Gurney, ibid., p.402.

73. J. Ramsay MacDonald, *Socialism and Society*, ILP, London, 1905, pp.13, 17, 61, for quotes in this paragraph, 92ff., 121–3 for critique of Marx.

74. MacDonald, ibid., p.164; J. Ramsay MacDonald, *Socialism: Critical and Constructive*, London, Waverley, [1921], pp.308–11 for stress on the socialist state characterized by 'communal service'.

75. Howell, *ILP*, p.357; pp.352–62 for an excellent discussion of ILP organicism and view of the state as the alternative to an analysis of capitalist contradiction and class struggle strategies of advance.

76. *Justice*, 16 Sept. 1905; *Labour Leader*, 20 Nov. 1908 on the occasion of the book reaching its sixth edition. *ILP* treasurer T. Benson used organic analogy to attack producer-led socialism in his article on 'Socialism and Syndicalism: a Biology Study', *Labour Leader*, 7 Jun. 1912, which insisted on 'a governing or organising class, corresponding to the brain, but an organising class whose only motive for existence is service to the community—a class which, also, may be hereditary under Socialism'.

77. Aveling 'Scientific Socialism', *Commonweal*, Apr. 1885; For the size of SDF membership, see C. Tsuzuki, *H.M. Hyndman and British Socialism*, Oxford University Press, Oxford, 1961, Appendix B.

78. S. Reynolds and Bob and Tom Woolley, *Seems So! A Working-class View of Politics*, Macmillan, London, 1911, p.283.

79. Ibid., p.278.

80 Ibid., pp.172, 282 on Fabians.

81. Ibid., pp.27, 284. Both H. Pelling 'The Working Class and the Welfare State', in *Popular Politics and Society in late Victorian Britain*, Macmillan, 1968 and P. Thane, 'The Working Class and State "Welfare" in Britain, 1880–1914', *Historical Journal*, vol.27 (1984), demonstrate labour movement reservations about state welfare especially while the working class did not control the state. S. Yeo, 'Working-class Association, Private Capital Welfare and the State in the late Nineteenth and Twentieth centuries', in N. Parry *et al.*, *Social Work, Welfare and the State*, Edward Arnold, 1979, explores Working-class friendly society practices of welfare and how these were defeated in the emerging welfare state.

82. Reynolds, *Seems*, p.118.
83. Perkins, *Professional Society*, pp.7–9, xiv, 11.
84. Ehrenreichs, 'PMC', pp.12, 17.
85. Ehrenreichs, 'Rejoinder', ibid., p.320.
86. Reynolds, *Seems*, p.17; p.278 on treating the poor like children.

9 WOMEN'S SOCIAL SCIENCE AND SOCIAL WORK

1. M. Sewell to Miss Clough, 30 Jun. 1937, WUS Archives.
2. Davin, 'Imperialism', pp.15ff.
3. S. Holton, *Feminism and Democracy: Women's Suffrage and Reform Politics in Britain*, Cambridge University Press, Cambridge, 1986, ch.1. Ellice Hopkins, the social purity campaigner in *Power*, 1900, pp.1–2, 160–1, eliding woman and mother, argued that national and imperial survival would depend upon moral redemption brought about by the 'mothers of our race'.
4. Attlee, *Social Worker*, pp.2, 32, 241. For use of term 'social work', D. Harrison, 'The Changing Meaning of Social Work', in Halsey, *Traditions*, pp.83ff.
5. For statistics, see p.218 above. Webb, *Apprenticeship*, p.275, used the word 'careers'; for earlier uses, Taylor, *Enfranchisement*, 1851, p.18 insisting that 'numbers of women are wives and mothers only because there is no other career open to them' and Martineau, *Autobiography*, 1877, vol.I, p. 149.
6. For nurses's associations between 1893 and state registration in 1919, see Holcombe, *Victorian*, pp.96–102. For Societies of women doctors and for the BMA endorsing equal pay for equal work, see for Fabian Women's Group survey, E. Morley (ed.), *Women Workers in Seven Professions: A Survey of their Economic Conditions and Prospects*, Routledge, London, 1914, pp.139, 163–4, also 194–201 for district nurses, p.233, for Sanitary Inspectors and health visitors. For the National Union of Teachers' efforts to involve women who formed over 70% of the profession, and for all–women Associations, ibid., pp.15, 34–5, 50. Walton, *Women*, pp.44, 48, for the Institute of Hospital Almoners (1907) and the Association of Probation Officers (1912). For a later survey, R. Strachey, *Careers and Openings for Women*, Faber and Faber, London, 1935, Appendix II, 'Professional Societies and Trade Unions'.
7. *The Official Report of the Central Conference of Women Workers held at Leeds, 7–10 November 1893*, Spark, Leeds, 1894, pp.231–2. B. Webb resigned from the Executive in 1897 over the issue of prayers but felt the NUWW to be doing good work: *Partnership*, pp.135–6.
8. M. Zimmeck, 'Strategies and Strategems for the Employment of Women in the British Civil Service, 1919–1939', *Historical Journal*, vol.27 (1984), pp.904–5 for women's role, 909 for evasion of the Law. See Morley, *Women*, for women in the higher civil service and their responsibility for women and children, pp.256ff., 237–49; pp.155, 167 for School Medical Officers or *Assistant* MOH posts and for the need for women's hospitals. Pioneer women often felt

undervalued and insecure. Clara Collet was furious when her superiors suppressed information collected by Sarah Reddish of the Women's Co-operative Guild, but reflected on 'how insecure my position is'. She later offered but then withdrew her resignation over 'capable women being subordinated (in the Labour Exchanges) to men who know nothing and care nothing about women's interests': Clara Collet, Diary, 20 Aug. 1904, 10 Aug. 1910, pp.19, 164, 165; also p.101 for the second annual dinner of Women Inspectors etc., Collet Papers, MSS. 29/8/1–146.

9. Morley asserted the freedom to choose, *Women*, p.xi, but the civil servant writing on women's prospects, p.253, argued in communion of labour terms that 'the most successful form of government and the happiest condition for the governed can only be attained, in the State as in the family, when masculine and feminine influences work in harmony'. See Davies, 'Health Visitor', pp.57–8, for defeat of women wanting to use feminine qualities but get equal status and pay.

10. C. Matheson, 'Training for Social Work: The New University Course in Birmingham', *Journal of Education* no.470 (1908), p.640; E. Cadbury, M. C. Matheson, G. Shann, *Women's Work and Wages: A Phase of Life in an Industrial City*, Fisher Unwin, London, 1906, ch.12, which argued for Wages Boards and a National Minimum: Matheson was also an active suffragist.

11. Miss Poole, 'The Classification of Homes', *Appendix to Report of the Central Conference of Women Workers*, 1892, Bristol, Arrowsmith, p.36. For legislation like the Industrial Schools, Prevention of Cruelty to Children and Custody of Children Acts between 1880 and 1891 making removal of children from parents easier, see G. Behlmer, *Child Abuse and Moral Reform in England, 1870–1908*, Stanford University Press, Stanford, 1982, ch.3; also A. Davin, 'When is a Child Not a Child?', in H. Corr and L. Jamieson (eds), *Politics of Everyday Life*, Macmillan, London, 1990, pp.47–8.

12. M. Pember Reeves, *Round About a Pound a Week*, 1913, Virago reprint, London, 1979, p.215; J. Ramsay MacDonald, *Socialism and Government*, ILP, London, 1909, pp.73–6.

13. WUS, Minutes, 25 Jun. 1888–21 Jan. 1889, *passim*.

14. For Sewell, see the obituary in *The Times*, 19 Nov. 1937; Hill declined the wardenship on the grounds of her commitment to the Marylebone neighbourhood: O. Hill to M. Sewell, 3 Dec. 1890; for connection with COS, WUS Minutes, 9 Oct. 1891; 26 Nov. 1887 for Helen Bosanquet (then Dendy) in residence.

15. Besides the COS and housing work, WUS settlers became School Managers, supplied workers for the Metropolitan Association for Befriending Young Servants, the Ladies' Sanitary Aid Association, the Children's Country Holiday Fund as well as for smaller neighbourhood projects like Saturday and evening classes for children, clubs for girls and for the handicapped and a Women's Friendly Society, a Maternity Club and a provident dispensary: ibid., 26 Nov. 1888, 23 Jan. 1891, 7 Feb. 1896. The WUS archive is sadly lacking

in material that gives insight into the inner thoughts and feelings of the settlers and any tension between these and public rhetoric. The most recent history is G. Barrett, *Blackfriars Settlement: A Short History, 1887–1987*, Blackfriars, London, 1985.

16. G. Lansbury, *My Life*, Constable, London, 1928, p.130; Attlee, *Social Worker*, pp.218–19 lists the principal settlements.

17. Bosanquet, *Strength*, pp.30, 181, 183, 121.

18. Bosanquet, *The Family*, Macmillan, New York, 1923, p.336.

19. For social economics as a practical and applied science: *Strength*, p.vi. WUS, Report...on the Training of Students, 22 May 1902, was amended by Mrs Alfred Marshall, wife of the economist, to include yet more practical subjects, domestic economy, sanitary science and bookkeeping—WUS Minutes, 6 Jun. 1902.

20. Bosanquet, *Strength*, pp.186–8.

21. Ibid., p.193; M.E. Loane, Point, pp.135–6.

22. Bosanquet, *Strength*, pp.vi, 327; WUS, Training [1893–4]; *Training*, 1902, WUS Arch.

23. M.E. Loane, *An Englishman's Castle*, Edward Arnold, London, 1909, p.231; Loane found single parent families and especially unmarried mothers inadequate, and felt that overindulgence of children required a different model of mothering, *Point*, pp.3, 108, 111, 130, 154. For WUS commitment to strengthening character and family life, WUS Leaflet d. 1910, no title, detailing aims etc., WUS Arch.

24. H. Bosanquet, *Rich and Poor*, Macmillan, London, 1899, p.103

25. H. Bosanquet, *Strength*, pp.120–1.

26. Patterson quoted in Barnett, *Canon Barnett*, vol.I, p.105 note. Both Vicinus, *Independent*, ch.6 and Koven, 'Culture', give helpful accounts of the compassionate side of scientific social work.

27. H. Bosanquet, Letter to *The Times*, 12 Dec. 1911. For her elation at getting the vote, 'Bernard and I find it much more interesting to talk now we both have the vote', letters to her mother, 16, 30 Nov. 1918, Bosanquet Papers.

28. Attlee, *Social Worker*, p.214; also E.J. Urwick, 'Settlement Ideals', *Charity Organisation Review*, n.s., vol.XIV (1904), p.338; L. Hamilton (warden), Victorian Women's Settlement, *First Annual Report*, 1898, p.6.

29. A. Hodson, *Letters from a Settlement*, Edward Arnold, London, 1909, p.53. My thanks to Roberta Staples, Librarian of Lady Margaret Hall, for helping me to trace Hodson.

30. Vicinus, *Independent*, p.220.

31. Barnett, *Canon Barnett*, vol.I, p.131; O. Hill, *Letter to my Fellow Workers*, for private circulation, London, 1908, p.6.

32. Chase, *Tenant*, pp.21, 25.

33. E. Pycroft to Bond, 6 Jan. 1886, in Katherine Buildings, Record of the Inhabitants during years 1885ff. begun by Beatrice Potter continued by Miss E. Pycroft, Misc. Coll. 43, no.41, British Library of Political and Economic Science.

34. M. Sewell, *District Visiting*, n.d., p.7, WUS Arch.; M. Sewell, 'Women's Settlements in England' in W. Reason (ed.), *University and*

Social Settlements, Methuen, London, 1898, p.98.
35. Attlee, *Social Worker*, p.64 for assumption that 'all applicants are frauds unless they prove themselves otherwise' which affected those trained by the COS and galled applicants; also Snell, *Men*, p.70 for danger of becoming 'a clever social detective instead of a sympathetic helper'. For descriptions of the casework procedure, A.F. Young and E.T. Ashton, *British Social Work in the Nineteenth Century*, Routledge and Kegan Paul, London, 1956, pp.103 and 100–2 for small percentage actually relieved; J. Fido, 'The Charity Organisation Society and Social Casework in London, 1869–1900', in A.P. Donajgrodski (ed.), *Social Control in Nineteenth Century Britain*, Croom Helm, London, 1977, pp.217ff.
36. Webb, *Apprenticeship*, p.203; Attlee, *Social Worker*, p.66; Sewell arguing no help was better than 'half-starved relief', *District*, p.10.
37. Hodson, *Letters*, pp.22, 31, 33, 178; irreverent Maude Royden also could 'think of nothing but the dangers of "giving". They appear to me so great as to be almost paralysing.' She kept feeling that if she were poor she would behave like them: 'I would infinitely prefer to loaf in the streets with a (presumably) attractive young man (than go to a 'girls' club)'; 'I should drink if I lived in Lancaster Street', quoted in S. Fletcher, *Maude Royden: A Life*, Basil Blackwell, Oxford, 1989, pp.32, 36. She soon left the Liverpool Victoria Women's Settlement and eventually became a minister, pacifist and socialist.
38. Hodson, *Letters*, p.142. More radically, some, like the Woolwich COS, simply ignored many of the guidelines and were disciplined in the end: Snell, *Men*, pp.73, 81. Other individual workers, like Emmeline Pethwick and Mary Neal, left their religious sisterhood to live in a small socialist household in East London: E. Pethick-Lawrence, *My Part in a Changing World*, Gollancz, London, 1938, pp.95–6.
39. Hodson, *Letters*, p.210; even the most rigid opponents of almsgiving recognized the emotional difficulty and Sewell tried to make witholding more acceptable by equating it with sacrifice or 'renunciation', urging the social worker 'to renounce the emotional satisfaction of superficial alms; to renounce the popularity which comes of doing what to the unthoughtful...appears the obvious action...to renounce, in fact, the easy paths of charity and take the hard ones': 'Charity Organisation: a Retrospect', *Charity Organisation Review*, n.s., vol.XI (1902), p.146.
40. D. Keeling, *The Crowded Stairs: Recollections of Social Work in Liverpool*, National Council of Social Service [1961], p.24; she indicated that they chose the name Personal Service Society very carefully and came into real conflict with Central Relief Society (a COS–type body) often disagreeing 'strongly with their reasons for witholding relief'. The Victoria Women's Settlement under Elizabeth Macadam also 'welcomed among our helpers some of our Working-class neighbours', *Annual Report*, 1908. For Guilds of Help, see S. Grundy, 'The Relations of the Charity Organisation Society and the Guilds of Help', *Charity Organisation Review*, n.s.,

vol. XXXII (1912) and Attlee, *Social Worker*, pp.78, 87; also M. Cahill and T. Jowitt, 'The New Philanthropy: the Emergence of the Bradford City Guild of Help', *Journal of Social Policy*, vol.IX (1980).

41. Llewelyn Davies quoted in G. Scott, '"The Working Class Women's Most Active and Democratic Movement": The Women's Co-operative Guild from 1883 to 1950', University of Sussex PhD thesis, 1988, p.49.

42. C. Mohanty, 'Under Western Eyes: Feminist Scholarship and Colonial Discourses', *Feminist Review*, no.30 (Autumn 1988).

43. J. Walkowitz, 'Science, Feminism and Romance: the Men and Women's Club 1885–1889', *History Workshop*, no.21 (Spring, 1986), pp.50–1. The protective mother stance was very visible in the NUWW in relation to prostitutes: e.g., a speaker counselled 'we must be as genial with them as with our own children; and some of them although perhaps twenty-five or thirty years of age, are the merest children in knowledge, except perhaps the knowledge of evil': *Report of the Conference of Rescue Workers held at Norwich*, Agas Goose, Norwich, 1898, p.11. Training also became available for moral welfare workers, e.g., in connection with the Josephine Butler Memorial Home: Liverpool University Department of Social Science, Practical Training Minute Book, 15 Nov. 1920 and passim 1919.

44. P. Beals, 'Fabian Feminism: Gender, Politics and Culture in London, 1880–1930', Rutgers Univ. PhD thesis, 1989, gives the fullest account of the Fabian Women's Group. See too, S. Alexander, 'Introduction', Reeves, *Round*, p.xviii; Fabian Women's Group, *Three Year's Work, 1908–1911*, [1911], p.20 for 'Group Record' listing members' 'avocations and interests'. C. Dyhouse, *Feminism and the Family in England 1880–1939*, Basil Blackwell, Oxford, 1989, pp.58–62, for FWG research concerns and relations with other women's groups.

45. Hutchins (1858–1935) served on the Executive both of the Fabian Society and the WIC whose journal *Women's Industrial News* she edited for a time. Having studied at the LSE, she then lectured there in social science and administration and is best known for her *Women in Modern Industry*, 1915, EP reprint, Wakefield, 1978. Bentham, a medical doctor and expert on child health, vounteered her services to the WLL baby clinic in North Kensington, served as a member of the National Executive Committee of the Labour Party and, became MP for E. Islington in 1929. For WLL, see L. Middleton (ed.), *Women in the Labour Movement: The British Experience*, Croom Helm, London, 1978, chs. 2, 4, pp.44–5 for Bentham; C. Collette, *For Labour and for Women: The Women's Labour League, 1906–1918*, Manchester University Press, 1989. For WIC, see E. Mappen, *Helping Women at Work: The Women's Industrial Council, 1889–1914*, Hutchinson, London, 1985.

46. FWG, *Three*, p.9.

47. Ibid., p.12.

48. E. Smith, *Wage-earning Women and their Dependants*, Fabian Society, London, 1915; Dyhouse, *Feminism*, for relations with WIC.

49. FWG, *A Summary of Six Papers and Discussions upon the Disabilities of Women as Workers*, FWG, 1909, p.23 for 'Scheme of Work'; *A Summary of Eight Papers and Discussion Upon the Disabilities of Mothers as Workers*, FWG, 1910.

50. FWG, *Disabilities of Women*, pp.8, 21.

51. FWG, *Disabilities of Mothers*, p.8; see too M. Atkinson for maternal citizenship, *The Economic Foundations of the Women's Movement*, Fabian Tract no.175, Jun. 1914, p.21.

52. FWG, *Disabilities of Mothers*, p.7, report of views of Lily Braun in *Die Frauenfrage*, pp.22ff., 24ff. report on American Mrs Stetson's book *Women and Economics*. Dyhouse, *Feminism*, p.123 notes the existence of a Committee to Reorganize Domestic Work.

53. FWG, *Three*, p.14

54. Atkinson, *Economic*, pp.15, 7, 16, 18; Hutchins, *Women*, pp.195–6.

55. Reeves, *Round*, pp.12–14.

56. Ibid., p.145; also Bermondsey settler, A. Martin, *The Mother and Social Reform*, National Union of Women's Suffrage Societies, London, 1913, pp.13, 36, for the construction of mothers as marvellous managers but oppressed victims, sometimes brutalized by male violence.

57. Reeves, *Round*, pp.89, 91.

58. Ibid., pp.224, 227.

59. Reynolds, *Seems*, p.17; A Chew, *The Life and Writings of Ada Nield Chew*, Virago, London, 1982, pp.37, 238; pp.46, 34 for her complex relations with middle-class women compounded of admiration, reserve and yet mutual misunderstanding; she worked for the National Union of Women's Suffrage Societies, the WLL and the Fabian Society.

60. See my 'Gender and Class: Women's Languages of Power', forthcoming in *Labour History Review*. D. Thom, 'The Bundle of Sticks: Women, Trade Unionists and Collective Organisation before 1918', in A. John (ed.), *Unequal Opportunities. Women's Employment in England 1800–1918*, Basil Blackwell, Oxford, 1986, p.280, argues that 'the principle of organization was one of protection, of help for the weak rather than of self-activity' and this sometimes led to tensions between leaders, philanthropic supporters and members.

61. M. Bondfield, *A Life's Work*, Hutchinson, London, 1949, p.38; B. Hutchins, 'Yorkshire', in C. Black (ed.), *Married Women's Work: Being the Report of an Enquiry undertaken by the Women's Industrial Council*, Bell, London, 1915. My thanks to Gerry Holloway for calling attention to this episode.

62. *Common Cause*, 5 Jan. 1911.

63. *The Times*, 14 Nov. 1912.

64. Women's Co-operative Guild, *Maternity: Letters from Working Women*, ed. M. Llewelyn Davies, 1915, Virago, London, 1978, pp.191, 2–3.

65. Letter to M. Llewelyn Davies, 5 Oct. 1921, vol.8, pp.46–7, WCG Coll.

66. WCG, *Life*, p.40.

67. *The Hospital*, 31 Jan. 1903, p.307. For accounts of this initiative, J.

Gaffin and D. Thoms, *Caring and Sharing: The Centenary of the Co-operative Women's Guild*, Co-operative Union, Manchester, 1983, pp.62–7 and Scott, 'WCG', pp.41–51.

68. M. Llewelyn Davies, *A Co-operative Colony: Papers reprinted from the 'Co-operative News', dealing with a Scheme of Co-operation for Poor Neighbourhoods*, Kirby Lonsdale, n.d., p.29; *A Co-operative Relief Column, or How to Adapt Co-operation to the Needs of Poor Districts*, Co-operative Union, Manchester, 1900, p.13. For survey procedure, Items 6 and 7, d. Feb. 18 1902, vol.6, WCG Coll.; for results: Women's Co-operative Guild, *The Extension of Co-operation to the Poor, Report of an Inquiry made by the Guild, Dec. 1901, Jan., Feb., 1902*, Manchester, 1902.

69. *Co-operative News*, 28 Mar. 1903; COS women were also contemptuous about irrelevant cooking advice but could not supply an alternative, e.g., Bosanquet, *Rich*, pp.89–90; M.E. Loane, *The Next Street But One*, Edward Arnold, London, 1907, pp.26, 28.

70. *Co-operative News*, 13 Dec. 1902; *The Hospital*, 31 Jan. 1903; Vicinus, *Independent*, pp.220–1.

71. *Co-operative News*, 9 May 1903; *Sunderland Co-operative Record*, Oct. 1902, p.81; for children's conversation, vol.2, item 7, WCG Coll.

72. *Co-operative News*, 25 Apr. 1903; 14 Feb. 1903 for success of Tuesday evening parties. Pleasant Tuesday afternoon socials were equally popular in London at the Robert Browning Settlement, *Eighteen Years in the Central City Swarm*, Hammond, London, 1913, pp.28–35.

73. Ibid., 14 Feb. 1903; Jenny Davies's exercise book, entry d. 1903, vol.6, WCG Coll.

74. M. McMillan, *The Life of Rachel McMillan*, Dent, London, 1927, pp.40–1. Girls' clubs were standard in the industrial women's movement and riddled with tensions between trying to control and/or to empower the 'girls': for subtle blending of the two tendencies, see E. Pethwick, 'Working Girls' Clubs', in Reason, *Settlements*, pp.110, 113.

75. For issues surrounding closure, *Co-operative News*, 24 Sept., 19 Nov. 1904; G.D.H. Cole, *Century*, p.223; Gaffin, *Caring*, pp.64, 47.

76. Loane, *Point*, p.92; Sewell's practice undermined her rhetoric on cultural difference, 'Conditions of Effectual Work amongst the Poor', NUWW, 1892, p.117. *Women Workers. Papers read at a Conference* (Bristol), Arrowsmith, Bristol, 1892.

77. Webb, *Apprenticeship*, p.260; Loane, *Englishman's Castle*, p.212; Bosanquet, *Rich*, p.169; but see Hodson, *Letters*, pp.37, 39, for fear of the 'School Board Man' and the 'Sanitary'.

78. Loane, *Point*, pp.63–4; for 'horror', M.E. Loane, *Queen's Poor*, p.127. Behlmer, *Child*, pp.167, 170–3. For tricking the factory inspector, Loane, *Next*, p.88; Rose Squire, *Thirty Years in the Public Service*, Nisbet, London, 1927, pp.69–70; McFeely, *Lady*, p.26 for warning to lady inspectors that 'women and girls lie awfully'. On the increase of state and voluntary visitors, J. Lewis, 'The Working-class Wife and Mother and State Intervention, 1870–1918', in J. Lewis (ed.), *Labour and Love: Women's Experience of Home and Family*,

1850–1914, Basil Blackwell, Oxford, 1986, p.101.

79. Loane, *Next*, p.79; Llewelyn Davies made a similar point in her evidence to the Royal Commission on Divorce when she talked about Guilders being 'the sort of women who have other people's troubles confided to them in a way no district visitor or such person, however kindly disposed, hears them', quoted by Scott, 'WCG', p.92. Reeves, *Round*, p.15 for informants as initially 'suspicous and reserved'. For discussion of the problems of interclass interaction, R.I. McKibbon, 'Social Class and Social Observation in Edwardian England', *Transactions of the Royal Historical Society*, 5th ser., vol.XXVIII (1978); also Anna Davin's *Growing Up Poor: Home, School and Street in London 1870–1914*, Rivers Oram Press, London, 1995.

80. Reeves, *Round*, p.16.

81. Bosanquet, *Rich*, p.202; Loane, *Next*, pp.13, also 99-100 for a Walworth mother's resentment at having to play to an audience, 'the poor is to them what a theatre is to me'; Ada Nield Chew's sketch 'All in a Day's Work: Mrs. Turpin' (1912), *Chew*, p.154 featured a mother who said yes to the social worker's question about giving her children a daily milk pudding, although she couldn't afford to, because 'it was easiest to get rid of her that way'.

82. Loane, *Neighbours and Friends*, Edward Arnold, London, 1910, pp.12–13; Bosanquet, *Rich*, p.225.

83. Bosanquet, *Rich*, p.129.

84. Hodson, *Letters*, pp.6, 254; National Union of Women Workers, *Hints for District Visitors (Sanitation)*, Tract no.2, NUWW, London, 1896, p.5, stresses the Christian reasons for a campaign against dirt.

85. B. Webb, Diary entries for 8 Mar., 4 Jun., early Dec. 1885, *Apprenticeship*, pp.264–5, 266, 276–7.

86. Ibid., p.277.

87. Quoted in Bell, *Hill*, p.88.

88. Attlee, *Social Worker*, p.127; also S. Chapman, 'Economic Studies in Relation to Social Work', *Charity Organisation Review*, n.s., vol.XXII (1907), p.281; E. Ross, 'Survival Networks: Women's Neighbourhood Sharing in London before World War One', *History Workshop*, no.15 (Spring 1983), pp.17–19.

89. Hodson, *Letters*, p.35.

90. E. Ross, 'Labour and Love: Rediscovering London's Working-Class Mothers, 1870–1918, in Lewis, *Labour*, pp.79–80; but also Martin ratifying the habits of the poor, *Mother*, p.37.

91. Barnett, *Canon Barnett*, vol.I, pp.30, 31; Bell, *Hill*, pp.82–3, 85.

92. Twining, *Recollections*, pp.193, 171.

93. Pethwick, 'Clubs', pp.102–3.

94. *Charity Organisation Review*, n.s., vol.XLI (1917), p.153.

10 UNIVERSITY CHALLENGE

1. B. Simon, *Education and the Labour Movement, 1870–1920*, Lawrence and Wishart, 1974, pp.221–35 for the 1902 Act. A.H. Halsey (ed.), *British Social Trends since 1900. A Guide to the Changing Social Structure*

of Britain, 2nd edn, Macmillan, London, 1988, pp.278–80 gives a useful summary of phases of university expansion, 1900–85; histories of redbricks and polytechnics include Armytage, *Civic Universities*; M. Sanderson, *The Universities and British Industry, 1850–1970*, Routledge and Kegan Paul, London, 1972.

2. For the School of Ethics, B. Bosanquet papers, Box N; lecturers included Urwick and G.E. Moore on ethics, Leslie Stephen on political philosophy and G.F. Stout on psychology.

3. A. Mansbridge, 'University Tutorial Classes', 1912, p.28; 'Co-operation, Trade Unionism and University Extension', 1903, both in *The Kingdom of the Mind, Essays and Addresses, 1903–37*, J.M. Dent, London, 1944. A. Mansbridge, *An Adventure in Working-class Education: Being the Story of the Workers' Educational Association 1903–1915*, Longmans, Green, London, 1920, pp.10, 12.

4. Joint Committee of University and Working Class Representatives on the Relation of the University to the Higher Education of Working People, *Oxford and Working-Class Education*, Clarendon Press, Oxford, 1908, pp.47–8.

5. MacDonald, quoted in Harrison, *Learning*, p.268; *Co-operative News*, 10 Sept. 1910; *Co-operative Congress Report*, 1910, p.447, quoted in Gurney, 'Co-operative Culture', p.98.

6. W.W. Craik, *The Central Labour College, 1902–29: A Chapter in the History of Adult Education*, Lawrence and Wishart, London, 1964, pp.85, 39, 41ff.

7. J.F. Horrabin, 'Plebs League', *WEA Yearbook*, 1918, pp.390–1. See too Craik, *Central*, chs. 4–6.

8. Commission of Enquiry into Industrial Unrest, No.7 Division, *Report of the Commissioners for Wales, including Monmouthshire, Parl. Sess.*, 1917–8, vol.XV, Cd. 8668, pp.20, 17–18.

9. B. Simon, 'The Struggle for Hegemony, 1920–1926', in *The Search for Enlightenment: The Working Class and Adult Education in the Twentieth Century*, Lawrence and Wishart, London, 1990, gives an excellent account of this complex episode of conflict. Craik, Central, chs 10–12, recounts the spread of the NCLC and relations with the TUC; S. Macintyre, *A Proletarian Science: Marxism in Britain, 1917–1933*, Cambridge University Press, Cambridge, 1980, pp.74–85; also 85–7 describes Communist Party education.

10. Thompson, quoted in Harrison, *Learning*, pp.297; 273, 293, 341 for Leeds and Hull. For E.P. Thompson, see D. Thompson, *Outsiders. Class, Gender and Nation*, Verso, London, 1993, pp.6–7; for Williams, *Politics*, part I, ch.6.

11. Halsey, *Social Trends*, pp.279, 291.

12. R. Titmuss, 'War and Social Policy', 1958, in *Essays on the Welfare State*, Unwin University Books, 5th impression, London 1964, pp.84–6; A. Oakley (Titmuss's daughter), *Taking it Like a Woman*, Flamingo, London, 1985, pp.6–7. For Halsey, see C. Crouch and A. Heath (eds), *Social Research and Social Reform*, Clarendon Press, Oxford, 1992, pp.v–vii; A.H. Halsey, 'Provincials and Professionals: the British post–war Sociologists', in M. Bulmer (ed.), *Essays on the*

History of British Sociological Research, Cambridge University Press, Cambridge, 1985, pp.153–5.

13. F. Whitehead, 'The Government Social Survey', in ibid.; L. Moss, *The Government Social Survey. A History*, OPCS, HMSO, London, 1991, pp.3–5.

14. Webb, *Partnership*, p.92. Heyck, *Transformation*, p.96 shows how the installation of science into the redbricks and polytechnics similarly made the middle-class literary and philosophical societies look amateurish. Gardner, *Lost*, pp.204–6.

15. Harding, *Science Question*, pp.70ff. for characteristic social relations in current scientific production. Edinburgh Weekend Return Group, *In and Against the State*, Pluto, London, 1979, a book by a group of radical social workers, envisions a changed form of welfare state in the control of workers and clients. For the preconceptualizing role of the PMC and for attempts to build solidarities between mental (PMC) and manual workers in imperial Chemical Industries and create counter-knowledge. M. Hales, *Living Thinkwork: Where do Labour Processes Come From?*, CSE Books, London, 1980, pp.100ff.

16. Maurice, *Lectures to Ladies*, p.19; Dowling, 'L.S.A.', pp.73, 90 for lectures and tracts.

17. For the division of labour in sanitary visiting, see ibid., pp.127, 132, 139, 162; for Twining's involvement as a superintendant, see her *Recollections*, pp.206–7. For Ellen Ranyard, see E. Platt, *The Story of the Ranyard Mission*, London, Hodder and Stoughton, London, 1937 and *Missing Link Magazine*, 1857ff.

18. H. Bosanquet, *Bosanquet*, p.52; Bernard Bosanquet did, however, enjoy talking to workmen about any piece of work.

19. B. Harrison, 'Miss Butler's Oxford Survey', in Halsey, *Traditions*, pp.47ff.; pp.55, 68 for Cambridge. The male Oxford scene is evoked in Richter, Green and the Cambridge scene in Collini, *Noble Science*.

20. Keynes quoted in M. Paley Marshall, *What I Remember*, intro. G.M. Trevelyan, Cambridge University Press, Cambridge, 1947, p.xi. C. Fay to E. Cann, 13 Oct. 1913, in *Memoirs of the British Library of Political and Economic Science*, LSE, London, 1978, pp.22–3 shows Mrs Marshall protecting her husband's ideas against supposed criticism.

21. Webb, *Apprenticeship*, p.352; for Marshall's treatment of women at Cambridge, see M. Berg, 'The First Women Economic Historians', *Economic History Review*, vol.XLV (1992), pp.315–16.

22. Webbs, *Industrial Democracy*, pp.xxvii; xxv–vi for value of documents; Lewis, *Women and Action*, pp.113–14; Berg, 'First' for prominence of women in policy-related economic history especially at the LSE, pp.317–20.

23. 'In Memoriam, Sybella Gurney, Mrs Victor Brandford', *Sociological Review*, vol.XIX (1927), p.140; at a Conference of the School of Sociology clergymen ratified the fact that training need not wither love, *Charity Organisation Review*, n.s., vol.XXV (1909), p.281. Sewell, 'The Beginnings of Social Work Training' in E. Macadam,

The Equipment of the Social Worker, Allen and Unwin, London, 1925, p.28.

24. Heyck, *Transformation*, pp.121ff.; Collini, *Public Moralists*, pp.216ff.

25. Richter, *Green*, p.191; A. Briggs, 'Social Welfare, Past and Present', in Halsey, *Traditions*, p.9.

26. *Charity Organisation Review*, n.s., vol.XIII (1903), pp.31–41 for Marshall paper, 'Economic Teaching at the Universities in Relation to Public Well–being'.

27. Ibid., p.54; further discussion, pp.41–5, 52–5.

28. Ibid., p.43.

29. Harris, 'Ratan Tata', p.36.

30. E.J. Urwick, 'Settlement Ideals. II', *Charity Organisation Review*, n.s., vol.XIV (1904), p.332; ibid., p.118 where B. Bosanquet drew attention to women's enthusiasm: 'men seem less disposed to attend lectures'.

31. Webb, *Partnership*, p.133.

32. Macadam, *Equipment*, pp.33–6. For Oxford's Barnett House, founded in 1914, see Briggs, in Halsey, *Traditions*, pp.6, 22.

33. Macadam, *Equipment*, pp.36–44; Sanderson, *Universities*, pp.315–7. For the self–effacing Macadam, see M. Stocks, *Eleanor Rathbone. A Biography*, Victor Gollancz, London, 1949, pp.7, 58, 92. Liverpool frequently noted and worried over the preponderance of women; also Macadam quoted in Walton, *Women*, p.159.

34. School of Social Science, University of Liverpool, typescript history, Box 826; Kelly, *Advancement*, p.230.

35. For America, R. Rosenberg, *Beyond Separate Spheres: Intellectual Roots of Modern Feminism*, Yale University Press, New Haven, 1982, p.50: Rosenberg gives a good account of feminization and gendering at the University of Chicago. Also Mary Jo Deegan, 'Women in Sociology: 1890–1920', *Journal of the History of Sociology*, vol.I (1978), pp.11–34, and 'Early Women Sociologists and the American Sociological Society: the Patterns of Exclusion and Participation', *The American Sociologist*, vol.XVI (1981), pp.14–24. J. Bernard tells about home economy and social work: *Academic Women*, Pennsylvania State University Press, University Park, 1964, Appendix A; also N. Cott, *The Grounding of Modern Feminism*, Yale University Press, New Haven, 1986, pp.163–5.

36. M. Stocks, *My Commonplace Book*, Peter Davies, London, 1970, p.82.

37. The annual LSE *Calendar* shows the consistent presence of women faculty in the Social Science and Administration faculty compared with Sociology. Ibid., 1910–11, p.77 also urged the study of Ethnology on 'everyone who proposes to carry out administrative and missionary work in the outlying parts of the British Empire'.

38. J. Atkins, Typescript 'Notes on the Origin and Development of Queen Elizabeth College...Oct. 27, 1956', QEPH/PBN 8, pp.1–8, Kings College Archives. F.J.C. Hearnshaw, *The Centenary History of King's College London, 1828–1928*, George Harrop, London, 1929, p.440; also appendix: Hilda Oakley, 'King's College for Women', pp.504, 507.

39. For the content and calibre of the course: *Morning Post*, 3 Jun. 1914; 'Report for the University Grants Commission', QAP/GPt6/2, UGC Visit 14 Mar. 1924.

40. For Headlam's resignation, Delegacy Minutes, item 648, d. 29 Oct. 1912, p.328; for postwar crisis, Minutes of the Special Investigation Commission, OA/CS/ME.

41. For remaining a separate college and later history: Atkins, 'Notes', p.8; M. Sargeaunt, typescript 'The Principal Looks Back', Q/OB 1–2. N. Marsh, *The History of Queen Elizabeth College*, King's College, London, 1986.

42. Barrett, *Blackfriars*, pp.26–7.

43. Universities Statistical Record, *University Statistics*, vol.I (1993–4), Table 28, p.82.

44. E.M. Burns, 'The Social Sciences as Disciplines: Great Britaiⁿ', *Encyclopaedia of the Social Sciences*, New York, 1935, p.231. Burns shows that anthropology and psychology were more professionalized than sociology. Both had professors and programmes at Cambridge, Oxford and London, while psychology also had chairs at Bristol, Liverpool, Aberdeen and St Andrews. Anthropology was given a separate section in the British Association. The British Psychological Society formed in 1901 and the *British Journal of Psychology* started publication in 1904; the journal *Mind* had existed since 1876. For economics, J. Hey, and D. Winch (eds) *A Century of Economics, 100 Years of the Royal Economic Society and the Economic Journal*, Basil Blackwell, Oxford, 1990, which also gives further bibliography.

45. D. Haraway, 'The Biopolitics of Postmodern Bodies: Constitutions of Self in Immune System Discourse' in *Simians*, p.205. For a good account of the dignified version of objectivity as asocial detachment, Harding, *Science Question*, p.25.

46. Ibid., p.71.

47. Quoted in Heyck, *Transformation*, p.91; Playfair also served on the Health of Towns Commission and advised the government on sanitation in Buckingham Palace and on the potato blight in Ireland.

48. Ibid., pp.96, 100ff., on Huxley as the exponent of non–utilitarian science replacing religion as a commitment to lofty ideals.

49. For Germany, see I. Gorges, 'The Social Survey in Germany Before 1933', in Bulmer, *Social Survey*, pp.329, 336–8. The discussion of the USA is based on M. Furner, *Advocacy and Objectivity: A Crisis in the Professionalization of American Social Science, 1865–1905*, University Press of Kentucky, Lexington, 1975, pp.313, 318.

50. Bemis recounting this to Ely quoted in ibid., p.177. For Columbia, see S. Turner, 'The World of the Academic Quantifiers: the Columbia University Family and its Connections' and for Wisconsin, S. Cohen, 'The Pittsburgh Survey and the Social Survey Movement: a Sociological Road Not Taken', both in Bulmer, *Social Survey*.

51. S. Slaughter and E. Silva, 'Looking Backwards: How Foundations Formulated Ideology in the Progressive Period', in R. Arnove (ed.), *Philanthropy and Cultural Imperialism*, Indiana University Press,

Bloomington, 1982, pp.60–1.
52. Abrams, *Origins*, pp.149, 66; T. Haskell, *The Emergence of Professional Social Science: The American Social Science Association and the Nineteenth-Century Crisis of Authority*, University of Illinois Press, Urbana, 1977.
53. K. Mannheim, *Ideology and Utopia: An Introduction to the Sociology of Knowledge*, 1929 and 1931, Routledge edn, London, 1960, pp.128, 140.
54. Marshall, 'Economic Teaching', p.37; D. Winch, 'Economic Knowledge and Government in Britain: some Historical and Comparative Reflections' in M. Furner and B. Supple (eds), *The State and Economic Knowledge*, Cambridge University Press, Cambridge, 1990, p.53 discusses Marshall's designation of the educated captain of industry as hero.
55. Marshall, 'Economic Teaching', p.40.
56. 'The Provision of Training in Social Science in the University of Liverpool', [1917–19], box 826.
57. Yeos, 'Uses of Community', pp.238–44 for Liverpool.
58. Mrs Simey, quoted in Kelly, *Advancement*, p.367; P. Abrams, 'The Collapse of British Sociology?'. in P. Abrams *et al.* (eds), *Practice and Progress: British Sociology 1950–1980*, George Allen and Unwin, London, 1981, pp.61–2 for statistics of expansion.
59. Ibid., pp.62–3 for contradictions between populism and 'adulation of technique'; also J. Barnes, 'Professionalism in British Sociology' in ibid., pp.14–15 and passim discusses the ongoing tensions over making the British Sociological Association (founded 1951) a professional or an open body. P. Abrams, 'The Uses of British Sociology, 1831–1981' in Bulmer, *History*, p.197, places Halsey in the advocacy' as well as the 'socio-technic' tradition.
60. M. Lacey and M. Furner discuss the concept of the 'knowledge base' in 'Social Investigation, Social Knowledge and the State: an Introduction', in Lacey and Furner (eds), *The State and Social Investigation in Britain and the United States*, Cambridge University Press, Cambridge, 1993.
61. Whitehead, 'Government', pp.87–90 for developments of technique.
62. Abrams gave his view of the crisis in 'Collapse?', in *Practice*, pp.54–5.
63. Harding, *Whose Science?*, pp.120–33.
64. Haraway, 'Situated Knowledges', p.190.
65. Ibid., p.191.
66. Two examples are Taylor's acknowledgment in *Eve*, p.vii and Davidoff and Hall in *Family Fortunes*, p.11.
67. H. Roberts (ed.), *Doing Feminist Research*, Routledge, London, 1981, 1992, helped open up the discussion and reflects on its course ten years on. M. Maynard, 'Methods, Practice and Epistemology: the Debate about Feminism and Research', in M. Maynard and J. Purvis (eds), *Researching Women's Lives from a Feminist Perspective*, Taylor and Francis, London, 1994, gives a clarifying account of the arguments.
68. Maguire, *Republic*, pp.129ff.
69. Haraway, 'Situated Knowledges', p.196.

SELECT BIBLIOGRAPHY

This bibliography lists a selection of the works which were cited in short form in the notes or were important in conceptualizing this book. Titles of newspapers, journals and periodicals will be found in the notes.

MANUSCRIPT COLLECTIONS

Bernard and Helen Bosanquet Papers, The Robinson Library, University of Newcastle upon Tyne

Lord Henry Brougham Papers, University College London Library

Josephine Butler Society Collection, at the Fawcett Library, London Guildhall University

Sir Edwin Chadwick Papers, University College London Library

Clara Collet Papers, Modern Records Centre, University of Warwick Library

Department of Household and Social Science Papers, King's College London Archives

Department of Social Science and Social Work Papers, The Archives, the University of Liverpool

Frederic Harrison Papers, London Library of Political and Economic Science, LSE

The Kay-Shuttleworth Papers deposited in John Rylands University Library of Manchester

John Stuart Mill-Harriet Taylor Papers, London Library of Political and Economic Science, LSE

Women's Co-operative Guild Collection, London Library of Political and Economic Science, LSE

Women's University Settlement Archives, Fawcett Library, London Guildhall University

PRINTED BOOKS AND ARTICLES

Abrams, P., *The Origins of British Sociology: 1834–1914*, University of Chicago Press, Chicago, 1968

Abrams, P., *et al.* (eds), *Practice and Progress: British Sociology 1950–1980*, George Allen and Unwin, London, 1981

Acton, W., *Prostitution Considered in its Moral, Social and Sanitary Aspects*, 2nd edn (1870), Cass reprint, London, 1972

Armytage, W.H.G., *Civic Universities*, Ernest Benn, London, 1956

Atkinson, M., *The Economic Foundations of the Women's Movement*, Fabian Tract no.175, June 1914

Attlee, C.R., *The Social Worker*, G. Bell and Sons, London, 1920

Babcock, B., *The Reversible World: Symbolic Inversion in Art and Society*, Cornell University Press, Ithaca, 1978

Bahmueller, C.F., *The National Charity Company: Jeremy Bentham's Silent Revolution*, University of California Press, Berkeley, 1981

Bakhtin, H.M., *Rabelais and His World*, trans. H. Iswolsky, MIT Press, Cambridge, Mass., 1966

Barnett, H., *Canon Barnett: His Life, Work and Friends by His Wife*, 2 vols, John Murray, London, 1918

Barrow, L., *Independent Spirits: Spiritualism and English Plebeians 1850–1910*, Routledge and Kegan Paul, London, 1986

Behlmer, G., *Child Abuse and Moral Reform in England, 1870–1908*, Stanford University Press, Stanford, 1982

Bell, E. Moberly, *Octavia Hill: A Biography*, Constable, London, 1942

Bentham, J., *Works*, ed. J. Bowring, 10 vols, William Tait, Edinburgh, 1843

Berg, M., 'The First Women Economic Historians', in *Economic History Review*, vol.XLV, 1992

Bestor, A., 'The Evolution of the Socialist Vocabulary', in *Journal of the History of Ideas*, vol.IX, 1948

Bodichon, B., *Women and Work*, Bosworth and Harrison, London, 1857

Bonar, J. and Macrosty, H.W., *Annals of the Royal Statistical Society, 1833–1934*, The Society, London, 1934

Booth, General W., *In Darkest England and the Way Out*, Salvation Army, London, 1890

Boralevi, L. Campos, *Bentham and the Oppressed*, Walter de Gruyter, Berlin, 1984

Bosanquet, B. (ed.), *Aspects of the Social Problem*, Macmillan, London, 1895

Bosanquet, B., *The Philosophical Theory of the State*, Macmillan, London, 1899

Bosanquet, C.B.P., *London: Some Account of its Growth, Charitable Agencies and Wants*, Hatchard, London, 1868

Bosanquet, H., *Rich and Poor*, Macmillan, London, 1899

Bosanquet, H., *The Strength of the People: A Study in Social Economics*, Macmillan, London, 1902

Bosanquet, H., *Social Work in London 1869–1912* (1914), Harvester reprint, Brighton, 1973

Bosanquet, H., *The Family*, Macmillan, New York, 1923

Bosanquet, H., *Bernard Bosanquet: A Short Account of His Life*, Macmillan, London, 1924

Bowley, A.L., *Livelihood and Poverty*, Bell, London, 1915

Branford, V., *Interpretations and Forecasts: A Study of Survivals and Tendencies in Contemporary Society*, Duckworth, London, 1914

Branford, V., 'On the Origins and Use of the Word Sociology and on the Relation of Sociology to other Studies and to Practical Problems' (1904), in *Sociological Papers*, 1905

Bray, C., *Phases of Opinion and Experience During a Long Life*, Longmans Green, London, 1879

Bray, C., *The Philosophy of Necessity*, 2 vols, Longman, Orme, Brown, Green, Longmans, London, 1841; 2nd edn, Longman, Green, Longman, Roberts, London, 1863

Briggs, A., 'Language of "Class" in Early Nineteenth-Century England', in Briggs, A., and Saville, J. (eds), *Essays in Labour History*, Macmillan, London, 1967

Briggs, A., 'Middle-Class Consciousness in English Politics 1780–1846', in *Past and Present*, no.9, 1956

Bristol Statistical Society, *Proceedings of the First to Fifth Annual Meetings*, Bristol, 1837–41, Bristol Central Library, College Green

Bulmer, M. (ed.), *Essays on the History of British Sociological Research*, Cambridge University Press, Cambridge, 1985

Bulmer, M. *et al.* (eds), *The Social Survey in Historical Perspective, 1880–1940*, Cambridge University Press, Cambridge, 1991

Burrow, J.W., *Evolution and Society: A Study of Victorian Social Theory*, Cambridge University Press, Cambridge, 1966

Burton, H., *Barbara Bodichon, 1827–1891*, John Murray, London, 1949

Butler, J. (ed.), *Woman's Work and Woman's Culture*, Macmillan, London, 1869

Butler, J., *The Duty of Women in Relation to Our Great Social Evil...25 Nov. 1870*, Fawcett Library

Butler, J., *The Constitution Violated*, Edmonston and Douglas, Edinburgh, 1871

Caine, B., *Victorian Feminists*, Oxford University Press, Oxford, 1992

Cameron, D., *Feminism and Linguistic Theory*, Macmillan, London, 1985

Carpenter, J.E., *The Life and Work of Mary Carpenter* (1879), Patterson Smith reprint, Montclair, 1974

Carpenter, M., *Reformatory Schools for the Children of the Perishing and Dangerous Classes, and for Juvenile Offenders* (1851), Woburn reprint, London, 1968

Carpenter, M., 'Women's Work in the Reformatory Movement', in *English Woman's Journal*, vol.I, 1858

Carr-Saunders, A.M., and Wilson, P.A., *The Professions* (1933), Cass reprint, London, 1964

Chadwick, E., *Report on the Sanitary Condition of the Labouring Population of Great Britain* (1842), ed. M. Flinn, Edinburgh University Press reprint, Edinburgh, 1965

Chadwick, E., 'The Development of Statesmanship as a Science by the

Investigation of the Phenomena of State Necessities', in Richardson, B. (ed.), *A Review of the Works of E. Chadwick* (1887), Dawson Reprint, London, 1965

Chalmers, T., *On the Sufficency of the Parochial System, without a Poor Rate, for a Right Management of the Poor*, William Collins, Glasgow, 1841

Chapman, S.J., 'Economic Studies in Relation to Social Work', in *Charity Organisation Review*, n.s., vol.XXII, 1907

Chase, E., *Tenant Friends in Old Deptford*, Williams and Norgate, London, 1929

Cherry, G., *The Evolution of British Town Planning*, Leonard Hill Books, Leighton Buzzard, 1974

Chew, A., *The Life and Writings of Ada Nield Chew*, ed. D. Chew, Virago, London, 1982

Chitty, S., *The Beast and the Monk: A Life of Charles Kingsley*, Hodder and Stoughton, London, 1974

Claeys, G., *Machinery, Money and the Millennium: From Moral Economy to Socialism, 1815–60*, Polity, Cambridge, 1987

Close, Rev. F., *A Sermon Addressed to the Female Chartists of Cheltenham... August 25*, 1839, Hamilton Adams, London, 1839

Cobbe, F.P., 'Social Science Congresses and Women's Part in Them', in *Macmillan's Magazine*, Dec. 1861

Cobbe, F.P., The Life of Frances Power Cobbe, 2 vols, Houghton Mifflin, Boston, 1894

Cole, G.D.H., *A Century of Co-operation*, Co-operative Union, Manchester [1944]

Collini, S., *Liberalism and Sociology: L.T. Hobhouse and Political Argument in England 1880–1914*, Cambridge University Press, Cambridge, 1979

Collini, S., *Public Moralists: Political Thought and Intellectual Life in Britain, 1850–1930*, Clarendon, Oxford, 1991.

Collini, S., Winch, D., and Burrow, J., *That Noble Science of Politics: A Study in Nineteenth-Century Intellectual History*, Cambridge University Press, Cambridge, 1983

Comte, A., *A General View of Positivism*, trans. J.H. Bridges, Trübner, London, 1865.

Comte, A., *The Positive Philosophy of Auguste Comte*, trans. and condensed H. Martineau, 2 vols, 2nd edn, Trübner, London, 1875

Corbin, A., 'Commercial Sexuality in Nineteenth-Century France: A System of Images and Regulations', in Gallagher, C., and Laqueur, T. (eds), *The Making of the Modern Body*, University of California Press, Berkeley, 1987

Corrigan, P., and Sayer, D., *The Great Arch: English State Formation as Cultural Revolution*, Basil Blackwell, Oxford, 1985

Craig, E.T., 'Socialism in England: Historical Reminiscences', in *American Socialist*, Oneida, New York, 23 August 1877–14 February 1878

Craik, W.W., *The Central Labour College, 1902–29: A Chapter in the History of Adult Education*, Lawrence and Wishart, London, 1964

Cullen, M.J., *The Statistical Movement in Early Victorian Britain: The Foundations of Empirical Social Research*, Harvester, Hassocks, 1975

Darwin, C., *The Descent of Man and Selection in Relation to Sex* (1874),

John Murray, London, 1901
Davidoff, L., 'Class and Gender in Victorian England', in Newton, J. *et al.* (eds), *Sex and Class in Women's History*, Routledge and Kegan Paul, London, 1983
Davidoff, L., and Hall, C., *Family Fortunes: Men and Women of the English Middle Class 1780–1850*, Hutchinson, London, 1987
Davidson, R., *Whitehall and the Labour Problem in Late-Victorian and Edwardian Britain: A Study in Official Statistics and Social Control*, Croom Helm, London, 1985
Davies, E., *The Higher Education of Women* (1866), AMS reprint, New York, 1973.
Davin, A., 'Imperialism and the Cult of Motherhood', in *History Workshop*, no.5, Spring 1978
Denison, E., *Letters and Other Writings of the Late Edward Denison*, ed. B. Leighton, Richard Bentley and Son, London, 1872
Dodd, P., 'Englishness and the National Culture', in Colls, R. and Dodd, P. (eds), *Englishness, Politics and Culture, 1880–1920*, Croom Helm, London, 1986
Douglas, M., *Purity and Danger: An Analysis of Concepts of Pollution and Taboo*, Routledge and Kegan Paul, London, 1966
Dyhouse, C., *Feminism and the Family in England 1880–1939*, Basil Blackwell, Oxford, 1989
Eagleton, T., *Literary Theory: An Introduction*, Blackwell, Oxford, 1983
Ehrenreich, B. and J., 'Professional-Managerial Class' and 'Rejoinder', in Walker, P. (ed.), *Between Labour and Capital*, Harvester, Hassocks, 1979
Ellis, H., *The Task of Social Hygiene*, Constable, London, 1912
[Empson, W.], 'Illustrations of Political Economy: Mrs Marcet–Miss Martineau', in *Edinburgh Review*, vol.LVII (1833)
Essays on Reform (1867), ed. V. Crick, Oxford University Press reprint, Oxford, 1967
Everett, C.W., *Jeremy Bentham*, Weidenfeld & Nicolson, London, 1966
Fabian Women's Group, *A Summary of Six Papers and Discussions upon the Disabilities of Women as Workers*, FWG, 1909
Fabian Women's Group, *A Summary of Eight Papers and Discussion upon the Disabilities of Mothers as Workers*, FWG, 1910
Fabian Women's Group, *Three Year's Work, 1908–1911* [1911]
Farquharson, D., 'The Dissolution of the Institute of Sociology', in *Sociological Review*, n.s., vol.III, 1955
Ferguson, A., *Essay on the History of Civil Society* (1767), ed. D. Forbes, Edinburgh University Press, Edinburgh, 1966
Feuchtwang, S., 'The Discipline and its Sponsors', in Asad, T. (ed.), *Anthropology and the Colonial Encounter*, Ithaca Press, London, 1973
Fido, J., 'The Charity Organisation Society and Social Casework in London, 1869–1900', in Donajgrodski, A.P. (ed.), *Social Control in Nineteenth Century Britain*, Croom Helm, London, 1977
Finer, S.E., *The Life and Times of Sir Edwin Chadwick*, Methuen, London, 1952
Finer, S.E., 'The Transmission of Benthamite Ideas 1820–1850', in Sutherland, G. (ed.), *Studies in the Growth of Nineteenth-Century Govern-*

ment, Routledge and Kegan Paul, London, 1972

Finnegan, F., *Poverty and Prostitution: A Study of Victorian Prostitutes in York*, Cambridge University Press, Cambridge, 1979

Foucault, M., *The Order of Things: an Archaeology of the Human Sciences*, Tavistock, London, 1970

Foucault, M., *The History of Sexuality*, vol.1, Penguin, Harmondsworth, 1981

Foucault, M. *Power/Knowledge, Selected Interviews and Other Writings 1972–77*, ed. C. Gordon, Harvester, Brighton, 1980

Furner, M., *Advocacy and Objectivity: A Crisis in the Professionalization of American Social Science, 1865–1905*, University Press of Kentucky, Lexington, 1975

Gallagher, C. and Laqueur, T. (eds), *The Making of the Modern Body: Sexuality and Society in the Nineteenth Century*, University of California Press, Berkeley, 1987

Gallie, W.B., 'Essentially Contested Concepts', in *Proceedings of the Aristotelian Society*, vol.LVI, 1955–6

Galton, F., *Hereditary Genius: An Inquiry into its Laws and Consequences* (1869), 2nd edn, Macmillan, London, 1892

Galton, F., 'The Possible Improvement of the Human Breed', in *Essays in Eugenics*, Eugenics Education Society, London, 1909

Gardner, P., *The Lost Elementary Schools of Victorian England: The People's Education*, Croom Helm, London, 1984

Gaskell, P., *Artisans and Machinery: The Moral and Physical Condition of the Manufacturing Population Considered with Reference to Mechanical Substitutes for Human Labour*, 1836, Cass reprint, London, 1968

Geddes, P., 'A Suggested Plan for a Civic Museum (or Civic Exhibition) and its Associated Studies' (1906), in *Sociological Papers*, 1907

Geddes, P., (ed.) *Cities in Evolution*, Outlook Tower Association Edinburgh and Association for Planning and Regional Reconstruction London (1915), new and revised edn, Williams and Norgate, London, 1949

Glasgow and Clydesdale Statistical Society, *Constitution and Regulations*, and *Transactions*, Glasgow, 1836

Goldman, L., 'A Peculiarity of the English? The Social Science Association and the Absence of Sociology in Nineteenth-Century Britain', in *Past and Present*, no.114, 1987

Gorham, D., 'Victorian Reform as a Family Business: the Hill Family', in Wohl, A. (ed.), *The Victorian Family: Structure and Stresses*, Croom Helm, London, 1978

Gould, S., *The Mismeasure of Man*, Penguin, Harmondsworth, 1981

Gray, J., *Lecture on Human Happiness* (1825), London School of Economics reprint, London, 1931

Gurney, P. 'The Middle-class Embrace: Language, Representation, and the Contest over Co-operative Forms in Britain, c.1860-1914', in *Victorian Studies*, vol.37, 1994

Hales, M., *Living Thinkwork: Where do Labour Processes Come From?*, CSE Books, London, 1980

Halévy, E., *The Growth of Philosophical Radicalism* (1928), Faber and

Faber, London, 1952

Hall, C., 'The Early Formation of the Victorian Domestic Ideology', in Burman, S. (ed.), *Fit Work for Women*, Croom Helm, London, 1978

Halsey, A.H. (ed.), *Traditions of Social Policy: Essays in Honour of Violet Butler*, Blackwell, Oxford, 1976

Halsey, A.H., 'Provincials and Professionals: the British Post-War Sociologists', in Bulmer, M. (ed.), *Essays on the History of British Sociological Research*, Cambridge University Press, Cambridge, 1985

Halsey, A.H., *British Social Trends since 1900: A Guide to the Changing Social Structure of Britain*, 2nd edn, Macmillan, London, 1988

Hamburger, J., *Intellectuals in Politics: John Stuart Mill and the Philosophic Radicals*, Yale University Press, New Haven, 1965

Hanna, Rev. W., *Memoirs of Thomas Chalmers*, 2 vols, Thomas Constable, Edinburgh, 1854

Haraway, D., 'The Biopolitics of Postmodern Bodies: Constitutions of Self in Immune System Discourse', in *Simians, Cyborgs and Women: The Reinvention of Nature*, Free Association Books, London, 1991

Haraway, D., 'Situated Knowledges: The Science Question in Feminism and the Privilege of Partial Perspective', in ibid.

Harding, S., *The Science Question in Feminism*, Cornell University Press, Ithaca, 1986

Harding, S., *Whose Science? Whose Knowledge? Thinking From Women's Lives*, Open University Press, Milton Keynes, 1991

Harris, J., 'The Webbs, The Charity Organisation Society and the Ratan Tata Foundation: Social Policy from the Perspective of 1912', in Bulmer, M. et al. (eds), *The Goals of Social Policy*, Unwin Hyman, London, 1989

Harrison, F., *Order and Progress* (1875), Harvester reprint, Hassocks, 1975

Harrison F., *Autobiographic Memoirs*, 2 vols, Macmillan, London, 1911

Harrison, J.F.C., *Learning and Living 1790–1960: A Study in the History of the English Adult Education Movement*, Routledge and Kegan Paul, London, 1961

Harrison, J.F.C., *Robert Owen and the Owenites in England and America*, Routledge, London, 1969

Harrison, R., *Before the Socialists: Studies in Labour and Politics 1861–1881*, Routledge, London, 1965

Hennell, M., *John Venn and the Clapham Sect*, Lutterworth, London, 1958

Hennock, E.P., 'The Measurement of Urban Poverty: from the Metropolis to the Nation, 1880–1920', in *Economic History Review*, 2nd series, vol.XL, 1987

Herstein, S., *A Mid-Victorian Feminist: Barbara Leigh Smith Bodichon*, Yale University Press, New Haven, 1985

Heyck, T., *The Transformation of Intellectual Life in Victorian England*, Croom Helm, London, 1982

Heywood, B., *Addresses Delivered at the Manchester Mechanics' Institution*, London, 1843

Hill, A.H., *Our Unemployed*, NAPSS, London, 1868

Hill, A.H., *Vagrancy, the Relations of Country Districts to Great Towns, with*

Suggestions for its more Uniform Treatment, Labour News, London, 1881
Hill, F., *An Autobiography of Fifty Years in Times of Reform*, Constance Hill (ed.), R. Bentley and Son, London, 1894
Hill, F., *The National Distress with its Remedies, Real and Imaginary*, Longman, London, 1830
Hill, Florence, *Children of the State: The Training of Juvenile Paupers*, Macmillan, London, 1868
Hill, O., *Letter to My Fellow-Workers*, for private circulation, London, 1908
Hill, R., and F. D., *The Recorder of Birmingham: A Memoir of Matthew Davenport Hill with Selections from his Correspondence*, London, 1878
Hobhouse, L.T., *The Labour Movement* (1893), 2nd edn, Unwin, 1898
Hobhouse, L.T., *Democracy and Reaction* (1904), Harvester reprint, Brighton, 1972
Hobhouse, L.T., 'Editorial', in *Sociological Review*, vol.I, 1908
Hobhouse, L.T., *Liberalism*, Home University Library, London, 1911
Hobhouse, L.T., 'Sociology', in *Encyclopaedia of Religion and Ethics*, vol.XI, 1920
Hobhouse, L.T., *Social Development. Its Nature and Conditions* (1924), George Allen and Unwin, London, 1966
Hobhouse, L.T., *Sociology and Philosophy: A Centenary Collection of Essays and Articles*, LSE and G. Bell, London, 1966
Hobson, J.A., *The Problem of the Unemployed: An Enquiry and an Economic Policy* (1896), 6th edn, Methuen, London, n.d.
Hobson, J.A., *The Social Problem: Life and Work*, James Nisbet, London, 1902
Hobson, J.A., *Confessions of an Economic Heretic* (1938), Harvester reprint, Brighton, 1976
Hodson, A., *Letters From a Settlement*, Edward Arnold, London, 1909
Holcombe, L., *Victorian Ladies at Work: Middle-Class Working Women in England and Wales, 1850–1914*, Archon, Hamden, Conn., 1973
Hole, J., *Lectures on Social Science and Organisation of Labour*, John Chapman, London, 1851
Holyoake, G.J., *John Stuart Mill, as some of the Working Class Knew Him*, Trübner, London, 1873
Holyoake, G.J., *Sixty Years of an Agitator's Life*, 2 vols, 3rd edn., Fisher Unwin, London, 1893
Holyoake, G.J., *The History of Co-operation*, 2 vols, Fisher Unwin, London, 1906
Howell, D., *British Workers and the Independent Labour Party, 1888–1906*, Manchester University Press, Manchester, 1983
Hutchins, B., *Women in Modern Industry*, 1915, EP reprint, Wakefield, 1978
Jameson, A., *Sisters of Charity and the Communion of Labour: Two Lectures on the Social Employment of Women*, Longman, Brown, Green, Longmans and Roberts, London, 1859
Johnson, G.W., and Johnson, L.A. (eds), *Josephine Butler: An Autobiographical Memoir*, Hamilton and Kent, London, 1909
Johnson, R., '"Really Useful Knowledge", Radical Education and

Working-Class Culture 1790–1848', in Clarke, J., et al., *Working-Class Culture, Studies in History and Theory*, Hutchinson, London, 1979

Joint Committee of University and Working-Class Representatives on the Relation of the University to the Higher Education of Working People, *Oxford and Working-Class Education*, Clarendon Press, Oxford, 1908

Jones, G. Stedman, *Outcast London: A Study in the Relationship between Classes in Victorian Society*, Clarendon Press, Oxford, 1971

Jones, G., *Social Darwinism and English Thought: The Interaction Between Biological and Social Theory*, Harvester Press, Brighton, 1980

Jones, G., *Social Hygiene in Twentieth-Century Britain*, Croom Helm, London, 1986

Jones, L., and Ludlow, J.M., *The Progress of the Working Class 1832–1867* (1867), Kelley reprint, Clifton, New Jersey, 1973

Kay-Shuttleworth, J., *The Moral and Physical Condition of the Working Classes Employed in the Cotton Manufacture in Manchester*, 2nd edn (1832), Cass reprint, London, 1970

Keeling, D., *The Crowded Stairs: Recollections of Social Work in Liverpool*, National Council of Social Service, London, 1961

Kelly, T., *For the Advancement of Learning: The University of Liverpool, 1881–1981*, Liverpool University Press, Liverpool, 1981

Kent, C.A., *Brains and Numbers: Elitism, Comtism, and Democracy in Mid-Victorian England*, University of Toronto Press, Toronto, 1978

Kevles, D., *In the Name of Eugenics: Genetics and the Uses of Human Heredity*, Alfred Knopf, New York, 1985

Kingsley, C., 'The Massacre of the Innocents: A Speech in Behalf of the Ladies' Sanitary Association...1859', in *Sanitary and Social Lectures and Essays*, Macmillan, London, 1892

Kingsley, C., *The Water-Babies: A Fairy Tale for a Land-Baby* (1863), abridged children's edn, Puffin Books, Harmondsworth, 1985

Lacey, M. and Furner, M., *The State and Social Investigation in Britain and the United States*, Cambridge University Press, Cambridge, 1993

Lambert, R., *Sir John Simon 1816–1904 and English Social Administration*, Macgibbon, London, 1963

Levine, P., *Victorian Feminism, 1850–1900*, Florida State University, Tallahassee, 1987

Levy, C. (ed.), *Socialism and the Intelligentsia, 1880–1914*, Routledge and Kegan Paul, London, 1987

Lewis, J., *The Politics of Motherhood: Child and Maternal Welfare in England 1900–1930*, Croom Helm, London, 1980

Lewis, J., *Women in England, 1870–1950: Sexual Divisions and Social Change*, Wheatsheaf, Sussex, 1984

Lewis, J., 'The Working-Class Wife and Mother and State Intervention, 1870–1918', in Lewis, J. (ed.), *Labour and Love: Women's Experience of Home and Family, 1850–1914*, Basil Blackwell, Oxford, 1986

Lewis, J., *Women and Social Action in Victorian and Edwardian England*, Edward Elgar, Aldershot, 1991

Lively, J. and Rees, J. (eds), *Utilitarian Logic and Politics: James Mill's Essay on Government, Macaulay's Critique and the Ensuing Debate*, Clarendon

Press, Oxford, 1978

Loane, M.E., *The Queen's Poor: Life as they Find it in Town and Country*, Edward Arnold, London, 1905

Loane, M.E., *The Next Street But One*, Edward Arnold, London, 1907

Loane, M.E., *From Their Own Point of View*, Edward Arnold, London, 1908

Loane, M.E., *An Englishman's Castle*, Edward Arnold, London, 1909

Loane, M.E., *Neighbours and Friends*, Edward Arnold, London, 1910

London Edinburgh Weekend Return Group, *In and Against the State*, Pluto, London, 1979

Lowndes, M., *I Too Have Lived in Arcadia*, Macmillan, London, 1941

Macadam, E., *The Equipment of the Social Worker*, Allen and Unwin, London, 1925

McBriar, A.M., *An Edwardian Mixed Doubles: The Bosanquets versus the Webbs: A Study in British Social Policy 1890–1920*, Clarendon Press, Oxford, 1987

McCormac, H., *An Appeal on Behalf of the Poor*, Archer, Hudgson and Jellett, Belfast, 1830

McCormac, H., *Moral-Sanatory Economy*, Belfast, 1853

McCrone, K., 'The National Association for the Promotion of Social Science and the Advancement of Victorian Women', in *Atlantis*, vol.VIII, 1982

McDougall, W., 'A Practicable Eugenic Suggestion' (1904), in *Sociological Papers*, 1905

McFeely, M., *Lady Inspectors: The Campaign for a Better Workplace, 1893–1921*, Basil Blackwell, Oxford, 1988

McGregor, O.R., 'Social Research and Social Policy in the Nineteenth Century', in *British Journal of Sociology*, vol.VIII, 1957

Macintyre, A., 'The Essential Contestability of Some Social Concepts', in *Ethics*, vol.LXXXIV, 1973

Macintyre, S., *A Proletarian Science: Marxism in Britain 1917-1933*, Cambridge University Press, Cambridge, 1980

McLeish, J., *Evangelical Religion and Popular Education*, Methuen, London, 1969

Maguire, P., et al., *The Republic of Letters: Working-class Writing and Local Publishing*, Comedia Publishing Group, London, 1982

Mairet, P., *Pioneer of Sociology: The Life and Letters of Patrick Geddes*, Lund Humphries, London, 1957

Manchester Statistical Society, Appendix to the Minutes, Local History Department, Manchester Central Library

Manchester Statistical Society, *Report of a Committee...On the State of Education in the Borough of Manchester in 1834*, London, 1835, 2nd edn revised, London, 1837

Manchester Statistical Society, *Report of a Committee...On the State of Education in the Borough of Salford in 1835*, London, 1836

Manchester Statistical Society, *Report of a Committee of a Manchester Statistical Society on the Condition of the Working Classes in an Extensive Manufacturing District in 1834, 1835 and 1836*, James Ridgway and Sons, London, 1838

Manchester Statistical Society, *Transactions*, Manchester, 1858-1887

Mannhelm, K., *Ideology and Utopia: An Introduction to the Sociology of Knowledge* (1929 and 1931), Routledge, London, 1960

Martin, A., *The Mother and Social Reform*, National Union of Women's Suffrage Societies, London, 1913

H. Martineau, *Autobiography*, 3 vols, Smith, Elder, London, 1877

Maurice, F.D. (ed.), *Lectures to Ladies on Practical Subjects*, 3rd edn revised, Macmillan, Cambridge, 1857

Maurice, J.F., *The Life of Frederick Denison Maurice, Chiefly Told in His Own Letters*, 2 vols, 4th edn, Macmillan, London, 1885

Mayhew, H., *London Labour and the London Poor*, 3 vols, London, 1851, 2nd edn, 4 vols, London, 1861-2, Cass reprint, London, 1967

Mayhew, H., *The Unknown Mayhew: Selections from the Morning Chronicle, Labour and the Poor*, eds E.P. Thompson and E. Yeo, Merlin, London, 1971

Meliora: or, Better Times to Come, Being the Contributions of Many Men Touching the Present State and Prospects of Society, ed. Viscount Ingestre, London, 1852, 2nd series, London, 1853

Mill, J., *An Essay on Government* (1819), in Lively, *Utilitarian Logic*, op.cit.

[Mill, J.], *A Fragment on Mackintosh*, Baldwin and Cradock, London, 1835

Mill, J.S., 'On the Definition of Political Economy and on the Method of Investigation Proper to it', in *Westminster Review*, vol.XXVI, 1836

Mill, J.S., *A System of Logic*, Book VI (1843), reprinted as *On the Logic of the Moral Sciences*, Bobbs Merrill, New York, 1965

Mill, J.S., *Principles of Political Economy with Some of their Applications to Social Philosophy* (1848), Sir John Lubbock's Hundred Books edn, Routledge, London, 1891

Mill, J.S., *Autobiography* (1873), Penguin, London, 1989

Millerson, G., *The Qualifying Associations: A Study in Professionalization*, Routledge, London, 1964

More, H., (ed.), *Memoirs of the Life and Correspondence of Mrs. Hannah More*, ed. W. Roberts, 3 vols, 2nd edn, Seeley and Burnside, London, 1834

More, M., *Mendip Annals: or a Narrative of the Charitable Labours of Hannah and Martha More in their Neighbourhood, Being the Journal of Martha More*, ed. A. Roberts, James Nisbet, London, 1859

Morley, E. (ed.), *Women Workers in Seven Professions: A Survey of their Economic Conditions and Prospects*, Routledge, London, 1914

The Morning Chronicle Survey of Labour and the Poor: The Metropolitan Districts, Caliban, Firle, 1980, vols.1–III.

Morris, R., *Cholera 1832: The Social Response to an Epidemic*, Croom Helm, London, 1976

Morris, W., 'How We Live and Might Live' (1888), in Cole, G.D.H. (ed.), *Studies in Prose* etc., Nonesuch, London, 1974

Morris, W., 'Communism' (1893), in *Collected Works*, vol.XXIII, Long - mans, Green, London, 1915

Morris, W., 'Useful Work Versus Useless Toil', in Briggs, A. (ed.), *Selected Writings and Designs*, Penguin, Harmondsworth, 1962

Mort, F., *Dangerous Sexualities: Medico-Moral Politics in England since 1830*, Routledge and Kegan Paul, London, 1987

National Association for the Promotion of Social Science, *Transactions*, London, 1857–1884

National Association for the Promotion of Social Science, *Report on Trades Societies and Strikes*, John W. Parker and Son, London, 1860

National Association for the Promotion of Social Science, Manchester Meeting, 1866, 'Collection of Printed Forms, Newspaper Cuttings etc.', Manchester Central Library Local History Collection

National Association for the Promotion of Social Science, *Sessional Proceedings*, London, 1867–84

National Association for the Promotion of Social Science, *Lectures on Economic Science*, Longmans, London, 1970

National Reformatory Union, *The Authorized Report of the First Provincial Meeting of the N.R.U....Bristol at 20–22 Aug. 1856*, London, 1856

Osborne, S. Godolphin, 'Immortal Sewerage', in *Meliora*, op.cit., 1853.

Owen, R., *Book of the New Moral World: Explanatory of the Elements of the Science of Society or the Social State of Man* (1844), Kelley reprint, New York, 1970

[Pare, W.], *An Address Delivered at the Opening of the Birmingham Co-operative Society*, 17 Nov. 1828, Birmingham Co-operative. Society, Birmingham, n.d.

Parry, N. and J., *The Rise of the Medical Profession*, Croom Helm, London, 1976

Pattison, M., *Suggestions on Academical Organisation with Especial Reference to Oxford*, Emonston and Douglas, Edinburgh, 1868

Pearse, I., and Crocker, L., *The Peckham Experiment*, Allen and Unwin, London, 1943

Pearson, K., *National Life From the Standpoint of Science*, 2nd edn, Cambridge University Press, Cambridge, 1904

Peel, J.D.Y., *Herbert Spencer, The Evolution of a Sociologist*, Heinemann, London, 1971

Perkin, H., *The Rise of Professional Society*, Routledge, London, 1989

Pethwick, E., 'Working Girls' Clubs', in *University and Social Settlements*, ed. W. Reason, Methuen, London, 1898

Prochaska, F.R., *Women and Philanthropy in Nineteenth-Century England*, Clarendon Press, Oxford, 1980

Reeves, M. Pember, *Round About a Pound a Week* (1913), Virago reprint, London, 1979

Rendall, J., *The Origins of Modern Feminism: Women in Britain, France and the US 1780–1860*, Macmillan, London, 1985

Rendall, J., '"A Moral Engine"? Feminism, Liberalism and the English Woman's Journal', in Rendall, J. (ed.), *Equal or Different: Women's Politics 1800–1914*, Basil Blackwell, Oxford, 1987

Reynolds, S., Woolley, B., and Woolley, T., *Seems So! A Working-Class View of Politics*, Macmillan, London, 1911

Richardson, R., *Death, Dissection and the Destitute*, Routledge and Kegan Paul, London, 1987

Richter, M., *The Politics of Conscience: T.H. Green and His Age*, Weidenfeld and Nicolson, London, 1964

Riley, D., *Am I That Name?', Feminism and the Category of 'Women' in History*, Macmillan, London, 1988

Rodgers, B., 'The Social Science Association 1857–1886', in *Manchester School of Economic and Social Studies*, vol.XX, 1952

Rossi, A., 'Sentiment and Intellect: The Story of John Stuart Mill and Harriet Taylor', in Rossi, A. (ed.), *Essays on Sexual Equality*, University of Chicago Press, Chicago, 1970

Rothblatt, S., *The Revolution of the Dons: Cambridge and Society in Victorian England*, Faber and Faber, London, 1968

Rowntree, B.S., *Poverty: A Study of Town Life*, 4th edn, Macmillan, London, 1902

Russett, C. Eagle, *Sexual Science: The Victorian Construction of Womanhood*, Harvard University Press, Cambridge, Mass., 1989

Sanderson, M., *The Universities and British Industry, 1850–1970*, Routledge and Kegan Paul, London, 1972

Scott, J., 'Deconstructing Equality-versus-Difference: or, the Uses of Poststructuralist Theory for Feminism', in *Feminist Studies*, vol.14, 1988

Searle, G.R., *Eugenics and Politics in Britain, 1900–1914*, Noordhoff, Leyden, 1976

Sewell, M., 'Women's Settlements in England', in Reason, W. (ed.), *University and Social Settlements*, Methuen, London, 1898

Simon, B., 'The Struggle for Hegemony, 1920–1926', in Simon, B. (ed.), *The Struggle for Enlightenment: the Working Class and Adult Education in the Twentieth Century*, Lawrence and Wishart, London, 1990

Smith, M.J., *Professional Education for Social Work in Britain: An Historical Account*, George Allen and Unwin, London, 1965

Smith, W. Hawkes, *The Errors of the Social System—Being an Essay on Wasted, Unproductive and Redundant Labour*, Longman, London, 1834

Smith, W. Hawkes, *Letters on the State and Prospects of Society, Birmingham*, 1838, Reprinted from the *Philanthropist* newspaper

Smith, W. Hawkes, *Letters on Social Science*, Flindell, Birmingham, 1839

The Society for Bettering the Condition and Increasing the Comforts of the Poor, *Reports*, 5 vols, London, 1798–1808

The Society for Bettering the Condition of the Poor at Clapham Surrey, *Rules and Regulations of the Society...Instituted February 11, 1799, to which is Prefixed an Account of the Origins and Designs of the Society*, 2nd edn, London, 1805

Sociological Papers, 1905-1907 then *Sociological Review*, 1908-1955

Soffer, R., *Ethics and Society in England: The Revolution in the Social Sciences 1870–1914*, University of California Press, Berkeley, 1978

Spencer, H., *The Principles of Sociology*, vol.1 (1876), in *Herbert Spencer: Structure, Function and Evolution*, S. Andreski (ed.), Michael Joseph, London, 1971

Spencer, H., *The Man Versus the State: With Four Essays on Politics and Society*, Penguin, Harmondsworth, 1969

Stallybrass, P., and White, A., *The Politics and Poetics of Transgression*, Methuen, London, 1986

Statistical Society of London, *Journal*, London, 1839–86

Steedman, C., *Childhood, Culture and Class in Britain. Margaret McMillan, 1860–1931*, Virago, London, 1990

Strachey, R. *The Cause: A Short History of the Women's Movement in Great Britain* (1928), Virago, London, 1978

Taylor, B., *Eve and the New Jerusalem: Socialism and Feminism in the Nineteenth Century*, Virago, London, 1983

Taylor, H., 'Enfranchisement of Women' (1851), in Mill, J.S., *The Subjection of Women etc.*, Virago, London, 1983

Thompson, E.P., *The Making of the English Working Class*, Pelican, Harmondsworth, 1968

Thompson, E.P., *The Poverty of Theory and Other Essays*, Merlin, London, 1978

Thompson, N., *The People's Science: The Popular Political Economy of Exploitation and Crisis 1816–1834*, Cambridge University Press, Cambridge, 1985

Thompson, W., *An Inquiry into the Principles of the Distribution of Wealth Most Conducive to Human Happiness*, 1824, Kelley reprint, New York, 1963

Twining, L., *Recollections of Life and Work*, London, Edward Arnold, 1893

Urwick, E.J., 'Settlement Ideals I and II', in *Charity Organisation Review*, n.s., vol.XIV, 1904

Urwick, E.J., 'Social Education of Yesterday and Today', in *Charity Organisation Review*, n.s., vol.XIV, 1904

Urwick, E.J., *A Philosophy of Social Progress*, Methuen, London, 1912

Vicinus, M., *Independent Women: Work and Commnuity for Single Women 1850–1920*, Virago, London, 1985

Vicinus, M., and Nergaard, B., *Ever Yours: Florence Nightingale, Selected Letters*, Virago, London, 1989

Vogeler, M., *Frederic Harrison: The Vocations of a Postivist*, Clarendon Press, Oxford, 1984

Voloshinov, V.N., *Marxism and the Philosophy of Language*, trans. Matejka, L., and Titunik, I., Harvard University Press, Cambridge, Mass., 1986

Waddington, I., *The Medical Profession in the Industrial Revolution*, Gill and Macmillan, Dublin, 1984

Wallas, G., *Human Nature in Politics*, Archibald Constable, London, 1908

Walton, R.G., *Women in Social Work*, Routledge and Kegan Paul, London, 1965

Watts, J., *The Facts and Fictions of Political Economists*, Abel Heywood, Manchester, 1842

Webb, B., *My Apprenticeship*, Longmans, Green, London, 1926

Webb, B., *Our Partnership*, eds B. Drake, and M.I. Cole, Longmans, Green and Co, London, 1948

Webb, R., *Harriet Martineau: A Radical Victorian*, Columbia University Press, New York, 1960

Webb, S., 'Historic', in *Fabian Essays* (1889), Allen and Unwin, London, 1962

Webb, S., and Webb, B., *Industrial Democracy* (1897), Longmans, Green,

London, 1920

Webb, S., and Webb, B., *The Prevention of Destitution* (1911), Longmans, Green, London, 1920

Webster, C. (ed.), *Biology, Medicine and Society 1840–1940*, Cambridge University Press, Cambridge, 1981

Whitehead, F. 'The Government Social Survey', in Bulmer, M., *Essays on the History of British Sociological Research*, op.cit.

Wilberforce, R.I., and Samuel, *The Life of William Wilberforce*, John Murray, London, 1838

Wilensky, H.L., 'The Professionalization of Everyone?', in American *Journal of Sociology*, vol.LXX, 1964

Williams, R., *Marxism and Literature*, Oxford University Press, Oxford, 1977

Williams, R., *Politics and Letters: Interviews with New Left Review*, Verso, London, 1981

Williams, R., *Keywords: A Vocabulary of Culture and Society*, Fontana, London, 1983

Women's Co-operative Guild, *The Extension of Co-operation to the Poor, Report of an Inquiry made by the Guild, Dec. 1901, Jan., Feb., 1902*, Manchester, 1902

Women's Co-operative Guild, *Maternity, Letters from Working Women* (1915), ed. M. Llewelyn Davies, Virago, London, 1978

Women's Co-operative Guild, *Life as We Have Known It* (1931), ed. M. Llewelyn Davies, Virago, London, 1977

Women Workers, *Papers Read at a Conference Convened by the Bristol and Clifton Ladies' Association for the Care of Girls* (1892), Arrowsmith, Bristol, 1893

Yeo, E., 'Christianity in Chartist Struggle', in *Past and Present*, no.91, 1981

Yeo, E., 'Culture and Constraint in Working-Class Movements', in Yeo, E. and S. (eds), *Popular Culture and Class Conflict*, (see below)

Yeo, E. and S. (eds), *Popular Culture and Class Conflict 1590–1914: Explorations in the History of Labour and Leisure*, Harvester, Brighton, 1981

Yeo, E. and S., 'On the Uses of "Community" from the Owenites to the Present', in Yeo, S. (ed.), *New Views of Co-operation*, Routledge, London, 1988

Yeo, S., 'Notes on Three Socialisms—Collectivism, Statism and Associationism', in Levy, C. (ed.), *Socialism and the Intelligentsia 1880–1914*, Routledge and Kegan Paul, London, 1987

Young, R., 'The Naturalization of Value Systems in the Human Sciences', Open University Course: Science and Belief From Darwin to Einstein, Block VI, *Problems in the Biological and Human Sciences*, Open University Press, Milton Keynes, 1981

Young, R., 'Darwinism is Social', in Kohn, D. (ed.), *The Darwinian Heritage*, Princeton University Press, Princeton, New Jersey, 1985

Young, R., *Darwin's Metaphor: Nature's Place in Victorian Culture*, Cambridge University Press, Cambridge, 1985

UNPUBLISHED WORKS AND THESES

Beals, P., 'Fabian Feminism: Gender, Politics and Culture in London, 1880–1930', PhD thesis, Rutgers University, 1989

Corrigan, P., 'State Formation and Moral Regulation in Nineteenth-Century Britain: Sociological Investigations', PhD thesis, University of Durham, 1977

Dowling, W.C., 'The Ladies' Sanitary Association and the Origins of the Health Visiting Service', MA thesis, University of London, 1963

Gurney, P., 'The Making of Co-operative Culture in England, 1870–1918', PhD thesis, University of Sussex, 1989

Koven, S., 'Culture and Poverty: The London Settlement House Movement 1870–1914', PhD thesis, Harvard University, 1987

Scott, G., '"The Working Class Women's Most Active and Democratic Movement": The Women's Co-operative Guild from 1883 TO 1950', PhD thesis, University of Sussex, 1988

Worzala, D., 'The Langham Place Circle: the Beginnings of the Organized Women's Movement in England', PhD thesis, University of Wisconsin, 1982

[Yeo], E. Janes, 'The Quest for the New Moral World: Changing Patterns of Owenite Thought, 1817–1870', MA thesis, University of Wisconsin, 1963

Yeo, E., 'Social Science and Social Change: A Social History of Some Aspects of Social Science and Social Investigation in Britain 1830–1890', PhD thesis, University of Sussex, 1972

Yeo, E. (ed.), 'Radical Femininity, Women's Self-Representation in Nineteenth and Twentieth Century Social Movements', forthcoming

INDEX